T0296001

Behavioral Finance
Beyond the Basics

World Scientific Lecture Notes in Finance

ISSN: 2424-9939

Series Editors: Professor Alexander Lipton and Professor Itzhak Venezia

This series provides high quality lecture note-type texts in all areas of finance, for courses at all levels: undergraduate, MBA and PhD. These accessible and affordable lecture notes are better aligned with today's classrooms and are written by expert professors in their field with extensive teaching experience. Students will find these books less formal, less expensive and also more enjoyable than many textbooks. Instructors will find all the material that they need, thus significantly reducing their class preparation time. Authors can prepare their volumes with ease, as they would be based on already existing, and actively used, lecture notes. With these features, this book series will make a significant contribution to improving the teaching of finance worldwide.

Published:

More information on this series can also be found at https://www.worldscientific.com/series/wslnf

World Scientific Lecture Notes in Finance – **Vol. 9**

Behavioral Finance
Beyond the Basics

Editors

Itzhak Venezia
The University of Limassol, Limassol, Cyprus

Rachel Calipha
Academic College of Tel-Aviv-Yaffo, Israel

World Scientific

NEW JERSEY · LONDON · SINGAPORE · BEIJING · SHANGHAI · HONG KONG · TAIPEI · CHENNAI · TOKYO

Published by

World Scientific Publishing Co. Pte. Ltd.
5 Toh Tuck Link, Singapore 596224
USA office: 27 Warren Street, Suite 401-402, Hackensack, NJ 07601
UK office: 57 Shelton Street, Covent Garden, London WC2H 9HE

Library of Congress Cataloging-in-Publication Data
Names: Venezia, Itzhak, editor. | Calipha, Rachel, editor.
Title: Behavioral finance : beyond the basics / [edited by]
    Itzhak Venezia, The University of Limassol, Limassol, Cyprus,
    Rachel Calipha, Academic College of Tel-Aviv-Yaffo, Israel.
Description: New Jersey : World Scientific, [2025] | Series: World Scientific lecture notes in finance,
    2424-9939 ; vol. 9 | Includes bibliographical references and index.
Identifiers: LCCN 2024017604 | ISBN 9789811290626 (hardcover) |
    ISBN 9789811290633 (ebook) | ISBN 9789811290640 (ebook other)
Subjects: LCSH: Finance--Psychological aspects. |
    Investments--Psychological aspects. | Investments--Decision making.
Classification: LCC HG4515.15 .B438 2025 | DDC 332.601/9--dc23/eng/20240529
LC record available at https://lccn.loc.gov/2024017604

British Library Cataloguing-in-Publication Data
A catalogue record for this book is available from the British Library.

For any available supplementary material, please visit
https://www.worldscientific.com/worldscibooks/10.1142/13771#t=suppl

Desk Editors: Balasubramanian Shanmugam/Catherine Domingo Ong

Typeset by Stallion Press
Email: enquiries@stallionpress.com

To my loved ones, Laurie, Dana, and Irit
— **Itzhak Venezia**

To my beloved family, Sasi, Shoham, Shachaf, and Ariel
In memory of Mom who passed away this year
— **Rachel Calipha**

Preface

Welcome to the fourth volume of edited books constituting an eclectic collection of chapters in behavioral finance based on contributions of participants in the Israel Behavior Finance conferences. Like its predecessors, this book continues to be edited by Professor Itzhak Venezia (in this book with Dr. Rachel Calipha), who carefully selected the chapters to be included in this volume.

Behavioral finance has evolved significantly since its inception, and the chapters in this collection reflect the diverse and dynamic nature of this field. The chapters featured here not only build upon the foundational concepts established in the earlier volumes but also explore novel financial products, themes, and ideas that have gained rapid prominence in recent years: From the integration of artificial intelligence into investment decision-making processes to the analysis of the alternative meats industry, and various other alternative investment instruments such as Non-Fungible Tokens (NFTs). This collection therefore pushes the boundaries of what is conventionally associated with behavioral finance.

We invite you to embark on this intellectual journey with us as we explore not only the tried-and-true concepts but also the emerging horizons that promise to shape the future of finance. Whether you are a scholar, practitioner, or simply an inquisitive mind interested in the realm of behavioral finance, this book offers a wealth of knowledge and ideas to explore.

The book is divided into four parts. The first part deals with anomalies, a topic that was essential in stimulating finance scholars to explore the possibility of employing psychological biases in their quest to explain some anomalous phenomena in finance. The first chapter, *Changes in Short Positions and Earnings Surprises* by Joshua Livnat, Dan Segal, and Kate Suslava, concerns one of the most intriguing anomalies, the Post Earnings Announcement Drift (PEAD).[1] The authors show that holders of short positions seem to behave in a manner inconsistent with the PEAD and suggest that the PEAD is the result of investor underreaction to earnings news. The next chapter, by Jacob Oded and Itzhak Venezia, analyzes the question: Why do firms pay dividends rather than resort to other cash distribution systems to their stockholders such as the more tax-efficient share repurchases? This anomaly is, to the best of our knowledge, the earliest anomaly for which a behavioral finance explanation was offered (Thaler and Shefrin, 1981). Since then, a plethora of alternative psychological explanations have been offered, none of which is completely satisfactory. This chapter adds to the discussion (although it does not attempt to resolve it), by tackling the problem from a novel angle, namely that behavioral differences between stockholders prevent them from agreeing on the exact terms of share repurchases, hence requiring firms to employ the inferior method of dividends for cash disbursement. The following chapter, *Energy Futures as an Inflation Hedge in a Time-Varying Coefficient Framework*, by Chunbo Liu, Cheng Zhang, and Zhiping Zhou, strives to determine which of the following two theories best explains recent increases in energy prices: Modigliani and Cohn's hypothesis that investors suffer from money illusion, discounting real cash flows at nominal discount rates and selling risky assets during high inflation periods (Modigliani and Cohn, 1979; Cohen *et al.*, 2005), or that nominal returns of assets contain market assessments of expected inflation rates, and investors are more likely to invest in various inflation hedging assets (Fama and Schwert, 1977).[2] The authors find support for the traditional rather than the behavioral explanation.

One of the main conundrums of behavioral finance is why anomalies persist when arbitrageurs can observe and eliminate them through trading. Guy Kaplanski's chapter, *Cross-Sectional Anomalies: Statistical*

---

[1] This is one of the lesser-known anomalies, but it is one of the first to be discovered (as early as 1984, Foster *et al.*, 1984), and one that is still being extensively researched.

[2] Questions about inflation have become more relevant recently as inflation has risen considerably since 2020 after trending down since the 1980s and exhibiting relatively low rates during the previous decades.

Phenomena or Free-Lunch Opportunities, makes a brave attempt at cracking this mystery and manages to inch us closer to finding the ever-elusive answer. Kaplanski explores the activity of arbitrage investors following the discovery of pricing anomalies and shows that they find these anomalies profitable in terms of risk-reward in the long run. This implies mispricing, which is difficult to reconcile with full rationality but can be explained via investors' behavioral biases. Additionally, since the chapter provides a thorough list of existing anomalies, it is very useful to any researcher in behavioral finance.[3]

Turning our attention to the behavior of professional investors, Part 2 starts with the chapter *Investor Sophistication and the Effect of Behavioral Biases in Structured Products Investment* by Moran Ofir and Zvi Wiener. This chapter delves into the world of structured product investments and examines the detrimental effects of behavioral biases on investors in these financial instruments. The chapter implies that professional investors, aware of the psychological biases of amateurs, exploit these biases to sell them overpriced structured products. The authors suggest that in these circumstances, some specific regulations are justified to protect individual investors. The next chapter, *Analysts' Unfavorable Recommendation Initiations* by Joshua Livnat, Kate Suslava, Yakun Wang, Li Zhang, and Chen Zhao also hints that analysts (another type of sophisticated market participants) might be guided by questionable motivations. In this chapter, the authors analyze why analysts initiate unfavorable coverage of firms. The naïve might find this question redundant. Aren't analysts supposed to provide "all the news that's fit to print?" The less naïve would assume that analysts strategically decide what to publish and what not to. The novel point of the current chapter is that it explores the particular motivations of analysts behind their strategy of when to initiate negative reports and suggest an innovative result. The authors show that the data support the hypothesis that analysts initiate such recommendations since this increases their credibility amongst investors.

Transitioning to Part 3 where we present chapters dealing with factors that affect individuals' behavior. It analyzes the extent of amateurs'

---

[3] About 70 anomalies are listed in the chapter. Some of them may overlap, but we imagine there might exist others that escaped Kaplanski's eyes and others that strategically were hidden from the public. Overall, the general picture we get from this list is that the number of anomalies is impressive.

cognitive and psychological biases, how good is their decision-making, and for those who err in their decisions, how can this be amended. The first chapter of this part *Annuity or Lump Sum: Getting Retiring Smokers to Make Better Savings Distribution Decisions* by Abigail Hurwitz, Yaniv Hanoch, Andrew Barnes, and Orli Sade investigates the relatively unexplored territory of the impact of smoking on retirement savings decisions. Whereas smokers should be better off choosing lump sum over annuity plans given their (lower) expected longevity, the authors show that on average they do not. The authors present and discuss several methods that could be used by policymakers to nudge those who go wrong to switch to better decisions. They then show which of these methods is the most efficient for achieving this goal. The next two chapters explore individuals' borrowing decisions. The first of these two, *The Effect of Income Inequality on Individuals' Loan Decision* by Shirit Katav Herz and Binyamin Berdugo, explores the "Keeping up with the Joneses" effect. They show that individuals exposed to information about others' superior achievements exhibit a heightened inclination to borrow. This underscores the significance of social comparisons in shaping loan choices that potentially are taken to finance "frivolous spending" thus exacerbating income inequality. The second of these two chapters, *Individual Differences and the Repayment of High- and Low-Consequences Debt*, by Yoav Ganzach and Asya Pazy, suggests that personality and intelligence may affect how individuals handle their debt repayment. Shifting our focus to a unique aspect of consumer behavior, the fifth chapter *It's Not about the Money...: Behavioral Aspects of Tipping* by Hana Medler-Liraz, explores the intricate world of tipping behavior. Tipping remains an intriguing phenomenon, driven more by psychological and social motivations than economic considerations. This chapter offers insights into why people tip and highlights the multifaceted behavioral factors at play in this voluntary payment practice.

Our journey then takes us to Part IV where we conclude with chapters that deal with markets based on technological innovations and the effect of technological innovations on financial markets. The first chapter in this part, *Non-Fruitful Token? Market Reactions to NFT-Related Disclosures* by Smadar Siev investigates how markets respond to firms' disclosures related to Non-Fungible Tokens (NFTs). As the chapter's title implies, the author is skeptical of the usefulness of these instruments, and her skepticism probably is based on her findings that the market shows doubt toward NFTs, particularly among new firms entering this space. Her analysis tracks market reactions to firms' NFTs disclosures filed with the SEC. Siev's analysis distinguishes between "Clear" disclosures, indicating actual NFT engagement, from "Vague" ones, referring to future intentions. Both types exhibit similar non-significant cumulative-average-abnormal-returns (CAAR) behavior upon announcement, followed by significant declines afterward. Segmenting by traits shows varied CAAR patterns, but overall, the study suggests that the market mistrusts NFTs.

Continuing our venture into the realm of innovations, Shlomith D. Zuta's chapter, *The Alternative Meat Industry: Fad or Disruption?* explores the world of alternative investments with a focus on the alternative meats industry. As investments in this novel sector gain momentum, Zuta suggests that behavioral biases might influence the evaluation and allocation of capital in these domains.

Consumption of plant-based meat has been booming over the past few years, accompanied by surging interest on the part of investors, traditional meat producers, and the media. But is the alternative meat industry a truly disruptive force for the meat industry, or is it just a fad? The case sets out to explore this question. Following an introduction of the issue at hand, it provides an overview of the reasons for the increase in the popularity of meat substitutes. Next, industry structure and competition are explored. An examination of the different types of investors is warranted since behavioral considerations might govern some of their decisions. The case concludes with a discussion of the challenges facing the industry and potential policy issues. One of the lessons learned from this chapter is that behavioral finance could be instrumental in exploring whether some other new markets/innovations are just fads or have the potential to become useful and long-lasting, and researchers in this area can add to the understanding the dynamics of evolving markets.

The concluding chapter *Understanding and Mitigating Biases in AI Systems: Insights and Recommendations* by Ruti Gafni, Boris Kantsepolsky, and Sofia Sherman resides in the captivating realm where artificial intelligence and finance intersect. The questions that revolve around AI relate to the extent that it would change the world of finance and if so, how. As AI continues to reshape human activities, the chapter highlights the potential negative consequences of embedding human biases into AI systems. It offers actionable recommendations for mitigating these biases and increasing trust and adoption of AI systems, bridging the gap between technology and behavioral considerations, thus rendering the world of finance more useful to society.

Each of the above chapters investigates a unique aspect of human behavior and its impact on financial decisions, from individual differences to societal and market-level dynamics. Together, they offer a rich tapestry of insights, bridging the gap between traditional concepts and the rapidly emerging frontiers of behavioral finance. They collectively emphasize the significance of understanding human behavior in financial decision-making, illuminating both well-trodden paths and uncharted territories within this ever-evolving discipline.

This collection would not have been possible without the dedication and expertise of both the authors and the referees. Hence, it is essential to express our heartfelt gratitude to the authors who have enriched this collection with their research and expertise. It is your rigorous work, thoughtful insights, and innovative contributions that make this collection a valuable resource for scholars, practitioners, and enthusiasts alike. We would also like to extend our sincere appreciation to the referees who played a crucial role in reviewing the chapters for this collection. Your meticulous evaluation and valuable feedback have ensured the excellence and credibility of the chapters included in this compilation.

References

Cohen, R.B., Polk, C., and Vuolteenaho, T. (2005). Money illusion in the stock market: The Modigliani–Cohn hypothesis. *The Quarterly Journal of Economics*, 120(2), 639–668.

Fama, E.F. and Schwert, G.W. (1977). Asset returns and inflation. *Journal of Financial Economics*, 5(2), 115–146.

Foster, G., Olsen, C., and Shevlin, T. (1984). Earnings releases, anomalies, and the behavior of security returns. *Accounting Review*, 59, 574–603.

Modigliani, F. and Cohn, R.A. (1979). Inflation, rational valuation and the market. *Financial Analysts Journal*, 35(2), 24–44.

Thaler, R.H. and Shefrin, H.M. (1981). An economic theory of self-control. *Journal of Political Economy*, 89(2), 392–406.

About the Editors

Itzhak Venezia, as of September 2024, is the Distinguished Research Professor of Behavioral Finance, Risk Management, and Insurance at the University of Limassol. He holds the Sanger Chair of Banking and Risk Management (emeritus) at the Hebrew University, Jerusalem, Israel, where he taught before assuming his current position. Professor Venezia is the Editor-in-Chief of the *Lecture Notes Series in Finance*, and the editor of the books *Behavioral Finance: Where do Investors Biases Come From?* and *Behavioral Finance: The Coming of Age*. He also authored the book *Lecture Notes in Behavioral Finance*. Itzhak has published numerous papers in leading journals such as *The Journal of Finance, Journal of Economic Theory, Journal of Banking and Finance*, and *Management Science* and is the Joint Editor of the book *Bridging the GAAP: Recent Advances in Accounting and Finance*. He taught as a Visiting Professor at Yale University, the University of California, Los Angeles, Rutgers University, and Northwestern University. Professor Venezia's research currently concentrates on Behavioral Finance and Insurance. In Behavioral Finance, he contributed profoundly to a better understanding of the disposition effect, herding, the differences in biases between amateurs and professionals, and other issues. In Insurance, he provided important insights about the demand for deductibles, suggesting several explanations for the deductible puzzle. His papers also shed light, among others, on the optimal construction of multi-period insurance con-tracts and on explaining the tie-in of savings and insurance contracts. Prof. Venezia holds a PhD from the University of California, Berkeley.

Rachel Calipha is a Senior Lecturer of Finance, the Head of Capital Market Specialty, and the Head of the Research Institute of Society and Economics (RISE Impact) at the Academic College of Tel Aviv-Yaffo, Israel. Before this appointment, she taught as a Visiting Professor at Yeshiva University, New York, where she received a teaching award.

Currently, Rachel teaches courses in Mergers and Acquisitions, Firm Valuation, Financial Statements, Investments, Financial Crises, and Social Impact Bonds at the Academic College of Tel Aviv Yaffo and at Ben Gurion University, Israel.

Rachel has published papers in the *Journal of Strategy and Management* and in *Advances in Mergers and Acquisitions*. In addition, she has published chapters in the *Encyclopedia of Finance* and in *Behavioral Finance: A Novel Approach*. She is the editor of the book *The Evolution of the Israeli Third Sector: A Conceptual and Empirical Analysis* and she has published several case studies such as *Social Impact Bond: Rehabili-tation of Prisoners Case*. Rachel Calipha's research currently concentrates on Impact Investments. Rachel holds a PhD from the Ben Gurion Univer-sity, Israel.

List of Contributors

Andrew Barnes
Virginia Commonwealth University
Richmond, Virginia, USA

Binyamin Berdugo
Academic College of Tel-Aviv-Yaffo, Israel

Ruti Gafni
Academic College of Tel-Aviv-Yaffo, Israel

Yoav Ganzach
Academic College of Tel-Aviv-Yaffo, Israel

Yaniv Hanoch
University of Southampton
Southampton, UK

Abigail Hurwitz
Hebrew University of Jerusalem, Israel

Boris Kantsepolsky
Academic College of Tel-Aviv-Yaffo, Israel

Guy Kaplanski
Bar-Ilan University Ramat-Gan, Israel

Shirit Katav-Herz
Academic College of Tel-Aviv-Yaffo, Israel

Chunbo Liu
Shanghai International Studies University
Shanghai, China

Joshua Livnat
New York University
New York, USA

Hana Medler-Liraz
Academic College of Tel-Aviv-Yaffo, Israel

Jacob Oded
Tel Aviv University, Israel

Moran Ofir
Reichman University
Israel

Asya Pazy
Tel Aviv University, Israel

Orly Sade
Hebrew University of Jerusalem, Israel

Dan Segal
Reichman University
Israel

Sofia Sherman
Academic College of Tel-Aviv-Yaffo, Israel

Smadar Siev
Ono Academic College
Israel

Kate Suslava
Bucknell University
Pennsylvania, USA

Itzhak Venezia
The University of Limassol
Limassol, Cyprus

Yakun Wang
The Chinese University of Hong Kong, Hong Kong

Zvi Wiener
Hebrew University of Jerusalem
Israel

Cheng Zhang
University of Denver
Denver, Colorado, USA

Li Zhang
Rutgers University
Newark, USA

Chen Zhao
Southwestern University of Finance and Economics
China

Zhiping Zhou
Tongji University Shanghai, China

Shlomith D. Zuta
Academic College of Tel-Aviv-Yaffo, Israel

Acknowledgments

We thank the Tel Aviv Yaffo Academic College, and Yoav Ganzach, Dean of the School of Management and Economics for their support in funding the Fourth Israel Conference in Behavioral Finance which led to the writing of this book. We are also grateful to the members of the steering committee of this conference, Sasson Bar Yosef, Rachel Gilo Shalom, Jacob Oded, and Yaron Lahav for participating in the organization and operation of this conference.

Contents

Part I

Anomalies

Chapter 1

Changes in Short Positions and Earnings Surprises

Joshua Livnat*, Dan Segal†, and Kate Suslava‡

*Stern School of Business, New York University,
New York, USA
jlivnat@ stern.nyu.edu

†Reichman University, Israel
dsegal@idc.ac.il

‡Freeman College of Management,
Bucknell University, Lewisburg, USA
kate.suslava@bucknell.edu

Abstract

Our study investigates how the existence of short interest affects the Post Earnings Announcement Drift (PEAD). When extremely negative or positive earnings are announced, investors with large short positions can either cover their short positions immediately or continue to hold and/or increase their short positions. Our combined evidence show that investors typically trim down short positions after earnings announcements, regardless of the direction of the earnings surprise. Also, investors seem to increase their short positions if they had low levels of short positions, especially for firms that reported positive earnings surprises. Investors seem to behave in a manner inconsistent with the PEAD, and support an explanation that PEAD is the result of investor underreaction to earnings news.

Keywords: Earnings surprise, Short positions, Stock market reaction

1. Introduction

The Post Earnings Announcement Drift (PEAD) is the tendency of equity returns of companies with extreme earnings surprises to drift in the direction of the earnings surprise after the earnings become public.[1] This persistent phenomenon is one of the most perplexing market anomalies — stock prices typically react immediately to the earnings surprises, so any further drift in returns should not occur in an efficient market. There are three potential explanations for this phenomenon. The most reasonable explanation is that there is an element of risk which our traditional stock pricing models do not capture. However, despite many various tests and methodologies over close to 50 years the phenomenon still exists. Another potential explanation is that there are impediments to arbitrage that prevent market participants from taking advantage of this phenomenon. However, the phenomenon exists also for large, very liquid stocks with low arbitrage risks. The third explanation, which is more behavioral, is that investors underreact to the extreme earnings surprises. They may be seeking further information to corroborate the initial extreme surprise, hence causing the PEAD.

The purpose of this study is to investigate how the existence of short interest affects the PEAD. Investors who hold short positions in a particular company are betting that the price of the stock will go down, so they can cover their short positions at a profit. Suppose that one holds a short position in a firm that has just announced an extremely negative earnings surprise. The negative earnings surprise is likely to cause the stock price to decline. The short position holder now faces the question of covering the short position and realizing an immediate profit, or holding onto the short position (and maybe adding to it) in anticipation of further declines as predicted by the PEAD. Other investors who wish to take advantage of the PEAD may also take short positions in the company with an extremely negative earnings surprise. Similarly, investors with short positions in companies that had extremely positive earnings surprises probably face a parallel dilemma. They can terminate the short position at a loss and avoid larger future losses if the stock price should continue to increase as predicted by the PEAD. On the other hand, if the holders of the short position had expected negative news to occur, they may now be inclined to assess the extremely positive earnings surprise as temporary with lower future

---

[1] Some examples of PEAD studies include Ball and Brown (1968), Bernard and Thomas (1990), and Livnat and Mendenhall (2006).

earnings that will drive future stock prices down. They may continue to hold onto their short positions, or even add to them. Similarly, other investors who also expect future earnings disappointments may also take initial short positions, adding to the short interest of the stocks with extremely positive earnings surprises.

It is not clear *a priori* which of the two effects of the initial short position will dominate. Will the immediate unwinding of the short position be stronger and the short interest will decline, or the expectations of future negative news will cause investors to build up the short position? The question is particularly intriguing given the long and convincing evidence about the PEAD. It has been shown that extremely positive earnings surprises are more likely to be followed by future positive earnings surprises and stock returns. The converse has been shown for extremely negative earnings surprises. If PEAD expectations dominate we should observe an increasing short interest for companies with extremely negative news and a decreasing short interest for companies with extremely positive earnings surprises. However, if the PEAD is driven by underreaction stemming from investors' lack of confidence about the continuing direction of future earnings surprises, then we would expect to mostly see an immediate unwinding of the short positions. Which of these two behavioral decisions will dominate is an interesting academic question, but it also has practical implications. We can construct portfolios based on earnings surprises and their associated short-interest movements, and observe subsequent market returns.

An earlier study by Lasser *et al.* (2010) examined the effects of short selling on market reactions to earnings announcements. They provide evidence that, for companies with extremely positive earnings surprises, immediate market returns of firms with high short interest are larger than those of firms with low short interest. This is attributed to the covering of short positions. In contrast, for extremely negative earnings surprises, firms with high levels of short interest have weaker (less negative) immediate returns than firms with low levels of short interest, again possibly due to the liquidation of short positions. They also show that the PEAD is smaller for firms with high short interest; less positive for extremely positive earnings surprises, and less negative for extremely negative earnings surprises. This is attributed to the short-term effects of unwinding the short positions. While appealing in shedding light on the effects of potential short covering after earnings announcements, their study is limited by the fact that they have not examined directly the changes in short interest from before the earnings announcements to those afterward. They also examined only the sub-sample with short interest data. These limitations are remedied in the current study.

2. Data and Research Design

The universe in this study is composed of the largest 3,000 firms with common stock on the CRSP database that are matched to the Compustat database, to resemble the Russell 3,000 Index. Consistent with prior studies, we delete firms with stock prices below $1.00 or market values below $10 million. At each month-end, we identify the closest earnings announcement in the prior 180 days from the Compustat quarterly database. We then construct the earnings surprise from the IBES detail database if the IBES actual announcement date and the Compustat earnings report date are within a day of each other. The standardized earnings surprise, *SUE*, is the actual IBES quarterly EPS minus the average forecast of all analysts in the 90-day period prior to the earnings announcement (with only the most recent forecast by each analyst), scaled by the standard deviation of these forecasts or 0.01, whichever is higher. We then select the closest short-interest ratio, the number of shorted shares divided by shares outstanding from the CRSP database as of the month-end, on either side of the earnings announcement date, as long as the short interest date is prior to the month-end date (the portfolio formation date) and no more than 180 days prior to the earnings announcement date. The change in the short-interest ratio, *DIFSHORT*, is the short-interest ratio immediately after the earnings announcement minus the one immediately prior to it. The frequency of reporting short-interest data was changed in 2007 from monthly to bi-weekly, which is another advantage of the current study over the Lasser *et al.* (2010) study that used only monthly data through 2003. At the portfolio formation date, we sort all firms into quintiles using the earnings surprise *SUE* and the change in short ratio *DIFSHORT*. The portfolio performance is assessed by the average buy-and-hold return on a stock minus the value-weighted buy-and-hold return on a portfolio of similar stocks in terms of size (market value of equity, 3 groups), book/market (B/M) ratio (book equity to market equity ratio, 3 groups) and 12-month momentum (in months $t - 12$ through $t - 1$, 3 groups). Portfolios are held for a month and are reconstituted at the end of the subsequent month-end.

In addition to the earnings surprise *SUE*, this study uses the abnormal buy-and-hold return in the three days centered on the earnings announcement date, *XRETPRELIM*. The abnormal return is the buy-and-hold return minus the buy-and-hold return on similar stocks in terms of size, B/M, and 11-month momentum as above. Prior studies have either used *XRETPRELIM* instead of *SUE* to determine the earnings surprise or in addition to *SUE* to take advantage of additional information beyond earnings available in their earnings releases or conference calls. We can also use *XRETPRELIM* to assess the differential market reactions to *SUE* for firms with different levels of short interest as in Lasser *et al.* (2010).

The following analyses use two approaches. A tabulation of mean abnormal monthly returns on the portfolios for the various quintiles of *SUE*, short interest prior to the earnings announcement and *DIFRATIO*. We also use Fama and MacBeth (1973) monthly cross-sectional regressions of abnormal returns on various factors. For the latter, we scale the quintile rank of the various variables by 4 (which is the highest value, with rank zero representing the lowest quintile), and subtract 0.5. The coefficients of the scaled variables in the regressions represent the return on a hedge portfolio holding long positions in the top quintile and short positions in the bottom quintile. The intercept measures the average abnormal return in the sample for that month. We use the average monthly coefficients (and their *t*-statistics) over the sample period that ends in December 2022 to assess the importance of variables in explaining portfolio abnormal returns.

Table 1 reports summary statistics for our sample.[2] The mean and median abnormal returns are very close to zero for both the month after portfolio formation and the short window around the earnings announcement. The mean and median earnings surprises are positive, which indicates that companies are typically able to beat analyst forecasts. The mean and median short-interest ratios are around 2–4%, with the short-interest ratio increasing slightly from before the earnings announcement to immediately afterward. The sample has a large variation in size, although the selected firms are typically larger than the CRSP population due to the sample selection criteria. Also notable in the table is that short interest and IBES data reduce the initial sample by about one-third.

Table 2 reports the correlations among the main variables in the study. For ease of interpretation, the independent variables have been assigned their quintile rank and scaled to fall in the range of [−0.5, +0.5]. There is a positive correlation between the abnormal return around the earnings announcement and that of the monthly abnormal return after the portfolio formation date, which is similar in size to that of the earnings surprise. This is consistent with prior evidence about the PEAD and the high

---

[2]All variables except the market value and number of forecasts have been multiplied by 100.

Table 1:   Summary statistics.

Variable	N	Mean	Std. dev.	P 10	P 25	P 50	P 75	P 90
XMONRET	1268223	−0.124	13.519	−13.565	−6.510	−0.707	5.249	13.128
XRETPRELIM	819541	0.234	8.581	−8.543	−3.552	0.094	3.967	9.181
SUE	816515	3.593	1557.720	−3.000	−0.611	0.523	2.021	4.965
SHORTINTPRIOR	886467	3.756	5.200	0.064	0.487	1.927	4.833	9.785
SHORTINTPOST	728382	3.849	5.269	0.072	0.527	2.000	4.967	9.987
DIFSHORT	715772	0.012	0.974	−0.569	−0.164	0.000	0.171	0.609
MARKET VALUE	1268223	4159	27003	41	98	348	1514	6009
N_FORECAST	819625	5.369	5.089	1	2	4	7	12

Notes: The table presents summary statistics of variables in the sample spanning July 1985 through December 2020. N is the number of observations. *Std. Dev* is the standard deviation. The table also reports various percentiles of the variables. *XMONRET* is the abnormal monthly return during the month after the portfolio formation date. *XRETPRELIM* is the abnormal return in the 3-day window centered on the earnings announcement date. Abnormal returns are buy-and-hold returns on the stock minus the value-weighted return on stocks with similar size (3 groups), B/M (3 groups), and momentum (return over months $t - 12$ through $t - 1$, 3 groups). *SUE* is IBES actual EPS minus IBES mean forecast by all analysts in the 90-day period prior to the earnings announcement divided by the standard deviation of the forecasts. *SHORTINTPRIOR* (*SHORTINTPOST*) is the closest ratio of shorted shares to shares outstanding prior to (after) the earnings announcement. *DIFSHORT* is *SHORTINTPOST* minus *SHORTINTPRIOR*. *MARKET VALUE* is market capitalization of the firm, and *N_FOREASCTS* is the number of analyst forecasts for a given firm. All variables except the market value and number of forecasts have been multiplied by 100.

correlation between the earnings surprise and its immediate market reaction (almost 30% in our sample). The short-interest ratios have low negative correlations with the returns after the portfolio formation date, and the change in the short-interest ratio has insignificant correlation with the return after the portfolio formation date. The short-interest ratio and the earnings surprise have a negative correlation, indicating that investors held higher short-interest positions in companies with negative earnings surprises than in companies with positive earnings surprises, consistent with the idea that the short interest can predict the sign of earnings surprises.

3. Results

Table 3 shows the relation between the earnings surprises and the abnormal returns in the 3-day window centered on the earnings announcement date in the "All" column. We can see that the quintile of firms with the most negative *SUE* had on average immediate negative abnormal returns

Table 2: Correlation matrix.

	XMONRET	XRETPRELIM	RSUE	RXRETPRELIM	RSHORTINTPRIOR	RSHORTINTPOST
XMONRET	1.00000 1268223					
XRETPRELIM	0.01173 <0.0001 819541	1.00000 819541				
RSUE	0.01175 <0.0001 816515	0.27300 <0.0001 816363	1.00000 816515			
RXRETPRELIM	0.01141 <0.0001 819541	0.82442 <0.0001 819541	0.29253 <0.0001 816363	1.00000 819541		
RSHORTINTPRIOR	-0.00216 0.0423 886467	-0.01281 <0.0001 649529	-0.02182 <0.0001 646507	-0.00941 <0.0001 649529	1.00000 886467	
RSHORTINTPOST	-0.00386 0.0010 728382	-0.01202 <0.0001 532794	-0.02713 <0.0001 530150	-0.00815 <0.0001 532794	0.94425 <0.0001 715772	1.00000 728382
RDIFSHORT	0.00082 0.4871 715772	-0.01101 <0.0001 526571	-0.02903 <0.0001 523932	-0.00678 <0.0001 526571	-0.06988 <0.0001 715772	0.07826 <0.0001 715772

Notes: Variable definitions can be found in the notes in Table 1. All the explanatory variables are ranked on each portfolio formation date into quintiles. The prefix *r* indicates that the variables are assigned their quintile rank (0 through 4), divided by 4 minus 0.5. These transform the variables into the [−0.5, +0.5] range.

Table 3. Short window returns around earnings announcements.

Ranked SUE	XRETPRELIM							XRETPRELIM						
	Ranked SHORTINTPRIOR							Ranked SHORTINTPRIOR						
	.	0	1	2	3	4	All	.	0	1	2	3	4	All
	Mean	Mean	Mean	Mean	Mean	Mean	Mean	N	N	N	N	N	N	N
.	−0.780	0.442	−0.187	0.138	−0.682	−0.652	−0.045	137	925	897	666	311	242	3178
0	−2.73	−2.27	−2.98	−3.50	−3.99	−4.48	−3.39	35717	17876	23715	26346	28339	31104	163E3
1	−0.905	−0.546	−1.14	−1.14	−1.39	−1.51	−1.17	33138	12090	25038	29194	31733	32788	164E3
2	0.601	0.638	0.309	0.582	0.498	0.646	0.541	32067	10919	26348	30622	31796	30964	163E3
3	1.520	1.426	1.553	1.700	2.067	2.269	1.789	33521	12259	27886	29751	30539	29400	163E3
4	3.121	3.163	3.026	3.452	3.761	3.949	3.417	35432	15792	27539	28659	28825	26966	163E3
All	0.313	0.395	0.268	0.288	0.197	0.027	0.234	17E4	69861	131E3	145E3	152E3	151E3	82E4

Notes: The table presents mean abnormal returns for the 3-day window centered on the earnings announcement date. Portfolios are sorted independently into quintiles each month-end on *SUE* and the closest short interest prior to the earnings announcement. Quintile 0 is the lowest values for each variable and "." represents missing values.

of −3.39%, whereas those of the most positive *SUE* had positive abnormal returns of 3.417% on average. There is a monotonic increase in abnormal returns across the earnings surprise quintiles. The table also shows the relationship between the short-interest ratio prior to the earnings announcement and the immediate abnormal returns around it in the "All" row. It shows a declining pattern, with firms that had the lowest short interest (column "0") having average abnormal return of 0.395%, as compared to 0.27% for firms with the highest short positions (column "4").

Consistent with Lasser *et al.* (2010), the table also shows that the abnormal returns for firms in the highest *SUE* quintile increase almost monotonically with the short-interest ratio. This is consistent with immediate short covering as a reaction to the positive earnings surprise. However, inconsistent with Lasser *et al.* (2010), we see that the abnormal returns around the earnings announcement for the lowest *SUE* quintile become monotonically more negative across the short-interest ratio quintiles. We would expect that immediate short covering will yield the opposite results.

Table 4 is similar to Table 3, except that it provides information on the abnormal returns during the month after the portfolio formation date. Examining the "All" column again shows monotonically increasing abnormal returns across *SUE* quintiles with −0.328% for the most negative earnings surprises and 0.120% for the most positive *SUE*, consistent with the PEAD. The effect of the short-interest ratio in the "All" row is less clear-cut. It is not monotonic, is small, and shows that firms with high short-interest ratios prior to the earnings announcement tend to have slightly more negative abnormal returns subsequently than those with low short-interest ratios. However, a more interesting observation in Table 4 is that subsequent abnormal returns for firms with the most positive earnings surprises are much higher for firms with low short interest of 0.598% on average than those with high short-interest ratios of −0.50%. The converse is true for firms with the most negative *SUE*. Firms with the lowest short-interest ratio prior to the earnings announcements had negative abnormal returns subsequently of −0.618% as compared to −0.224 for those with the highest short-interest positions before the earnings announcement. In fact, the table shows that most of the action in the month following the earnings announcement is in the firms with the lowest short ratio. These results are consistent with Lasser *et al.* (2010).

Table 5 provides information about the relationship between subsequent abnormal returns and both the earnings surprises, *SUE*, and the

Table 4. Abnormal monthly portfolio returns.

Ranked SUE	XMONRET							XMONRET						
	.	Ranked SHORTINTPRIOR					All	.	Ranked SHORTINTPRIOR					All
		0	1	2	3	4			0	1	2	3	4	
	Mean	Mean	Mean	Mean	Mean	Mean	Mean	N	N	N	N	N	N	N
.	−0.481	−0.116	−0.165	−0.045	−0.212	−0.524	−0.316	212E3	108E3	46870	32798	26156	25974	452E3
0	−1.02	−0.618	0.001	0.049	−0.010	−0.224	−0.328	35741	17876	23715	26347	28340	31105	163E3
1	−0.376	−0.137	0.024	−0.064	0.007	−0.038	−0.100	33154	12090	25038	29195	31735	32788	164E3
2	0.087	0.219	0.252	0.136	0.150	0.029	0.133	32096	10919	26348	30622	31801	30964	163E3
3	0.118	0.190	0.139	0.122	−0.008	0.028	0.088	33545	12260	27886	29751	30539	29400	163E3
4	0.052	0.598	0.222	0.198	−0.076	−0.050	0.120	35472	15796	27539	28662	28825	26966	163E3
All	−0.372	−0.063	0.054	0.064	−0.018	−0.121	−0.124	382E3	177E3	177E3	177E3	177E3	177E3	127E4

Notes: The table presents mean abnormal returns for the month after the portfolio formation date. Portfolios are sorted independently into quintiles each month-end on *SUE* and the closest short interest prior to the earnings announcement. Quintile 0 is the lowest values for each variable and "." represents missing values.

Table 5. Abnormal monthly portfolio returns.

Ranked SUE	XMONRET — Ranked XRETPRELIM							XMONRET — Ranked XRETPRELIM						
	.	0	1	2	3	4	All	.	0	1	2	3	4	All
	Mean	Mean	Mean	Mean	Mean	Mean	Mean	N	N	N	N	N	N	N
.	−0.318	−0.416	−0.148	−0.676	0.584	0.699	−0.316	449E3	490	774	864	615	435	452E3
0	−5.18	−0.439	−0.266	−0.294	−0.308	−0.157	−0.328	27	58357	39044	28738	20530	16428	163E3
1	4.398	−0.113	−0.172	−0.107	−0.058	0.004	−0.100	19	39140	39032	35155	29038	21616	164E3
2	−1.65	−0.112	0.085	0.126	0.197	0.337	0.133	34	26883	33827	35799	35508	30699	163E3
3	−2.75	−0.258	0.132	0.058	0.205	0.154	0.088	25	21452	28237	33876	39228	40563	163E3
4	−4.45	−0.271	0.075	−0.001	0.137	0.321	0.120	47	17401	23090	29573	39084	54065	163E3
All	−.318	−0.266	−0.054	−0.039	0.078	0.194	−0.124	449E3	164E3	164E3	164E3	164E3	164E3	127E4

Notes: The table presents mean abnormal returns for the month after the portfolio formation date. Portfolios are sorted independently into quintiles each month-end on *SUE* and the 3-day abnormal return is centered on the earnings announcement. Quintile 0 is the lowest value for each variable and "." represents missing values.

abnormal return around the earnings announcement, *XRETPRELIM*. It shows that for each *SUE* quintile, firms with the highest immediate abnormal returns have also higher subsequent abnormal returns than those with the lowest *XRETPRELIM*. The converse is also true; subsequent abnormal returns are always higher for firms with the highest *SUE* than those with the lowest *SUE* for each *XRETPRELIM* quintile. Thus, future portfolio returns can be enhanced by using both the earnings surprise, *SUE*, and the abnormal return around the earnings announcement, *XRETPRELIM*, likely because of additional non-earnings information released with earnings or in the immediate conference calls afterward.[3]

Next we examine whether the changes in the short-interest ratios are dependent on the earnings surprise. If investors holding large short position in a company cover immediately their positions after the earnings announcement, we would expect to see similar changes in short-interest ratios across all *SUE* quintiles. Differences in short interest changes across *SUE* quintiles may be attributed to differential risk aversion levels, with short covering stronger for the most positive SUE quintile to reduce future losses. If investors completely believe past studies about PEAD, then we expect to see increases in the short-interest ratios of firms with the most negative *SUE*, and decreases for firms with the most positive earnings surprises.

Table 6 shows the mean change in the short-interest ratios for *SUE* quintiles and different levels of the short-interest ratio prior to the earnings announcement. Looking at the "All" column, we see that during the sample period the short-interest ratios increased slightly from before the earnings announcement to immediately afterward. It is also evident that the short interest increased more for the lowest quintile *SUE* than for the quintiles with the most positive earnings surprises, consistent with investors expecting the PEAD. The "All" row shows that short-interest positions tend to decline for companies with the highest short positions prior to the earnings announcements but increase for all other firms.

A closer examination of Table 6 reveals a few interesting phenomena. Relatively large increases in short-interest ratios occur for firms with the most negative earnings surprises, except for those with the highest

---

[3] Examples of studies into the information content of conference calls include Bushee *et al.* (2003), Price *et al.* (2012), Brockman *et al.* (2015), Druz *et al.* (2015), and Klevak *et al.* (2019).

Table 6. Changes in short interest around earnings announcements.

Ranked SUE	DIFSHORT — Ranked SHORTINTPRIOR							DIFSHORT — Ranked SHORTINTPRIOR						
	.	0	1	2	3	4	All	.	0	1	2	3	4	All
	Mean	Mean	Mean	Mean	Mean	Mean	Mean	N	N	N	N	N	N	N
.	.	0.026	0.040	0.036	0.008	-0.115	0.013	0	86056	37008	26365	21203	21208	192E3
0	.	0.039	0.080	0.093	0.078	-0.014	0.053	0	14576	19476	21742	23572	26190	106E3
1	.	0.043	0.051	0.045	0.045	-0.070	0.017	0	9651	20076	23671	25949	27138	106E3
2	.	0.056	0.053	0.042	-0.002	-0.114	-0.003	0	8658	20895	24420	25565	25254	105E3
3	.	0.040	0.039	0.026	-0.004	-0.117	-0.010	0	9645	22129	23739	24584	23822	104E3
4	.	0.051	0.053	0.031	0.007	-0.112	0.002	0	12653	22139	23141	23295	21952	103E3
All	.	0.034	0.051	0.044	0.022	-0.088	0.012	0	141E3	142E3	143E3	144E3	146E3	716E

Notes: The table presents mean changes in short-interest ratios from immediately before the earnings announcement to immediately after it. Portfolios are sorted independently into quintiles each month-end on SUE and the short interest immediately prior to the earnings announcement. Quintile 0 is the lowest value for each variable and "." represents missing values.

short-interest ratios prior to the earnings announcements. This is consistent with both investors who pile in after extreme negative earnings to take advantage of PEAD expectations, but also short covering and profit realization by those investors who held the largest short positions prior to the earnings announcement. The table also shows a reasonably high buildup of short positions for firms with the most positive earnings surprises, consistent with betting against the PEAD and assessments that the extremely positive earnings surprise is temporary and will reverse. On the other hand, for the highest prior short interest quintile (column "4") investors tend to cover their short positions and trim their losses. Further, we observe an increase in the short position across all *SUE* quintiles for quintiles 0–2 of the short position prior to the earnings announcement. In other words, it appears that the level of the short position drives the change in the position post-earnings announcement and not the earnings surprise *per se*. Thus, Table 6 does not provide clear-cut evidence that will point to how investors assess the expectations for future price drifts from their changes in short-interest positions. However, we can examine whether the change in short-interest ratios around earnings announcements, *DIFRATIO*, are related to subsequent portfolio returns.

Table 7 shows the subsequent abnormal returns to different combinations of *SUE* and *DIFSHORT*. For the most negative earnings surprises, decreases in short ratios actually have more subsequent negative abnormal returns than for firms with the highest *DIFRATIO*. This is consistent with the PEAD effect dominating and implying that it pays to increase the short positions on earnings disappointments. The results for the most positive earnings surprises are more ambiguous and both extreme changes in short-interest ratios tend to have the lowest subsequent returns. Hence, it seems reasonable to examine all the factors together in a multivariate regression.

Table 8 presents time-series means and *t*-statistics of monthly cross-sectional regressions in the manner of Fama and MacBeth (1973). The dependent variable is the abnormal return during the month after the portfolio formation date. In Model 1, the independent variable is the scaled *SUE* rank, a number in the range [−0.5, +0.5]. The coefficient on *RSUE* has a mean of 0.318 with a *t*-statistic of 3.71, highly significant, and consistent with prior studies of the PEAD. Note that our study is closer to a practical application of a portfolio strategy since it assumes a portfolio rebalancing each month-end using all available data as of that

Table 7. Abnormal monthly portfolio returns.

| Ranked SUE | XMONRET | | | | | | | XMONRET | | | | | | |
| | · | Ranked DIFSHORT | | | | | All | · | Ranked DIFSHORT | | | | | All |
	Mean	0 Mean	1 Mean	2 Mean	3 Mean	4 Mean	Mean	N	0 N	1 N	2 N	3 N	4 N	N
·	−0.440	−0.303	−0.151	−0.217	0.103	−0.249	−0.316	26E4	22208	40831	64310	41768	22723	452E3
0	−0.794	−0.164	0.053	−0.257	−0.026	−0.005	−0.328	57568	21736	19246	17794	21141	25639	163E3
1	−0.211	−0.025	−0.032	−0.053	−0.042	−0.054	−0.100	57515	24674	20859	15445	20224	25283	164E3
2	0.059	0.217	0.246	0.200	0.098	0.115	0.133	57958	25408	20517	14875	19860	24132	163E3
3	0.146	−0.015	0.077	0.116	0.193	−0.048	0.088	59462	25090	20619	15597	19625	22988	163E3
4	0.188	−0.022	0.047	0.246	0.265	−0.071	0.120	60080	23857	20381	16581	20055	22306	163E3
All	−0.270	−0.044	0.012	−0.072	0.098	−0.049	−0.124	552E3	143E3	142E3	145E3	143E3	143E3	127E4

Notes: The table presents mean abnormal returns for the month after the portfolio formation date. Portfolios are sorted independently into quintiles each month-end on *SUE* and the change in the short-interest ratio from immediately prior to the earnings announcement to immediately following it. Quintile 0 is the lowest value for each variable and "·" represents missing values.

Table 8.   Regressions of returns on signals.

	Model 1	Model 2	Model 3	Model 4
Intercept	−0.035	−0.036	−0.030	−0.036
	−0.70	−0.71	−0.61	−0.72
RSUE	0.318	0.255	0.252	0.253
	3.71	2.92	2.92	2.900
RXRETPRELIM		0.247	0.252	0.265
		2.88	2.97	3.08
RSHORTINTPRIOR			−0.130	
			−1.11	
RDIFSHORT				−0.152
				−2.66
N	1162	1162	1162	1162
R-square	0.003	0.006	0.011	0.007

Notes: The table presents the time series means (and *t*-statistics) of 450 monthly cross-sectional regressions where the dependent variable is the abnormal return during the month after the portfolio formation date. The independent variables are the earnings surprise, *SUE*, the abnormal returns around the earnings announcement date, *XRETPRELIM*, the short-interest ratio immediately prior to the earnings announcement date, *SHORTINTPRIOR*, and the change in the short-interest ratio from immediately prior to the earnings announcement to immediately afterward, *DIFSHORT*. All the independent variables are sorted on the portfolio formation date into quintiles. Each independent variable is assigned its rank (0 to 4), divided by 4, minus 0.5. *N* represents the average number of firms in the cross-sectional regressions. *R*-square is the average *R*-square of the 450 monthly regressions. Further information on the variables is available in Table 1 notes.

date. Each firm in our initial sample with IBES forecast in the prior 180 days is included in the portfolio. Model 2 adds the scaled rank of the 3-day return around the earnings announcement, *RXRETPRELIM*. Now both *RSUE* and *RXRETPRELIM* have positive and highly significant coefficients, indicating that both contribute significantly to portfolio abnormal returns. The sum of the two coefficients is about 0.5% abnormal return per month, greater than just 0.32% for *SUE*, indicating the additional information beyond earnings released during the earnings announcement window.

Model 3 in Table 8 adds the scaled short-interest ratio immediately prior to the earnings announcement. Both *SUE* and *XRETPRELIM* maintain their coefficients and significance levels, but the short interest has a negative and statistically insignificant coefficient. The negative coefficient indicates that high short-interest position prior to the earnings announcements tends to reduce the subsequent PEAD, consistent with Lasser *et al.* (2010), but the effect is not strong enough to be significant. Model 4 maintains the two variables that measure the surprise in the earnings announcement, *RSUE* and *RXRETPRELIM*, but now adds the scaled rank of the change in the short-interest ratio from before to after the earnings announcement, *RDIFRATIO*. The two information variables are still positive and significant, and the sum of their returns is slightly higher than in Model 2, where *RDIFRATIO* was not included. However, the coefficient on *RDIFRATIO* is negative and significant, indicating that increases in the short positions actually reduce subsequent portfolio returns. Since Table 6 shows that most of the increases in short positions occurred for positive earnings surprises with relatively lower short-interest positions prior to the earnings announcements, this result indicates that betting against PEAD resulted in lower returns.

4. Summary and Conclusions

This study investigates the relationship of short interest to the PEAD. When extremely negative earnings are announced, investors with large short positions face a dilemma. They can cover their short positions immediately, harvesting their likely gains on the declines in stock prices as a result of the negative news. Alternatively, they can continue to hold their short positions or even increase the short positions in anticipation of further negative news, as previous studies of the PEAD have shown. A similar dilemma exists for short positions when extremely positive news is announced. Do they capitulate and terminate their short positions in an effort to avoid larger future losses, or alternatively bet that the current extreme positive news is transitory and hold on to their short positions or even increase them? If short investors are more sophisticated and are aware of the PEAD, they should increase their short positions after extreme negative announcements and reduce their short positions after extremely positive earnings surprises.

Our combined evidence show that investors typically trim down short positions after earnings announcements, regardless of the direction of the earnings surprise. Also, investors seem to increase their short positions if they had low levels of short positions, especially for firms that reported positive earnings surprises. Thus, we find that investors seem to behave in a manner inconsistent with the PEAD. This strengthens the likelihood that the PEAD is the result of underreaction to the news by investors. It also shows that professional investors can not only take advantage of the PEAD in obtaining abnormal portfolio returns but can also enhance those returns by betting against companies that increase their short positions after the earnings announcements.

References

Ball, R. and Brown, P.R. (1968). An empirical evaluation of accounting income numbers. *Journal of Accounting Research*, 6, 159–178.

Bernard, V.L. and Thomas, J.K. (1990). Evidence that stock prices do not fully reflect the implications of current earnings for future earnings. *Journal of Accounting and Economics*, 13(4), 305–340.

Brockman, P., Li, X., and Price, S.M. (2015). Differences in conference call tones: Managers versus analysts. *Financial Analyst Journal*, 71(4), 24–42.

Bushee, B.J., Matsumoto, D.A., and Miller, G.S. (2003). Open versus closed conference calls: The determinants and effects of broadening access to disclosure. *Journal of Accounting and Economics*, 34(1–3), 149–180.

Druz, M., Wagner, A., and Zeckhauser, R. (2015). Tips and tells from managers: How the market reads between the lines of conference calls. NBER Working Paper No. 20991.

Fama, E.F. and MacBeth, J.D. (1973). Risk, return, and equilibrium: Empirical tests. *Journal of Political Economy*, 81(3), 607–636.

Klevak, J., Livnat, J., and Suslava, K. (2019). A practical approach to advanced text mining in finance. *The Journal of Financial Data Science*, 1(1), 122–129.

Lasser D.J., Wang, X., and Zhang, Y. (2010). The effect of short selling on market reactions to earnings announcements. *Contemporary Accounting Research*, 27(2), 609–638.

Livnat, J. and Mendenhall, R.R. (2006). Comparing the post-earnings announcement drift for surprises calculated from analyst and time series forecasts. *Journal of Accounting Research*, 44(1), 177–205.

Price, S.M., Doran, J.S., Peterson, D.R., and Bliss B.A. (2012). Earnings conference calls and stock returns: The incremental informativeness of textual tone. *Journal of Banking & Finance*, 36, 992–1011.

Chapter 2

Behavioral Explanations for the Preferences of Dividends Over Stock Repurchases

Jacob Oded* and Itzhak Venezia[†]

*Coller School of Management,
Tel Aviv University, Tel Aviv 69978, Israel
oded@tauex.tau.ac.il

[†]The University of Limassol, Limassol, Cyprus
itzhakvenezia@gmail.com

Abstract

This chapter adopts a behavioral approach to explain why firms prefer dividends over stock repurchases (a tender offer auction) as a payout mechanism despite the significant tax disadvantage that dividends yield. We suggest that different shareholders might have different preferences toward stock repurchases, which may stem from differences in their financial literacy, their diverse discount factors, or from similar other idiosyncratic preferences. This divergence of behavior may lead to differences in the number of shares the various groups of shareholders would agree to sell under the tender offer. If the shareholders cannot coordinate so that they all buy the same number of shares, and if the firm makes an underpriced offer, then a value transfer would occur from those who bought more to those who purchased fewer shares. The stockholders, not knowing *a priori* to which category they belong, will object to this cash disbursement mechanism and may prefer dividends. This chapter develops a formal two-stockholder model that proves the above assertions.

Keywords: Payout policy, Stock repurchases, Dividends, Behavioral finance

1. Introduction

Firms return cash to their shareholders using both dividends and stock buybacks (repurchases). An important question in payout policy is why firms pay dividends although repurchases have a substantial tax advantage over dividends. In most countries, dividends are taxed at the investor's marginal tax rate while stock buybacks are subject to capital gains tax, which is generally substantially lower. More importantly, when the cash is distributed in the form of stock repurchase, only the capital gain is taxed. This creates a tax deferral effect which becomes even more valuable the longer the investor holds the stock.[1] This question was first pointed out in Black (1976) as the "dividend puzzle" in which he questions why firms distribute dividends at all. Miller (1986) also addresses the question and suggests that it may be driven by behavioral/cognitive motives, but does not explore this path.

To demonstrate the huge difference in tax liability, consider, for example, IBM's payout policy. In 2022, IBM paid shareholders about $6 billion in dividends, but repurchased stock only for $400 million. The tax rate on dividends in the US in 2002 ranged 20–37% and on capital gains ranged 0–20%, depending on the investor's income. Suppose we assume an average tax rate of 30% on dividends and 10% on capital gains. This implies IBM investors paid $1.8 billion dividend taxes and $40 million in capital gains tax, a total of $1.84 billion. Had IBM instead paid the cash out only in the form of repurchases, investors would have paid only 10% × 6.4 = $0.64 billion in taxes, i.e. $1.16 billion less. Moreover, we have assumed here that the tax base for the capital gains tax is zero. But if the average investor bought the stock when the price was 50% lower, then the tax investors would pay if only repurchase are used for payout would be down to 50% × 10% × 6.4 = $0.32 billion only!

---

[1] Ordinary dividends are taxed at income tax rate which can reach 37%, while capital gains are taxed only at 20% at most. In the past, the gap between these tax rates used to be substantially higher.

The two common forms of stock repurchase are a tender offer repurchase and an open market repurchase program. In a tender offer repurchase, the firm specifies a number of shares it will buy at a given price, which is usually above the market price. In an open market program, the firm repurchases its share through a broker at the prevailing market price over some period of time. Although they are not legally required to, most firms announce open market repurchase. In the past, dividend was much more widespread as a form of payout. Barclay and Smith (1988) found for the period 1983–1986 that while 80% of the firms listed in the NYSE paid dividends, only 10% used open market repurchase and only 1% used tender offer repurchase.

Over the years, repurchases experienced dramatic growth, and since 1996, firms have been paying out cash in the form of repurchases more than they do so with dividends (see, for example, Grullon and Michaely, 2002; Farre-Mensa *et al.*, 2014). The growth in repurchase activity, however, has been in addition to dividend distribution and not as an alternative (e.g. Skinner 2008). For example, in 2022, the S&P 500 firm repurchased shares for about $920 billion and dividends for about $560 billion, i.e. dividends still account for about 38% of S&P 500 firms payout. So, the question remains, why firms pay dividends despite their substantial tax disadvantage.

One branch of the literature about payout policy that tries to explain why firms pay dividends builds on information asymmetry. This literature suggests that because of information asymmetry, firms pay dividends to signal undervaluation (e.g. Bhattacharya, 1979; Miller and Rock, 1985; John and Williams, 1985). In particular, a trade-off where repurchases have tax advantage but dividends have information advantage is suggested (e.g. Ofer and Thakor, 1987). However, repurchases can also be used to signal undervalutaion and likely provide an even stronger signal. This is because when firms repurchase stock, they not only signal they have cash to pay as they do with dividends but also commit to the market price, something dividends do not do (e.g. Vermaelen, 1981; Oded, 2005; Babenko, Tserlukevich and Verdashko, 2012, Bond and Zhong, 2016). Brennan and Thakor (1990) provide an asymmetric information model in which they suggest that since dividend distribution is *pro rata* and stock repurchase is not, the latter payout method gives informed stock-holders an advantage over uninformed stock-holders and hence creates wealth transfer from uninformed stockholders to informed stockholders.[2] Brennan and Thakor's model assumes homogeneity of shareholder taxation, so that for tax levels above the level where adverse selection can explain the dividend dominance, all shareholders will tender and hence the stock repurchase will be taxed as a dividend, leaving stock repurchase without any tax advantage over dividends.

A different friction that the literature builds on is agency costs of free cash. This literature originates in Jensen's (1986) argument that managers will spend free cash on excess executive compensation and empire building. He suggests debt takes free cash out of the firm, thus preventing its waste. Following studies apply this idea to payout policy, which like debt removes free cash, thereby preventing its waste (e.g., Chowdhry and Nanda, 1994; Oded 2020). Oded (2011) considers how agency costs of free cash and information asymmetry interact to determine the choice between open market programs and tender offer repurchases. Agency costs of free cash may explain why firms both repurchase and pay dividends. Dividends are more committing than repurchases (in fact many announced repurchases are not executed (Stephens and Weisbach, 1998; Ben-Rephael *et al.*, 2014), while dividends once announced are committing and they also informally commit the firm to pay dividends in the future. Firms that reduce dividends are punished by the market, but no such penalties are reported in the literature for dividends. On the other hand, because they are not committing, repurchases give firms the financial flexibility to stop payout or not execute at all an announced repurchase program if, for example, the cash is unexpectedly needed for investment. This is an advantage dividends do not share.

In this chapter, we adopt a behavioral approach to the dividend conundrum and provide an explanation for why firms may prefer dividends over repurchases despite their disadvantages described above. Behavioral explanations for the preference for dividends were offered already in the 1980s. Shefrin and Statman (1984) provide a behavioral explanation based on arguments of self-control (Thaler and Shefrin, 1981) and mental accounting (Kahneman and Tversky, 1979). They argue

---

[2]The SEC regulations require that if stock repurchase is performed *pro rata*, then it will be considered as dividend and accordingly be taxed as dividend. Hence, it is useless for stockholders to agree on a *pro-rata* stock repurchase in order to circumvent the dividend tax.

that dividends and capital gains cannot be treated as perfect substitutes and that some investors would be willing to pay a premium (in the form of higher taxes) for cash dividends because of self-control reasons, the desire to segregate different types of income, or the wish to avoid regret. They argue that because of mental accounting investors might be averse to losing on their stocks' mental account even if they are compensated by dividends, a compensation which is recorded on a mentally different "current" account. In addition, they suggest that selling stocks in lieu of dividends requires an active action that they later may regret, whereas receiving dividends is a passive behavior that usually will not entail regret. Dong *et al.* (2005) tested Shefrin and Statman's theory via questionnaires filled out by a Dutch investor panel. They could not confirm this theory. Rather, they found that the respondents in this survey seem to prefer dividends partly because the cost of cashing them is lower than the cost of selling shares. Our model is in some way supported by Dong *et al.*'s finding because the coordination difficulties could be interpreted as a special type of cost, albeit different from the costs relevant to the respondents in Dong *et al.* (2005)'s paper. A different viewpoint on the relationship between dividends and behavior is provided by Bar-Yosf and Venezia (1991). They show that expectation formations cause dividends to perpetuate in a particular form, thus preventing firms to fluctuate between distribution methods and forcing the firms to stick with dividend payments. Yet another view on dividends and behavior is provided by Breuer *et al.* (2014). They examined the relevance of behavioral patterns for corporate dividend policy in a multiple-country study. They find that while individuals' preferences may affect dividend policy, cultural differences do not. These findings support the idea that behavioral aspects are partly responsible for the prevalence of choosing dividends over other payout methods and reinforce the theory that payout methods are globally stable. Hasan and Islam (2022) review the literature concerned with behavioral explanations for paying dividends, and one of the lessons of this review is that there is a need for examining this issue from a different perspective, and this is what this chapter strives to do.

As in Brennan and Thakor (1990), we take the optimal amount of payout as given and deliberately ignore the motives for payout (signaling, agency costs of free cash flow, etc.) in order to focus on the comparison between dividends and stock repurchase as a periodical payout mechanism.

We suggest a simple model with two investors (shareholders) who delegate the control to a manager who acts to maximize firm value. These shareholders only vote on the payout method: either dividend or stock repurchase. If they choose a repurchase, then the manager/firm sets the repurchase price. We show that this creates a coordination problem between shareholders which under some circumstances prevents the use of the repurchase tax advantage. Since coordination among shareholders has to do with the relation among them, we regard this coordination problem as a behavioral issue. We suggest that because dividends do not engender coordination issues, they have a behavioral advantage over repurchases. This coordination problem demonstrates an additional manner, to those described above, in which behavioral aspects affect payout policy and help explain investors' behavior.

The rest of this chapter is organized as follows. In Section 2, we present our model. In Section 3, we consider an extension with asymmetric taxation. Section 4 offers directions for further research. Section 5 concludes.

2. The Model

2.1. *MM World Without Taxes*

We start with the Modigliani and Miller (henceforth MM) settings: no taxes, symmetric information, no transaction costs, no agency costs of free cash and no benefits of control (i.e. complete markets). For analytical convenience, the discount rate is assumed to be zero. We consider a model with two dates. There is an equity-financed firm. For simplicity, we assume that the firm is owned by only two investors, both risk-neutral. For now, since we are in the MM world, there is no difference between the investors, except in their level of holdings. The investors objective is to maximize their terminal wealth which is the value of their cash and stock at the terminal date. The firm is run by a manager, identified with it, whose function is to maximize the firm's terminal value.[3]

The firm and the two investors play the following game: At $t = 0^-$, the firm announces the amount of payout C which is determined by the

---

[3] Here, we make our only deviation from the MM world. We do not have the complete contracting possibility. The manager actions are not contractible and are determined by maximizing the firm's value.

technology (nature) and has to be distributed to the investors, the investors then vote immediately on the payout form: either a dividend or a stock repurchase. At $t = 0$, the vote results are announced. If the investors vote for a dividend, then at $t = 1$, the dividend is paid to the investors in proportion to their holdings and the game ends. If the investors vote for a repurchase, then at $t = 0^+$, the firm holds an auction in which it announces a fixed price at which it offers to repurchase stocks for a total amount of C. Investors have no control over the auction price. They immediately bid the number of shares they wish to tender up to their holdings. At $t = 1$, the repurchase results are announced and performed. If the repurchase is undersubscribed, then it fails, C is paid as a dividend and the game ends. If the repurchase succeeds, the firm repurchases shares from the investors in proportion to their bids for the amount of C and the game ends. At $t = 0$, there is a market in which the investors can sell any quantity to a market maker as long as he can sell it without loss at $t = 1$ or as long as he serves as an intermediate who clears demand and supply between the two investors. The market price at $t = 0$ is the price he is willing to buy stock for. At $t = 1$, the investors can sell any quantity of shares in the market at fair value.

Notation:

$t \in \{0, 1\}$ dates.

$i \in \{a\ b\}$ investors.

$j \in \{D,R\}$ payout methods (either D for dividend of R for repurchase).

N_t is the number of stocks outstanding at time t.

N_t^i is the number of stocks investor i holds at time t so that $N_t^a + N_t^b = N_t$.

α_t is the fraction of the firm investor a holds at t. Thus, $\alpha_t = N_t^a/N_t$.

W_t^i is the investor i's wealth at period t which is the value of his cash + stock at t.

V_{tj} is the firm's market value at time t when the payout form is j.

P_{tj} is the stock market price at time t when the payout form is j.

P_R is the fixed repurchase price which the firm announces.

N_R is the number of shares repurchased.

C is the payout amount.

Just after the manager announces C, the rest of the firm's assets have a market value of A_0 which reflects all (symmetric) information available. This value is unchanged by the vote since the vote regards C only. Without loss of generality, we assume $N_0^a > N_0^b$ so that agent a has the choice of payout in the vote.

At $t = 0$, the vote is over. If the investors vote for dividend, then $V_{0D} = A_0 + C$ and the stock price is $P_{0D} = (A_0 + C)/N_0$, thus

$$W^a_{0D} = \alpha_0[C + A_0] \qquad W^b_{0D} = (1 - \alpha_0)[C + A_0] \tag{1}$$

At $t = 1$, the dividend is paid, $N^a_{1D} = N^a_0$ and $N^b_{1D} = N^b_0$, and hence, $\alpha_1 = \alpha_0$. The firm's ex-dividend value is then $V_{1D} = A_0$ and $P_{1D} = A_0/N_0$. Investors a and b get dividend of $\alpha_0 C$ and $(1 - \alpha_0)C$, respectively. The value of investors positions (cash + stock) respectively after the dividend is paid is thus

$$W^a_{1D} = \alpha_0[C + A_0] \qquad W^b_{1D} = (1 - \alpha_0)[C + A_0] \tag{2}$$

so that the investors wealth is unchanged.

If on the other hand the investors vote for a repurchase, then at $t = 0$, the firm's market value is still $V_{0R} = A_0 + C$, and hence, $P_{0R} = P_{0D}$.

We denote with Q the fraction that the net payout amount consists out of the firm's post-announcement but pre-repurchase *value* so that here

$$Q = C/(A_0 + C) \tag{3}$$

The firm now proposes to repurchase N_R shares from the investors at a fixed price P_R such that $P_R \times N_R = C$. Only if shares are repurchased at market value ($P_R = P_{0R}$), then $Q = N_R/N_0$. Given the proposed repurchase price, each investor bids a number of shares to be repurchased up to the number of shares he owns. Let B^a and B^b represent the bids of investors a and b, respectively, (the fraction of the firm each offers to tender), then the strategy space for the subgame (which starts after a vote for repurchase) is $P_R \in [C/N_0, C]$, $B^a \in [0, N^a_0]$, $B^b \in [0, N^b_0]$. At $t = 1$, the repurchase auction results are announced and performed. According to our assumption above, if $B^a + B^b \geq N_R$, then C is purchased from the investors in proportion to their bids. Else, the repurchase fails and the cash C is paid as dividend.

Proposition 1. *In a two investors MM world without taxes, the firm is indifferent to the form of payout and in the case of a repurchase to the repurchase price.*

Proof. Regardless of what the repurchase price P_R is, since $V_{OR} = A_0 + C$ and since an amount of C will be taken out of the firm either in the form of repurchase or in the form of dividend (if the repurchase fails), then the ex-payout firm value is $V_{1R} = A_0 = V_{1D}$.   ∎

Proposition 2. *In a two investors MM world without taxes, the investors are indifferent between a stock repurchase and dividend. Further, in the case of repurchase, investors are indifferent to their bids whenever $P_R = P_{OR}$, and they submit maximum bid whenever $P_R > P_{OR}$. Whenever $P_R < P_{OR}$, the investors refrain from participating (bid 0), so that the repurchase fails and C is distributed as dividend.*

Proof. Having assumed $N_0^a > N_0^b$ (w.l.o.g), then investor a has the choice of mechanism. He will prefer a repurchase if $W_{1R}^a > W_{1D}^a$ and prefer dividend otherwise. Suppose that he chooses a repurchase. If the repurchase auction fails, then $W_{1R}^i = W_{1D}^i$ so that both investors are indifferent between repurchase and dividend.

(i)   Suppose the firm sets $P_R = P_{OR}$. Let N_R^a and N_R^b represent the number of shares each investor gets to tender, respectively. If the repurchase succeeds, we have $N_R^a + N_R^b = N_R$, and the auction results are

$$N_R^a = \frac{B^a}{B^a + B^b} N_R \qquad N_R^b = \frac{B^b}{B^a + B^b} N_R \qquad (4)$$

Investor a gets $N_R^a P_{OR}$ in cash and holds $N_0^a - N_R^a$ in stocks priced at P_{1R} each. Since $P_R = P_{OR}$, then $N_R = QN_0$, so that $P_{1R} = A_0/(N_0(1 - Q)) = P_{OR}$, that is, tendered shares are worth the same as non-tendered shares, so that the value of his position is $W_{1R}^a = N_0^a P_{OR}$ regardless of his bid. This is equal to W_{1D}^a and to the initial value of his position. Consequently, he is indifferent to the form of payout. Now, since no value is generated or lost through the repurchase, then investor b is indifferent too.

(ii)   Suppose the firm sets $P_R > P_{OR}$. This results in $N_R < QN_0$ so that non-tendered shares will be worth $P_{1R} < P_{OR}$. Investors then want to repurchase as many shares as they can. They submit maximum bids, the repurchase succeeds, and each share holder tenders a number of shares proportional to his holdings. Hence, $\alpha_1 = \alpha_0$, investor a ends up with $\alpha_0 C$ in cash and $\alpha_0 A_0$ in stocks which implies $W^a_{1R} = W^a_{1D}$. Consequently, $W^b_{1R} = W^b_{1D}$ so that in this case too, investors are indifferent between repurchase and dividend.

(iii) Setting $P_R < P_{0R}$ results in $N_R > QN_0$, so that the non-tendered shares will be worth $P_{1R} > P_{0R}$, the investors will not want to tender any shares, the repurchase will fail and C will be paid as dividend. ∎

In a pure MM world, firm actions are contractible and the investors can set the repurchase price. Our model deviates from pure MM world in restricting contracting ability. Investors cannot control this price. Still, we derive investors indifference results.

2.2. *MM World with Taxes*

Next, we introduce taxation into the model. Assume that both investors (and the market maker) pay a fraction τ tax on dividends and that stock repurchase is not taxed at all.

If the investors vote for dividend, then at $t = 0$, the firm's market value is[4] $V_{0D} = A_0 + (1 - \tau)C$ and the stock price is $P_{0D} = [A_0 + C(1 - \tau)]/N_0$ and thus

$$W^a_{0D} = \alpha_0[A_0 + C(1 - \tau)] \qquad W^b_{0D} = (1 - \alpha_0)[A_0 + C(1 - \tau)] \qquad (5)$$

At $t = 1$, the dividend is paid, $\alpha_1 = \alpha_0$, the firm's ex-dividend value is $V_{1D} = A_0$, and the stock price is $P_{1D} = A_0/N_0$. Investors a and b get dividend of $\alpha_0(1 - \tau)C$ and $(1 - \alpha_0)(1 - \tau)C$, respectively. The value of their positions (cash and stock) after the dividend is paid is thus

$$W^a_{1D} = \alpha_0[A_0 + C(1 - \tau)] \qquad W^b_{1D} = (1 - \alpha_0)[A_0 + C(1 - \tau)] \qquad (6)$$

Here too, the investors wealth is unchanged.

If on the other hand, the investors vote for repurchase, the firm and the investors play the same game with same strategy space, only the payoffs are different. Stock price and firm value will reflect no taxation, however, only if repurchase success is warranted.

---

[4]Assets value is not affected. This can be justified by assuming that the cost was A_0 and that they are sold at cost at the terminal date.

Proposition 3. *In a two investors MM world with taxes, the firm is indifferent to the form of payout and in the case of a repurchase to the repurchase price.*

Proof. As in the no-tax world, regardless of what the repurchase price P_R is, the ex-payout firm value is $V_{1R} = A_0 = V_{1D}$, hence the firm is indifferent to the repurchase price it sets. ∎

The firm is indifferent to the price, so when voting about the payout mechanism, investors should speculate about the consequences of different prices the firm may set. The stock price at $t = 0$ depends on investors' conception of what price the manager will set and whether the auction will succeed.

Denote with P_{0R}^* the stock price at $t = 0$, when the investors vote for repurchase under beliefs that the repurchase will succeed, then $P_{0R}^* = [A_0 + C]/N_0$. Next, suppose repurchase is chosen and suppose the manager sets the repurchase price at fair value, i.e. $P_R = P_{0R}^*$. Then $N_R = QN_0$ stocks are offered for repurchase. As in the non-tax case, this implies that upon repurchase success, we get $P_{1R} = P_{0R}^*$. Hence, both investors are indifferent to tendering or not as long as they are sure the auction will succeed. Each investor can assure this at no cost by bidding at least N_R stocks. We summarize this result in the following proposition.

Proposition 4. *In a two investors MM world with taxes, there is a set of Nash equilibria in which investors vote for a repurchase, and the firm sets the repurchase price at the fair value $P_R = [A_0 + C]/N_0$, this set includes all investors' bids such that $N_R^a + N_R^b \geq N_R$. Of these equilibria, only the ones in which investors submit bids higher than N_R are sequential. In these equilibria, both investors are strictly better off than in the case of dividends.*

Now, suppose the investors believe that if they choose a repurchase, the firm will set a repurchase price $P_R > P_{0R}^*$. If they vote for a repurchase, then still $P_{0R} = P_{0R}^*$ because the repurchase will succeed. This is because now $P_{1R} < P_{0R} < P_R$. Investors will submit maximum bids and the repurchase will be *pro rata*.

Before considering the case where the firm will set a repurchase price $P_R < P_{0R}^*$, we prove the following theorem.

Theorem 5. *In a two investors MM world with taxes, stock repurchase weakly dominates dividend. Hence, in all sequential equilibria, investors will vote for repurchase.*

Proof. If the firm sets $P_R > P_{0R}^*$, then both investors submit maximum bids, the repurchase succeeds and their terminal wealth is as in the non-taxed case which is strictly higher than the terminal wealth with taxed dividend. If $P_R = P_{0R}^*$, then Proposition 4 yields this result. If the firm sets $P_R < P_{0R}^*$, an investor can always avoid tendering. If the repurchase fails, he gets the same payout as when the payout is in the form of a dividend. If the repurchase succeeds, he is better off because this means that there is no taxation and the repurchase only transferred wealth to him from the other investor. Investors never know what repurchase price the firm will choose. Under any beliefs which assign positive probability to a repurchase price higher than P_{0R}^*, they will always vote for repurchase. ∎

In order to complete the equilibria analysis for the taxed MM world, we need to solve for investors' bids for $P_R < P_{0R}^*$. For such prices, an investor will never bid a quantity for which a repurchase success results in total wealth lower than wealth under dividend. Consider investor a. His concern when bidding is not about selling his shares cheap to the company but about a possible wealth transfer to investor b which will happen whenever he tenders more than his proportional shares. Whenever this wealth transfer is higher than τC, then he is better off with a dividend, that is, with repurchase cancellation.

Proposition 6. *In a two investors MM world with taxes, any price $P_R < P_{0R}^*$ can be supported in a Nash equilibrium in which the repurchase succeeds.*

Proof. The number of shares offered for repurchase is $N_R = C/P_R$. Suppose investor a bids $\alpha_0 N_R$ and investor b bids $(1 - \alpha_0)N_R$, then the repurchase succeeds and each investor's terminal wealth is as in the non-taxed case. To see that neither of them will deviate, consider investor a. Bidding more than $\alpha_0 N_R$ results in wealth transfer to investor b. Bidding less will result in repurchase failure and terminal wealth as in the taxed dividend case which is strictly lower. ∎

In any Nash equilibrium with $P_R > P_{0R}^*$ investors bids are unique (maximum bid). When $P_R = P_{0R}^*$, any bid combination such that $N_R^a + N_R^b \geq N_R$ will hold. In both cases, in any equilibrium, the repurchase succeeds.

For $P_R < P_{0R}^*$, the set of equilibria is more interesting. On the one hand, it is in the investors' best interest not to tender shares, since if the repurchase succeeds, non-tendered shares are worth more than tendered ones. On the other hand, if the repurchase fails, then C is taxed. Given that investor b bids less than a bid proportional to his holdings, investor a will not deviate from a bid $N_R^a = N_R - N_R^b$ as long as the wealth transfer to investor b is less than $\alpha_0 \tau C$ so that he is still better off with a repurchase than with dividend and the repurchase will succeed. Whenever the implied wealth transfer is higher than $\alpha_0 \tau C$, investor a will submit a bid lower than $N_R - N_R^b$ so that we get Nash equilibria in which the repurchase fails. For these equilibria to arise, we need P_R to be substantially below P_{0R}^* and investor b's bid to be low enough. We get symmetric arguments for investor b's bids given investor a's bids.

Although we would expect that in a taxed MM world, investors will strictly prefer repurchase, in our model, since the firm's objective is maximizing its value, then it is indifferent to the repurchase price. Thus, whenever the price is less than the fair value, there can be a wealth transfer between investors. Whenever this price is substantially less than the fair value, then since investors are unable to coordinate their bids, the repurchase may fail so that they will lose the tax benefit.

3. Extension

3.1. *Asymmetric Taxation*

Suppose now that investor b is tax-exempt and that investor a and the market maker are taxed at τ on dividends only. If dividend is chosen, then at $t = 0$, investors will not agree on the value of the payout. A stock is worth $[A_0 + C]/N_0$ to investor b but only $[A_0 + C(1 - \tau)]/N_0$ to investor a. Investor a would sell all his shares to investor b through the market at a price in this range and taxes will not be paid. The price will depend on the investors' market power. If repurchase is chosen, then as in the case of symmetric taxation, for $P_R > P_{0R}^*$ (P_{0R}^* is the market price under symmetric taxation), investors submit maximum bids and the repurchase will succeed. For $P_R = P_{0R}^*$, investor b is indifferent to his bid since he is not taxed. The set of Nash equilibria will then include any bid combination such that $N_R^a + N_R^b \geq N_R$, but only the equilibria in which $N_R^a \geq N_R$ will be sequential. When $P_R < P_{0R}^*$, investor b is indifferent to auction results while investor a prefers bids such that $N_R^a + N_R^b \geq N_R$ as long as the wealth transfer due to the auction is less than $\alpha_0 \tau C$.

If investor a has full market power at $t = 0$, then he is better off with voting for a dividend because he is able to sell his shares for the non-taxed value under dividend, while under repurchase he can be sure there will not be wealth transfer only as long as $P_R \geq P_{0R}^*$. We summarize this discussion in the following proposition without proof.

Proposition 7. *Under asymmetric taxation in which only investor a is taxed, whenever investor a has the market power or no market power, he is weakly better off with a dividend. Hence, under full or no market power to investor a, in all sequential equilibria, the payout form is a dividend.*

Whenever he does not have full market power, he is strictly better off with a repurchase when $P_R \geq P_{0R}^*$. When $P_R < P_{0R}^*$, there is some K such that for $P_R > K$ investor a is strictly better of with a repurchase, while for $P_R < K$ he is weakly better off with a dividend. K depends on investor a's market power.

4. Conclusion

We develop a simple model in which the stockholders delegate control of the payout policy to a manager who acts to maximize firm value. The manager executes the payout policy dictated by the shareholders: a stock repurchase (a tender offer auction) or a dividend. If the manager chooses to repurchase shares, this creates a coordination problem which prevents the investors from using the tax benefits from stock repurchase. The problem arises even at the primitive level of the MM world with taxes and becomes more severe under asymmetric taxation. It would be interesting to investigate whether these characterizations persist or even become stronger in a more complicated model. It would also be interesting to look at the implications of transaction costs, size of payout and introducing a shock to the firm's value between the time the manager announces the price and the time the repurchase auction takes place.

Acknowledgments

The financial support from the Jeremy Coller Institute and the Henry Crown Institute of Business Research in Israel is gratefully acknowledged.

References

Babenko, I., Tserlukevich, Y., and Vedrashko, A. (2012). The credibility of open market share repurchase signaling. *Journal of Financial and Quantitative Analysis*, 47, 1059–1088.

Barclay, M.J. and Smith, C.W. (1988). Corporate payout policy: Cash dividend vs. open market repurchases. *Journal of Financial Economics*, 22(1), 61–82.

Bar-Yosef, S. and Venezia, I. (1991). Earnings information and the determination of dividend policy. *Journal of Economics and Business*, 43(3), 197–214.

Ben-Rephael, A., Oded, J., and Wohl, A. (2014). Do firms buy their stock at bargain prices? Evidence from actual stock repurchase disclosures. *Review of Finance*, 18, 1299–1340.

Bhattacharya, S. (1979). Imperfect information, dividend policy, and 'the bird in hand' fallacy. *Bell Journal of Economics*, 10(1), 259–270.

Black, F. (1976). The dividend puzzle. *Journal of Portfolio Management*, 2, 5–8.

Bond, P. and Zhong, H. (2016). Buying high and selling low: Stock repurchases and persistent asymmetric information. *Review of Financial Studies*, 29, 1409–1452.

Brennan, M. and Thakor, A. (1990). Shareholder preferences and dividend policy. *Journal of Finance*, 45, 993–1018.

Breuer, W., Rieger, M.O., and Soypak, K.C. (2014). The behavioral foundations of corporate dividend policy a cross-country analysis. *Journal of Banking & Finance*, 42, 247–265.

Dong, M., Robinson, C., and Veld, C. (2005). Why individual investors want dividends. *Journal of Corporate Finance*, 12(1), 121–158.

Farre-Mensa, J., Michaely, R., and Schmalz, M. (2014). Payout policy. *Annual Review of Financial Economics*, 6, 75–134.

Grullon, G. and Michaely, R. (2002). Dividends, share repurchases, and the substitution hypothesis. *Journal of Finance*, 57, 1649–1684.

Hasan, F. and Islam, M.R. (2022). The relationship between behavioral finance and dividend policy: A literature review. *Academy of Accounting and Financial Studies Journal*, 26(5), 1–11.

Jensen, M. (1986). Agency costs of free cash flow, corporate finance, and takeovers. *American Economic Review*, 76, 323–329.

John, K. and Williams, J. (1985). Dividends, dilution and taxes: A signaling equilibrium. *Journal of Finance*, 40(4), 1053–1070.

Kahneman, D. and Tversky, A. (1979). Prospect theory: An analysis of decision under risk. *Econometrica*, 47, 263–291.

Miller, M. (1986). Behavioral rationality in finance: The case of dividends. *Journal of Business*, S461–S468.

Miller, M. and Rock, K. (1985). Dividend policy under asymmetric information. *Journal of Finance*, 40(4), 1031–1051.

Oded, J. (2005). Why do firms announce open-market stock repurchase programs? *Review of Financial Studies*, 18, 271–300.

Oded, J. (2011). Stock repurchases: How firms choose between a self tender offer and an open-market repurchase program. *Journal of Banking and Finance*, 35, 3174–3187.

Oded, J. (2020). Payout policy, financial flexibility, and agency costs of free cash flow. *Journal of Business, Finance, and Accounting*, 47, 218–252.

Ofer, R. and Thakor, A. (1987). A theory of stock price responses to alternative corporate cash disbursement methods: Stock repurchases and dividends. *Journal of Finance*, 42, 365–394.

Shefrin, H.M. and Statman, M. (1984). Explaining investor preference for cash dividends. *Journal of Financial Economics*, 13(2), 253–282.

Skinner, D. (2008). The evolving relation between earnings, dividends, and stock repurchases. *Journal of Financial Economics*, 87, 582–609.

Stephens, C. and Weisbach, M. (1998). Actual share reacquisition in open-market repurchase programs. *Journal of Finance*, 53, 313–333.

Thaler, R.H. and Shefrin, H.M. (1981). An economic theory of selfcontrol. *Journal of Political Economy*, 89(2), 392–406.

Vermaelen, T. (1981). Common stock repurchase and market signaling: An empirical study. *Journal of Financial Economics*, 9, 139–183.

Chapter 3

Energy Futures as an Inflation Hedge in a Time-Varying Coefficient Framework

Chunbo Liu[*], Cheng Zhang[†], and Zhiping Zhou[‡]

[*]School of Business and Management, Shanghai International
Studies University, Shanghai, China
bernard.cliu@shisu.edu.cn

[†]Daniels College of Business, University of Denver, Denver,
CO 80210, United States
cheng.zhang161@du.edu

[‡]Corresponding author, School of Business, Macau University
of Science and Technology, Macau, China
zhiping.zhou@phd.unibocconi.it

Abstract

This study investigates whether energy futures provide the ability to hedge against inflation. Using a Markov-switching vector error correction model (MS-VECM), we find that the Brent crude oil futures index is the only index that exhibits significant inflation hedging capability, among the subindexes of energy futures. Moreover, its inflation hedging capacity exhibits substantial variation over time, with most of the hedging power emerging under the relatively longer and more common regime. Results are robust to include common stocks and bonds in the model. We do not find evidence that unleaded gas, heating oil, gas oil, and natural gas futures have inflation hedging ability. Overall, our results suggest that crude oil futures are alternative candidates for well-diversified investment portfolios with inflation protection ability.

Keywords: Inflation hedge, Energy futures, Markov switching, Vector error correction

1. Introduction

The recent surge in inflation becomes a focal point for investors and induces behavioral changes that respond to macroeconomic shifts. Behavioral finance theory provides conflicting hypotheses on this issue. On the one hand, Modigliani and Cohn hypothesize that investors suffer from money illusion, discounting real cash flows at nominal discount rates and selling risky assets during high inflation periods (Cohen *et al.*, 2005). On the other hand, the inflation hedging hypothesis posits that nominal returns of assets contain market assessments of expected inflation rates, and investors are more likely to invest in various inflation hedging assets (Fama and Schwert, 1977). In this chapter, we examine the inflation protection ability of energy futures and stand on the latter hypothesis.

Energy has long been recognized as a key factor influencing inflation. The 1973 oil crisis and the 1979 energy crisis had a substantial impact on the Great Inflation of the 1970s. Moreover, the energy price surge in 2007–2008 is believed to have contributed to the early stages of the 2008 financial crisis (Bernanke, 2009; Hamilton, 2009). Recently, the surge in energy prices has contributed to a broader increase in inflation worldwide, posing a threat to post-pandemic economic recovery. The co-movement between energy prices and general CPI makes energy a potential candidate as an inflation hedge. As a result, some non-commercial investors have turned to energy futures (e.g., crude oil futures) to hedge inflation, representing a significant demand for commodities in the financial sector. Various studies have found that such demand has become more prominent in the past decade (Hamilton and Wu, 2014; Basak and Pavlova, 2016; Kang *et al.*, 2020). However, the literature is inconclusive about whether and when energy futures can effectively hedge against inflation. In particular, the distinct nature of regimes in the energy futures markets is often overlooked.

We investigate this research question by employing a Markov-switching vector error correction model (MS-VECM), which provides a comprehensive framework to capture the relationship that changes from state to state. This model enables us to distinguish between regimes in which long-run inflation hedging is statistically significant and the pace of adjustment is relatively fast, and regimes where no inflation hedging can be observed, or even regimes where asset prices diverge from inflation. Our study uses monthly returns on the S&P Goldman Sachs Commodity Index (GSCI) from January 1983 to December 2018. We examine the hedging ability of individual indexes of energy futures, including Brent crude oil (BCO), unleaded gas, heating oil, gas oil, and natural gas. Finally, we conduct a robustness test by including common stocks and bonds into the model and re-examining the inflation hedging ability of energy futures.

The main findings of this study are as follows. Over the whole sample period, we dive into exploring the inflation protection ability of individual indexes of energy futures. According to the coefficients related to the error-correction mechanism, BCO provides the best inflation hedges. Moreover, the effectiveness of BCO futures as an inflation hedge varies considerably over time. Inflation hedging is relatively fast in pace and of high statistical significance in a stable regime, which prevails more than 77.3% of the time. During this period, low inflation tends to coincide with low BCO futures returns. However, we do not find statistically significant error correction (EC) coefficients on the other four energy futures subindexes, indicating that these futures may not provide effective inflation hedging.

Previous studies, such as Becker and Finnerty (2000) and Gorton and Rouwenhorst (2006), have found that incorporating commodity futures into portfolios can enhance performance, especially when those futures are used to hedge against inflation risk. To test the robustness of our findings, we also include common stocks and government bonds in our model. This is important because in real-world portfolio allocations, investors typically overweight stocks and bonds and include commodities to hedge against unexpected inflation. Our results show that BCO futures exhibit significant hedging ability, while other futures do not offer inflation protection.

Our chapter makes several contributions to the existing literature. Firstly, it adds to the ongoing debate on the inflation hedging ability of energy futures specifically, and commodity futures more broadly. While this topic has been extensively studied, existing methodologies do not fully account for the distinct nature of regimes present in the futures markets. Secondly, we examine the inflation hedging ability of energy futures within a framework that includes stocks and bonds. This is particularly useful in light of recent developments in commodity markets. Numerous studies examine the performance of portfolios composed of stocks and bonds and demonstrate the advantages of adding new asset classes to portfolios (Becker and Finnerty, 2000; Jensen *et al.*, 2000; Gorton and Rouwenhorst, 2006; Demidova-Menzel and Heidorn, 2007). Our results suggest that some energy futures indexes exhibit significant inflation hedging ability, providing an economic rationale for including commodity futures in portfolios. We are among the few studies that adopt a time-varying coefficient framework in commodity research (Alizadeh *et al.*, 2008; Balcilar *et al.*, 2015; Uddin *et al.*, 2018; Liu *et al.*, 2023). Our focus is on investigating energy's time-varying inflation hedging ability, as opposed to the time-varying moments in commodity returns, which is the focus of existing studies. Lastly, we contribute to the methodology by extending previous models to include latent regime shifts governed by one ergodic and irreducible Markov chain. We investigate whether additional parametric flexibility is needed to examine the long-run relationship between energy futures and inflation.

2. Literature Review

From a theoretical perspective, the existing literature provides several explanations for the relationship between energy prices and inflation. The first explanation is the supply shock channel in which rising energy prices indicate a scarcity of energy and a fall in output. Consumers may choose to save less and borrow more, leading to an increase in the price level. The second explanation is the distribution channel (Gospodinov and Ng, 2013), which argues that rising energy prices could be considered a tax imposed on energy-importing countries. Consumers may demand fewer goods, which could cause downward pressure on the price level. The third explanation is the real balance effect channel (Cologni and Manera, 2008), which proposes that investors would rebalance their portfolios toward money after an increase in energy prices. The price level will increase if monetary authorities fail to meet the growing money demand. Although it is widely accepted that energy prices have inflation implications, whether energy futures can be used to hedge inflation risk is under-explored in the literature.

The findings of prior research on the inflation hedging ability of energy futures are not conclusive. Several studies document that energy futures provide a hedge against inflation (Herbst, 1985; Erb and Harvey,

2006; Kat and Oomen, 2007; Spierdijk and Umar, 2014). For instance, Erb and Harvey (2006) use annual data to perform linear regression analysis and find that the sensitivity to inflation varies widely across different commodities. Their results show that the roll returns of energy and heating oil futures index are positively correlated with the unexpected inflation component. However, Kat and Oomen (2007) distinguish between spot and roll returns and find that the correlation between energy futures and unexpected inflation primarily stems from the spot market. The correlation of roll returns with unexpected inflation is largely insignificant, which contradicts the findings by Erb and Harvey (2006). In a more recent study, Spierdijk and Umar (2014) implemented a rolling-window analysis and showed that the inflation hedging capacity of energy futures varies substantially over time.

Our chapter is directly related to the literature investigating the performance of portfolios incorporating energy futures (Becker and Finnerty, 2000; Gorton and Rouwenhorst, 2006; Demidova-Menzel and Heidorn, 2007). Becker and Finnerty (2000) show that including commodity futures contracts improved the performance of equity and bond portfolios from 1970 to 1990, especially during the high inflation of the 1970s. Gorton and Rouwenhorst (2006) construct an equally weighted index of commodity futures monthly returns, including energy and other futures contracts. They find that commodities are positively correlated with inflation at all horizons, while stocks and bonds are negatively correlated with inflation. Demidova-Menzel and Heidorn (2007) explore the risk-return relationships of equity and bond portfolios after including commodities, and their findings suggest that commodities can be a sensible addition to portfolios during high inflationary periods.

Our chapter is also related to the extensive literature on the inflation-hedging ability of various asset classes, including inflation-linked bonds (Dudley, 1996; Kothari and Shanken, 2004) and common stocks (Ely and Robinson, 1997; Ahmed and Cardinale, 2005; Luintel and Paudyal, 2006; Kim and Ryoo, 2011). We contribute to this literature by investigating the inflation hedging ability of energy futures. In recent years, there has been growing interest in the relationship between energy commodities and other asset classes, such as common stocks (Sadorsky, 1999; Kilian, 2007; Apergis and Miller, 2009; Kilian and Park, 2009; Kilian, 2010; Balcilar and Ozdemir, 2013; Balcilar *et al.*, 2015). We contribute to this line of research by examining the dynamics of energy commodities and inflation, with the latter being the most important macroeconomic variable that also affects common stocks.

We are among the few who apply the regime-switching methodology when studying commodity markets. Prior studies have utilized a range of empirical techniques to investigate this relationship. Conventional tools include (1) the Fisher coefficient, which is based on linear regression models of Fama and Schwert (1977); (2) the Pearson correlation, which is proposed by Bodie (1982); (3) the Johansen (1991) cointegration vector, as adopted by Mahdavi and Zhou (1997), and later by Bilgin *et al.* (2018) who refine the model to make the cointegration nonlinear; (4) the VECM model, as utilized by Levin *et al.* (2006) and Lucey *et al.* (2017); (5) the VAR model, as provided by Hoevenaars *et al.* (2008) and Spierdijk and Umar (2014); (6) the structural VAR model, as implemented by Blanchard and Gali (2007); Cologni and Manera (2008); Lippi and Nobili (2012) and Blanchard and Riggi (2013); (7) the NARDL model, as used by Van Hoang *et al.* (2016). However, none of these methods account for the distinct nature of regimes present in the energy futures markets. As one exception, Beckmann and Czudaj (2013) examine the inflation hedging ability of gold using the MS-VECM approach and find that the effectiveness of gold as an inflation hedge depends on the time horizon. Apergis and Miller (2009) use the same method and show that the relationship between gold prices and real interest rates exhibits substantial variations over time. Chinn and Coibion (2014) document significant heterogeneity within the sample period in terms of inflationary regimes and energy futures prices. The ambiguous results of previous studies and the evidence of the unstable relationship between energy futures prices and inflation call for the application of the time-varying coefficient framework.

3. Econometric Methodology and Data

3.1. *Econometric Methodology*

Single-state models used in previous research may not be the best description of the dynamic relationships in the data when examining the inflation hedging characteristics of different asset classes. One appealing model, the Markov-switching approach proposed by Hamilton (1990), can provide multiple states and contain time-varying parameters. It falls within the category of nonlinear models that can capture the nonlinear dynamic process in the time series data. While the literature has utilized Markov-switching models in the context of stocks and bonds (Guidolin and Timmermann, 2006), the application of these time-varying coefficient models to energy commodities is rather limited (Alizadeh *et al.*, 2008; Bae *et al.*, 2014; Giampietro *et al.*, 2017).

This chapter considers an *M*-regime, *p*th order autoregressive with *r* cointegrating vectors, Markov-switching vector error-correction model.

$$\Delta Y_t = \mu(s_t) + \sum_{i=1}^{p} A_i(s_t)\Delta Y_{t-i} + \sum_{j=1}^{r} \alpha_j(s_t)Z_{t-1} + \varepsilon_t, \varepsilon_t|s_i \sim NID\left(0, \Sigma_{s_t}\right) \quad (1)$$

where Y_t denotes the column vector of observations at time t, $s_t = 1, 2, \ldots,$ *M* represents the regime in time *t*, $\mu(s_t)$ collects the regime-dependent intercepts, $A_i(s_t)$ is a row vector of *i*th order autoregressive parameters in regime s_t, $\alpha_j(s_t)$ measures the speed of EC in regime s_t, and Z_t is the column vector containing the residuals from the error-correction equation, i.e., $Z_t = \hat{C}_y - \hat{C}\bar{Y}_t$, where $\hat{C}$ is the estimated cointegration matrix. These unobservable states are generated by a discrete-state, irreducible, and ergodic first-order Markov chain: $Pr(s_t = j|s_{t-1} = 1) = p_{ij}$, where p_{ij} is the generic $[i, j]$ element of the $M \times M$ transition matrix *P*.

The long-run EC and cointegration are explained as a mixture of *M* different regime-specific equilibrium adjustments.

$$\Delta Y_t|I_{t-1} \sim \begin{bmatrix} N(\mu(s_{1,t}) + \sum_{i=1}^{p} A_i(s_{1,t})\Delta Y_{t-i} + \sum_{j=1}^{r} \alpha_j(s_{1,t})Z_{t-1}, \Sigma_1)Pr = q_{s_{1,t}} \\ N(\mu(s_{2,t}) + \sum_{i=1}^{p} A_i(s_{2,t})\Delta Y_{t-i} + \sum_{j=1}^{r} \alpha_j(s_{2,t})Z_{t-1}, \Sigma_2)Pr = q_{s_{2,t}} \\ \vdots \\ N(\mu(s_{M,t}) + \sum_{i=1}^{p} A_i(s_{M,t})\Delta Y_{t-i} + \sum_{j=1}^{r} \alpha_j(s_{M,t})Z_{t-1}, \Sigma_2)Pr = q_{s_{M,t}} \end{bmatrix}$$

$$(2)$$

where I_{t-1} is information set at time $t-1$ and $q_{s_{j,t}}$ is the predicted probability of being in regime *j* at time *t* and $q_{s_{j,t}} = e_j'P\xi_{t-1|F_{t-1}}$. Here, e_j is a unit column vector with a unit value at the *j*th position, $\xi_t|I_t$ is a column vector of the filtered regime probabilities at time *t*, and $\bar{\xi}$ is defined as ergodic probabilities of the long-run equilibrium.

$$
\xi_{t|I_t} = \begin{bmatrix} Pr(s_t = 1|I_t) \\ Pr(s_t = 2|I_t) \\ \vdots \\ Pr(s_t = M|I_t) \end{bmatrix} \quad \text{with } \bar{\xi_t} = \begin{bmatrix} Pr(s_t = 1) \\ Pr(s_t = 2) \\ \vdots \\ Pr(s_t = M) \end{bmatrix} \tag{3}
$$

Based on the analysis, it can be concluded that the MS(M)-VECM(p,r) has a long-run equilibrium and provides an unconditional cointegration if the long-run error-correction coefficients are negative and statistically different from zero.

Krolzig (1998) provides an exhaustive overview of the MS model. First, the Johansen (1991) cointegration test is applied to check for the presence of cointegration. We use both the trace test and the L-Max test of Johansen's procedure, with the former testing the null hypothesis that the number of cointegrating vectors is equal to r, and the latter testing the null hypothesis that the number of cointegrating vectors is no greater than r. Next, we use OxMetrics with the MS-VECM code reported in Krolzig (1998) to estimate the MS model. Estimation and inferences are based on the expectation-maximization algorithm, which is a filter that enables the iterative calculation of the one-step ahead forecast of the state vector $\xi t|_{t-1}$ given the information set and the construction of the log-likelihood function of the data. The cointegration matrix estimated in the first stage is used to calculate the error-correction residuals, which enter Equation (1) as Z_t.

3.2. Data

We first obtain the aggregate energy futures index from the S&P GSCI Energy Futures Index. More importantly, we look into the components of energy futures and select five individual subindexes, namely Brent crude oil (BCO), unleaded gas (UG), heating oil (HO), gas oil (GO), and natural gas (NG). We adopt the U.S. seasonally adjusted CPI for all urban consumers as our inflation index. We obtain the monthly returns on the S&P GSCI Total Return Index from Thomson Reuters Datastream and the inflation index from the Bureau of Labor Statistics. We also use the CRSP U.S. Treasury 10-Year Bond Index and the CRSP value-weighted U.S. market index. Our sample covers the period from January 1983 to December 2018.

We choose January 1983 as our starting month as it is when we begin to have non-missing observations of the energy futures indexes. Figure 1 illustrates the evolution of these energy futures indexes in our sample

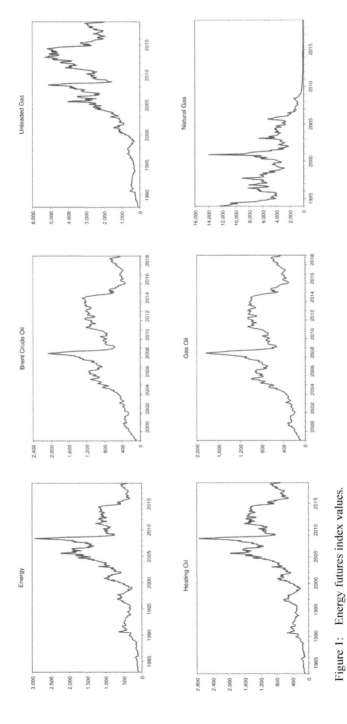

Figure 1: Energy futures index values.

Notes: All futures index values are in U.S. dollars. The X-axis plots the period in months from 1983 to 2018. The Y-axis denotes the value of energy futures. All data are extracted from Thomson Reuters DataStream.

Table 1:   Summary statistics.

	Mean	Median	Max.	Min.	S.D.	Skewness	Kurtosis	JB p-values
CPI	0.221	0.221	1.377	−1.771	0.251	−1.361	14.389	0.000
Bonds	0.598	0.601	8.538	−6.682	2.106	0.108	3.721	0.006
Stocks	0.930	1.339	12.850	−22.536	4.336	−0.880	5.852	0.000
BCO	1.049	1.322	36.561	−33.755	9.027	−0.187	4.227	0.000
Unleaded gas	1.276	1.320	49.461	−39.519	9.807	0.397	5.609	0.000
Heating oil	0.877	0.498	37.596	−28.860	9.078	0.379	4.629	0.000
Gas oil	1.083	0.809	31.185	−30.925	9.157	−0.079	3.957	0.009
Natural gas	−1.099	−1.266	53.076	−37.633	14.462	0.540	4.445	0.000

Notes: The table presents sample statistics (in %) of the inflation rate, the nominal returns on bonds, stocks, and five individual energy futures subindexes from January 1983 to December 2018. It shows mean, median, maximum, minimum, standard deviation, skewness, excess kurtosis, and the *p*-value of the Jarque–Bera (JB) test, which assesses the normality of the series. All sample statistics are computed on a monthly basis.

period. Note that some series have a shorter sample period, with the natural gas index starting in January 1994, and the gas oil and BCO subindexes having their first data point in January 1999. Not surprisingly, the individual subindexes of energy futures are highly correlated with each other, except for the natural gas index, which exhibits a downward trend throughout the sample period.

Table 1 presents summary statistics for the main variables. The monthly returns of BCO have an average of 1.049% and a standard deviation of 9.027%. The average monthly returns of the five energy subindexes are very close to each other, except for natural gas, which has an average monthly return of −1.099% and a much larger standard deviation compared to the returns of the other four indexes. The average monthly inflation rate is 0.221%, and its volatility is 0.251%. The kurtosis of the returns of the energy futures subindexes ranges from 3.957 to 5.609, while the inflation index has excess kurtosis, with a statistic as high as 14.389. The Jarque–Bera statistics reject the null of normality in all series.

3.3. Johansen's Cointegration Test

We first investigate whether there is a cointegration between the energy futures subindexes and CPI in our sample period. Panel A of Table 2

Table 2: Johansen cointegration test.

Model	BCO	UG	HO	GO	NG
Panel A: Johansen cointegration test					
Null: *No cointegration*					
Trace	72.271	116.793	142.272	66.408	77.826
p-value	0.000	0.000	0.000	0.000	0.000
Null: *One cointegration vector*					
Trace	8.276	4.877	5.074	6.062	4.354
p-value	0.074	0.297	0.275	0.186	0.362
	(1)	**(2)**	**(3)**	**(4)**	**(5)**
Index	**BCO**	**UG**	**HO**	**GO**	**NG**
Panel B: Cointegration vectors					
Commodity	−0.593	−0.093	−0.132	−0.255	0.125
	[−1.934]	[−3.070]	[−3.117]	[−1.466]	[4.051]
Constant	−3.488	−5.114	−5.014	−4.864	−5.296
	[−1.767]	[−22.393]	[−18.011]	[−4.438]	[−24.940]

Notes: The table presents the results of cointegration tests conducted on monthly index series between January 1983 and December 2018 to examine whether the five subindexes have a cointegration relationship with CPI. The subindexes include Brent crude oil (BCO), unleaded gas (UG), heating oil (HO), gas oil (GO), and natural gas (NG). Panel A reports the Trace statistics and the corresponding *p*-values for testing the null hypotheses of cointegration and one cointegration vector, respectively. Panel B displays the estimated coefficients of the cointegration vector, along with the corresponding *t*-statistics provided in brackets below.

presents the results of Johansen's cointegration test and shows the trace test statistics. For the first model, which examines the cointegration between CPI and the BCO futures, Johansen's trace test suggests the existence of one cointegrating vector. The *p*-value of the trace test suggests that the null hypothesis of no co-integration is rejected at the 1% level (Mackinnon *et al.*, 1999). However, the trace test cannot reject the null hypothesis of one cointegrating vector at the 5% level. Thus, there is one cointegrating vector in the model and a long-run relationship between CPI and the BCO futures. Panel B reports the results of the cointegrating vector, including the corresponding *t*-statistics. Note that the coefficients are normalized with respect to the inflation index. For brevity, we only show the normalized coefficient of the corresponding energy subindexes. As shown in the first column, the coefficient attached to the BCO futures has a negative sign, indicating that the widening gap between the two series tends to strengthen the error-correction mechanism.

We also identify one cointegrating vector in the model of CPI and unleaded gas index (UG), with the coefficient statistically significant at 1% level. For the model of CPI and the heating oil (HO) index, we identify one cointegration vector, with a statistically negative coefficient shown in column (3). However, we fail to find a statistically significant coefficient in the cointegration vector of the gas oil (GO) model. The coefficient estimate in column (5) suggests the absence of an error-correction mechanism in the model of CPI and natural gas (NG). Our findings support that there exists some heterogeneity within subindexes of energy futures regarding their cointegration relationship with inflation.

4. Markov-Switching Multistate VECM Analysis

4.1. *The BCO Futures Analysis*

We investigate the inflation hedging ability of several energy futures subindexes, starting with BCO. Note that the BCO futures series has a shorter sample period, covering only 1999–2018. We compare the information criteria statistics between linear and Markov-switching vector error-correction models to determine the appropriate model specification for the BCO futures. For MS-VECM models, we allow for multiple regimes (e.g., two or three) and different forms of VECM. Table 3 presents the relevant statistics. AIC and SIC statistics imply that Markov-switching models are superior to linear ones. In particular, the AIC shows that the best model specification is an MSIAH(3)-VECM(1,1), while the SIC suggests MSIAH(2)-VECM(1,1). Since SIC is known to suggest more parsimonious, the latter model is chosen. Therefore, we estimate a model that features two regimes, heteroscedastic errors, and an autoregressive order of 1. The Krolzig (1997) algorithm converged after 36 iterations. The number of observations in the system is 476, and the number of parameters in the Markov switching system equals 24, while the corresponding linear model has 11 parameters. With two nuisance parameters specified in the multi-state model, the linearity test should be implemented under a Chi-square with 11 degrees of freedom. The *p*-value of the Davies (1977)

Table 3: Model selection for BCO futures.

		Max log-likelihood	No. obs.	No. parameters	Saturation ratio	SIC	AIC	HQIC	LR linearity	Davies	Iterations
Model 1	Linear-VECM (1,1)	1392.40	238	11	21.64	−11.45	−11.61	−11.54	NA	NA	NA
	Linear-VECM (2,1)	1398.54	237	15	15.80	−11.46	−11.68	−11.59	NA	NA	NA
2 States	MSIA(2)-VECM(1,1)	1418.90	476	21	22.67	−11.44	−11.75	−11.62	52.99	0.000	55
	MSIA(2)-VECM(2,1)	1424.20	474	29	16.34	−11.35	−11.77	−11.60	51.32	0.000	45
	MSIAH(2)-VECM(1,1)	1440.23	476	24	19.83	**−11.55**	−11.90	**−11.76**	95.65	0.000	36
	MSIAH(2)-VECM(2,1)	1434.83	474	32	14.81	−11.37	−11.88	−11.75	72.59	0.000	40
3 States	MSIA(3)-VECM(1,1)	1434.77	476	33	14.42	−11.30	−11.78	−11.59	84.74	0.000	72
	MSIA(3)-VECM(2,1)	1448.78	474	45	10.53	−11.19	−11.85	−11.58	100.47	0.000	33
	MSIAH(3)-VECM(1,1)	1465.96	476	39	12.21	−11.42	**−11.99**	−11.76	147.12	0.000	70
	MSIAH(3)-VECM(2,1)	1469.84	474	51	9.29	−11.23	−11.97	−11.67	142.60	0.000	75

Notes: The table presents the AIC and SIC for various specifications of linear and Markov-switching vector error-correction models of the inflation index and BCO futures. MSIA stands for the Markov-switching model with regime-dependent intercepts and autoregressive coefficients, while MSIAH stands for the Markov-switching model with regime-dependent intercepts, autoregressive parameters, and heteroskedasticity. The sample period spans from January 1999 to December 2018.

Table 4: MSIAH(2)-VECM(1,1) model estimates for CPI and BCO futures.

Parameter	Regime 1		Transition matrix		Regime 2	
	ΔCPI(t)	ΔBCO(t)	0.727	0.273	ΔCPI(t)	ΔBCO(t)
Const.	0.002	−0.070	0.080	0.920	0.002	0.040
	[2.526]	[−2.854]			[10.584]	[4.303]
ΔCPI($t-1$)	0.281	2.313	Implied durations		0.027	−5.676
	[2.250]	[0.622]	Regime 1	3.660	[0.472]	[−2.141]
ΔBCO($t-1$)	0.028	0.097	Regime 2	12.460	0.016	−0.031
	[4.662]	[0.545]			[9.673]	[−0.358]
EC	0.002	−0.013	Ergodic prob.		−0.001	0.044
	[0.950]	[−0.240]	Regime 1	0.227	[−1.767]	[2.293]
SE	0.003	0.092	Regime 2	0.773	0.001	0.066

Notes: This table presents the results of the estimation of an MSIAH(2)-VECM(1,1) model for CPI and energy futures index, using monthly series during the period from 1999 to 2018. The coefficient estimates under the two regimes are presented, with the corresponding t-statistics shown in brackets below. The table also provides the transition matrix between regimes, along with the implied durations and ergodic probabilities of each regime.

test indicates the rejection of the null hypothesis at the 1% level. As a result, the test confirms that the Markov-switching model is better than the linear model.

Table 4 presents the results of the MSIAH(2)-VECM(1,1) model that examines the relation between CPI and crude oil futures. As expected, we obtain statistically positive coefficient estimates of ΔBCO ($t-1$) in both regimes, indicating a short-term dependence of inflation on lagged BCO futures. A significant EC mechanism of inflation exists in regime 2 (coefficient = −0.001, t-statistic = −1.767), while such equilibrium adjustment cannot be identified in the other regime. More importantly, the estimated EC coefficient of the BCO equation is positive and statistically significant in regime 2 (coefficient = 0.044, t-statistic = 2.293), indicating a significant inflation hedging ability of BCO futures in the long run. The regime-specific EC coefficient implies that under regime 2, with the most persistent regime prevailing during 77.3% of months, inflation hedging is relatively fast in pace and of very high statistical significance. Our results are consistent with the findings of Erb and Harvey (2016) and Spierdijk and Umar (2014), who identify a significant hedging ability of energy futures. Compared to existing studies, our chapter is based on more up-to-date data and relies on a more flexible framework to draw inferences.

Figure 2 depicts the two regimes identified by the MS model, showing the smoothed probabilities of being in regimes 1 and 2. Regime 1 prevailed in 2005–2006, 2008–2009, and from mid-2014 to 2015, while regime 2 prevailed during the rest of the sample period. The estimated transition matrix and ergodic probabilities suggest that regime 2 predominates, characterizing 77.3% of months with spells lasting 12.46 months on average, regime 1 occurs during only 22.7% of months, with spells lasting just 3.66 months on average. These results suggest that BCO futures provide a long-run hedge against inflation for most of the sample period.

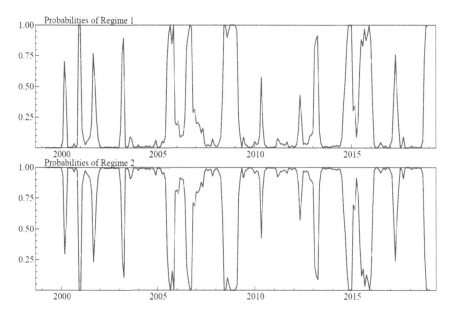

Figure 2:   Smoothed state probabilities of a MSIAH(2)-VECM(1,1) for CPI and BCO futures.

Notes: The X-axis plots the period in months from 1999 to 2018, while the Y-axis denotes the probability value ranging from 0 to 1.

4.2. *Other Subindexes Analysis*

4.2.1. *The unleaded gas futures analysis*

We next examine the inflation hedging ability of the other four energy futures subindexes, including unleaded gas, heating oil, gas oil, and natural gas. For brevity, the information criteria statistics of the other energy futures subindexes are not presented in the chapter and are available upon request. For the model that includes CPI and unleaded gas futures, we select the MSIAH(2)-VECM(1,1) model, which features two regimes, heteroscedastic errors, and an autoregressive order of 1. Panel A of Table 5 summarizes the estimation results. In regime 1, the EC coefficient on inflation is negative and statistically significant, indicating an error-correction in inflation. At the same time, the negative sign of EC coefficient on unleaded gas futures provides an indication that it diverges from the inflation index. In regime 2, there is a significant error-correction in inflation, confirmed by the negative EC coefficient on the inflation index (coefficient = -0.002, t-statistic = -3.720). The negative sign of EC

Table 5: Estimates of MS-VECM models for CPI and prices of other energy subindexes.

Parameter	Regime 1		Transition matrix		Regime 2	
	ΔCPI(t)	ΔUG(t)	0.888	0.112	ΔCPI(t)	ΔUG(t)
Panel A: CPI and the unleaded gas subindex						
Const.	0.002	0.014	0.053	0.947	0.001	0.008
	[6.556]	[1.005]			[11.189]	[0.941]
ΔCPI($t-1$)	0.127	-3.740	Implied durations		0.253	-0.504
	[2.014]	[-1.081]	Regime 1	8.940	[5.011]	[-0.159]
ΔUG($t-1$)	0.022	0.061	Regime 2	19.000	0.011	0.163
	[10.903]	[0.590]			[9.494]	[2.393]
EC	-0.007	-0.225	Ergodic prob.		-0.002	-0.024
	[-2.550]	[-1.569]	Regime 1	0.320	[-3.720]	[-0.743]
SE	0.002	0.128	Regime 2	0.680	0.001	0.066

Table 5:   (*Continued*)

Parameter	Regime 1 ΔCPI(*t*)	ΔHO(*t*)	Transition matrix 0.763	0.237	Regime 2 ΔCPI(*t*)	ΔHO(*t*)
Panel B: CPI and the heating oil subindex						
Const.	0.002	−0.002	0.106	0.894	0.002	0.008
	[5.347]	[−0.134]			[12.787]	[0.982]
ΔCPI(*t* − 1)	0.226	−1.326	Implied durations		0.251	0.282
	[2.990]	[−0.413]	Regime 1	4.22	[5.336]	[0.096]
ΔHO(*t* − 1)	0.020	0.092	Regime 2	9.47	0.009	0.084
	[6.766]	[0.792]			[8.252]	[1.066]
EC	−0.004	−0.083	Ergodic prob.		−0.002	0.003
	[−2.383]	[−1.015]	Regime 1	0.308	[−3.967]	[0.141]
SE	0.003	0.122	Regime 2	0.692	0.001	0.062

Parameter	Regime 1 ΔCPI(*t*)	ΔGO(*t*)	Transition matrix 0.696	0.305	Regime 2 ΔCPI(*t*)	ΔGO(*t*)
Panel C: CPI and the gas oil subindex						
Const.	0.002	−0.107	0.059	0.942	0.002	0.035
	[1.580]	[−3.255]			[11.274]	[3.961]
ΔCPI(*t* − 1)	0.300	3.773	Implied durations		0.047	−5.845
	[1.944]	[1.053]	Regime 1	3.28	[0.869]	[−2.206]
ΔGO(*t* − 1)	0.027	−0.106	Regime 2	17.09	0.015	−0.002
	[3.380]	[−0.521]			[10.010]	[−0.022]
EC	0.003	−0.189	Ergodic prob.		−0.002	−0.009
	[0.492]	[−1.194]	Regime 1	0.161	[−1.740]	[−0.207]
SE	0.004	0.090	Regime 2	0.839	0.001	0.072

(*Continued*)

Table 5:   (*Continued*)

Parameter	Regime 1		Transition matrix		Regime 2	
	ΔCPI(*t*)	ΔNG(*t*)	0.818	0.182	ΔCPI(*t*)	ΔLS(*t*)
Panel D: CPI and the natural gas subindex						
Const.	0.001	−0.016	0.067	0.933	0.001	−0.026
	[1.339]	[−0.519]			[6.595]	[−1.868]
ΔCPI(*t* − 1)	0.365	2.084	Implied durations		0.301	3.527
	[3.487]	[0.359]	Regime 1	5.49	[3.342]	[0.657]
ΔNG(*t* − 1)	0.009	−0.032	Regime 2	14.99	0.003	0.044
	[3.979]	[−0.253]			[2.986]	[0.616]
EC	0.003	−0.201	Ergodic prob.		0.001	−0.038
	[0.859]	[−0.991]	Regime 1	0.268	[1.703]	[−0.614]
SE	0.004	0.211	Regime 2	0.732	0.001	0.106

Notes: This table presents the results of the estimation of MS-VECM models using various subindexes of energy futures, including unleaded gas (Panel A), heating oil (Panel B), gas oil (Panel C), and natural gas (Panel D). The sample contains monthly time series covering January 1983 to December 2018. Coefficient estimates under the two regimes are reported, with the corresponding *t*-statistics shown in brackets below. The transition matrix between regimes, implied durations, and ergodic probabilities are also provided.

coefficient in the UG equation suggests the unleaded gas futures subindex lacks the ability to hedge inflation. Both regimes last for a fairly long time period. Regime 1 lasts 8.94 months on average, and prevails 32.0% of the time. Regime 2 lasts 19 months on average and prevails during 68.0% of months. The transition matrix indicates that both regimes, especially regime 2, are highly persistent. There is a 94.7% probability of no shift within one month in regime 2, while this probability equals 88.8% in regime 1. Figure 3(a) depicts the smoothed probabilities of being in regime 2, which prevailed during 1999–2001, 2004–2006, 2008–2009, and 2012, and regime 1, which prevailed during the rest of the sample period. These results show that UG futures cannot provide a hedge against inflation in either of these two regimes.

4.2.2. *The heating oil futures analysis*

Based on the information criteria, we choose the MSIAH(2)-VECM(1,1) specification for the heating oil index. As shown in Panel B of Table 5, the

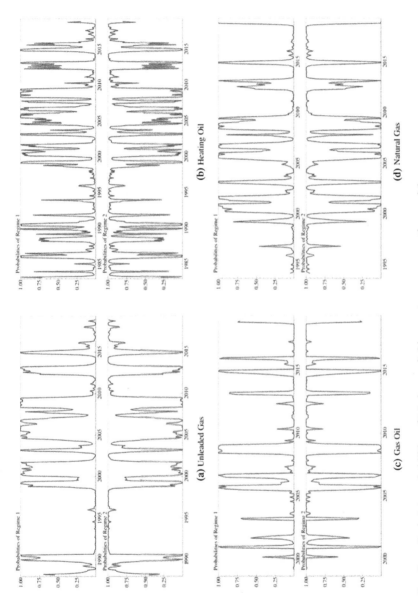

Figure 3: Smoothed state probabilities of Markov-switching vector error-correction models.

Notes: The X-axis plots the period in months during the sample period. The Y-axis denotes the probability value ranging from 0 to 1.

EC coefficients of CPI in both regimes are negative and highly significant, implying a significant equilibrium adjustment mechanism embedded in CPI in both regimes. However, the EC coefficients of the heating oil futures subindex are statistically insignificant in both regimes, indicating that we cannot use this subindex to hedge inflation risk. This finding is inconsistent with the results of Erb and Harvey (2006), who found a positive correlation between heating oil futures return and inflation. It is worth noting that the results presented in our chapter might not be directly comparable to those in the chapter of Erb and Harvey (2006), given that they use linear regressions to study the correlation between commodity futures roll returns and unexpected inflation and our sample period does not fully overlap with theirs (1959–2004). Regime 1 is relatively short-lived, occurring around once in every three observations, while Regime 2 prevails during 69.2% of our sample period and lasts an average of 9.47 months. The smoothed state probabilities depicted in Figure 3(b) show that regime 2 dominated during the periods of 1991–1999, 2001–2002, and 2016–2018, while both regimes seem to have been present during the rest of the sample period.

4.2.3. *The gas oil futures analysis*

The estimation results of the MSIAH(2)-VECM(1,1) for the model of CPI and the gas oil index are presented in Panel C of Table 5. In regime 1, we do not find a significant equilibrium adjustment in the inflation index based on the EC coefficient (coefficient = 0.003, t-statistic = 0.492). Regime 2 features an EC mechanism in inflation, as reflected by the negative EC coefficient on the CPI (coefficient = −0.002, t-statistic = −1.740). The EC coefficients on the GO futures in both regimes are negative and statistically insignificant. It can be concluded that the GO futures cannot provide a hedge against inflation. Regarding the prevalence of the two regimes, regime 1 lasts a relatively short period, namely 3.28 months on average, and prevails during 16.1% of months, while regime 2 lasts more than 17.09 months and appears in 83.9% of the time. The smoothed probabilities of being in regimes 1 and 2 are depicted in Figure 3(c). It suggests that regime 1 occurs during 2005–2006, 2008–2009, and 2014–2015, while regime 2 dominates the rest of the sample period.

4.2.4. *The natural gas futures analysis*

Based on the information criteria, we adopt the MSIAH(2)-VECM(1,1) model as the appropriate specification for the natural gas futures index. The results are presented in Panel D of Table 5. The transition matrix suggests that both regimes are persistent, with regime 2 showing a probability of not switching to another regime within one month of 93.3%, and regime 1 showing a probability of 81.8%. The expected duration of regime 2 is 14.99 months, which is substantially longer than that of regime 1. Figure 3(d) shows that regime 2 prevailed in the years 1994–1998, 2002, 2003–2004, 2007, 2010–2011, 2013–2014, and 2015–2018, while regime 1 prevailed during the rest of the sample period. In regime 2, we obtain a significantly positive EC coefficient on CPI, indicating the absence of an EC mechanism in inflation. Similarly, the EC mechanism cannot be found in regime 1. In both regimes, the estimated EC coefficients for the natural gas futures index are negative and statistically insignificant, implying that NG futures lack the ability to hedge inflation risk.

4.3. *Robustness*

In this section, we enrich the empirical model by including common stocks and government bonds as a robustness test of our main findings. This is to bring the model closer to real-world asset management practices, as portfolios usually consist primarily of stocks and bonds. Commodity futures are commonly used by fund managers to hedge against inflation risk, and this exercise adds to the recent literature that examine the performance of portfolios that include commodity futures.

We examine the inflation hedging ability of the five subindexes of energy futures using the new model specification. Consistent with the main results, only BCO futures exhibit the ability to hedge against inflation risks during our sample period. For brevity, the estimation results of the other four subindexes are not presented in the chapter and are available upon request. Table 6 presents the estimates of the new model of BCO. The estimated implied durations and ergodic probabilities suggest that regime 2 dominates, characterizing 73.4% of months with spells lasting 8.76 months on average, while regime 1 occurs during 26.7% of months with spells lasting just 3.18 months. The coefficients of $\Delta BCO(t-1)$ in

Table 6:　Estimates of an MSIAH(2)-VECM(1,1) model with common stocks and government bonds.

Parameter	Regime 1				Transition matrix		Regime 2			
	ΔCPI(t)	ΔBCO(t)	ΔStock(t)	ΔBond(t)			ΔCPI(t)	ΔBCO(t)	ΔStock(t)	ΔBond(t)
Const.	0.001	−0.041	−0.022	0.011	0.686	0.314	0.002	0.043	0.020	−0.001
	[1.854]	[−2.038]	[−1.614]	[1.286]	0.114	0.886	[10.232]	[4.599]	[5.060]	[−0.235]
ΔCPI(t − 1)	0.339	0.492	0.374	−0.741			0.003	−4.737	−2.096	0.947
	[2.709]	[0.128]	[0.154]	[−1.046]	Implied durations		[0.040]	[−1.757]	[−1.796]	[1.563]
ΔBCO(t − 1)	0.020	0.146	−0.081	−0.027	Regime 1	3.180	0.016	−0.019	0.009	0.018
	[3.180]	[1.034]	[−0.923]	[−0.497]	Regime 2	8.760	[7.325]	[−0.218]	[0.249]	[0.840]
ΔStock(t)	0.020	0.913	0.317	−0.096			−0.005	−0.245	−0.144	−0.064
	[2.131]	[3.130]	[1.630]	[−1.374]	Ergodic prob.		[−1.145]	[−1.380]	[−1.543]	[−1.219]
ΔBond(t)	0.024	0.033	0.097	−0.006	Regime 1	0.267	−0.010	−0.380	0.213	−0.106
	[0.714]	[0.056]	[0.287]	[−0.046]	Regime 2	0.734	[−0.680]	[−1.163]	[1.388]	[−1.294]
EC	0.003	0.524	−0.060	0.118			−0.008	0.457	0.145	−0.054
	[0.137]	[0.947]	[−0.162]	[0.948]			[−1.863]	[2.421]	[1.613]	[−1.106]
SE	0.003	0.084	0.052	0.021			0.001	0.067	0.029	0.15

Notes: This table presents the results of estimating an MSIAH(2)-VECM(1,1) model that investigates the interdependence between BCO futures, CPI, common stocks, and government bonds. The sample contains monthly time series from January 1999 to December 2018. Coefficient estimates under the two regimes are reported, with the corresponding *t*-statistics shown in the brackets. The transition matrix between regimes, implied durations, and ergodic probabilities are also provided.

the CPI equations are positive and significant in both regimes, indicating a significant short-term dependence of the inflation index on lagged BCO futures returns. A similar relationship can be found between inflation and lagged stock returns in regime 1. However, we fail to identify such a relationship between CPI and bonds in both regimes.

The error-correction coefficient explains the direction and pace of the long-run adjustment mechanism. In regime 2, we observe a statistically significant negative EC coefficient for the inflation index (coefficient = −0.008, t-statistic = −1.863), indicating the presence of a significant long-run equilibrium adjustment. However, the EC coefficient of the CPI equation is positive but statistically insignificant in regime 1. Most importantly, the inflation hedging properties of BCO futures are evident in regime 2, as reflected by a positive and statistically significant EC coefficient (coefficient = 0.457, t-statistic = 2.421). The EC coefficient of the BCO equation is not statistically significant in regime 1. The smoothed probabilities of being in regimes 1 and 2, depicted in Figure 4, indicate that regime 1

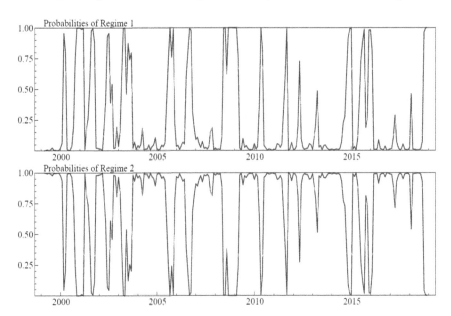

Figure 4: Smoothed state probabilities of an MSIAH(2)-VECM(1,1) for CPI, BCO futures, common stocks, and government bonds.

Notes: The X-axis plots the period in months from 1999 to 2018, while the Y-axis denotes the probability value ranging from 0 to 1.

prevailed during the periods of 2001–2002, 2005–2006, 2008–2009, and from mid-2014 to 2015, while regime 2 prevailed during the rest of the sample period. In summary, BCO futures continue to provide an effective hedge against inflation when we include common stocks and government bonds.

5. Conclusion

This study explores the effectiveness of energy futures as a hedge against inflation. We adopt an MS-VECM approach to account for heterogeneity in inflationary regimes and energy futures over the whole data sample. We investigate the inflation hedge capacity of five subindexes of energy futures separately. Empirical results indicate that BCO futures provide the best hedge against inflation. Moreover, their hedging capacity exhibits substantial variation over time. Most of the actual inflation hedging is obtained under the relatively longer and more common regime, in which the long-run equilibrium EC coefficient is positive and highly significant. We do not find evidence in support of the inflation hedging ability of other subindexes, including unleaded gas, heating oil, gas oil, and natural gas.

We conduct a robustness test by including common stocks and bonds in the analysis and find that our main findings are robust. Consistent with the estimation results of the model without stocks and bonds, we find that only BCO futures can hedge against inflation. These results suggest that our main findings are robust to the inclusion of stocks and bonds. To accurately assess the hedging capacity of energy futures, it is crucial to capture the time-varying relationship between inflation rates and energy futures returns. Our MS-VECM framework serves as a first step in this direction. Future research may apply time-varying parameter vector autoregressions to investigate the inflation protection ability of energy futures covering the COVID-19 periods. It might also be interesting to calculate hedge ratios and the degree of hedging effectiveness of energy futures. We leave this as a direction for future research.

References

Ahmed, S. and Cardinale, M. (2005). Does inflation matter for equity returns? *Journal of Asset Management*, 6, 259–273.

Alizadeh, A., Nomikos, N., and Pouliasis, P. (2008). A Markov regime switching approach for hedging energy commodities. *Journal of Banking & Finance*, 32, 1970–1983.

Apergis, N. and Miller, S. (2009). Do structural oil-market shocks affect stock prices? *Energy Economics*, 31, 569–575.

Bae, G., Kim, W. C., and Mulvey, J. (2014). Dynamic asset allocation for varied financial markets under regime switching framework. *European Journal of Operational Research*, 234, 450–458.

Balcilar, M. and Ozdemir, Z.A. (2013). The causal nexus between oil prices and equity market in the US: A regime switching model. *Energy Economics*, 39, 271–282.

Balcilar, M., Gupta, R., and Miller, S.M. (2015). Regime switching model of US crude oil and stock market prices: 1859 to 2013. *Energy Economics*, 49, 317–327.

Basak, S. and Pavlova, A. (2016). A model of financialization of commodities. *Journal of Finance*, 71, 1511–1555.

Becker, K.G. and Finnerty, J.E. (2000). Indexed commodity futures and the risk and return of institutional portfolios. Office of Futures and Options Research. Working paper.

Beckmann, J. and Czudaj, R. (2013). Gold as an inflation hedge in a time-varying coefficient framework. *The North American Journal of Economics and Finance*, 24, 208–222.

Bernanke, B.S. (2009). Outstanding issues in the analysis of inflation. In *Understanding Inflation and the Implications for Monetary Policy: A Phillips Curve Retrospective*, p. 447.

Bilgin, M.H., Gogolin, F., Lau, M.C.K., and Vigne, S.A. (2018). Time-variation in the relationship between white precious metals and inflation: A cross-country analysis. *Journal of International Financial Markets, Institutions and Money*, 56, 55–70.

Blanchard, O.J. and Gali, J. (2007). The macroeconomic effects of oil shocks: Why are the 2000s so different from the 1970s? Discussion paper, National Bureau of Economic Research.

Blanchard, O.J. and Riggi, M. (2013). Why are the 2000s so different from the 1970s? A structural interpretation of changes in the macroeconomic effects of oil prices. *Journal of the European Economic Association*, 11, 1032–1052.

Bodie, Z. (1982). Inflation risk and capital market equilibrium. *Financial Review*, 17, 1–25.

Chinn, M.D. and Coibion, O. (2014). The predictive content of commodity futures, *Journal of Futures Markets*, 34, 607–636.

Cohen, R.B., Polk, C., and Vuolteenaho, T. (2005). Money illusion in the stock market: The Modigliani–Cohn hypothesis. *The Quarterly Journal of Economics*, 120, 639–668.

Cologni, A. and Manera, M. (2008). Oil prices, inflation and interest rates in a structural cointegrated var model for the G-7 countries. *Energy Economics*, 30, 856–888.

Davies, R.B. (1977). Hypothesis testing when a nuisance parameter is present only under the alternative. *Biometrika*, 64, 247–254.

Demidova-Menzel, N. and Heidorn, T. (2007). Commodities in asset management. Frankfurt School-Working Paper Series.

Dudley, W. (1996). Treasury inflation-protection securities: A useful tool, but not a cure-all. Goldman Sachs Investment Research Report (October).

Ely, D.P. and Robinson, K.J. (1997). Are stocks a hedge against inflation? International evidence using a long-run approach. *Journal of International Money and Finance*, 16, 141–167.

Erb, C.B. and Harvey, C.R. (2006). The strategic and tactical value of commodity futures. *Financial Analysts Journal*, 62, 69–97.

Fama, E.F. and Schwert, G.W. (1977). Asset returns and inflation. *Journal of Financial Economics*, 5, 115–146.

Giampietro, M., Guidolin, M., and Pediu, M. (2017). Estimating stochastic discount factor models with hidden regimes: Applications to commodity pricing. *European Journal of Operational Research*, 265, 685–702.

Gorton, G. and Rouwenhorst, K.G. (2006). Facts and fantasies about commodity futures. *Financial Analyst Journal*, 62, 47–68.

Gospodinov, N. and Ng, S. (2013). Commodity prices, convenience yields, and inflation. *Review of Economics and Statistics*, 95, 206–219.

Guidolin, M. and Timmermann, A. (2006). An econometric model of nonlinear dynamics in the joint distribution of stock and bond returns. *Journal of Applied Econometrics*, 21, 1–22.

Hamilton, J.D. (1990). Analysis of time series subject to changes in regime. *Journal of Econometrics*, 45, 39–70.

Hamilton, J.D. (2009). Causes and consequences of the oil shock of 2007–08. Discussion Paper, National Bureau of Economic Research.

Hamilton, J.D. and Wu, J.C. (2014). Risk premia in crude oil futures prices. *Journal of International Money and Finance*, 42, 9–37.

Herbst, A.F. (1985). Hedging against price index inflation with futures contracts. *Journal of Futures Markets*, 5, 489–504.

Hoevenaars, R.P.M.M., Molenaar, R.D.J., Schotman, P.C., and Steenkamp, T. (2008). Strategic asset allocation with liabilities: Beyond stocks and bonds. *Journal of Economic Dynamics and Control*, 32, 2939–2970.

Jensen, G.R., Johnson, R.R., and Mercer, J.M. (2000). Efficient use of commodity futures in diversified portfolios. *Journal of Futures Markets*, 20, 489–506.

Johansen, S. (1991). Estimation and hypothesis testing of cointegration vectors in Gaussian vector autoregressive models. *Econometrica: Journal of the Econometric Society*, 59, 1551–1580.

Kang, W.K., Rouwenhorst, G., and Tang, K. (2020). A tale of two premiums: The role of hedgers and speculators in commodity futures markets. *Journal of Finance*, 75, 377–417.

Kat, H.M. and Oomen, R.C.A. (2007). What every investor should know about commodities part ii: Multivariate return analysis. *Journal of Investment Management*, 5, 16–40.

Kilian, L. (2007). The economic effects of energy price shocks. *Journal of Economic Literature*, 46, 871–909.

Kilian, L. (2010). Not all oil price shocks are alike: Disentangling demand and supply shocks in the crude oil market. *The American Economic Review*, 99, 1053–1069.

Kilian, L. and Park, C. (2009). The impact of oil price shocks on the U.S. stock market. *International Economic Review*, 50, 1267–1287.

Kim, J.H. and Ryoo, H.H. (2011). Common stocks as a hedge against inflation: Evidence from century-long US data. *Economics Letters*, 113, 168–171.

Kothari, S.P. and Shanken, J. (2004). Asset allocation with inflation-protected bonds. *Financial Analysts Journal*, 60, 54–70.

Krolzig, H.-M. (1997). *Markov-Switching Vector Autoregressions: Modelling, Statistical Inference, and Application to Business Cycle Analysis*, Vol. 454. Berlin: Springer.

Krolzig, H.-M. (1998). *Econometric Modelling of Markov-Switching Vector Autoregressions using MSVAR for Ox*. Oxford, United Kingdom: University of Oxford.

Levin, E.J., Montagnoli, A., and Wright, R.E. (2006). *Short-Run and Long-Run Determinants of the Price of Gold*. World Gold Council, Research Study No. 32.

Lippi, F. and Nobili, A. (2012). Oil and the macroeconomy: A quantitative structural analysis. *Journal of the European Economic Association*, 10, 1059–1083.

Liu, C., Zhang, X., and Zhou, Z. (2023). Are commodity futures a hedge against inflation? A Markov-switching approach. *International Review of Financial Analysis*, 86, 102492.

Lucey, B.M., Sharma, S.S., and Vigne, S.A. (2017). Gold and inflation(s) — A time-varying relationship. *Economic Modelling*, 67, 88–101.

Luintel, K.B. and Paudyal, K. (2006). Are common stocks a hedge against inflation? *Journal of Financial Research*, 29, 1–19.

Mackinnon, J.G., Haug, A.A., and Michelis, L. (1999). Numerical distribution functions of likelihood ratio tests for cointegration. *Journal of Applied Econometrics*, 14, 563–577.

Mahdavi, S. and Zhou, S. (1997). Gold and commodity prices as leading indicators of inflation: Tests of long-run relationship and predictive performance. *Journal of Economics and Business*, 49, 475–489.

Sadorsky, P. (1999). Oil price shocks and stock market activity. *Energy Economics*, 21, 449–469.

Spierdijk, L. and Umar, Z. (2014). Are commodity futures a good hedge against inflation. *Journal of Investment Strategies*, 3, 35–57.

Uddin, G.S., Rahman, Md.L., Shahzad, S.J.H., and Rehman, M.Ur. (2018). Supply and demand-driven oil price changes and their non-linear impact on precious metal returns: A Markov regime switching approach. *Energy Economics*, 73, 108–121.

Van Hoang, T.H., Lahiani, A., and Heller, D. (2016). Is gold a hedge against inflation? New evidence from a nonlinear ARDL approach. *Economic Modelling*, 54, 54–66.

Chapter 4

Cross-Sectional Anomalies: Statistical Phenomena or Free-Lunch Opportunities

Guy Kaplanski

Bar-Ilan University, Ramat-Gan, Israel
guykap@biu.ac.il

Abstract

I extend the analysis of Kaplanski (2023) to explore arbitrage activity following the discovery of cross-sectional anomalies. After anomaly discovery, arbitrage capital reshapes out-of-sample returns, thereby creating a contrarian effect on top of the general decay in returns. As a result, the monthly first-day return is responsible for more than 10% of the portfolio value, which increases to 30% in case of monthly based anomalies. The continuous arbitrage activity suggests that arbitrageurs find anomalies profitable in the long run. This implies mispricing, which is difficult to reconcile with full rationality but can be explained via investors' behavioral biases.

Keywords: Market efficiency, Cross-sectional anomalies, Arbitrage trading activity, Exploiting mispricing

1. Introduction

According to the efficient market theory (Fama, 1970), market prices reflect all contemporaneous available information. While market efficiency in the case of private information is questionable, the consensus in the literature is that stock markets are efficient as regards public information.

Therefore, it is surprising that in the half-century since Fama's seminal work, numerous studies have reported on quantitative measures that systematically predict future stock returns. Jensen's (1978) economic definition of market efficiency may partially explain such predictors. According to this definition, prices reflect the information until the marginal profit from this information does not exceed the cost involved in exploiting it. This is only a partial explanation because many of those studies also show that trading on those predictors yields persistent excess returns, which compensate for the costs of trading, the costs of acquiring and processing information, and the risks involved. Those results challenge the market efficiency hypothesis and are commonly considered anomalies not fully explained. The debate as to whether they indicate mispricing still needs to be resolved. On the one hand, the anomalies produce abnormal profits. On the other hand, many studies correctly claim that the intensive search within the same data of stock market returns is expected to identify distinct patterns that are formed randomly by pure chance (see, e.g., Fama, 1998; Hou et al., 2015, 2020; Harvey et al., 2016; Martin and Nagel, 2019).

If an anomaly reflects mispricing, it should diminish after discovery. In line with this claim, Chordia et al. (2014), McLean and Pontiff (2016), and Jacobs and Müller (2020) show that the returns on anomalies declined by half after their discovery. However, while this decline supports the existence of a mispricing component in anomalies, it does not refute the possibility that anomalies are spurious phenomena found by coincidence. According to this possibility, the decline in out-of-sample returns occurs randomly, as there is no actual cause behind the observed initial anomaly.

To account for such a possibility, Kaplanski (2023) examines directly arbitrage trading activity. Kaplanski (2023) shows that arbitrageurs persistently exploit anomalies, indicating that anomalies represent arbitrage opportunities rather than random patterns. The current study extends this approach to study further how arbitrage capital reshapes out-of-sample returns. The enhanced analysis includes daily analysis while studying monthly data anomalies on a standalone basis. Studying 71 well-known anomalies shows that the discovery of anomaly shifts returns to the beginning of the month, and this phenomenon repeats every month. The shift occurs across the weeks of the month, as Kaplanski (2023) shows, and it is substantially more profound within the days of the first week. This shift creates a jump in returns on the anomaly in the opposite direction to the general decay in returns after anomaly discovery. Therefore, this jump is neither explained by this decline nor by spurious effects. Instead, the findings suggest that arbitrageurs shift realized returns in their efforts to exploit the mispricing after discovering the anomaly.

Figure 1 illustrates the economic value of arbitrage trading activity after discovering anomalies. The figure shows the percentage loss from a delay of one day in updating the anomalies portfolio. The investment

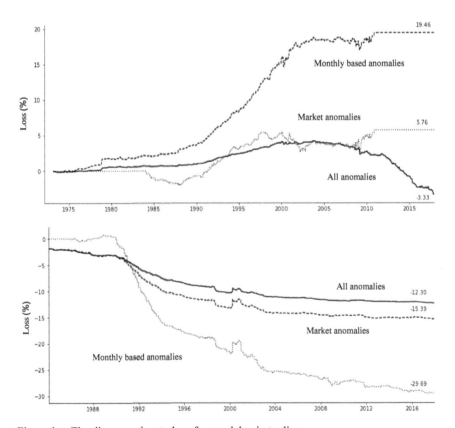

Figure 1: The disproportionate loss from a delay in trading.

Notes: This figure shows the percentage loss from a single-day delay in updating anomalies' portfolios at the beginning of each month. The long-minus-short investment strategy holds long top-quintile and short-selling bottom-quintile stocks at equal proportions per anomaly. The upper (lower) figure corresponds to anomalies before (after) their discovery. The loss is presented separately for all anomalies (solid), market-based anomalies (dashed), and monthly-based anomalies (dotted).

strategy is holding top-quintile and short-selling bottom-quintile stocks at equal weights per each anomaly. To isolate the impact of anomaly discovery, Panel A shows the loss of anomalies before discovery, while Panel B shows the loss of anomalies after their discovery.

The loss from a single-day delay on pre-discovery anomalies (the solid curve in Panel A) is positive for most of the sample period, indicating profits. The dashed and dotted curves show the losses for anomalies based on market data, like past prices, and anomalies based on monthly data, like monthly returns and volume. The delay in updating pre-discovery anomalies portfolios leads mostly to profits rather than losses for all types of anomalies. In sharp contrast, the loss for post-discovery anomalies (the solid curve in Panel B), which declines during most of the sample period, drops to −12.3% by the end of the sample period. This value is more than fifteen times the loss of −0.8% predicted from a naïve model that assumes a linear proportion of loss from missing out on investing one day each month. Moreover, this post-discovery loss increases to −15.39% and −29.69% in the case of market-based and monthly based anomalies compared to −0.95% and −3.66% predicted from the naïve model, respectively.

According to Figure 1, the impact of a delay in updating anomalies' portfolios is in opposite signs before and after anomalies discovery. While the loss on pre-discovery anomalies is close to zero and primarily positive, implying profits for most of the sample period, it is negative and large in absolute terms on post-discovery anomalies. This loss is several times larger than the loss predicted from a naïve model that assumes a loss that is linearly proportional to the delay's length and the portfolio's outdated portion. This loss confirms that after discovering anomalies, a large portion of their profits is realized at the beginning of the month. As a result, missing out only a single day each month in updating the portfolio ends up with a total loss of more than 12% of the portfolio value. Furthermore, in line with the hypothesis that monthly based anomalies attract more monthly trading activity, the loss increases to about 30% in the case of those anomalies, which are also easier to apply and more exposed to less sophisticated arbitrageurs.

These results show that the stock markets settled a long time ago the debate of whether anomalies indicate mispricing and an opportunity for arbitrage profits. The discovery of anomalies leads to persisting trading activity, which has strengthened over the years. This intensified activity shows that investors find the implied mispricing in anomalies profitable in the long run after accounting for trading costs and the risks involved. It also sheds more light on how the market becomes more efficient over time. Differently from the idea that the knowledge about the mispricing in anomaly would prevent its appearance from the first place, at least part of the correction occurs through periodical pressure from arbitrage trading activity (see Green *et al.*, 2011; Akbas *et al.*, 2015; Kokkonen and Suominen, 2015; McLean and Pontiff, 2016; Jacobs and Müller, 2020). These results support Lo's (2004) adaptive market theory and emphasize the importance of complementary theories to full rationality as in behavioral finance.

The rest of the chapter is as follows. Section 2 presents the data and the methodology. Section 3 explores the changes in returns caused by arbitrageurs' trading activity after anomaly discovery. Section 4 concludes. The list of cross-sectional anomalies is in the Appendix.

2. Data and Methodology

The data includes all U.S. firms listed on the NYSE, AMEX, and NASDAQ with share codes 10 and 11. Stocks with end-of-month prices below $5, stocks not traded during the month, stocks that do not have monthly returns or quarterly earnings for the previous 12 months, and stocks with negative equity book values for the previous year are excluded. A firm must be listed on Compustat (annual) for at least two years to mitigate backfilling biases (Fama and French, 1993). These filters conform to conventional filters in the literature on cross-sectional anomalies (e.g., Avramov *et al.*, 2021, 2022). Based on financial statements data from 1971, the firm-month sample starts in January 1973. The next-month returns start in February 1973 and end in December 2018, with 29.5 million firm-day observations across 14,111 firms.

For the financial statements data, the previous fiscal year's annual data are updated at the end of June every year to ensure that the information for predicting future stock returns is available in real time. In addition, the previous quarter's financial statements data are updated each month, provided that the release date was in the past. If no release date is given, it is assumed to be public by the end of the fourth month after the reporting period to guarantee data availability without look-ahead bias. Following Shumway (1997), daily delisting returns are also incorporated.

To explore the impact of the discovery of anomalies on trading activity, I constructed a comprehensive anomalies net trading (AT) index similar to Kaplanski (2023). AT index is constructed from 71 cross-sectional anomalies reported in the academic literature that produce continuous predictors of stock returns. A famous example of an anomaly is the momentum of Jegadeesh and Titman (1993). According to this phenomenon, stocks that have been profitable in the last six months tend to be further profitable in the following months and *vice versa*. Similar examples are the short-term and long-term reversals of Jegadeesh (1990) and Debondt and Thaler (1985), where returns tend to reverse after one month and five years, respectively. An example of a fundamental anomaly is the surprise in earnings of Foster *et al.* (1984). According to this anomaly, the sign and the extent of the surprise in the most recent quarterly reported earnings predict future returns. The Appendix lists all anomalies, while Kaplanski (2023) provides a detailed description of their construction.

In constructing AT, stocks are sorted every month on each anomaly. The anomaly's long and short portfolios comprise stocks of extreme quintiles. AT equals the sum of changes in the firm-month observation in long-side anomalies portfolios minus changes in short-side anomalies portfolios. According to this definition, AT measures the monthly net change in the number of anomalies portfolios to which the firm-month observation belongs. For instance, if a stock is added to two long portfolios and one short portfolio, then $AT = 2 - 1 = 1$. AT aggregates net changes in stock holdings in all anomalies' portfolios rather than the holdings to identify actual trading. For instance, consider a stock that belongs to a portfolio for two months in a row. While this stock affects returns over two months, arbitrageurs buy it mainly in the first month as it is already in their portfolio in the second month. By the same reasoning, arbitrageurs sell this stock only in the third month when the stock is taken out of the portfolio. Thus, AT represents the net demand from the trading activity of anomalies portfolios.

To compare the AT results to the general performance of investing in the anomalies, I also constructed an anomalies portfolios index (AI).

AI equals the sum of long-side anomalies portfolios minus short-side anomalies portfolios that the firm-month observation belongs to. This index is identical to the aggregate anomalies index of Engelberg *et al.* (2018).

To estimate the time of anomaly discovery, I adopt McLean and Pontiff's (2016) clearly defined two points in time for each anomaly: the end of the original study's sample period and the publication date of the original study. Each anomaly pre-discovery period starts at the beginning of the original study's sample period and lasts until December of the last year in the original study's sample period. The post-discovery period starts immediately afterward, in January of the subsequent year. The assumption here is that once the authors discover the anomaly, the information about it may start propagating and affecting the market. To test this hypothesis, I divide the post-discovery period of each anomaly into two sub-periods. The post-discovery pre-publication period starts in January, following the last year of the anomaly original study's sample period. It ends in December of the publication year, which is the year on the journal's cover. The post-publication period starts immediately afterward, in January of the subsequent year.

3. Shifts in Returns Following Anomaly Discovery

In this section, I show how the discovery of anomalies affects trading activity and, thus, the returns on the relevant stocks. In the main tests, I compare daily reruns at the beginning of each month, immediately when the previous month's information is available. Comparing subsequent days identifies arbitrage trading activity from two different sources. First, trading activity can be the residual from non-monthly arbitrage activity. This non-monthly trading activity may occur at different times and continue for several days. Therefore, comparing sequential trading days can detect residual arbitrage activity, even if actual trading of some and even most arbitrageurs started earlier. The other source is monthly periodical arbitrage trading activity. This monthly periodical trading activity is expected because significant anomalies like momentum require full-month data. In addition, it is common in the literature to consider the relative strength of stocks at time points when the market situation is the same, usually at the end of each month. Thus, it is sufficient that marginal

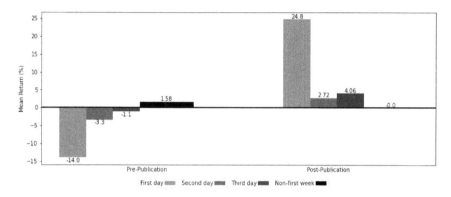

Figure 2: The change in daily mean returns after publication.

Notes: The figure shows the mean returns on long-minus-short anomalies portfolios before and after the publication of anomalies in academic journals. Annual returns are 252 times the daily returns (no compounding).

arbitrageurs rank stocks and correspondingly update their portfolios on a monthly (or quarterly) basis or rebalance their portfolios during different times to generate the effect.

Figure 2 demonstrates how the anomaly discovery reshapes the returns within the first week of each month. The figure shows the annualized mean return on anomalies' portfolios before and after the publication of the anomaly in an academic journal. The investment strategy is holding top-quintile and shorting bottom-quintile per each anomaly at equal weights. The bar on each graph's left side corresponds to the month's first day. The annualized mean return of −14% before anomaly publication jumps to +28.8% after publication. A similar, albeit less profound, pattern is observed in the second and third days of the month. The mean returns of −3.3% and −1.1% before the discovery turn 2.72% and 4.06% after discovery. This is compared to the mean return in all other weeks (the wide bar) of 1.58% before publication, which turns zero afterward. Figure 2 indicates that after the publication of the anomaly, the returns on it shift to the beginning of the month. The mean return on the first day jumps, and the same holds for the second and third days. In line with Kaplanski (2023), who finds a shift across the weeks of the month, the returns on the other weeks of the month decrease.

3.1. *The Impact of Anomaly Discovery on Returns*

To test the impact of anomaly discovery on returns, I employ the following regression equation:

$$R_{i,t} = \gamma_{0t} + \gamma_1 AT_{i,t} + \gamma_2 PD_{AT_{i,t}} + \sum_{j=1}^{3} \gamma_{3,j} AT_{i,t}(Dj_t - Dj + 1_t)$$

$$+ \sum_{j=1}^{3} \gamma_{4,j} PD\_AT_{i,t} \times (Dj_t - Dj + 1_t) + \sum_{j=1}^{4} \gamma_{5,j} Di_t + \gamma_6 AI_{i,t}$$

$$+ \gamma_7 PD\_AT_{i,t} + \sum_{j=1}^{4} \gamma_{8,j} R_{i,t-j} + \sum_{j=1}^{4} \gamma_{9,j} R^2_{i,t-j} + \sum_{j=1}^{4} \gamma_{10,j} V_{i,t-j} + \varepsilon_{i,t} \quad (1)$$

where $R_{i,t}$ is the daily return of stock i on day t; γ_{0t} accounts for the fixed effect of day t; $AT_{i,t}$ is the stock i anomalies net trading index; $PD\_AT_{i,t}$ is the post-discovery AT; and Dj_t (j = 1, 2, 3, and 4) are daily dummy variables for the first four days of the month. AI and PD_AI control variables correspond to returns on all and post-discovery anomalies. The regression controls also for lagged values over the last week (4 trading days) for returns ($R_{i,t-j}$), volatility ($R^2_{i,t-j}$), and volume ($V_{i,t-j}$). According to Engelberg *et al.* (2018), these control variables assess the robustness of the results. For brevity, the coefficients are not reported. In all regressions, standard errors are clustered by time and firm.

In Equation (1), the interaction variables $AT \times (Dj - Dj + 1)$ capture returns on anomalies net trading (AT) index in the first three days of the month above the returns in the subsequent days. Likewise, the interaction variables $PD\_AT \times (Dj - Dj + 1)$ capture excess daily returns on post-discovery AT (PD_AT), confined to discovered anomalies.

Table 1 reports the regression results. The values in the table are in basis points. The first test does not include control variables. The post-discovery slope coefficient of $PD\_AT \times (D1 - D2)$ of 1.54 is highly significant (t = 3.76). The all-time $AT \times (D1 - D2)$ negative slope coefficient of −0.72 is also significant (t = −2.96). A similar pattern, albeit weaker, is observed in the second and third days. The $PD\_AT \times (D2 - D3)$ and $PD\_NT \times (D3 - D4)$ slope coefficients are 1.44 (t = 3.52) and 0.84 (t = 2.58), and the $AT \times (D2 - D3)$ and $AT \times (D3 - D4)$ slope coefficients are −0.81 (t = −3.09) and −0.50 (t = −2.43). These coefficients show that the lower

G. Kaplanski

Table 1: The changes in returns on anomalies after their discovery.

$PD\_AT \times (D1 - D2)$	1.54	1.43	1.53	1.43	0.91
	(3.76)***	(3.82)***	(3.74)***	(3.83)***	(2.65)***
$PD\_AT \times (D2 - D3)$	1.44	1.32	1.43	1.32	0.91
	(3.52)***	(3.60)***	(3.51)***	(3.60)***	(2.46)**
$PD\_AT \times (D3 - D4)$	0.84	0.92	0.84	0.92	0.69
	(2.58)***	(3.13)***	(2.57)**	(3.13)***	(2.31)**
$AT \times (D1 - D2)$	−0.72	−0.69	−0.71	−0.69	−0.37
	(−2.96)***	(−3.33)***	(−2.93)***	(−3.33)***	(−1.80)*
$AT \times (D2 - D3)$	−0.81	−0.75	−0.80	−0.75	−0.48
	(−3.09)***	(−3.45)***	(−3.06)***	(−3.45)***	(−2.21)**
$AT \times (D3 - D4)$	−0.50	−0.53	−0.50	−0.53	−0.38
	(−2.43)**	(−3.02)***	(−2.42)**	(−3.02)***	(−2.17)**
PD_AT	−0.07	−0.07	0.02	−0.13	−0.21
	(−0.88)	(−0.92)	(0.26)	(−1.64)	(2.69)***
AT	0.12	0.12	0.03	0.06	0.10
	(2.57)**	(3.11)***	(0.69)	(1.37)	(2.52)**
$D1$	11.41	72.60	5.62	72.77	7.70
	(2.65)***	(1.20)	(1.27)	(1.20)	(1.27)
$D2$	8.25	73.01	2.46	73.22	7.95
	(2.07)**	(1.33)	(0.60)	(1.34)	(1.43)
$D3$	6.67	20.43	0.88	20.58	2.86
	(1.57)	(0.44)	(0.20)	(0.65)	(0.62)
$D4$	−1.04	13.18	−0.68	13.29	1.68
	(0.79)	(0.79)	(−1.66)	(0.78)	(0.35)
PD_AI				0.37	0.44
				(3.37)***	(4.01)***
AI				0.92	1.03
				(9.59)***	(10.39)***

Table 1: (*Continued*)

Lagged control variables	−	−	−	−	+
Daily fixed effects	−	+	−	+	+
Firm fixed effects	−	−	+	−	−

Notes: This table reports the results of the regression in Equation (1). I regress the daily returns on the anomalies portfolios net trading (AT) index, post-discovery AT (PD_AT), the dummy variables for the days of the first week of the month ($D1$, $D2$, $D3$, and $D4$), the interactions between AT and PD_AT with the differences in the daily variables, and the lagged values of the last week (4 trading days) for stock returns, squared returns, and trading volume (the slope coefficients are not reported). AT is the sum of changes in long-side minus changes in short-side anomalies portfolios that the firm-month observation belongs to. PD_AT is calculated similarly to AT, with anomalies limited to the post-discovery period. The anomalies portfolios index (AI) controls for the returns on anomalies. PD_PI is calculated similarly to AI, with anomalies limited to the post-discovery period. The sample period is from 1973 to 2018. The slope coefficients in the table are multiplied by 10^4. The standard errors are clustered by time and firm. The t-statistics are in parentheses. *, **, and *** indicate significance at the 10%, 5%, and 1% levels, respectively.

daily average returns on AT relative to the subsequent days become significantly higher after the anomalies' discovery. The other tests in Table 1 confirm that the main results are not sensitive to model specifications. The $PD\_AT \times (Dj - Dj + 1)$ ($j = 1$, 2, and 3) coefficients in the second test with time-fixed effects are 1.43, 1.32, and 0.92, and they are significant at the 1% level ($t = 3.82$, 3.60, and 3.13, respectively). They are 1.53, 1.43, and 0.84 and significant ($t = 3.74$, 3.50, and 2.57, respectively) in the third test with firm fixed effects.

The last two tests control for the returns on anomalies and both the returns on anomalies and lagged control variables for past daily returns, volatility, and volume. Controlling for the returns on anomalies enables comparing the size of the shift in returns to the mean return on anomalies. The $PD\_AT \times (Dj - Dj + 1)$ slope coefficients are significantly positive in both tests and $AT \times (Dj - Dj + 1)$ slope coefficients are significantly negative. These opposite signs confirm that the returns' significant daily post-discovery effect is above and beyond the all-month daily mean return on anomalies. Moreover, in both tests, the $PD\_AT \times (Dj - Dj + 1)$ coefficients are of the same size order as the AI coefficients of 0.92 and 1.03 ($t = 9.59$ and 10.39), at the bottom of the table, which stand for returns on all anomalies. This same-size order indicates that the daily shift in returns across the days of the week is economically large relative to the general mean return on anomalies.

According to the results in Table 1, the returns on post-discovery anomalies are shifted toward the beginning of the month. As a result, the post-discovery first-day average return on anomalies is significantly larger than the second-day average return. The second-day average return, in turn, is significantly larger than that on the third day. This daily shift is of the same size order as the average daily return on anomalies. The daily post-discovery effect is robust to serial correlations in returns, volatility, trade volume, and time- and firm-fixed effects. Kaplanski (2023) conducts a similar analysis across the weeks of the month, showing an analogous shift in returns across all weeks of the month. Combining all results suggests anomaly discovery shifts return to the beginning of the month, particularly to the first day. Presumably, arbitrageurs who look to exploit anomalies advance trading activity towards the beginning of the month.

3.2. *The Evolution of the Post-Discovery Effect over Time*

In this subsection, I explore the development of the daily effect over time by running regressions like those in Equation (1) with two adjustments. First, I divide the post-discovery period into pre- and post-publication sub-periods. This division allows us to determine the exact time arbitrageurs start trading anomalies. The pre-publication sub-period starts in January of the year following the last year of the original study's sample period and ends in December of the publication year. The post-publication sub-period starts in January immediately afterward. The post-discovery AT indices, termed PD_AT and PP_AT, are calculated the same way as AT, except that the anomalies are confined to the two post-discovery sub-periods, respectively. Second, I distinguish between early and more recent years by splitting the post-discovery variables into early and late AT indices corresponding to 1973–1993 and 1994–2018. This separation accounts for the results of Chordia *et al.* (2014), who show that after 1993, the returns on anomalies declined by half. They attribute this decline to the growing hedge fund industry and reduced trading costs. Finally, the regressions include all lagged control variables and time-fixed effects (slope coefficients are not reported). The results of regressions with other specifications are not reported because the results are not very sensitive to model specifications, as shown in Table 1.

The post-publication slope coefficients of $PP\_AT \times (Dj - Dj + 1)$ before 1994, in the first column in Table 2, are large (3.47, 4.31, and 2.16) and highly significant (t = 3.98, 4.47, and 2.74). They are smaller after 1993 but still significant (1.12, 0.94, and 0.78; t = 2.47, 2.12, and 2.24, respectively). The post-discovery pre-publication slope coefficients of $PD\_AT \times (Dj - Dj + 1)$ are small and insignificant in both periods. These results show that the shift in returns across the first days of the month is stable over time. There is no shift in returns before the formal publishing of the anomaly in an academic journal. After publication, the mean return is significantly higher than that on the subsequent day. The smaller coefficients after 1993 are well expected and consistent with the general decline in returns on anomalies.

The second column in Table 2 reports the results of a similar regression with additional weekly variables analogously to the daily variables. Adding those variables allows me to explore the shift in returns across all

Table 2: Time development in arbitrage trading activity.

After publication	1973–1993	$PP\_AT \times (D1 - D2)$	3.47	3.16
			(3.98)***	(3.71)***
		$PP\_AT \times (D2 - D3)$	4.31	3.89
			(4.47)***	(4.15)***
		$PP\_AT \times (D3 - D4)$	2.16	1.85
			(2.74)**	(2.43)**
	1994–2018	$PP\_AT \times (D1 - D2)$	1.12	0.93
			(2.47)**	(2.07)**
		$PP\_AT \times (D2 - D3)$	0.94	0.68
			(2.12)**	(1.54)
		$PP\_AT \times (D3 - D4)$	0.78	0.58
			(2.24)**	(1.66)*
After discovery before publication	1973–1993	$PD\_AT \times (D1 - D2)$	−0.14	−0.05
			(−0.15)	(−0.05)
		$PD\_AT \times (D2 - D3)$	−1.65	−1.54
			(−1.67)*	(−1.52)

(Continued)

Table 2: (Continued)

		PD_AT × (D3 − D4)	−1.15	−1.66
			(−1.43)	(−1.29)
	1994–2018	PD_AT × (D1 − D2)	−0.38	−0.60
			(−0.81)	(−1.28)
		PD_AT × (D2 − D3)	0.33	0.04
			(0.63)	(0.07)
		PD_AT × (D3 − D4)	0.22	−0.00
			(0.48)	(−0.01)
After publication	1973–1993	PP_AT × (W1 − W2)		1.54
				(3.91)***
		PP_AT × (W2 − W3)		1.66
				(4.01)***
		PP_AT × (W3 − W4)		0.85
				(2.37)**
	1994–2018	PP_AT × (W1 − W2)		0.53
				(2.74)***
		PP_AT × (W2 − W3)		0.18
				(0.91)
		PP_AT × (W3 − W4)		0.03
				(0.07)
After discovery before publication	1973–1993	PD_AT × (W1 − W2)		−0.44
				(−0.92)
		PD_AT × (W2 − W3)		−0.34
				(−0.71)
		PD_AT × (W3 − W4)		0.03
				(0.07)

Table 2: *(Continued)*

1994–2018	$PD\_AT \times (W1 - W2)$	0.68
		(2.86)***
	$PD\_AT \times (W2 - W3)$	0.35
		(1.40)
	$PD\_AT \times (W3 - W4)$	0.25
		(1.29)

Notes: This table reports the results of regressions like those in Table 1 with the following changes in the interaction variables: (i) Post discovery AT index is split into the post-discovery pre-publication index (PD_AT) and post-publication index (PP_AT) and, separately, into the early period (1973–1993) and late period (1994–2018). The daily returns are regressed on AT, the post-discovery AT indices, the dummy variables for the days of the month, the interactions between AT with the differences in the days' variables, and the control variables (the slope coefficients are not reported) for the returns on anomalies (AI), post-discovery pre- and post-publication anomalies, dummies for the first four days of the week and lagged stock returns, squared returns, and trading volume. The second column includes additional weekly dummies and their corresponding control variables (the slope coefficients are not reported). The regressions include the time-fixed effects. The slope coefficients in the table are multiplied by 10^4. The standard errors are clustered by time and firm. The t-statistics are in parentheses. *, **, and *** indicate significance at the 10%, 5%, and 1% levels, respectively.

weeks of the month, as in Kaplanski (2023). Here, I combine this weekly analysis with daily-resolution analysis. The slope coefficients of the daily interaction variables are very similar to those in the first column, indicating a shift in daily returns within the first week of the month, particularly before 1994. Before 1994, the shift in returns across the weeks of the months was also very similar to that across the days in the first column. The shift starts after the publication of the anomalies as $PD\_AT \times (Wj - Wj + 1)$ slope coefficients are small and insignificant. The post-publication slope coefficients of $PP\_AT \times (Wj - Wj + 1)$ are large and significant at 1.54, 1.66, and 0.85 ($t = 3.91$, 4.01, and 2.37). These values indicate that in the early years of the sample, there is also a shift in returns across the weeks of the month toward the beginning of the month. Thus, the daily returns on the first week, which incline by themselves towards the beginning of the week, are higher on average than the returns on the second week. The returns on the second week are higher, on average, than on the third week, and the same holds for the returns on the third and fourth weeks. Those shifts occur only after publication, as no similar effect is observed in the post-discovery pre-publication sub-period.

The results are different after 1993. First, only the first-week post-publication $PP\_AT \times (W1 - W2)$ coefficient of 0.68 is significant ($t = 2.86$). Second, the first-week pre-publication $PD\_AT \times (W1 - W2)$ slope coefficient of 0.53 is also significant ($t = 2.74$). These results show two significant developments in the more recent years. First, the first-week excess returns start even before publication, as indicated by the significant $PP\_AT \times (W1 - W2)$ slope coefficient. Second, in both post-discovery sub-periods, the effect is concentrated mainly in the first week, as the coefficients for the other weeks are positive but insignificant. Both developments, which are further analyzed in Kaplanski (2023), are consistent with the hypothesis of Chordia *et al.* (2014) of increasing competition after 1993 in exploiting anomalies. Arbitrageurs start exploiting anomalies without waiting for publication, and they trade earlier, closer to the end of the previous month, when they first have the complete dataset required for ranking stocks. The concurrent decline in the differences across the days of the first weeks is probably due to the increasing trading activity during this week relative to other weeks.

Finally, focusing on weekly analysis, Kaplanski (2023) shows that the weekly shift exists in both long-side and short-side portfolios, as well as in bought stocks of both kinds of portfolios and sold stocks of short-side portfolios. He also shows that the differences between the long-side and short-side portfolios have diminished in recent years, which is consistent with the hypothesis of increasing market efficiency after the reduction in arbitrage costs. The analysis here complements this analysis by showing that the phenomenon also exists in daily returns, reinforcing the claim that arbitrage trading activity generates it.

3.3. *Is the Monthly Effect Driven by Arbitrage Trading Activity?*

If the observed shift in returns is due to arbitrage trading activity, I expect two results: First, there should be no effect before anomaly discovery. Second, the effect should be more intense in anomalies based on monthly data because they are more exposed to monthly trading immediately after the previous month's data is available.

In the previous sections, I show no shift before the anomaly discovery because the slope coefficients of $PD\_AT \times (Dj - Dj + 1)$ and $PD\_AT \times (Wj - Wj + 1)$ are insignificant. To verify that this is not a spurious result caused by the calculation of the *AT* index, I next repeat the regression in Equation (1) while replacing the *AT* index with one anomaly with a single date: The momentum anomaly of Jegadeesh and Titman (1993). This anomaly is commonly referred to as a premier anomaly (Daniel *et al.*, 1998; Hong and Stein, 1999; George and Hwang, 2004) due to its economic size, stability, and persistency. Finally, to test the second hypothesis, I ran the regression with the *AT* index, composed only of monthly data anomalies. This index is composed of the following anomalies: Bid–Ask Spread, Firm Age-Momentum, Information Discreteness and Momentum, Lagged Momentum, Long-Term Reversal, Max, Momentum, Momentum and LT Reversal, Momentum-Reversal, Momentum-Volume, Recency Ratio, Seasonality, Short-Term Reversal, Turnover, Volume/Market Value of Equity, and Xmax.

Table 3 reports the regression results. The regressions include the daily and weekly variables and their corresponding control variables. For brevity, I unify the two post-discovery sub-periods, as in Table 1, and the slope coefficients of the control variables are not reported. The first column in Table 3 corresponds to all anomalies. As with the previous results in Table 2, the slope coefficients of $PD\_AT \times (Dj - Dj + 1)$ and $PD\_AT \times (Wj - Wj + 1)$ before 1994 are positive and significant. Also consistent, after 1993, $PD\_AT \times (Dj - Dj + 1)$ slope coefficients are positive and significant, albeit to a lesser extent. Similarly, only the first-week slope coefficient of $PD\_AT \times (W1 - W2)$ is significantly positive after 1993. Thus, in line with the results in Table 2 in the more recent years, excess returns are mainly realized in the first week of the month. Nevertheless, the daily effect during the first week has continued.

The second column in Table 3 reports the results of the regression in which a single anomaly index for momentum replaces the *AN* index. The slope coefficients of both $PD\_AT \times (Dj - Dj + 1)$ and $PD\_AT \times (Wj - Wj + 1)$ before 1994 are mainly negative (−8.22, −6.75, −3.41, and −2.80, −1.39, 0.52) and tend to be mildly significant ($t = -2.39$, −2.00, −1.33, and −1.99, −0.97, 0.45, respectively). Indeed, up to 1993, there was no shift of returns towards the beginning of the month. On the contrary, the return on anomaly tilts backward such that the average return on the first day is significantly smaller than that on the second day, which, by itself, is significantly smaller than that on the third day. Moreover, the average daily returns on the first week are significantly smaller than those on the second week,

Table 3: The change in returns depends on anomaly characteristics.

Daily shift	1973–1993	$PD\_AT \times (D1 - D2)$	3.24	−8.22	4.85
			(3.78)***	(−2.39)**	(4.06)***
		$PD\_AT \times (D2 - D3)$	3.98	−6.75	5.66
			(4.24)***	(−2.00)**	(4.18)***
		$PD\_AT \times (D3 - D4)$	1.91	−3.41	2.86
			(2.52)**	(−1.33)	(2.48)**
	1994–2018	$PD\_AT \times (D1 - D2)$	1.00	1.03	1.23
			(2.27)**	(0.41)	(1.99)**
		$PD\_AT \times (D2 - D3)$	0.71	3.28	0.61
			(1.65)*	(1.32)	(0.97)
		$PD\_AT \times (D3 - D4)$	0.61	0.96	0.74
			(1.77)*	(0.49)	(1.46)
Weekly shift	1973–1993	$PD\_AT \times (W1 - W2)$	1.48	−2.80	2.29
			(3.75)***	(−1.99)**	(4.01)***
		$PD\_AT \times (W2 - W3)$	1.63	−1.39	2.70
			(3.95)***	(−0.97)	(4.54)***
		$PD\_AT \times (W3 - W4)$	0.81	0.52	1.30
			(2.28)**	(0.45)	(2.51)**
	1994–2018	$PD\_AT \times (W1 - W2)$	0.46	1.05	0.60
			(2.40)**	(0.98)	(2.19)**
		$PD\_AT \times (W2 - W3)$	0.15	2.83	0.14
			(0.76)	(2.66)***	(0.50)
		$PD\_AT \times (W3 - W4)$	0.08	1.37	−0.05
			(0.50)	(1.65)*	(−0.24)

Notes: This table reports the results of similar regressions to those in Table 2 with a separate AT depending on the types of anomalies. The daily returns are regressed on AT, the post-discovery AT indices, the dummy variables for the days and the weeks of the month, the interactions between AT with the differences in the days and weeks variables, and the control variables (the slope coefficients are not reported) for the returns on anomalies (AI), post-discovery pre- and post-publication anomalies, dummies for the weeks and lagged stock returns, squared returns, and trading volume. The three columns correspond to AT, composed of all anomalies, momentum anomaly, and monthly based anomalies. The regressions include the time-fixed effects. The slope coefficients in the table are multiplied by 10^4. The standard errors are clustered by time and firm. The t-statistics are in parentheses. *, **, and *** indicate significance at the 10%, 5%, and 1% levels, respectively.

which tend to be smaller than those on the third week. This increasing return tendency completely reveres after 1993, when the anomaly was formally published in Jegadeesh and Titman (1993). The sign of the slope coefficients of $PD\_AT \times (Dj - Dj + 1)$ and $PD\_AT \times (Wj - Wj + 1)$ turn positive (1.03, 3.28, 0.96, and 1.05, 2.83, 1.37, respectively). Moreover, $PD\_AT \times (W2 - W3)$, and $PD\_AT \times (W3 - W4)$ are significant ($t = 2.66$, and 1.65). The positive coefficients indicate that the increase in returns over the month completely disappears.

Moreover, according to the significantly positive weekly coefficients, the average daily returns over the first two weeks are significantly higher than those on the third week. The same applies to the average daily returns over the third week relative to the fourth week. In sum, the results of the momentum anomaly are entirely in line with the general results of the broad all-anomaly AT index. Once the momentum phenomenon has been officially published, there is a significant shift of returns on this anomaly towards the beginning of the month.

The third column in Table 3 corresponds to anomalies based on monthly data. As previously explained, those anomalies are prone to monthly trading strategies; hence, they are exposed to a more significant shift in returns over the days of the month. Comparing the slope coefficients in the first and third columns shows that the effect in both the days and weeks of the month is substantially more profound in monthly based anomalies. For example, the slope coefficients of $PD\_AT \times (D1 - D2)$ and $PD\_AT \times (D2 - D3)$ in the third column are 4.85 and 5.66 compared to 3.24 and 3.98 in the first column. Similarly, the slope coefficients of $PD\_AT \times (W1 - W2)$ and $PD\_AT \times (W2 - W3)$ are 2.29 and 2.70 vs. 1.48 and 1.68, respectively. These results align with the hypothesis that the effect is more intense in anomalies prone to monthly trading and exposed to less sophisticated arbitrageurs. Finally, it is worth mentioning that Kaplanski (2023) shows that the weekly shift is more profound in market-based than fundamental-based anomalies. Here, I show that the effect is the strongest in monthly based anomalies, and this effect also exists across the days of the first week.

In sum, the shift in returns appears only after discovering the anomaly. As expected, it is also more profound in monthly based anomalies like the momentum anomaly, in line with the assumptions that those anomalies are traded more often at the beginning of each month and are exposed to additional arbitrage activity of the less sophisticated arbitrageurs.

4. Conclusion

This study extends the analysis of Kaplanski (2023) on how arbitrage capital reshapes the returns after discovering anomalies. I find an intense and persistent return effect in the first days of the month, which appears only after the publication of the anomaly. This effect is opposite in sign to the general tendency of returns on anomalies to decay. As a result, a large portion of profits on anomalies is realized at the beginning of the month, with the highest shift across the first three days of the first week. For instance, the first-day return on anomalies accounts for more than 10% of the portfolio value, increasing to 30% in monthly based anomalies. Thus, the monthly seesaw pattern in returns across the weeks following the discovery of anomalies, first shown by Kaplanski (2023), is more profound across the days of the first week, particularly in monthly based anomalies.

This long-lasting trading activity of arbitrageurs suggests that the market has already decided that at least some anomalies point to persistent mispricing and offer ongoing abnormal profits. The evidence indicates that arbitrageurs find these opportunities profitable after considering the costs and risks involved despite the increasing competition in exploiting anomalies. This mispricing component in anomalies is difficult to reconcile with full rationality but can be explained via investors' behavioral biases.

Appendix: List of Anomalies

52-Week High, George and Hwang (2004); Accruals, Sloan (1996); Advertising/Market Value of Equity, Chan *et al.* (2001); Amihud's Measure (Illiquidity), Amihud (2002); Asset Growth, Cooper *et al.* (2008); Asset Turnover, Soliman (2008); Beta, Fama and MacBeth (1973); Bid-Ask Spread, Amihud and Mendelsohn (1986); Book Equity/ Market Value of Equity, Fama and French (1992); Cash Flow/Market Value of Equity, Lakonishok *et al.* (1994); Change in Asset Turnover, Soliman (2008); Change in Profit Margin , Soliman (2008); Change in Recommendation, Jegadeesh *et al.* (2004); Earnings Acceleration, He and Narayanamoorthy (2020); Earnings Surprise, Foster *et al.* (1984); Enterprise Component of Book / Penman *et al.* (2007); Enterprise Multiple, Loughran and Wellman (2011); Firm Age, Barry and Brown (1984); Firm Age-Momentum, Zhang (2006); Gross Profitability, Novy-Marx (2013); Change in Inventory, Thomas and Zhang (2002); Growth in LTNOA,

Fairfield *et al.* (2003); F-Score, Piotroski (2000); Fundamental Mispricing Characteristic, Bartram and Grinblatt (2018); G-score, Mohanram (2005); Idiosyncratic Risk, Ang *et al.* (2006); Information Discreteness and Momentum, Da *et al.* (2014); Investment, Titman *et al.* (2004); Investment-to-Assets, Chen Novy-Marx, Zhang (2011); Lagged Momentum, Novy-Marx (2012); Leverage , Bhandari (1988); Leverage Component of Book, Penman *et al.* (2007); Long-Term Reversal, Debondt and Thaler (1985); M/B and Accruals, Bartov and Kim (2004); Max, Bali *et al.* (2011); Momentum, Jegadeesh and Titman (1993); Momentum and LT Reversal, Chan and Kot (2006); Momentum-Reversal, Jegadeesh and Titman (1993); Momentum-Volume, Lee and Swaminathan (2000); Net Operating Assets, Hirshleifer *et al.* (2004); Net Working Capital Changes, Soliman (2008); Noncurrent Operating Assets Changes, Soliman (2008); Operating Leverage, Novy-Marx (2010); Organization Capital, Eisfeldt and Papanikolaou (2013); O-Score, Dichev (1998); Percent Operating Accrual, Hafzalla *et al.* (2011); Percent Total Accrual, Hafzalla *et al.* (2011); Profit Margin, Soliman (2008); Profitability, Balakrishnan *et al.* (2010); R&D/ Market Value of Equity, Chan *et al.* (2001); Return-on-Assets, Cooper *et al.* (2008); Return-on-Equity, Haugen and Baker (1996); Recency Ratio, Bhootra and Hur (2013); Revenue Surprises, Jegadeesh and Livnat (2006); Sales/Price, Barbee *et al.* (1996); Seasonality, Heston and Sadka (2008); Share Issuance (1-Year), Pontiff and Woodgate (2008); Share Issuance (5-Year), Daniel and Titman (2006); Share Volume, Datar *et al.* (1998); Short-Term Reversal, Jegadeesh (1990); Size, Banz (1981); Sustainable Growth, Lockwood and Prombutr (2010); Tax, Lev and Nissim (2004); Total XFIN, Bradshaw *et al.* (2006); Turnover, Haugen and Baker (1996); Volume/Market Value of Equity, Haugen and Baker (1996); Volume Trend, Haugen and Baker (1996); Volume Variance, Chordia *et al.* (2001); Xmax, Li and Yu (2012); ΔSales $-$ ΔInventory, Abarbanell and Bushee (1998); ΔSales $-$ ΔSG&A, Abarbanell and Bushee (1998).

References

Abarbanell, J. and Bushee, B. (1998). Abnormal returns to a fundamental analysis strategy. *Accounting Review*, 73, 19–45.

Akbas, F., Armstrong, W., Sorescu, S., and Subrahmanyam, A. (2015). Smart money, dumb money, and equity return anomalies. *Journal of Financial Economics*, 118, 355–382.

Amihud, Y. (2002). Illiquidity and stock returns: Cross-section and time-series effects. *Journal of Financial Markets*, 5, 31–56.

Amihud, Y. and Mendelsohn, H. (1986). Asset pricing and the bid-ask spread. *Journal of Financial Economics*, 17, 223–249.

Ang, A., Hodrick, R., Xing, Y., and Zhang, X. (2006). The cross-section of volatility and expected returns. *Journal of Finance*, 61, 259–299.

Avramov, D., Kaplanski, G., and Subrahmanyam, A. (2021). Moving average distance as a predictor of equity returns. *Review of Financial Economics*, 40, 127–145.

Avramov, D., Kaplanski, G., and Subrahmanyam, A. (2022). Post-fundamentals price drift in capital markets: A regression regularization perspective. *Management Science*, 68, 7065–7791.

Balakrishnan, K., Bartov, E., and Faurel, L. (2010). Post loss/profit announcement drift. *Journal of Accounting and Economics*, 50, 20–41.

Bali, T., Cakici, N., and Whitelaw, R. (2011). Maxing out: Stocks as lotteries and the cross-section of expected returns. *Journal of Financial Economics*, 99, 427–446.

Banz, R. (1981). The relationship between return and market value of common stocks. *Journal of Financial Economics*, 9, 3–18.

Barbee, W., Mukherji, S., and Raines, G. (1996). Do sales-price and debt-equity explain stock returns better than book-market and firm size? *Financial Analysts Journal*, 52, 56–60.

Barry, C. and Brown, S. (1984). Differential information and the small firm effect. *Journal of Financial Economics*, 13, 283–294.

Bartov, E. and Kim, M. (2004). Risk, mispricing, and value investing. *Review of Quantitative Finance and Accounting*, 23, 353–376.

Bartram, S. and Grinblatt, M. (2018). Agnostic fundamental analysis works. *Journal of Financial Economics*, 128, 125–147.

Bhandari, L. (1983). Debt/equity ratio and expected common stock returns: Empirical evidence, *Journal of Finance*, 43, 507–528.

Bhootra, A. and Hur, J. (2013). The timing of 52-week high price and momentum. *Journal of Banking and Finance*, 37, 3773–3782.

Bradshaw, M., Richardson, A., and Sloan, R. (2006). The relation between corporate financing activities, analysts' forecasts and stock returns. *Journal of Accounting and Economics*, 42, 53–85.

Chan, K. and Kot, H. (2006). Price reversal and momentum strategies. *Journal of Investment Management*, 4, 70–89.

Chan, L., Lakonishok, J., and Sougiannis, T. (2001). The stock market valuation of research and development expenditures. *Journal of Finance*, 56, 2431–2456.

Chen, L., Novy-Marx, R., and Zhang, L. (2011). An alternative three-factor model. Working Paper, University of Rochester.

Chordia, T., Subranhmanyam, A., and Anshuman, V. (2001). Trading activity and expected stock returns. *Journal of Financial Economics*, 59, 3–32.

Chordia, T., Subrahmanyam, A., and Tong, Q. (2014). Have capital market anomalies attenuated in the recent era of high liquidity and trading activity? *Journal of Accounting and Economics*, 58, 41–58.

Cooper, M., Gulen, H., and Schill, M. (2008). Asset growth and the cross-section of stock returns. *Journal of Finance*, 63, 1609–1651.

Da, Z., Gurun, U., and Warachka, M. (2014). Frog in the pan: Continuous information and momentum. *Review of Financial Studies*, 27, 2171–2218.

Daniel, K., Hirshleifer, D., and Subrahmanyam, A. (1998). Investor psychology and security market under- and over-reactions. *Journal of Finance*, 53, 1839–1885.

Daniel, K. and Titman, S. (2006). Market reactions to tangible and intangible information. *Journal of Finance*, 61, 1605–1643.

Datar, V., Naik, N., and Radcliffe, R. (1998). Liquidity and stock returns: An alternative test. *Journal of Financial Markets*, 1, 203–219.

DeBondt, W. and Thaler, R. (1985). Does the stock market overreact? *Journal of Finance*, 40, 793–805.

Dichev, I. (1998). Is the risk of bankruptcy a systematic risk? *Journal of Finance*, 53, 1131–1147.

Eisfeldt, A. and Papanikolaou, D. (2013). Organization capital and the cross-section of expected returns. *Journal of Finance*, 68, 1365–1406.

Engelberg, J., Mclean, R., and Pontiff, J. (2018). Anomalies and news. *Journal of Finance*, 73, 1971–2001.

Fairfield, P., Whisenant, S., and Yohn, T. (2003). Accrued earnings and growth: Implications for future profitability and market mispricing. *Accounting Review*, 78, 353–371.

Fama, E. (1970). Efficient capital markets: A review of theory and empirical work. *Journal of Finance*, 25, 383–417.

Fama, E. (1998). Market efficiency, long-term returns, and behavioral finance. *Journal of Financial Economics*, 49, 283–306.

Fama, E. and French, K. (1992). The cross-section of expected stock returns. *Journal of Finance*, 47, 427–466.

Fama, E. and French, K. (1993). Common risk factors in the returns of stocks and bonds. *Journal of Financial Economics*, 33, 3–56.

Fama, E. and MacBeth, J. (1973). Risk, return, and equilibrium: Empirical tests. *Journal of Political Economy*, 81, 607–636.

Foster, G., Olsen, C., and Shevlin, T. (1984). Earnings releases, anomalies, and the behavior of security returns. *Accounting Review*, 59, 574–603.

George, T. and Hwang, C. (2004). The 52-week high and momentum investing. *Journal of Finance*, 59, 2145–2176.

Green, J., Hand, J., and Soliman, M. (2011). Going, going, gone? The demise of the accruals anomaly. *Management Science*, 57, 797–816.

Hafzalla, N., Lundholm, R., and Van Winkle, M. (2011). Percent accruals. *Accounting Review*, 86, 209–236.

Harvey, C., Liu, Y., and Zhu, H. (2016). … and the cross-section of expected returns. *Review of Financial Studies*, 29, 5–68.

Haugen, R. and Baker, N. (1996). Commonality in the determinants of expected stock returns. *Journal of Financial Economics*, 41, 401–439.

He, S. and Narayanamoorthy, G. (2020). Earnings acceleration and stock returns. *Journal of Accounting and Economics*, 69, 101238.

Heston, L. and Sadka, R. (2008). Seasonality in the cross-section of stock returns. *Journal of Financial Economics*, 87, 418–445.

Hirshleifer, D., Hou, K., Teoh, S., and Zhang, Y. (2004). Do investors overvalue firms with bloated balance sheets? *Journal of Accounting and Economics*, 38, 297–331.

Hong, H. and Stein, J. (1999). A unified theory of underreaction, momentum trading and overreaction in asset markets. *Journal of Finance*, 54, 2143–2184.

Hou, K., Xue, C., and Zhang, L. (2015). Digesting anomalies: An investment approach. *Review of Financial Studies*, 28, 650–705.

Hou, K., Xue, C., and Zhang, L. (2020). Replicating anomalies. *Review of Financial Studies*, 33, 2019–2133.

Jacobs, H. and Müller, S. (2020). Anomalies across the globe: Once public, no longer existent? *Journal of Financial Economics*, 135, 213–230.

Jegadeesh, N. (1990). Evidence of predictable behavior of security returns. *Journal of Finance*, 45, 881–898.

Jegadeesh, N. and Livnat, J. (2006). Revenue surprises and stock returns. *Journal of Accounting and Economics*, 41, 147–171.

Jegadeesh, N. and Titman, S. (1993). Returns to buying winners and selling losers: Implications for stock market efficiency. *Journal of Finance*, 48, 65–91.

Jegadeesh, N., Kim, J., Krische, S., and Lee, C. (2004). Analyzing the analysts: When do recommendations add value? *Journal of Finance*, 59, 1083–1124.

Jensen, M.C. (1978). Some anomalous evidence regarding market efficiency. *Journal of Financial Economics*, 6, 95–101.

Kaplanski, G. (2023). The race to exploit anomalies and the cost of slow trading. *Journal of Financial Markets*, 62, 100754.

Kokkonen, J. and Suominen, M. (2015). Hedge funds and stock market efficiency. *Management Science*, 61, 2890–2904.

Lakonishok, J., Shleifer, A., and Vishny, R. (1994). Contrarian investment, extrapolation, and risk. *Journal of Finance*, 49, 1541–1578.

Lee, C. and Swaminathan, B. (2000). Price momentum and trading volume. *Journal of Finance*, 55, 2017–2069.

Lev, B. and Nissim, D. (2004). Taxable income, future earnings, and equity values. *Accounting Review*, 79, 1039–1074.

Li, J. and Yu, J. (2012). Investor attention, psychological anchors, and stock return predictability. *Journal of Financial Economics*, 104, 401–419.

Lo, A. (2004). The adaptive markets hypothesis: Market efficiency from an evolutionary perspective. *Journal of Portfolio Management*, 30, 15–29.

Lockwood, L. and Prombutr, W. (2010). Sustainable growth and stock returns. *Journal of Financial Research*, 33, 519–538.

Loughran, T. and Wellman, J. (2011). New evidence on the relation between the enterprise multiple and average stock returns. *Journal of Financial and Quantitative Analysis*, 46, 1629–1650.

Martin, I. and Nagel, S. (2019). Market efficiency in the age of big data. National Bureau of Economic Research Working Paper Series No. 26586.

McConnell, J. and Wei, X. (2008). Equity returns at the turn of the month. *Financial Analysts Journal*, 64, 49–64.

McLean, D. and Pontiff, J. (2016). Does academic research destroy stock return predictability? *Journal of Finance*, 71, 5–32.

Mohanram, P. (2005). Separating winners from losers among low book-to-market stocks using financial statement analysis. *Review of Accounting Studies*, 10, 133–170.

Novy-Marx, R. (2010). Operating leverage. *Review of Finance*, 15, 103–134.

Novy-Marx, R. (2012). Is momentum really momentum? *Journal of Financial Economics*, 103, 429–453.

Novy-Marx, R. (2013). The other side of value: The gross profitability premium. *Journal of Financial Economics*, 108, 1–28.

Penman, S., Richardson, S., and Tuna, I. (2007). The book-to-price effect in stock returns: Accounting for leverage. *Journal of Accounting Research*, 45, 427–467.

Piotroski, J. (2000). Value investing: The use of historical financial statement information to separate winners from losers. *Journal of Accounting Research*, 38, 1–41.

Pontiff, J. and Woodgate, A. (2008). Share issuance and cross-sectional returns. *Journal of Finance*, 63, 921–945.

Shumway, T. (1997). The delisting bias in CRSP data. *Journal of Finance*, 52, 327–340.

Sloan, R. (1996). Do stock prices fully reflect information in accruals and cash flows about future earnings? *Accounting Review*, 71, 289–315.

Soliman, M. (2008). The use of DuPont analysis by market participants. *Accounting Review*, 83, 823–853.

Thomas, J. and Zhang, H. (2002). Inventory changes and future returns. *Review of Accounting Studies*, 7, 163–187.

Titman, S., Wei, J., and Xie, F. (2004). Capital investments and stock returns. *Journal of Financial and Quantitative Analysis*, 39, 677–700.

Zhang, L. (2006). Information uncertainty and stock returns. *Journal of Finance*, 61, 105–137.

Part II

Professional Investors and Analysts Behavior

Chapter 5

Investor Sophistication and the Effect of Behavioral Biases in Structured Products Investment

Moran Ofir[*] and Zvi Wiener[†]

*Reichman University, PO Box 167, 8 Ha'universita Street,
Herzliya 4610101, Israel
mofir@idc.ac.il*

*†Hebrew University Business school Finance Department,
Mount Scopus, Jerusalem 91905, Israel
zvi.wiener@huji.ac.il*

Abstract

We examine the effects of behavioral biases among professional investors using the case of structured product (SP) investments. We outline key features embedded in SP and associate each with a specific behavioral bias. Our findings reveal that, to varying degrees, the biases examined affect professional investors. As the findings show that even professional investors are not immune to biases, we try to ascertain whether there are certain personal characteristics that influence the magnitude of bias within this group of professionals. Using logit, probit, and linear probability models, we show that the behavioral patterns examined are so deeply rooted in human behavior that they are difficult to overcome, and that this holds true with regard to any of the personal characteristics analyzed. By demonstrating these behavioral biases' impact on investors, our results lend support to applying specific regulation to SP investments, aimed at improving investor protection. The regulation should apply to both professional and non-professional investors.

Keywords: Behavioral biases, Professional investors, Structured products, Securities regulation

1. Introduction

It is a convention in financial literature that the behavior of individual investors is less relevant since it is institutional investors who drive financial markets. These professional investors are assumed to be rational and base their investment decisions on efficient analytical tools. Therefore, it is the marginal professional investor who, by exploiting arbitrage opportunities, sets the prices in the market. For instance, it is argued that any research that ignores the influence of professional traders is less relevant because non-professional individuals are unlikely to have any substantial impact on market prices since they are too far removed from the price discovery process (Locke and Mann, 2005).

There are numerous reasons to believe that the behavior of financial professionals differs from that of non-professionals, including their training, market experience, and access to information, as well as the regulations applied to them. However, it is unclear whether professional investors are really immune to behavioral biases. Hirshleifer (2001) argues that many financial behavioral patterns are so deeply rooted that they are difficult to overcome by learning. Menkhoff and Nikiforow (2009) provide evidence for Hirshleifer's hypothesis by testing it among fund managers; their findings support the hypothesis that many behavioral biases are difficult to overcome by learning, even though the fund managers analyzed have very strong incentives to learn efficient behavior.

In this chapter, we examine the performance of behavioral biases among professional investors in the case of structured product (SP) investments. SPs are prepackaged instruments comprising securities and derivatives bundled into a single derivative instrument. One of the key characteristics of SPs is that the return is determined by a predetermined formula, which specifies the product's performance in any possible future scenario.

SPs were first sold in the U.S. in the 1980s, but interest in SPs as a method of portfolio diversification and as an independent investment developed chiefly in the last decade. In Ofir and Wiener (2016), we provide evidence that the global market for SPs experienced massive growth in the last years. As we demonstrate there, analyzing typical SPs by discerning and pricing their underlying financial assets indicates a large implicit premium charged by issuers.[1]

---

[1] Support for this finding may be found in Stoimenov and Wilkens (2005), Benet *et al.* (2006), Wilkens and Stoimenov (2007), Hens and Rieger (2009, 2011), and Henderson and Pearson (2011).

Considering this riskless transfer of wealth, neoclassical economic theory fails to explain the consistent growth of the SP market. We argue that most SPs available are designed to exploit a number of common behavioral biases in decision-making under uncertainty. Several papers show that *retail* investors tend to be affected by these biases in their investment decisions involving SPs.[2] In this chapter, we focus on *professional* investors and analyze their investment decisions involving these products. We identify several features of SPs associated with specific behavioral biases. The insights we present are derived from various concepts in the realm of decision theory: loss aversion, the disposition effect, herd behavior, the ostrich effect, and the recency effect.

In order to examine professional investors' decision-making with regard to investment in SPs, we conduct an experiment that tests each bias individually to determine whether professional investors are influenced by it to the extent that they favor investment in an SP over another, equally profitable alternative. Our findings demonstrate that professional investors, much like non-professionals, tend to be affected by these behavioral biases. Next, we examine whether within this group of professional investors, certain personal characteristics may influence the magnitude of bias. In our analysis we use logit, probit, and linear probability models. All three models tell a consistent story regarding each of the biases: the signs of coefficients match across the board, and the statistical significance of coefficients is uniform. Overall, personal characteristics carry little explanatory power regarding biases. Apparently, these are so deeply rooted in human behavior that their effects are difficult to overcome regardless of personal characteristics.

By demonstrating the impact of these behavioral biases on investors, our results can support the application of specific regulation for SPs, designed to improve investor protection. Moreover, the proposed regulation should be applied to both professional and non-professional investors, since both groups are affected by the behavioral biases tested. Specifically, we propose regulative measures that would compel issuers to reveal the effective fees they charge investors. Equipping investors with disclosure of effective fees enables them to conduct a straightforward comparison of investment alternatives and decide whether the fees are

---

[2]E.g., Breuer and Perst (2007), Fischer (2007), Dobeli and Vanini (2010), Rieger (2012), Rieger and Hens (2012), Ofir and Wiener (2016).

justified, given bias. The aforementioned effective value is known to issuers; thus, no additional costs need to be borne.

The chapter proceeds as follows. Section 2 reviews the literature on the behavioral biases tested and analyzes the relation between identified features in SP investments and their correlative behavioral biases. In this section, we also summarize existing literature concerning the chosen behavioral biases. In Section 3 we review the literature regarding each bias, as performed by professional investors. Next, Section 4 describes the experiment and its results. In Section 5 we test whether certain personal characteristics affect the magnitude of bias within the group of professional investors. Finally, Section 6 presents the policy implications of our findings, concluding remarks and, implications and recommendations for SP regulation.

2. A Behavioral Analysis of Structured Products

This chapter focuses on five features commonly found in SPs and the behavioral biases associated with them. In this section, we review the literature about these biases and analyze the relation between each and its corresponding feature.

2.1. *Loss Aversion*

Loss aversion refers to people's tendency to strongly prefer avoiding losses to acquiring gains. A key conclusion of Kahneman and Tversky's (1979) classic study of decision-making under uncertainty is that choices are best explained by assuming that the significant carriers of utility are not states of wealth, but rather changes relative to a neutral reference point such as the status quo. According to their theory, value is assigned to gains and losses rather than to final assets. The value function is concave for gains and convex for losses and is steeper for losses than for gains. Empirical estimates of loss aversion demonstrate that the perceived disutility of loss is twice as high as the utility of gain (Tversky and Kahneman, 1991).

Investors consider SPs as less risky investments, primarily because most promise principal protection. Principal protection enables loss-averse investors to avoid losses and enjoy gains in certain circumstances.

Investors, especially retail investors, consider principal protection a very attractive feature, and their decisions pertaining to investment in SPs are strongly affected by it.

Note that principal protection is usually nominal and not real, and does not carry any compensation for the time value of money. Moreover, in some SPs the principal protection is in foreign currency, which exposes the principal to exchange rate risks. In short, principal protection is not necessarily what one would wish it to be, nor perhaps what investors assume it to be.

2.2. The Disposition Effect

Also identified by Kahneman and Tversky (1979), the disposition effect refers to an aversion to loss realization. Shefrin and Statman (1985) examine this feature within the context of financial markets. Specifically, they examine decisions to realize gains and losses in a market setting. They develop a descriptive theory of capital gain and loss realization in which investors tend to "sell winners too early and ride losers too long", relative to normative theory prescriptions (Shefrin and Statman, 1985). Following this research, the disposition effect has been studied intensively.[3] Using evidence that suggests that this tendency applies in real-life financial markets, Shefrin and Statman demonstrate how the tendency to sell winners and ride losers emerges in prospect theory in the following example.

Consider an investor who purchased a stock one month ago for $50 and finds that the stock is now selling at $40. The investor must now decide whether to realize the loss or hold the stock for one more period. In addition, suppose that at the end of the second period, one of two equiprobable outcomes will emerge: either the stock will increase in price by $10 or decrease in price by $10. According to prospect theory, our investor frames his choice as a choice between the following two lotteries:

A. Sell the stock now and realize a $10 loss.
B. Hold the stock for one more period, given 50-50 odds between losing an additional $10 and "breaking even."

---

[3]Odean (1998), Weber and Camerer (1998), Grinblatt and Keloharju (2000), Shapira and Venezia (2001), Locke and Mann (2005), Kumar (2009), and Ben-David and Hirshleifer (2012).

Since the choice between these lotteries is associated with the convex portion of the S-shaped value function, prospect theory implies that B would be selected over A. That is, the investor will ride his losing stock. An analogous argument demonstrates how prospect theory accounts for a propensity towards profit-taking.

In our research, the relevant behavioral phenomenon is aversion to loss realization, or in other words, the disposition to "ride losers". Many SPs include mandatory conversion provisions. Conversion is triggered when the price of the underlying asset falls past a predetermined threshold during the investment period. If the price does not cross this threshold, the investor receives the principal plus a relatively high return. The conversion into the "losing" asset typically reflects a higher price (i.e., the market price at the time of issue) than the asset's market price at the time of the SP's maturity.

The mandatory conversion feature is activated by the investor's tendency to "ride losers", since conversion into "losing" assets delays loss realization. Investors will continue to ride the losing asset in the near future, and refrain from realizing losses caused by investment in the SP. Investors tend to continue holding "losing" shares after the SP matures. This behavior enables them to avoid loss realization.

2.3. *Herd Behavior*

Herd behavior occurs when large numbers of people act in the same way at the same time. Substantial stock market trends, bubbles, and crashes often begin and end with periods in which a large number of investors buy or sell stocks. Individual investors join the crowd in a rush to enter or exit the market. The literature on herd behavior is extensive. Leibenstein (1950) defined it as the extent to which demand for an asset grows as others purchase it. He explained the motivations underlying herd behavior as "the desire of people to purchase a commodity in order to get into 'the swim of things'; in order to conform with the people they wish to be associated with; in order to be fashionable or stylish; or, in order to appear to be 'one of the boys'."

Herd behavior has also been explained in terms of the *network effect*, first defined by Katz and Shapiro (1985) as follows: "There are many products for which the utility that a user derives from consumption of the good increases with the number of other agents consuming the good. ... The utility that a given user derives from the good depends on the number of other users who are in the same 'network' as he or she." The main assumption underlying the effect is the existence of complete information. It is assumed that individuals possess identical motivations and expectations regarding the benefits of goods.

Bikhchandani *et al.* (1992) modeled herd behavior under *imperfect* information. Under their model, herd behavior occurred "when it was optimal for an individual, having observed the actions of those ahead of him, to follow the behavior of the preceding individual without regard to his own information". The decision-maker observes the actions of others and assumes that they hold more valuable information than he or she.

The most common explanation for herd behavior in financial markets is this last one. Non-professional investors follow the behavior of other investors, assuming that the latter holds more valuable information on market conditions and trends. Since our research focuses on professional investors in financial markets and assumes complete information, the network effect explanation is not valid; and so we focus on Leibenstein's explanation, which is a purely behavioral one.

Investment in SPs enables the investor not only to conform to the people with whom she wishes to be associated but also to do so without risking the entire funds invested in a specific instrument. Thus, on the one hand, an investor motivated solely by the information presumably held by other investors would invest directly in the underlying asset. On the other hand, an investor motivated by a desire to be fashionable, but is uncertain about the value of third-party information, would invest in SPs. These provide her with only partial exposure to the underlying asset, while providing the full benefit of conformity with the people with whom she wishes to be affiliated.

SPs, which provide investors with exposure to commodities, emerging markets, and exotic financial products, can exploit herd behavior. For example, structured notes linked to emerging market indices facilitate portfolio diversification in potential growth economies. Investors who purchase these market-linked products can conform to people with whom they wish to be associated without exposing the entire fund to the risk of the specific emerging market.

2.4. *The Ostrich Effect*

The impact of liquidity on the prices of financial assets occupies center stage in finance literature. Rational pricing of financial assets is informed by the assessment of a positive correlation between liquidity and prices; i.e., illiquidity has an adverse impact on asset value. When compared with otherwise identical illiquid assets, liquid assets should have a lower yield to maturity, given the option to liquidate the position at any stage and the possibility to realize an even larger return in the market, without risking the expected return for holding the investment to maturity.[4]

Galai and Sade (2006) found that investors prefer to hold illiquid assets and are even willing to pay a premium for them. They attribute this seemingly anomalous behavior to an aversion to receiving information on potential interim losses. The ostrich effect is defined as a tendency to avoid cognitive perception or internalization of apparently risky financial situations by pretending they do not exist. In other words, certain individuals, when faced with uncertainty, prefer investments for which the risk is unreported to similar investments (as far as risk and return are concerned) for which the risks are reported frequently. Support for ostrich effect behavior can be found in various types of financial markets and countries.[5]

Most SPs are illiquid. Investors can avoid apparently risky financial situations throughout the lifetime of an illiquid structure by assuming these situations do not exist. The only situation with which the investors are concerned is that occurring at maturity.

2.5. *Recency Effect*

An order effect occurs when the order of the information impacts the decision made by the decision-makers. Hogarth and Einhorn (1992) define order effects with the following example: "There are two pieces of evidence, A and B. Some participants express an opinion after seeing the information in the order A-B; others receive the information in the order B-A. An order effect occurs when opinions after A-B differ from

---

[4]See, e.g., Amihud and Mendelson (1991), Silber (1991), Kadlec and McConnel (1994), Amihud *et al.* (1997), Brenner *et al.* (2001).
[5]As demonstrated in Galai and Sade (2006), pp. 2757–2758.

those after B-A. The recency effect is a specific type of order effect in which the most recent information has a greater influence on the decision-makers than any other available information.

Hogarth and Einhorn (1992) present a theory of belief updating that explicitly accounts for order-effect phenomena and provides experimental evidence to support the theory. These effects have been observed in several areas of study. For instance, Tuttle *et al.* (1997) examine whether the order of information releases affects market prices. Economic theory would suggest that in a market context, information order is a variable irrelevant to the price decision. Nevertheless, significant evidence is found for a recency effect in their experimental asset markets.

Most SPs rely on an outcome that occurred in the recent past and are based on the presumed increase in the probability that the same outcome would recur in the near future. These products guarantee investors relatively high returns should a recent outcome recur at maturity. The recency effect influences the investor to attribute unrealistically high probability to this recurrence and tends to favor investment in the SP.

3. Investor Sophistication and Behavioral Biases

In this section, we discuss four of the five behavioral biases presented above from the perspective of professional investors. We analyze the literature regarding the effect each has on sophisticated investors. The ostrich effect is excluded from this section since to the best of our knowledge it has not been tested among professional investors.

3.1. *Loss Aversion*

Kahneman and Tversky (1979) revealed that individual decision-makers are primarily concerned with *changes* in their financial wealth and are particularly averse to losses from these changes. Their descriptive model does not differentiate between professional and non-professional decision-makers in that regard.

Coval and Shumway (2005) found strong evidence that Chicago Board of Trade (CBOT) traders are highly loss-averse. These traders generally close out their positions by the end of each trading day, providing a clean horizon over which they can evaluate their performance. To test loss aversion, they split the trading day into two periods and test whether traders with profitable mornings increase or reduce their afternoon risk-taking. Loss aversion suggests that traders who have experienced losses are most inclined to take subsequent risks and that traders with profitable mornings reduce their exposure to afternoon risk. Coval and Shumway (2005) found that traders are far more likely to take on additional afternoon risk following morning losses than following morning gains.

These findings suggest that the expected utility theory might not provide an accurate model for explaining the behavior of professional traders. Since CBOT traders can affect market prices, the findings lend credence to behavioral economics and finance models, which relax inherent assumptions used in standard financial economics asset pricing models.

3.2. The Disposition Effect

The disposition effect has been extensively researched, including studies that focus on the influence of investor sophistication and market experience on this bias. In general, the literature shows that this bias uniformly affects multiple investor types, including individual investors, futures traders, professional account managers, experimental laboratory participants, and financial institutions.

Odean (1998) tested the disposition effect by analyzing trading records for 10,000 accounts at a large discount brokerage house. He found that these investors sell winners more rapidly than losers. Even when all alternative rational motivations (such as rebalancing portfolios, avoiding higher trading costs of low-priced stocks, or tax motivations) are controlled for, these investors continue to prefer selling winners and holding losers. Their behavior is consistent with prospect theory, the disposition effect, and a mistaken belief that their winners and losers will mean revert.

Shapira and Venezia (2001) analyzed the investment patterns of a large number of clients of a major Israeli brokerage house. They compared the behavior of clients making independent investment decisions to that of investors whose accounts were managed by brokerage professionals, in order to test whether the tendency to sell winners more quickly than losers held for professional investors as well. Their results demonstrate that the disposition effect applies not only to independent investors but also to professionals, suggesting that the effect may exercise an even greater influence on pricing than commonly assumed. However, they also show that the effect is significantly weaker for professional investors than for amateurs, indicating that professional training and experience may, albeit not eliminate biases.

Grinblatt and Keloharju (2001) used a unique data set describing the buys, sells, and holds of individuals and institutions in the Finnish stock market on a daily basis. They found that investors are reluctant to realize losses and that past returns and historical price patterns affect trading. Sophisticated investor classes place less weight on past returns in deciding whether to buy or sell. By contrast, less sophisticated investors (house-holds, general government, and non-profit institutions) are more predis-posed to sell than to buy stocks with large past returns.

Based on data from a highly profitable stock trading team Garvey and Murphy (2004) found that professional traders held their losing trades much longer than their winning trades. The group of traders studied earned more than $1.4 million in intraday trading profits, but they realized their winning trades at a much faster rate than their losing trades, lowering their profitability. Moreover, when the traders limited their risk exposure by trading in small share sizes, in low-priced stocks, or during periods of low volatility, the discrepancy between losing and winning holding times increased.

Similarly, Locke and Mann (2005) studied the trading behavior of professional futures traders on the Chicago Mercantile Exchange (CME). They examined the discipline of professional traders and their tendency to exhibit the disposition effect. "Discipline" is defined as adherence to trade exit strategies, measured by either the general speed of trading or by avoidance of riding losses. Locke and Mann found that traders consist-ently hold losing trades for significantly longer periods than winning trades. Moreover, they found that traders who liquidated losing trades more promptly were more likely to be successful in the future, while trad-ers who held onto relatively large losing trades for longer periods (more than 10 minutes) were less likely to be successful. However, as opposed to Odean (1998), they were unable to discover any contemporaneous measurable costs associated with the apparent aversion to loss realization. To conclude, no evidence is available of a costly disposition effect among professional futures traders, but a relative lack of discipline in realizing both gains and losses promptly is harmful to the probability of success.

Feng and Seasholes (2005) analyzed the influence of sophistication and trading experience on the performance of the disposition effect. They found that together, sophistication and trading experience eliminate the reluctance to realize losses and reduce the propensity to realize gains by 37%. Moreover, sophisticated investors are 67% less prone to the disposition effect than the average investor. Trading experience on its own attenuates up to 72% of the disposition effect but does not totally eliminate it. Neither sophistication nor trading experience alone eliminates the disposition effect. However, a combination of the two does. While the reluctance of investors to realize losses can be eliminated, however, there is no amount of investor sophistication and trading experience capable of eliminating an investor's propensity to realize gains.

In contrast to the studies reviewed above, which have demonstrated the disposition effect by aggregating across investors, Dahr and Zhu (2006) analyzed the trading records of a major discount brokerage house, with the objective of identifying individual differences in the disposition effect. Using demographic and socioeconomic variables as proxies for investor literacy, they found that wealthier individuals and professionals exhibit a lower disposition effect. Moreover, they found that trading frequency helps reduce the disposition effect, which supports other findings showing that trading frequency can eliminate some market anomalies (List, 2003).

To conclude, the disposition effect is one of the most widely documented biases in investor behavior. Based on a wide range of investor databases, which reflect different levels of investor sophistication, all studies reviewed clearly document it, and most find that sophistication tends to reduce the magnitude of the bias.

3.3. *Herd Behavior*

Ascertaining the degree to which professional investors follow others' lead when trading is central to understanding their impact on financial markets, and to understanding how information becomes incorporated into market prices.

Lakonishok *et al.* (1992) presented evidence of herd behavior on the part of pension fund managers. They tested the herding behavior by assessing the degree of correlation across money managers in buying and selling a given stock. The evidence suggests that pension fund managers herd relatively little when trading in large stocks (those in the top two quintiles by market capitalization), but more so in smaller stocks.

Graham (1999) developed a model that implies that if an analyst has a high reputation or low ability, he is likely to herd. The model was tested using data from analysts who publish investment newsletters. Consistent with the model's implications, the findings indicate that a newsletter analyst is likely to herd if his reputation is high, and if his ability is low.

Wermers (1999) studied the tendency of mutual fund managers to herd in their stock trades from 1975 to 1994. Although he found an average level of herding similar to that found by Lakonishok *et al.* (1992), he found much higher levels of herding in small stocks and trading in growth-oriented mutual funds. Moreover, he found that future returns for stocks *bought* by herds are, on average, higher than for stocks *sold* by herds. Stocks that herds buy outperform stocks they sell by 4% during the subsequent six months, and this difference in returns is even more pronounced among small stocks.

Nofsinger and Sias (1999) compare herding by institutional and individual investors. They provide evidence that returns are strongly correlated with changes in institutional ownership over the herding period. They attribute this correlation to the hypothesized phenomenon whereby herding tendencies of institutional investors have a larger impact on returns than those of individual investors. They too found that stocks purchased by institutional investors subsequently outperform those they sell.

In a similar vein, Venezia *et al.* (2010) investigated the factors affecting herding behavior by amateurs and professionals. They found that both tend to herd, but that the former tend to do so to a greater extent. Moreover, their data reveal a weak correlation between amateurs' herding and stock market returns. Finally, herding is positively and significantly correlated with stock market volatility, and there is a causal relationship between the two, especially among amateurs, suggesting that amateurs pose a greater threat to market stability. Therefore, Venezia *et al.* conclude that improving transparency, education, and information will help mitigate market instability.

To conclude, herding behavior by both professional and retail investors is important because of its potential effect on fluctuations in prices and returns. The literature on herding behavior documents both professional and individual investors' tendencies to herd, with a stronger tendency among the latter. The findings imply that both groups have the potential to influence market prices and returns by herding behavior.

3.4. *Recency Effect*

Decision-making in financial markets relies crucially on learning and information processing by professional investors. Efficient learning requires the comparison of new information with previous expectations. The recency effect may be described as an inability to correctly recall prior expectations after being exposed to pieces of information in a specific order. Therefore, recency-biased professional investors lack the ability to process information efficiently.

The belief-adjustment model (Hogarth and Einhorn, 1992) predicts the recency effect would occur in complex decision domains regardless of the decision maker's experience. Indeed, Arnold *et al.* (2000) study the relationship between experience and recency effect by testing it on professional accountants. They find significant order and recency effects in the decisions of these experienced and professional participants. Moreover, they examine the effects of differing levels of experience and find that more experienced participants endure higher levels of order and recency effects than did their less experienced counterparts.

4. Behavioral Biases in Structured Product Investments by Professional Investors: Experimental Evidence

We designed a controlled experiment to test our hypothesis concerning the effects of behavioral biases on investment decisions involving SPs. The experiment's purpose was to assess each bias's influence on investment decisions made by professional investors with regard to SPs. These products incorporate a bundle of features associated with different behavioral biases. Each was examined separately in order to demonstrate its independent impact on investment decisions.

In order to compare decisions made by professionals and non-professionals (examined in Ofir and Wiener, 2016), both groups experienced the exact same experimental manipulation. To avoid inconsistent incentive schemes that could influence decision-making processes, participants from both groups were asked to make their own investment decisions, as opposed to their customers'. (The original experiment was conducted in Hebrew; its translation to English is provided in Appendix B.)

The experiment comprises seven investment decisions, each involving a choice between two mutually exclusive alternatives. The distinction between the two is based on the particular behavioral bias tested by that specific investment decision and is emphasized in order to make it salient for the participants. The experiment also contains three additional ranking questions, intended to neutralize the potential impact of other variables. These questions are only relevant to the part of the experiment that tests the influence of herd behavior.

The general instructions described a situation where the participants have a certain amount of money they wish to invest. The participants were instructed to choose only one of the two investment alternatives for each investment decision. They were told that each investment decision should be considered separately, and that in each decision the same amount of money was available. The exact initial fund was not specified, in order to guarantee that the experiment results would be independent of the magnitude of funds.

4.1. *Data*

Our sample consists of 573 Israeli professional investors, 75% of whom are investment advisors and 25% portfolio managers. The Law for the Regulation of Investment Advice, Investment Marketing and Investment Management, 1995 (Investment Advice Law) regulates the licensing and supervision of portfolio management and investment advisory services in Israel. It defines investment advisor as a person engaged in advising others in matters pertaining to acquiring, holding, acquiring, or selling securities and financial assets. Portfolio manager is defined as a person engaged in discretionary execution of investment transactions on behalf of others.

According to the Investment Advice Law, any legal person engaged in either activity in Israel, or with investors in Israel, must be licensed by the Israel Securities Authority (ISA). Having successfully completed the professional exams administered by the ISA, as well as an internship period of six and nine months for investment advisors and portfolio managers, respectively.

Among the professional group, 74% of participants were male and 26% female, 5% were board members and 20% were members of

Table 1:　Descriptive statistics.

Gender	Male: 74%			Female: 26%	
License	Inv. Adv: 75%	Port. man: 25%			
Board membership	No: 95%	Yes: 5%			
Invest. comm. mem	No: 80%	Yes: 20%			
Higher education (in years)	Min: 0	Max: 10	Mean: 3.7	Median: 4	SD: 1.97
Professional exper. (in years)	Min: 0	Max: 55	Mean: 13.26	Median: 11	SD: 9.94

investment committees. The average professional investor respondent had a university degree and professional experience of 13.26 years (Table 1).

4.2. *Loss Aversion*

In order to examine the impact of loss aversion on professionals faced with an SP investment opportunity, the participants were presented with two investment decisions. Both investment decisions offer the investor a choice between a risky investment in a one-year deposit dependent on the exchange rate between the Swiss franc and the Israeli shekel, and a safe investment in a one-year deposit that ensures the investor a certain return independent of the aforementioned exchange rate.

The two investment decisions can be illustrated as follows:

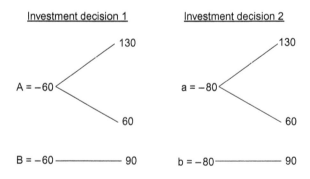

One of the risky investments was designed with some probability of loss (a). The other risky investment did not face the investors with a possible loss (A). The outcome of the two risky alternatives is equal as is the outcome of the two riskless alternatives is equal. We would expect a risk-averse investor to prefer the riskless investment to the risky one in both investment decisions; in other words, to reduce the variance of their investment's outcomes in both decisions. Likewise, we would expect risk-prone investors to prefer the risky investment to the safe one in both decisions. Choosing the risky investment in the first decision and the risk-less investment in the second decision can only be explained by loss aversion.

5. Results

The participants' choices in the two investment decisions are summarized in Table 2. The rows reflect the choice between a risky investment with no potential losses (denoted as A) and a safe investment (denoted as B) — the first investment decision. The columns reflect the choice between a risky investment with potential losses (denoted as a) and a safe investment (denoted as b) — the second investment decision.

The findings show that 60.88% of the professional participants pre-ferred the safe investment to the risky one in both investment decisions — at a highly significant level, $\chi^2(1) = 60.36$, $p < 0.001$. Consequently, it was not loss aversion alone, but mainly risk aversion, that influenced most professional participants in their decision. In comparison, the non-professionals' decisions did not significantly involve risk aversion, but were significantly influenced by loss aversion.

Table 2(a): Loss aversion: Households

	A (%)	B (%)
A	27.61	33.21
B	8.21	30.97

Table 2(b): Loss aversion: Professionals

	A (%)	B (%)
A	12.82	11.12
B	15.18	60.88

5.1. The Disposition Effect

In order to examine the disposition effect's impact on professionals faced with an SP investment opportunity, participants were presented with two investment alternatives. Both represented two very similar SPs. The only difference between them was that in the first, in the worst-case scenario, the initial fund was mandatorily converted into equity, while in the second, in the worst-case scenario, the investor was given a cash settlement. The participants were informed that the implied price of the underlying asset upon conversion exceeded the market price of the share at maturity, i.e., losses, while not realized, would be accrued. If a majority of investors prefer the mandatory conversion structure to the cash alternative, the results would constitute evidence of the prevalence of the disposition effect.

5.2. Results

The professional participants' choices are summarized in Table 3(a) and (b). The left column represents the percentage of investors who preferred the mandatory convertible structure product to the non-convertible one.

As shown above, 60.5% of the participants preferred mandatory conversion to liquidation — a highly significant difference ($\chi^2(1) = 26.26$, $p < 0.001$) indicating a disposition effect among the professional participants. As in the literature, we also found strong evidence that investor sophistication reduced the magnitude of the bias. The non-professional participants' decisions were influenced more by the disposition effect.

Table 3(a): Disposition: Households.

Shares	Cash
71.27%	28.73%

Table 3(b): Disposition: Professionals.

Shares	Cash
60.5%	39.5%

5.3. *Herd Behavior*

To test the impact of herd behavior on investment decision-making for SPs, the participants were faced with two choices between two SPs each. In one of them, the return was linked to the performance of a "fashionable" financial asset, and in the other, it was linked to the performance of an "unfashionable" financial asset.

A financial asset was considered "fashionable" when it was frequently referred to in the media. The first fashionable asset was a cleantech fund investing in environmental technologies. The second was an emerging market index. In each investment decision, the participants were asked to choose between a fashionable and an unfashionable SP, all the other conditions being equal. The participants were informed that both underlying assets in each investment decision (the fashionable and unfashionable) performed equally over the past year.

The experiment also included three ranking questions in order to ensure that the investment decisions were not affected by other variables. The professional participants were asked to rank the values appearing in every investment alternative according to importance. We did not find any significant discrepancies between the importance rankings of the different values, and therefore did not consider them a satisfactory explanation of investor choice.

Should the majority of investors prefer the "fashionable" over the "unfashionable" structure in each case, the results would support the hypothesis that herd behavior comes into play in investor decision-making.

5.4. *Results*

Investment decision preferences are summarized in Table 4(a)–(d). Table 4(a) and (b) represents the choice between an SP specializing in cleantech enterprises and an SP specializing in startups, all other conditions being equal. Table 4(c) and (d) represent the choice between an SP tracking an

Table 4(a):   Herding environ: Households.

Start-up fund	Environmental fund
31.93%	68.07%

Table 4(b):   Herding environ:
Professionals.

Start-up fund	Environmental fund
27.61%	72.39%

Table 4(c): Herding EM: Households.

Indian index	Italian index
82.46%	17.54%

Table 4(d):   Herding EM: Professionals.

Indian index	Italian index
85.86%	14.14%

emerging market index and one tracking a developed market index, all other conditions being equal.

As seen in Table 4(b), 68.07% of the participants preferred the "fashionable" cleantech product to the less fashionable startup fund, with a highly significant difference ($\chi^2(1) = 77.69$, $p < 0.001$). As reported in Table 4(b), 85.86% of the participants preferred the "fashionable" emerging market product to the "less fashionable" developed market alternative. The difference was highly significant ($\chi^2(1) = 305.5$, $p < 0.001$), suggesting that herd behavior affected the decisions made by the participants. Interestingly, herd behavior affected professionals slightly *less* than nonprofessionals in the environmental investment decision, while affecting them slightly *more* in the emerging market decision. Overall, the herding tendency was very similar for both groups, suggesting that sophistication has a weak mitigation effect when it comes to this bias.

5.5. *The Ostrich Effect*

To examine the impact of the ostrich effect on SP investments, the professional participants faced two similar alternatives, the only difference between which was that the first was non-negotiable, while the second was a highly liquid product, which could be redeemed by the issuer or traded on a secondary market. All other conditions were equal.

When compared with an otherwise identical illiquid asset, a liquid asset should have a lower yield to maturity, given the opportunity to liquidate the position on demand and the possibility of realizing higher market returns without jeopardizing the locked-in yield to maturity. Accordingly, we would expect rational investors to prefer liquid instruments to non-negotiable structures.

Unlike other investment decisions in our experiment, in which we presented investors with two alternatives to which they should be indifferent, this investment decision included an objectively preferable alternative. A result in which any significant portion of investors preferred the inferior illiquid to the liquid structure would thus provide evidence for an ostrich effect.

5.6. *Results*

Professional investors' choices are summarized in Table 5(a) and (b). The left columns represent the proportion of investors who preferred the inferior illiquid structure to the superior liquid product.

As shown in Table 5(b), 20.24% of the participants preferred the non-negotiable product to the liquid structure; the difference was highly significant. Thus, the ostrich effect did have an impact on decision-making. Compared to the non-professionals' decisions, the ostrich effect influenced the professionals' decisions less markedly.

5.7. *Recency Effect*

To examine the impact of recency on investments in SPs, the professional participants were given two similar investment alternatives, the only difference between which was that returns on the first were contingent on an outcome in the recent past, while those of the second were contingent on an outcome not recently experienced. All other conditions were equal.

Table 5(a): Ostrich effect: Households.

Illiquid investment	Liquid investment
35.58%	64.42%

Table 5(b): Ostrich effect: Professionals.

Illiquid investment	Liquid investment
20.24%	79.76%

Table 6(a):   Recency effect: Households.

Recent outcome	Non-recent outcome
77.24%	22.76%

Table 6(b):   Recency effect: Professionals.

Recent outcome	Non-recent outcome
63.36%	36.64%

The recency effect would be supported if the majority of investors preferred to invest in a product with returns contingent on an outcome that has recently occurred.

5.8. *Results*

Professional investors' selections are summarized in Table 6(a) and (b). The left column represents the proportion of investors who preferred the "recency effect" SP to the alternative.

Table 6(b) reveals that 63.36% of the participants preferred the "recency effect" structure. The difference was significant, $\chi^2(1) = 42.48$, $p < 0.001$, indicating that the recency effect comes into play in professional investors' decision-making. Compared to non-professionals, professionals were less recency-biased.

6. Analysis: Do Personal Characteristics Affect the Magnitude of the Behavioral Bias?

The experiment demonstrates that even professional investors are not immune to behavioral biases. In this section, we try to ascertain whether within the group of professional investors, certain personal characteristics may influence the magnitude of bias. We asked our participants to complete a short survey on personal characteristics. To measure the influence of personal characteristics, we applied three different econometric models to each tested bias.

6.1. *Methodology*

In the classical regression model, the dependent variable can take any value on the real line. In our case, the dependent variable y is a discrete outcome of a decision made by the participants. In other words, y is a binary variable that takes only two values: 0 when the participant is not biased and 1 when the participant is. The linear probability model (LPM) is simple to estimate and use, but has some drawbacks in dealing with binary dependent variables.

LPM's limitations can be overcome by using a more sophisticated binary response model (Wooldridge, 2009). The binary response model we use is of the form:

$$P(y = 1|x) = G(\beta_0 + \beta_1 x_1 + \cdots + \beta_k x_k) = G(\beta_0 + x_\beta)$$

where y is the conviction of a specific behavioral bias and x is the full set of explanatory variables, i.e., personal characteristics, including gender, higher education, professional experience, license, investment committee membership, and board membership. G is a function taking on values strictly between zero and one: $0 < G(z) < 1$, for all real numbers z.

For the function G, we use the two nonlinear functions used in the vast majority of applications (Wooldridge, 2009). In the *logit model*, G is the logistic function:

$$G(z) = \exp(z)/[1 + \exp(z)]$$

$G(z)$ is between zero and one for all real numbers z. This is the cumulative distribution function for a standard logistic random variable. In the *probit model*, G is the standard normal cumulative distribution function, which again ensures that the regression equation is strictly between zero and one for all parameter values and for x_j.

We also report the LPM estimates, using heteroscedasticity-robust standard errors. For the LPM, we report the usual R^2 reported for OLS models, while for the logit and probit models we report the pseudo R^2.

6.2. Loss Aversion

The estimates from all three models tell a consistent story. The signs of coefficients are uniform across models, and the same variables are statistically significant throughout. The only significant explanatory variable in all models is investment committee membership. We found that this variable reduces the tendency for loss aversion by around 11%. The other explanatory variables do not carry any significant marginal effect on loss aversion (Table 7).

Table 7:   Dependent variable: Loss aversion.

Independent variables	LPM	Logit	Probit
Gender	−0.011	−0.011	−0.011
	(0.043)	(0.043)	(0.043)
Education	−0.012	−0.012	−0.012
	(0.009)	(0.01)	(0.01)
Experience	0.003*	0.003*	0.003
	(0.001)	(0.002)	(0.002)
License	−0.062	−0.062	−0.062
	(0.047)	(0.048)	(0.049)
Invest. comm.	−0.113**	−0.116**	−0.114**
membership	(0.054)	(0.056)	(0.056)
Board membership	0.049	0.043	0.042
	(0.093)	(0.087)	(0.089)
No. of observations	573	573	573
R^2/pseudo R^2	0.018	0.015	0.015

Notes: Standard errors are in parentheses. ***Significant at the 1% level, **Significant at the 5% level, *Significant at the 10% level.

6.3. *The Disposition Effect*

The estimates from all three models tell a consistent story. The signs of coefficients are uniform across models, and the same variables are statistically significant throughout. The only significant explanatory variable in all models is board membership. We found that this variable reduces the disposition effect by around 29%. The other explanatory variables do not carry any significant marginal effect on the tendency for the disposition effect (Table 8).

6.4. *Herd Behavior*

6.4.1. *The emerging markets investment decision*

The estimates from all three models tell a consistent story. The signs of coefficients are uniform across models, and the same variables are statistically significant throughout. The only significant explanatory variable in all models is professional experience, but its coefficient's magnitude is extremely low. The other explanatory variables do not carry any

Table 8: Dependent variable: The disposition effect.

Independent variables	LPM	Logit	Probit
Gender	0.036	0.037	0.037
	(0.046)	(0.047)	(0.047)
Education	0.003	0.003	0.003
	(0.01)	(0.01)	(0.01)
Experience	−0.002	−0.002	−0.002
	(0.002)	(0.002)	(0.003)
License	0.01	0.011	0.011
	(0.054)	(0.054)	(0.054)
Invest. comm.	−0.018	−0.018	−0.018
membership	(0.058)	(0.059)	(0.059)
Board membership	−0.289***	−0.293***	−0.292***
	(0.099)	(0.102)	(0.101)
No. of observations R^2/	573	573	573
pseudo R^2	0.016	0.017	0.018

Notes: Standard errors are in parentheses. ***Significant at the 1% level;
**Significant at the 5% level; *Significant at the 10% level.

significant marginal effect on herding tendencies in this part of the experiment (Table 9).

6.4.2. *The environmental fund investment decision*

The estimates from all three models tell a consistent story. The signs of coefficients are uniform across models, and the same variables are statistically significant throughout. We found two significant explanatory variables in all models: education and the license type. We found that each year of higher education reduces the herding tendency by around 2.5%, and that possession of an investment advisor's license increases that tendency by around 11%, as opposed to the portfolio management license. The other explanatory variables do not carry any significant marginal effect on herding tendency in this part of the experiment (Table 10).

6.5. *The Ostrich Effect*

The estimates from all three models tell a consistent story. The signs of coefficients are uniform across models, and the same variables are

Table 9:   Dependent variable: Herd behavior (emerging markets).

Independent variables	LPM	Logit	Probit
Gender	−0.046	−0.049	−0.052
	(0.034)	(0.035)	(0.036)
Education	0.006	0.006	0.007
	(0.007)	(0.006)	(0.006)
Experience	−0.003**	−0.003**	−0.003**
	(0.001)	(0.001)	(0.001)
License	−0.0005	−0.0001	0.001
	(0.037)	(0.039)	(0.038)
Invest. comm. membership	0.02	0.021	0.022
	(0.04)	(0.04)	(0.039)
Board membership	−0.048	−0.053	−0.052
	(0.08)	(0.085)	(0.083)
No. of observations	573	573	573
R^2/pseudo R^2	0.016	0.02	0.021

Notes: Standard errors are in parentheses. ***Significant at the 1% level; **Significant at the 5% level; *Significant at the 10% level.

Table 10:   Dependent variable: Herd behavior (environmental).

Independent variables	LPM	Logit	Probit
Gender	0.061	0.061	0.061
	(0.044)	(0.044)	(0.044)
Education	−0.024**	−0.025**	−0.025**
	(0.009)	(0.01)	(0.01)
Experience	0.0003	0.0003	0.0003
	(0.001)	(0.002)	(0.002)
License	0.115**	0.111**	0.113**
	(0.051)	(0.048)	(0.049)
Invest. comm. membership	0.085	0.08	0.082
	(0.053)	(0.049)	(0.05)
Board membership	−0.009	−0.01	−0.009
	(0.101)	(0.097)	(0.098)
No. of observations	573	573	573
R^2/pseudo R^2	0.027	0.021	0.021

Notes: Standard errors are in parentheses. ***Significant at the 1% level; **Significant at the 5% level; *Significant at the 10% level.

Table 11:   Dependent variable: The Ostrich effect.

Independent variables	LPM	Logit	Probit
Gender	−0.061*	−0.06*	−0.063*
	(0.037)	(0.035)	(0.036)
Education	−0.013	−0.013	−0.012
	(0.009)	(0.009)	(0.009)
Experience	0.002	0.002	0.002
	(0.001)	(0.001)	(0.001)
License	0.078*	0.084*	0.084*
	(0.04)	(0.046)	(0.045)
Invest. comm. membership	0.014	0.014	0.013
	(0.046)	(0.049)	(0.048)
Board membership	−0.043	−0.045	−0.045
	(0.078)	(0.081)	(0.08)
No. of observations	573	573	573
R^2/pseudo R^2	0.022	0.022	0.022

Notes: Standard errors are in parentheses. ***Significant at the 1% level; **Significant at the 5% level; *Significant at the 10% level.

statistically significant throughout. We did not find any explanatory variables in all models related to the ostrich effect at an adequate level of significance (Table 11).

6.6. Recency Effect

The estimates from all three models tell a consistent story. The signs of coefficients are uniform across models, and the same variables are statistically significant throughout. We did not find any explanatory variables in all models related to the recency effect at an adequate level of significance.

To conclude, personal characteristics do not, overall, carry any meaningful explanatory power on the tendency for behavioral biases. With regard to several biases, we found that specific personal characteristics do have a significant marginal effect on the conviction of behavioral bias. However, we did not find any consistency across these characteristics, nor with respect to their causal relationship with the relevant behavioral bias.

Table 12:   Dependent variable: Recency effect.

Independent variables	LPM	Logit	Probit
Gender	−0.034	−0.034	−0.034
	(0.047)	(0.047)	(0.047)
Education	−0.008	−0.008	−0.008
	(0.011)	(0.011)	(0.01)
Experience	0.0007	0.0007	0.0007
	(0.002)	(0.002)	(0.002)
License	−0.025	−0.025	−0.025
	(0.051)	(0.052)	(0.052)
Invest. comm.	0.039	0.04	0.04
membership	(0.054)	(0.054)	(0.055)
Board membership	−0.038	−0.039	−0.039
	(0.102)	(0.106)	(0.105)
No. of observations	573	573	573
R^2/pseudo R^2	0.004	0.003	0.003

Notes: Standard errors are in parentheses. ***Significant at the 1% level; **Significant at the 5% level; *Significant at the 10% level.

Evidently, these behavioral biases are so deeply rooted in human behavior that the personal traits we analyzed are inadequate to overcome them (Table 12).

7. Discussion and Conclusions

Structured products (SPs) are synthetic investment instruments specifically designed to meet needs unmet by standard financial instruments. SPs can be used as an alternative to direct investments in financial assets, as a means to mitigate a portfolio's risk exposure, or as a way of exploiting market trends.

We outlined several key features of various SPs and associated each with specific behavioral biases identified in the decision-making literature. These include loss aversion, the disposition effect, herd behavior, the ostrich effect, and recency effect. We then conducted an experiment to test the possible impact of each bias on decisions pertaining to investment in SPs. Our findings reveal that, to varying degrees, the examined behavioral biases affect professional investors. Moreover, using logit, probit, and linear probability models we showed that the tested biases are so deeply rooted in human behavior that they are difficult to overcome by any one of the personal characteristics we analyzed.

In demonstrating the impact of these behavioral biases on investors, our results can support the application of specific regulation for SPs to improve investor protection. The recommended regulation should apply to both professional and non-professional investors but can vary and can be shaped in different forms, for example as sale prohibition or as different levels of mandatory disclosure.

As a modern alternative for household investment, SPs contribute to the completeness of financial markets by adding to the alternatives open to investors. SPs offer investors a different range of investment alternatives than that offered by traditional instruments. Therefore, regulation that includes sale prohibitions can save tremendous costs to the completeness of financial markets and to investors as consumers.

Mandatory disclosure is a less extreme regulatory solution and can vary across different levels of disclosure. The optimal level of disclosure is the specific level at which we achieve the highest available ratio between added value to the investor's protection as a result of the disclosure and the cost of disclosure.

We recommend regulation that would compel issuers to reveal the effective fees they charge investors. Full disclosure would enable investors to simply compare investment alternatives and decide whether and how much they are willing to pay for the recognized effects of each behavioral bias. This effective fee value is known to issuers; therefore, its calculation will not involve any additional cost.

In many cases, we can rely on the competitive forces of an economy to drive abnormal returns in financial markets back down to marginal cost. Our analysis, which provides a behavioral explanation for the abnormal returns in SP markets, sheds light on why competitive forces may not be sufficient in this case. An additional explanation for the ineffectiveness of competitive forces in the context of SPs is provided by Carlin (2009). He found that complexity increases the market power of firms. In his model, as competition increases, firms tend to add more complexity to their pricing schemes as the best response, rather than make their disclosures more transparent.

Disclosure of effective fees in SPs can improve competition in the market. The diversity of the SPs offered in the market and their complexity makes the comparison between any two SPs difficult. Without a regulatory solution, such as mandatory disclosure, issuing firms will continue to convolute products and consequently raise their profit margins. Therefore, increasing market competition would increase consumer surplus and contribute to market efficiency.

In conclusion, our research demonstrates that in the context of SPs, there is persuasive evidence that professional investors make major systematic errors. In Ofir and Wiener (2016), we obtained similar results regarding the decisions of retail investors. Since all market players make these errors, the tested behavioral biases clearly affect market prices and market efficiency substantially. Furthermore, as a result of mispricing, there is a substantial misallocation of resources in the economy. Thus, we suggest that in the SP case, regulatory and legal policy can limit the damage caused by imperfect rationality.

Appendix A: Relations between Structured Product Features and Behavioral Biases

Feature	Behavioral bias	References	Examples
Principal protection	Loss aversion	Kahneman and Tversky (1979)	Principal-protected market-linked instruments
Mandatory conversion to a "loser" asset	The disposition effect	Shefrin and Statman (1985)	Mandatory convertible bonds
Investment in emerging markets and exotic instruments	Herd behavior	Leibenstein (1950) Bikhchandani *et al.* (1992)	Market-linked structured notes on emerging market indices
Illiquidity	The Ostrich effect	Galai and Sade (2006)	Non-negotiable structured products
Reliance on a recent outcome	Recency effect	Hogarth and Einhorn (1992)	Most structured products

Appendix B: The Experiment

Instructions:
- A given sum of money is at your disposal for investment in the best possible way.
- You are presented with a number of investment decisions. You must choose only one of the mutually exclusive alternatives for each decision.
- The investment decisions are unrelated and each should be considered separately.
- The funds available to you are equal for each decision, and hence for each mutually exclusive investment alternative.

Investment decision 1:
(a) Investing the money at your disposal in a one-year deposit contingent on the exchange rate between the Israeli shekel (ILS) and the Swiss franc. For every ILS 60 invested in the deposit, at the end of the year you will receive ILS 130 if the ILS/ Swiss franc exchange rate increases, or ILS 60 if it decreases.
(b) Investing the money in a one-year deposit. For every ILS 60 invested you will receive ILS 90 at the end of the year.

The amount remitted at the end of the year includes the principal and no additional amounts will be paid.

Investment decision 2:
(a) Investing the money at your disposal in a one-year deposit with a guaranteed interest rate of 9% at the end of the year. The outcome of the principal is contingent on the rate of return on specific shares during the year. If the price of Teva shares fall by 15% or more in relation to the quoted price of the shares on the date of investment during this period, the principal of the deposit will be converted into Teva shares, based on their value at the beginning of the year. The conversion will take place at the end of the year and you will receive an additional 9% interest. If this condition is not met, the principal will be repaid in full, with an additional 9% interest.

(b) Investing the money in a one–year deposit with a guaranteed interest rate of 9% at the end of the year. The outcome of the deposit principal is contingent on the quoted price of specific shares. If the share price falls over the year by 15% or more in relation to the quoted price of the shares on the date of investment, 85% or less of the initial amount invested, respectively, will be paid *in cash* with an additional 9% interest. If this condition is not met, the principal will be repaid in full, with an additional 9% interest.

Investment decision 3:
(a) Investing the money at your disposal in a one-year deposit linked to the increase in the *Indian* share price index. If the index increases, the principal will appreciate pro-rata with the relative increase of the index. If the index decreases or remains unchanged, the principal will be repaid at the end of the year with no additional payments.
(b) Investing the money in a one-year deposit linked to the increase in the *Italian* Stock Exchange share price index. If the index increases, the principal will appreciate *pro-rata* with the relative increase of the index. If the share price index decreases or remains unchanged, the principal will be repaid at the end of the year and no additional payments.

The rates of return for the two indexes in the past year were identical.

Investment decision 4:
(a) Investing the money at your disposal in a one-year deposit that is dependent on the exchange rate of the Swiss franc. For every ILS 80 invested in the deposit, at the end of the year you will receive either ILS 130, if the exchange rate increases, or ILS 60 if it decreases.
(b) Investing the money in a one-year deposit. For every ILS 80 invested you will receive ILS 90 at the end of the year.

The amount remitted at the end of the year includes the principal and no additional sums will be paid.

Investment decision 5:
(a) Investing the money at your disposal in a one-year deposit that is linked to the performance of a fund that invests in *hi-tech startups*. If the fund's worth increases, the principal invested will appreciate pro-rata with the relative increase of the fund's worth. If the fund's worth decreases or remains unchanged, the principal will be repaid at the end of the year and no additional sums will be paid.
(b) Investing the money in a one-year deposit linked to the performance of a cleantech fund, which invests in companies engaged in *environmental technologies*. If the value of the fund increases, the principal will appreciate pro–rata with the increase in the fund's value. If the fund's value decreases or remains unchanged, the principal will be repaid at the end of the year and no additional sums will be paid.

In the past year, both funds yielded the same returns.

Investment decision 6:
(a) Investing the money at your disposal in a one-year deposit that pays ILS 110 at the end of the year for every ILS 100 invested, *with no option for early withdrawal.*
(b) Investing the money in a one-year deposit that pays ILS 110 at the end of the year for every ILS 100 invested. *The deposit may be withdrawn during the year at the market value on the date of withdrawal, which may be lower than ILS 100.*

Investment decision 7:
(a) Investing the money at your disposal in a one-year deposit that pays 10% interest, provided that the quoted price of a given share increases by at least 10% during the year. In the past year, *the share price increased by 10%.* If this condition is not met, the investment will be repaid in full and no additional amounts will be paid.
(b) Investing in a one-year deposit that pays 10% interest, provided that the quoted price of a given share increases by at least 10% during the year. In the past year, the *share price did not increase by 10%.* If this condition is not met, the investment will be repaid in full and no additional amounts will be paid.

To what extent do you identify with each of the following statements?

Rank on a scale of 1–10, with 1 = *not at all* and 10 = *very much*
Protecting the environment is important _____
Supporting entrepreneurial startups is important _____
Investment in emerging markets is important _____

References

Amihud, Y. and Mendelson, H. (1991). Liquidity, maturity and the yields on U.S. government securities. *Journal of Finance*, 46, 1411–1426.

Amihud, Y., Mendelson, H., and Lauterbach, B. (1997). Market microstructure and securities values: Evidence from the Tel-Aviv Stock Exchange. *Journal of Financial Economics*, 45, 365–395.

Arnold, V., Collier, P.A., Leech, S.A., and Sutton, S.G. (2000). The effect of experience and complexity on order and recency bias in decision making by professional accountants. *Accounting and Finance*, 40, 109–134.

Ben-David, I. and Hirshleifer, D. (2012). Are investors really reluctant to realize their losses? Trading responses to past returns and the disposition effect. *Review of Financial Studies*, 25, 2485–2532.

Benet, B., Giannetti, A., and Pissaris, S. (2006). Gains from structured product market: The case of reverse-exchangeable securities (RES). *Journal of Banking and Finance*, 30, 111–132.

Bikhchandani, S., Hirschleifer, D., and Welch, I. (1992). A theory of fad, fashion, custom and cultural change as informational cascades. *Journal of Political Economy*, 100, 992–1026.

Brenner, M., Eldor, R., and Hauser, S. (2001). The price of option illiquidity. *Journal of Finance*, 56, 789–805.

Breuer, W. and Perst, A. (2007). Retail banking and behavioral financial engineering: The case of structured products. *Journal of Banking and Finance*, 31, 827–844.

Carlin, B.I. (2009). Strategic price complexity in retail financial markets. *Journal of Financial Economics*, 91, 278–287.

Coval, J.D. and Shumway, T. (2005). Do behavioral biases affect prices? *Journal of Finance*, 60, 1–34.

Dhar, R. and Zhu, N. (2006). Up close and personal: Investor sophistication and the disposition effect. *Management Science*, 52, 726–740.

Dobeli, B. and Vanini, P. (2010). Stated and revealed investment decisions concerning retail structured products. *Journal of Banking and Finance*, 34, 1400–1411.

Lei, F. and Seasholes, M.S. (2005). Do investor sophistication and trading experience eliminate behavioral biases in financial markets? *Review of Finance*, 9, 305–351.

Fischer, R. (2007). Do investors in structured products act rationally? Working Paper.

Galai, D. and Sade, O. (2006). The "Ostrich effect" and the relationship between the liquidity and the yields of financial assets. *Journal of Business*, 79(5), 2741–2759.

Garvey, R. and Murphy, A. (2004). Are professional traders too slow to realize their losses? *Financial Analysts Journal*, 60, 35–43.

Graham, J.R. (1999). Herding among investment newsletters: Theory and evidence. *Journal of Finance*, 54, 237–268.

Grinblatt, M. and Keloharju, M. (2000). The investment behavior and performance of various investor types: A study of Finland's unique data set. *Journal of Financial Economics*, 55, 43–67.

Grinblatt, M. and Keloharju, M. (2001). What makes investors trade? *Journal of Finance*, 56, 589–616.

Henderson, B.J. and Pearson, N.D. (2011). The dark side of financial innovation: A case study of the pricing of a retail financial product. *Journal of Financial Economics*, 100, 227–247.

Hens, T. and Rieger, M.O. (2009). The dark side of the moon: Structured products from the customer's perspective. NCCR FINRISK Working Paper 459, University of Zurich.

Hens, T. and Rieger, M.O. (2011). Why do investors buy structured products? EFA 2009 Bergen Meetings Paper.

Hirshleifer, D. (2001). Investor psychology and asset pricing. *Journal of Finance*, 56, 1533–1597.

Hogarth, R.M. and Einhorn, H.J. (1992). Order effects in belief updating: The belief-adjustment model. *Cognitive Psychology*, 24, 1–55.

Kadlec, G.B. and McConnell, J.J. (1994). The effect of market segmentation and illiquidity on asset prices: Evidence from exchange listings. *Journal of Finance*, 49, 611–635.

Kahneman, D. and Tversky, A. (1979). Prospect theory: An analysis of decision under risk. *Econometrica*, 47(2), 263–291.

Katz, M.L. and Shapiro, C. (1985). Network externalities, competition, and compatibility. *American Economic Review*, 75, 424–440.

Kumar, A. (2009). Hard-to-value stocks, behavioral biases, and informed trading. *Journal of Financial and Quantitative Analysis*, 44, 1375–1401.

Lakonishok, J., Shleifer, A., and Vishny, R.W. (1992). The impact of institutional trading on stock prices. *Journal of Financial Economics*, 32, 23–43.

Leibenstein, H. (1950). Bandwagon, Snob, and Veblen effects in the theory of consumers' demand. *Quarterly Journal of Economics*, 64, 183–207.

List, J.A. (2003). Does market experience eliminate market anomalies? *Quarterly Journal of Economics*, 118, 41–71.

Locke, P.R. and Mann, S.C. (2005). Professional trader discipline and trader disposition. *Journal of Financial Economics*, 76, 401–444.

Menkhoff, L. and Nikiforow, M. (2009). Professionals' endorsement of behavioral finance: Does it impact their perception of markets and themselves? *Journal of Economic Behavior and Organization*, 71, 318–329.

Nofsinger, J.R. and Sias, R.W. (1999). Herding and feedback trading by institutional and individual investors. *Journal of Finance*, 54, 2263–2295.

Odean, T. (1998). Are investors reluctant to realize their losses? *Journal of Finance*, 53, 1775–1798.

Ofir, M. and Wiener, Z. (2016). Individuals investment in financial structured products from rational and behavioral choice perspectives. In I. Venezia (Ed.), *Behavioral Finance: Where do Investors' Biases Come From?* World Scientific Publishers, pp. 33–65, Ch. 2.

Rieger, M.O. (2012). Why do investors buy bad financial products? Probability misestimation and preferences in financial investment decision. *Journal of Behavioral Finance*, 13, 108–118.

Rieger, M.O. and Hens, T. (2012). Explaining the demand for structured financial products: Survey and field experiment evidence. *Zeitschrift für Betriebswirtsch*, 82, 491–508.

Shapira, Z. and Venezia, I. (2001). Patterns of behavior of professionally managed and independent investors. *Journal of Banking and Finance*, 25, 1573–1587.

Shefrin, H. and Statman, M. (1985). The disposition to sell winners too early and ride losers too long: Theory and evidence. *Journal of Finance*, 40, 777–790.

Silber, W.L. (1991). Discounts on restricted stock: The impact of illiquidity on stock prices. *Financial Analyst Journal*, 47, 60–64.

Stoimenov, P.A. and Wilkens, S. (2005). Are structured products "fairly" priced? An analysis of the German market for equity-linked instruments. *Journal of Banking and Finance*, 29, 2971–2993.

Tuttle, B., Coller, M., and Burton, F.G. (1997). An examination of market efficiency: Information order effects in a laboratory market. *Accounting, Organization and Society*, 22, 89–103.

Tversky, A. and Kahneman, D. (1991). Loss aversion and riskless choice: A reference dependent model. *Quarterly Journal of Economics*, 106, 1039–1061.

Venezia, I., Nashikkar, A., and Shapira, Z. (2011). Firm specific and macro herd-ing by professional and amateur investors and their effects on market volatil-ity. *Journal of Banking and Finance*, 35, 1599–1609.

Weber, M. and Camerer, C.F. (1998). The disposition effect in securities trading: An experimental analysis. *Journal of Economic Behavior and Organization*, 33, 167–184.

Wermers, R. (1999). Mutual fund herding and the impact on stock prices. *Journal of Finance*, 54, 581–622.

Wilkens, S. and Stoimenov, P.A. (2007). The pricing of leverage products: An empirical investigation of the German market for 'long' and 'short' stock index certificates. *Journal of Banking and Finance*, 31, 735–750.

Wooldridge, J.M. (2009). *Introductory Econometrics: A Modern Approach*, 4th edn. South-Western Cengage Learning.

Chapter 6

Analysts' Unfavorable Recommendation Initiations

Joshua Livnat[*], Kate Suslava[†], Yakun Wang[‡], Li Zhang[§],
and Chen Zhao[¶]

[*]*Stern School of Business, New York University,
44 West 4th Street, New York, NY 10012, USA
jlivnat@stern.nyu.edu*

[†]*Freeman College of Management, Bucknell University,
1 Dent Dr., Lewisburg, PA 17837, USA
kate.suslava@bucknell.edu*

[‡]*The Chinese University of Hong Kong, Central Ave, Hong Kong
wangyakun@cuhk.edu.cn*

[§]*Rutgers Business School, Rutgers University,
Washington Pl., Newark, NJ 07102, USA
lizhang@business.rutgers.edu*

[¶]*Southwestern University of Finance and Economics,
Qingyang District, Chengdu, Sichuan, China
zhaochen@swufe.edu.cn*

Abstract

Surprisingly, analysts initiate unfavorable coverage nearly as often as they initiate positive coverage. We show that analysts do this to build their reputation. First, they are more likely to initiate unfavorable recommendations when their reports include more discussions about firm uncertainty. This suggests that analysts are dissuaded from issuing favorable forecasts when they perceive the firm's future prospects to be unclear. Second, we find that analysts gain credibility from investors after

131

they begin coverage with unfavorable recommendations. Specifically, the market reactions to subsequent upgrade recommendations are significantly stronger when analysts initiate unfavorable coverage than benchmark returns.

Keywords: Analyst recommendations, Coverage initiation, Uncertainty, Stock market reaction

1. Introduction

Analyst coverage initiations are significant information events. Prior studies find more positive stock market responses to initial recommendations than to secondary, or follow-up recommendations (McNichols and O'Brien, 1997; Demiroglu and Ryngaert, 2010; Crawford *et al.*, 2012; Li and You, 2015). Analysts' initiation decisions depend on the benefits and costs of following a firm. The costs of analyst coverage include information gathering, information processing, and free-riding (O'Brien and Bhushan, 1990; Lang and Lundholm, 1996). Benefits include the expected commission revenue from trades, potential financing and consulting revenue for the brokerage company from the covered firm, as well as an opportunity to provide information to important investment clients (Irvine, 2003; Brown *et al.*, 2015). Initiations with favorable stock investment opinions (i.e., *strong buy/buy*) are likely to generate these benefits. For example, issuing favorable recommendations helps analysts build good relationships with the firms they choose to cover, which may lead to potential underwriting businesses for the corporate finance department of the brokerage firm. Favorable initiations can also help analysts curry favor with management who may share more information with analysts both before and after Regulation Fair Disclosure (Chen and Matsumoto, 2006; Green *et al.*, 2014). These benefits explain why recommendations by sell-side analysts are known to be optimistic (Francis and Philbrick, 1993; Dugar and Nathan, 1995; Cowen *et al.*, 2006; Chen and Matsumoto, 2006; Mayew, 2008).

However, there is no comprehensive explanation for unfavorable coverage initiations (i.e., *hold/sell/strong sell*), which constitute a significant portion (almost 50% in our sample) of all analyst coverage initiations. The initiation of unfavorable coverage is unlikely to generate incremental revenue streams for a brokerage firm. Due to short-sale constraints, trading commissions that could result from unfavorable recommendations are limited. Expressing a reserved opinion about a firm is also unlikely to contribute to future underwriting revenue or curry favor with management, as analysts with unfavorable recommendations are less likely to have access to managers (Brown *et al.*, 2015). Therefore, it is unclear why a financial analyst would initiate unfavorable coverage instead of simply withholding it altogether.

We argue that analysts initiating unfavorable coverage due to reputation concerns. Specifically, when analysts are uncertain (negative) about the future performance of a company but decide to initiate coverage because of corporate finance department's request or their clients' information demand, more reputable analysts will issue *hold* (*sell/strong sell*) recommendations. The reputation concern could be related to brokerage firms' overall work standards. For example, more reputable brokerage firms would require their analysts to make more unbiased recommendations. Analysts may also initiate unfavorable coverage out of their own career concerns if they want to build a good reputation in the labor market. Once investors are aware of analysts' reputation-building efforts by initiating unfavorable coverage, the stock market reaction to subsequent upgrades or downgrades should also reflect analysts' credibility.

We start with all coverage initiations for the S&P 1500 Index firms from 1996 to 2015 and our final sample includes 9,673 observations. Around 49.27% of our sample consists of unfavorable initiations (*hold/sell/strong sell*), of which *hold* is the most frequent (43.86% of all initiations). The proportion of unfavorable recommendation initiations ranges from approximately 20–30% before 2002 and increases to 40–50% after 2002. This increase can be attributed to the Global Analyst Research Settlement, as well as NASD and NYSE rule changes.[1] Comparing firms with unfavorable initiations to companies with favorable ones, we find that their financial and stock performance is weaker. However, firms with unfavorable initiations are still large firms with a stable sales growth, good earnings news and positive past stock returns. They have a fair analyst following and are covered by large brokerage houses. Therefore, it appears that a firm's size and financial performance indicators do not explain much about its unfavorable analyst initiations.

---

[1]The revised NASD and NYSE rule stipulates that analyst firms must disclose the recommendation distribution. Barber *et al.* (2006) document a clear shift in the recommendation distribution toward less favorable recommendations coinciding with the rule changes' effective date.

To examine whether analysts are more likely to initiate unfavorable coverage when there is higher uncertainty, we examine the text of analyst initiation reports. We obtain the texts of analyst reports from Thomson Reuters Investext® ("Investext"), a database that includes analyst reports for companies in the S&P 1500 Index starting in 1995. We find some anecdotal evidence consistent with analysts initiating unfavorable coverage when they are uncertain about companies' future performance or business strategy. For example, Lebenthal and Co. initiated coverage of Nordstrom with a *hold* rating in January 2016. In the initial analyst report, they admit that the company "is considered one of the best-in-class retailers in the US," but then explain that their conservative rating is due to the lack of "clarity as to when comps will be positive and EBIT dollars will grow at a high single-digit percent range." Similarly, when Aegis Capital Corporation initiated coverage on Abaxis in June 2017, they stated that they view the company shares as "potentially attractive in the companion animal diagnostics space." However, they decided to rate the company shares as a *hold* because "Abaxis continues to be a 'show me' story."

We apply a Natural Language Processing algorithm (the Loughran and McDonald Sentiment Word Lists) to count the number of "uncertain" words in the content of analyst reports.[2] The univariate analysis shows that unfavorable initiations contain more frequent discussions of uncertainty than favorable initiations do on average. We then run Logistic regressions to examine the association between unfavorable initiations and uncertainty. The dependent variable is an indicator variable equal to 1 if the initiation recommendation is *hold*, *sell*, or *strong sell*, and 0 if it is *buy* or *strong buy*. Our main independent variable of interest is the analysts' perceived uncertainty measure (*Uncertainty*) which is the frequency of uncertain words in the main content of an analyst report. Control variables include firm characteristics, analyst characteristics, industry fixed effect, and year fixed effect. Our regression results show that analysts' perceived uncertainty is positively associated with unfavorable initiation recommendations. This evidence suggests that analysts are cautious and start their coverage with more reserved recommendations when initiating coverage for less predictable companies, which gives them the option to upgrade the recommendation in the future when the uncertainty is resolved. We also find that initiating analysts tend to herd with existing

---

[2] https://sraf.nd.edu/textual-analysis/resources/#LM%20Sentiment%20Word%20Lists.

recommendations. Analysts from larger brokerage firms are more likely to initiate unfavorable recommendations, possibly due to reputation concerns. Further, prior analyst experience with unfavorable initiations and the breadth of their portfolio are both positively associated with the likelihood of unfavorable recommendation initiations, suggesting analysts learn from past experience of initiating unfavorable coverage.

If analysts initiate unfavorable coverage because they are genuinely uncertain about companies' future performance or operating strategy and stay relatively neutral instead of overly optimistic, market participants should be able to detect this phenomenon and react more strongly to subsequent upgrades or downgrades when analysts' uncertainty is (partially) resolved. In other words, unfavorable initiations are likely to help analysts gain credibility with investment clients and investors. To test whether analysts gain credibility from initiating unfavorable coverage, we first examine the market reaction to subsequent *buy* or *strong buy* recommendations after unfavorable initiating recommendations. We calculate the market reaction to analyst recommendations as the buy-and-hold abnormal returns over the three trading days centered on the analyst recommendations. To assess whether the market reaction is stronger for upgrades from the unfavorable initiation recommendations, we use two benchmarks: (1) market reactions to subsequent *buy* or *strong buy* recommendations after non-initiating unfavorable recommendations; and (2) market reactions to *buy* or *strong buy* initiation recommendations.

Univariate analysis shows that the mean (median) of market returns to upgrades after unfavorable initiations is 3.2% (2.4%), significantly higher than 2.5% (1.5%) market return for upgrades after unfavorable non-initiating recommendations. The market returns to upgrades after unfavorable initiations are also significantly higher than the market returns to favorable initiations.

We then examine the association between stock market reactions and unfavorable initiations using multivariate regression analyses. Our main independent variable of interest is an indicator variable (*Unfavorable_ Initiation*) equal to 1 if the *buy/strong buy* recommendation is an upgrade from an unfavorable initiation, and 0 if the *buy/strong buy* recommendation is an upgrade from a non-initiating unfavorable recommendation or it is a *buy/strong buy* initiation. Other control variables include the recommendation level, firm size, book-to-market, number of firms covered by the analyst, brokerage firm size, the difference between the analyst recommendation and the existing consensus, and industry and year fixed effects. We find that the stocks returns are significantly and positively associated with *Unfavorable_Initiation*, suggesting market reactions to upgrades after unfavorable initiations are higher than both benchmarks (market reactions to upgrades after unfavorable non-initiating recommendations and market reactions to favorable initiations), controlling other firm and analyst characteristics. These results suggest analysts gain credibility from initiating unfavorable coverage.

Our chapter contributes to the literature about analyst coverage decisions. Initiation of coverage by a sell-side analyst represents a commitment of resources by the brokerage firm. Prior studies find that analysts initiate coverage to generate lucrative trading commissions, to drum-up investment banking business and to provide information to important institutional clients (Irvine, 2003). These reasons explain why analyst initiations are overly optimistic (Ertimur *et al.*, 2011; Crawford *et al.*, 2012). Our chapter attempts to explain the large proportion of unfavorable initiations, which has not been previously explored. Our findings also contribute to the literature on analysts' reputation concerns and reputation-building process. Certain analysts, such as analysts from large brokerage firms or analysts with a good breadth of portfolio, start building reputation and credibility with the investment community from the coverage initiation.

The rest of the chapter is organized as follows: Section 2 describes our data and sample. Section 3 presents the summary statistics. Section 4 shows the empirical analysis of the uncertainty and credibility hypotheses. Section 5 provides our conclusion.

2. Data and Sample Selection

We obtain our data about analyst coverage initiations from the I/B/E/S recommendations detail history file. We consider an analyst recommendation to be an initiation if it is the first recommendation issued by an analyst for a particular firm in the I/B/E/S database.[3] We impose a number of requirements on the recommendations to be included in our sample of

---

[3]Our results remain the same if we define initiating recommendations as the first recommendation issued by a certain analyst and a specific brokerage firm in the I/B/E/S database.

initiations. First, it should be issued after the first two years of the I/B/E/S recommendation data (starting in 1996) to exclude recommendations added due to I/B/E/S backfilling. Second, we exclude initiations within the first six months of the analyst's first appearance in I/B/E/S, to exclude initiations by new analysts who are just beginning their coverage. Finally, we exclude all initiations that occur in the first 60 days of the firm's IPO date.

We measure analysts' perceived uncertainty about a firm by performing textual analysis of analyst reports collected from Investext (the database includes about 1.1 million analyst reports for companies in the S&P 1500 Index from 1995 to 2016). Stock price and stock return information are from the Center for Research in Security Prices (CRSP), and the companies' financial information is from Compustat.

Our sample selection process is as follows. First, we identify 45,728 initiating recommendations from I/B/E/S for S&P 1,500 firms from 1996 to 2015. We then match the I/B/E/S initiation sample with analyst reports from Investext following Huang *et al.* (2014). Specifically, we match an I/B/E/S recommendation with a report if the report date falls within the "matching window," which begins two days before the I/B/E/S recommendation announcement date and ends two days after the I/B/E/S review date. In the cases when one I/B/E/S recommendation matches with several reports, we keep the report that is closest to the I/B/E/S announcement date. The matching resulted in 12,997 observations. Requiring non-missing values for regression variables, our final sample includes 9,673 observations. The sample selection process is presented in Table 1.

Table 2 shows the sample distribution by Fama–French industries and by year. As shown in Panel A, our sample covers all 12 industries. More than half of all initiations occur in three growth industries: Business Equipment, which includes Computers, Software, and Electronic

Table 1:   Sample selection.

Step 1: Initiating recommendations for S&P 1500 firms from 1996 to 2015	45,728
Step 2: Merge with analyst report following Huang *et al.* (2014)	12,997
Step 3: Non-missing values of regression variables	9,673
Our sample	9,673

Notes: This table shows our sample selection process.
Source: I/B/E/S, Investex, Compustat and CRSP, Thomson Reuters. As of May 21, 2019.

Table 2:   Sample distribution by industry and year.

Industries	Frequency	Percentage
Panel A: Distribution by industry		
Business equipment	1,935	20.00
Finance	1,762	18.22
Wholesale, retail, and some services	1,204	12.45
Other	1,203	12.44
Manufacturing	832	8.60
Healthcare, medical equipment, and drug	673	6.96
Consumer non-durables	593	6.13
Oil, gas, and coal extraction and product	417	4.31
Utilities	339	3.50
Chemicals and allied products	281	2.90
Telephone and television transmission	255	2.64
Consumer durables	179	1.85
Total	9,673	100

Year	Frequency	Percentage	Cumulative
Panel B: Distribution by year			
1996	1	0.01	0.01
1997	14	0.14	0.16
1998	101	1.04	1.2
1999	167	1.73	2.93
2000	177	1.83	4.76
2001	257	2.66	7.41
2002	424	4.38	11.8
2003	479	4.95	16.75
2004	487	5.03	21.78
2005	569	5.88	27.66
2006	528	5.46	33.12
2007	659	6.81	39.94
2008	671	6.94	46.87
2009	922	9.53	56.4

Table 2:   (*Continued*)

Year	Frequency	Percentage	Cumulative
2010	822	8.5	64.9
2011	889	9.19	74.09
2012	819	8.47	82.56
2013	706	7.3	89.86
2014	737	7.62	97.48
2015	244	2.52	100
Total	9,673	100	

Notes: This table shows our sample distribution by 12 Fama–French industries (Panel A) and by year (Panel B).
Source: Sample selection per authors' analysis. Fama–French Industry classification. As of May 21, 2019.

Equipment (20% of all initiations); Finance (18%); and Wholesale and Retail (12%). Regarding the sample distribution across time, our observations span from 1996 to 2015 and are concentrated in recent years. For example, initiations from 2006 to 2015 comprise about two-thirds of our sample size. This increase is mainly driven by the availability of analyst reports in later years.

3. Summary Statistics

3.1. *Distribution of Initiations by Rating*

We first describe the distribution of recommendations in our initiation sample. I/B/E/S classifies stock recommendations into five categories: *strong buy, buy, hold, sell*, and *strong sell*. *Strong buy* and *buy* recommendations are usually considered favorable, while *hold, sell* and *strong sell* are regarded as unfavorable (or reserved) recommendations (Ertimur *et al.*, 2011; Crawford *et al.*, 2012). This is consistent with the market reaction to coverage initiations: *strong buy* and *buy* initiations are followed by significant positive stock returns. *Hold, sell*, and *strong sell* initiations, however, generate insignificant or significant negative returns (Irvine, 2003; Demiroglu and Ryngaert, 2010).

Table 3:   Distribution of initiating recommendations.

	Recommendation	Frequency	Percentage	Cumulative
Favorable	*Strong buy*	1,701	17.59	17.59
	Buy	3,206	33.14	50.73
		4,907	50.73	50.73
Unfavorable	*Hold*	4,243	43.86	94.59
	Sell	448	4.63	99.22
	Strong sell	75	0.78	100
		4,766	49.27	100
	Total	9,673	100	100

Notes: This table shows the frequency, percentage, and cumulative percentage of *strong buy, buy, hold, sell,* and *strong sell* opinions in our initiating recommendation sample. *Source*: Sample selection per authors' analysis. Fama–French Industry classification. As of May 21, 2019.

As shown in Table 3, unfavorable recommendations (*hold, sell,* and *strong sell*) account for nearly half of initiating recommendations in our sample, with the majority belonging to the *hold* recommendation (about 44%). *Sell* and *strong sell* initiations together comprise only about 5% of the sample. Approximately 18% and 33% of initiations in our sample fall into the *strong buy* and *buy* categories, respectively.[4]

To see how the pattern varies across years, we plot the percentage of recommendation types in our sample across the years. Figure 1 shows how the percentage of *strong buy, buy* and unfavorable initial recommendations (*hold, sell,* and *strong sell*) changed for each year from 1996 to 2015. Due to the Global Analyst Research Settlement, which addressed issues of conflicts of interest faced by financial analysts, there has been a large increase (decrease) of unfavorable (favorable) recommendations after 2002. Before 2002, the proportion of unfavorable recommendations accounted for 20–30% of all initiations.

---

[4]The proportion of unfavorable recommendations in our sample is slightly higher than what is documented in the literature. For example, Ertimur *et al.* (2011) find that unfavorable initiations account for about 35% of all initiations between 1994 and 2007. The difference is mainly driven by the sample period, as there is a higher percentage of unfavorable initiations in more recent years.

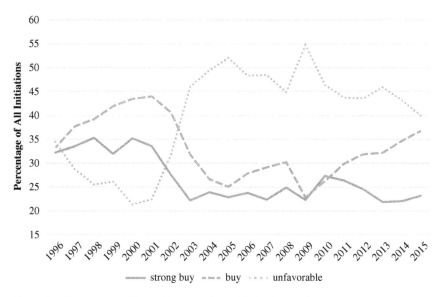

Figure 1:   Percentage of favorable vs. unfavorable initiations by year.

Notes: This figure shows the percentage of unfavorable (*hold, sell,* or *strong sell*) and favorable (*buy* or *strong buy*) initiating analyst recommendations from 1996 to 2015. We consider an analyst recommendation to be an initiating recommendation if it is the first recommendation issued by a certain analyst in the I/B/E/S database. The blue line represents the percentage of *strong buy* recommendations. The red line shows the percentage of *buy* recommendations. The gray line is the percentage of unfavorable recommendations. We calculated these percentages based on all of the initiating recommendations in the I/B/E/S sample.

Source: I/B/E/S and authors' analysis. As of May 21, 2019.

After 2003, this number has risen to include 40–50% of all initiating recommendations.

3.2. *Favorable vs. Unfavorable Initiations*

Next, we look at the characteristics of stocks with unfavorable initiations and compare them to those with favorable initiations. As shown in Table 4, stocks receiving unfavorable initiations are comparable in size to the companies with favorable initiations: *Size* (natural log of total equity) is around 8.4 for both groups of companies, which equates to about $5 billion in market capitalization. Firms with unfavorable initiations have a

Table 4:   Comparison between favorable and unfavorable initiations.

Variables	Unfavorable (N = 4,766)	Favorable (N = 4,907)	Difference
Size	8.432	8.367	0.066**
BM	0.464	0.411	0.054***
Leverage	0.146	0.124	0.022***
Sales_Growth	0.028	0.033	−0.005***
SUE	0.064	0.092	−0.028***
Stock_Return	0.058	0.162	−0.104***
Stock_Volatility	0.389	0.41	−0.021***
Institutional_Ownership	0.759	0.756	0.003
Avgrec	2.476	2.224	0.252***
Stdrec	0.826	0.814	0.012**
Nrec	10.127	9.526	0.601***
Broker_Size	68.296	57.85	10.446***
Ncover	10.113	9.658	0.455***
Unfavorable_Pct	0.563	0.496	0.067***
Uncertainty	11.976	10.833	1.143***

Notes: This table compares firms that receive unfavorable initiating recommendations and those that receive favorable initiating recommendations. Mean values of
each group and the difference between the two groups are displayed. A *t*-test is
used to examine the statistical significance of the difference in means. ***, **, and
* denote significance at the 1%, 5%, and 10% levels, respectively. Individual variable definitions are outlined in the Appendix.
Source: I/B/E/S, Investex, Compustat, CRSP and Thomson Reuters. As of May 21,
2019.

smaller magnitude of earnings surprises (the difference in *SUE* is 0.028
and statistically significant), but they still outperform analyst earnings
forecasts with a positive *SUE* of 0.064. Sales growth is slightly higher for
the firms with favorable initiations at 3.3% vs. 2.8%, with the statistically
significant difference of 0.5%. Firms with unfavorable initiations have
higher levels of debt (*Leverage* of 15% vs. 12% for favorable initiations)
and cheaper value of equity (*BM* of 0.46 vs. 0.41). At the time of initiations, their stock, on average, outperforms the market (*Stock_Return* of
5.8%) but gives way to the stock performance of firms with positive initiations (*Stock_Return* of 16.2%). These results seem to indicate that firms

that receive a favorable recommendation initiation are recent market winners, with superior operating performance and a low level of financial leverage. Analysts seem to be playing it safe with their initial recommendations, assigning unfavorable recommendations to good firms that still outperform the market and beat earnings forecasts but grow their sales at a slower rate. This provides some support to our uncertainty hypothesis that analysts might be hedging their bets with some less predictable firms.

The rest of Table 4 presents the analyst characteristics for the two groups of firms. Firms with unfavorable initiations have a larger number of analysts following them before the initiation (*Nrec* of 10.1 vs. 9.5 for the favorable ones), which is also consistent with slightly higher institutional ownership (*Institutional_Ownership* is 75.9% for unfavorable vs. 75.6% for favorable initiations). Analysts that issue unfavorable initiations work at larger brokerage houses (*Broker_Size* of 68.3 vs. 57.9 for the favorable ones), follow a larger number of stocks (*Ncover* is 10.1 vs. 9.7 for the favorable ones), and are more experienced with issuing unfavorable recommendations (56.3% of the stocks they follow have unfavorable initiations vs. 49.6% for the other group). Analyst characteristics seem to support our credibility hypothesis. For these analysts, initiations might be driven by institutional owners' demand for more reliable information.

Finally, our textual measure of analyst uncertainty confirms that analysts use more tentative verbiage in their reports when initiating unfavorable coverage (*Uncertainty* of 11.97 for unfavorable vs. 10.83 for favorable initiations). This is also supported by the higher standard deviation of existing analyst recommendations for this group of companies: *Stdrec* is higher for firms with unfavorable initiations.

Overall, although the financial and stock performance of firms with unfavorable coverage initiations are inferior to those with favorable coverage, they are still relatively large firms with positive sales growth rates, good earnings news, and positive past stock returns. Analysts might be initiating their coverage with unfavorable recommendations due to higher levels of uncertainty surrounding these firms. The analysts that initiate such unfavorable coverage belong to large brokerage houses and have other unfavorable recommendations in the portfolio of firms they follow. This indicates that the demand for unfavorable initiations might be driven by institutional clients, and/or the analysts' investment clients requesting more reliable information about firm performance for their investment decisions.

4. Main Results

4.1. *Uncertainty Hypothesis*

In our uncertainty hypothesis, we predict that analysts are more likely to initiate unfavorable coverage when they perceive that a firm is facing more uncertainty. To test this hypothesis, we run the following logistic regression with industry and year-fixed effects:

$$
\begin{aligned}
Unfavorable_{jt} = {} & \propto + \beta_1 Ucertainty_{jt} + \beta_2 Size_{jt} + \beta_3 BM_{jt} + \beta_4 Leverage_{jt} \\
& + \beta_7 SalesGrowth_{jt} + \beta_5 SUE_{jt} + \beta_6 StockReturn_{jt} \\
& + \beta_8 StockVolatility_{jt} + \beta_9 InstitutionalOwnership_{jt} \\
& + \beta_{10} Avgrec_{jt} + \beta_{11} Nrec_{jt} + \beta_{12} Stdrec_{jt} \\
& + \beta_{13} LogBrokerSize_{jt} + \beta_{14} LogNcover_{jt} \\
& + \beta_{15} UnfavorablePct_{jt} + f_{jt} + \varepsilon_{jt}
\end{aligned} \tag{1}
$$

The dependent variable (*Unfavorable*) represents an analyst decision to initiate unfavorable firm coverage; it is equal to 1 if the initiating recommendation is *hold*, *sell* or *strong sell* and equal to 0 if the initiating recommendation is *buy* or *strong buy*. Our main variable of interest (*Uncertainty*) is a proxy for the perceived analyst uncertainty. To capture the level of analysts' uncertainty about a firm, we perform textual analysis of analyst reports by searching the content of a report for the words classified under an uncertainty category in the Loughran and McDonald Sentiment Word Lists (available at https://sraf.nd.edu/textual-analysis/). If higher levels of perceived uncertainty are indeed associated with unfavorable initiations, we expect the coefficient of *Uncertainty* to be positive.

Following prior studies on analyst initiations, we include controls for firm, brokerage, and analyst characteristics previously shown to be related to analyst coverage decisions (Ertimur *et al.*, 2011). We control for firm size with the natural logarithm of the market value of equity (*Size*). We use two proxies to capture firm growth opportunities: (1) Leverage, the book value of debt scaled by the book value of debt and market value of equity; (2) the Book-to-Market ratio (BM). We control the firm operating performance with sales growth rate (*Sales_Growth*). We also include a measure of the most recent earnings surprise (*SUE*), calculated as the difference between actual EPS and analyst consensus forecast of EPS divided by the stock price prior to the recommendation announcement, and recent excess 12-month stock return over the CRSP value-weighted index (*Stock_Return*). We expect a positive association between firms' operating performance and favorable initiations.

Prior studies show that the demand for new initiations might be driven by investment client requests for more reliable information about a firm (Brown *et al.*, 2015). Both analysts associated with larger brokerage houses with investment clients and analysts covering firms with higher institutional ownership are more likely to be susceptible to this type of demand. We control for it with the natural log of *Broker_Size*, the number of analysts affiliated with a certain broker, and *Institutional_Ownership*, a ratio of shares held by institutional investors scaled by total shares outstanding. We expect both of these variables to be positively associated with the likelihood of unfavorable recommendations.

Analysts tend to release recommendations similar to those previously released by other analysts (Trueman, 1994). We control for this herding behavior with *Avgrec*, calculated as a mean of all recommendations issued for a given company by other analysts in the 365-day period before the initiation. Higher *Avgrec* implies a more unfavorable existing recommendation, as it is based on the numbers 1–5, where the recommendation is *strong buy*, *buy*, *hold*, *sell*, and *strong sell*, respectively. We expect that more unfavorable existing recommendations (higher *Avgrec*) are positively associated with unfavorable initiations. We control for the existing level of analyst uncertainty by including *Stdrec*, measured as the standard deviation of recommendations issued for a stock by other analysts in the 365 days before an analyst starts following a stock. We control for stock visibility with *Nrec*, the number of recommendations issued for a stock by other analysts.

Finally, per revised NASD and NYSE rules, analyst firms must disclose their recommendation distribution. This resulted in less favorable analyst opinions following the ruling (Barber *et al.*, 2006). Therefore, it is reasonable to assume that, subsequent to the ruling, analysts that cover more firms would have a more balanced mix of favorable/unfavorable recommendations in their portfolio. We control for the extent of analyst coverage with the natural log of *Ncover*, the total count of stocks an analyst covers. We control for analysts' prior experience with unfavorable coverage with *Unfavorable_Pct*, as the percentage of stocks that get *hold*, *sell*, or *strong sell* recommendations in the analyst's portfolio. We expect that both of these variables, proxies for analyst experience with conservative recommendations, will be positively associated with unfavorable initiations.

Table 5 shows the results of the estimating Equation (1). In the first specification, we include only *Uncertainty* as an independent variable, and observe a positive and statistically significant relationship. The coefficient is 0.013 with a *t*-statistic of 4.48. This result confirms our prediction that analysts are more likely to initiate unfavorable recommendations

Table 5:   Logistic regression analysis of uncertainty hypothesis.

| | \multicolumn{4}{c}{Dependent variable = Unfavorable} | | | |
	Coefficient	*t*-statistics	Coefficient	*t*-statistics
Intercept	−0.206	(−0.60)	−3.085***	(−6.49)
Uncertainty	0.013***	(4.48)	0.010***	(3.13)
Size			−0.093***	(−4.49)
BM			0.109	(1.11)
Leverage			−0.016	(−0.08)
Sales_Growth			−0.543	(−0.79)
Sue			−0.173***	(−2.69)
Stock_Return			−0.298***	(−4.68)
Stock_Volatility			−0.638***	(−3.46)
Institutional_Ownership			−0.14	(−0.84)
Avgrec			0.982***	(18.04)
Nrec			0.019***	(3.58)
Stdrec			0.024	(0.30)
Log_Broker_Size			0.281***	(11.19)
Log_Ncover			0.079**	(2.07)
Unfavorable_Pct			0.527***	(5.37)
Industry FE	Yes		Yes	
Year FE	Yes		Yes	
N	9,673		9,673	

Notes: The table reports the logistic regressions of the *Unfavorable* dummy variable, which is equal to 1 for *hold, sell,* or *strong sell* recommendations and 0 otherwise, on the proxy for analyst uncertainty (*Uncertainty*) and various firm and analyst control variables. The numbers in parenthesis are heteroscedasticity-robust *t*-statistics adjusted for clustering within firms. ***, **, and * denote significance at the 1%, 5%, and 10% levels, respectively. Individual variable definitions are outlined in Appendix.
Source: I/B/E/S, Investex, Compustat, CRSP, and Thomson Reuters. As of May 21, 2019.

when they perceive the covered firm to be facing higher uncertainty. As we include controls for firm and analyst characteristics in the second specification, we observe that our main variable of interest remains significantly positive, further confirming our uncertainty hypothesis.

The coefficients on firm controls in the regression are consistent with our expectations. All measures of operating performance are negatively associated with the likelihood of unfavorable initiations: the coefficients on *Sales_Growth* (−0.54), *SUE* (−0.17), and *Stock_Return* (−0.29) are all negative and statistically significant. Turning to analyst controls, we find that analysts tend to herd, as previous unfavorable recommendations (*Avgrec*) are positively and significantly associated with more conservative initiations. We also observe that, as expected, analysts from larger brokerage houses tend to issue more unfavorable initiations, as they are more likely to face pressures for reliable information from their investment clients: the coefficient on *Log_Broker_Size* is positive and significant. Prior analyst experience with unfavorable initiations (*Unfavorable_Pct*) and the breadth of their portfolio (*Log_Ncover*) both positively contribute to the likelihood of unfavorable initiations, consistent with our prior observations about regulatory changes.

4.2. *Credibility Hypothesis*

To test the credibility hypothesis, we examine the market reaction to subsequent *buy* or *strong buy* recommendations after unfavorable coverage is initiated. A stronger market reaction to these upgrades would imply that analysts gain additional credibility from investors after issuing unfavorable initiations. We use two benchmarks for our comparison analysis. First, we compare market reactions around the upgrades from unfavorable initiations to upgrades from unfavorable non-initiating recommendations. We consider this a valid benchmark because the magnitude of the upgrades are the same, and the only difference is the starting point: it is either an unfavorable initiation or an unfavorable non-initiation. Therefore, it is reasonable to assume that the difference in market reaction would capture the premium that investors place on a more credible upgrade. Our secondary benchmark is the market reaction to favorable initiations when similar to upgrades from unfavorable initiations, analysts issue a *buy* or a *strong buy* recommendation for a company. The market reaction to analyst recommendations (*XRET*) is calculated as the buy-and-hold abnormal return over the three trading days centered on analyst recommendations. Following Daniel and Titman (1997), we measure abnormal returns as the buy-and-hold return over the designated window, minus the value-weighted buy-and-hold return on a portfolio of stocks with similar size: market value of equity (three groups), book-to-market ratio (three groups) and 12-month momentum (three groups). Table 6 reports the results of our univariate analysis.

In Panel A of Table 6 we report the mean and median abnormal returns of 3.2% and 2.4%, respectively, for upgrades that occurred after unfavorable initiations. In contrast, the mean and median abnormal returns of upgrades that follow unfavorable non-initiating recommendations are only

Table 6:   Univariate analysis of credibility hypothesis.

XRET	Upgrades after unfavorable initiations	Upgrades after unfavorable non-initiations	Difference
Panel A: Comparison of *XRET* to the upgrades after unfavorable non-initiating recommendations			
Mean	0.032	0.025	0.007***
Median	0.024	0.015	0.009***
N	726	27,693	

XRET	Upgrade after unfavorable initiations	Favorable initiations	Difference
Panel B: Comparison of *XRET* to the favorable initiations			
Mean	0.032	0.013	0.019***
Median	0.024	0.009	0.015***
N	726	2,836	

Notes: This table shows the univariate analysis of the credibility hypothesis. Panel A compares the market reaction to *buy* or *strong buy* recommendations after unfavorable initiations and to *buy* or *strong buy* recommendations after unfavorable non-initiating recommendations. Panel B compares the market reaction to *buy* or *strong buy* recommendations after unfavorable initiations and to *buy* or *strong buy* initiating recommendations. *XRET* is the buy-and-hold abnormal return over the three trading days centered on analyst recommendations. Abnormal returns are measured over matched size, book-to-market, and momentum portfolios. A *t*-test is used to test the statistical significance of the difference in mean values. We use Wilcoxon signed-rank tests to examine the statistical significance of the difference in median values. Individual variable definitions are outlined in the Appendix.

Source: I/B/E/S, Investex, Compustat, CRSP and Thomson Reuters. As of May 21, 2019.

2.5% and 1.5%. The differences between the two groups are both economically and statistically significant: the upgrades from unfavorable initiations, on average, result in 0.7 percentage points higher abnormal returns. These results provide some support to the credibility hypothesis, which predicts that analysts gain some additional credibility with investors by starting with more conservative coverage. Investors tend to rely more on subsequent upgrades by such seemingly trustworthy analysts.

In Panel B, we compare the market reaction to upgrades after unfavorable initiations with market reactions to upgrades after *buy* or *strong buy* initiating recommendations. The mean and median of market reactions to the latter are 1.3% and 0.9%, both significantly lower than the corresponding statistics of the market reaction to upgrades after unfavorable initiations. This result further supports our credibility hypothesis.

The above univariate analysis provides some preliminary evidence for the credibility hypothesis. However, the market reaction to analyst recommendations may be driven by other factors as well. To control for such influence, we perform multivariate regression analyses. Specifically, the regression is as follows:

$$XRET_{jt} = \propto + \beta_1 UnfavorableInitiation_{jt} + \beta_1 Size_{jt} + \beta_3 BM_{jt}$$
$$+ \beta_4 Ireccdn_{jt} + \beta_7 LogNcover_{jt} + \beta_5 LogBrockerSiz_{jt}$$
$$+ \beta_1 Innovative_{jt} + f_{jt} + \varepsilon_{jt} \tag{2}$$

The main variable of interest is *UnfavorableInitiation*, a dummy variable equal to 1 if an analyst starts following a stock with an unfavorable recommendation and then upgrades the recommendation to either *buy* or *strong buy*, and 0 otherwise. If these types of initiations earn analysts some additional credibility, this variable should contribute positively to abnormal stock returns around the upgrade announcement. We control for firm size (*Size*) and value (*BM*) characteristics. Recommendation level (*Ireccdn*) measures the ratings by analysts (i.e., *buy* or *strong buy*). We add the number of firms covered by an analyst (*Ncover*) to capture the amount of time and effort an analyst can invest in following the given firm. Brokerage firm size (*Broker_Size*) is the number of analysts employed by the analyst's brokerage house. Larger brokerages offer greater resources to analysts and are deemed to be more prestigious, so recommendations by analysts affiliated with larger brokerage firms are likely to generate stronger market reactions (Clement 1999; Hong and Kubik 2003). Jegadeesh and Kim (2009) find that stock price reactions following recommendation revisions are stronger when the new recommendations stray further away from consensus than when they remain closer to it. We control for the difference between a given recommendation and the consensus (*Innovative*). The variable f_{it} represents a vector of fixed effects that includes the year and Fama–French industry dummies.

Our first set of results in Table 7 is based on a sample that includes *buy* or *strong buy* recommendations that are either upgraded from unfavorable initiations (*Unfavorable_Initiation* = 1) or upgraded from unfavorable non-initiating recommendations (*Unfavorable_Initiation* = 0). The results in Panel A demonstrate that the coefficient of *Unfavorable_Initiation* is positive and significant (0.007, *t*-stat = 2.55), suggesting that the market reaction to *buy* or *strong buy* recommendations is significantly stronger for those upgraded from unfavorable initiations than for those upgraded from unfavorable non-initiating recommendations. After we add firm and analyst control variables in the second specification, the coefficient of

Table 7:   Regression analysis of credibility hypothesis.

	Dependent variable = *XRET*			
	Coefficient	*t*-statistics	Coefficient	*t*-statistics
Panel A: Favorable upgrades from unfavorable initiations and non-initiations				
Intercept	0.029***	(8.89)	0.068***	(12.95)
Unfavorable_Initiation	0.007**	(2.55)	0.007**	(2.57)
Size			−0.007***	(−20.68)
BM			0.015***	(6.26)
Ireccdn			−0.001	(−0.29)
Log_Ncover			−0.001	(−0.27)
Log_Broker_Size			0.004***	(12.16)
Innovative			−0.001	(−0.22)
Industry FE	Yes		Yes	
Year FE	Yes		Yes	
N	28,063		27,827	
R^2	2%		6%	

Table 7:   (*Continued*)

	Dependent variable = *XRET*			
	Coefficient	*t*-statistics	Coefficient	*t*-statistics
Panel B: Favorable upgrades from unfavorable initiations and favorable initiations				
Intercept	0.068***	(20.12)	0.024***	(3.10)
Unfavorable_Initiation	0.020***	(7.08)	0.020***	(6.86)
Size			−0.005***	(−7.44)
BM			0.007**	(2.02)
Ireccdn			−0.001	(−0.55)
Log_Ncover			0.001	(0.15)
Log_Broker_Size			0.003***	(3.21)
Innovative			−0.004*	(−1.79)
Industry FE	Yes		Yes	
Year FE	Yes		Yes	
N	3,562		3,562	
R²	6%		8%	

Notes: This table reports the OLS regressions of abnormal returns (*XRET*) on the *Unfavorable_ Initiation* dummy variable and firm and analyst controls for two samples. In Panel A, the sample includes *buy* or *strong buy* recommendations that are upgraded either from unfavorable initiations or from unfavorable non-initiating recommendations. In Panel B, the sample includes *buy* or *strong buy* recommendations that are either upgraded from unfavorable initiations or are favorable initiations. The dependent variable (*XRET*) is the buy-and-hold abnormal return over the three trading days centered on analyst recommendations. *Unfavorable_ Initiation* is equal to 1 if the *buy* or *strong buy* recommendations are upgraded from unfavorable initiations, and 0 otherwise. The numbers in parenthesis are heteroscedasticity-robust *t*-statistics adjusted for clustering within firms. ***, **, and * denote significance at the 1%, 5%, and 10% levels, respectively. Individual variable definitions are outlined in the Appendix. *Source*: I/B/E/S, Investex, Compustat, CRSP and Thomson Reuters. As of May 21, 2019.

Unfavorable_Initiation remains positive and significant (*Coef* = 0.007, *t*-stat = 2.57). Consistent with prior literature, firm size loads negatively, and value factor loads positively (Fama and French, 1993), while brokerage size is significantly positive (Hong and Kubik, 2003).

In Panel B, the sample includes *buy* or *strong buy* recommendations that are either upgraded from unfavorable initiations (*Unfavorable_ Initiation* = 1) or are favorable initiating recommendations (*Unfavorable_ Initiation* = 0). Similar to the results in Panel A, the market reaction to *buy* or *strong buy* recommendations that are upgraded from unfavorable initiations is significantly stronger than the market reaction to *buy* or *strong buy* initiating recommendations. The results remain consistent after controlling for firm and analyst characteristics. Overall, the multivariate regression analyses provide further support for the credibility hypothesis.

4.3. *Robustness Tests*

Because our test sample is limited to firms in the S&P 1500 Index and to analyst initiation reports in Investext, we re-perform our tests using a larger sample of all I/B/E/S initiations, to assess the robustness of our main findings. This sample consists of 158,955 initiations spanning 1996 to 2015. Table 8 shows the distribution of all initiation recommendations that are available in I/B/E/S. The results demonstrate that our main sample has a similar distribution of favorable vs. unfavorable initiations: 59% of favorable and 41% of unfavorable initiations in the larger I/B/E/S sample vs. 51% of favorable and 49% of unfavorable initiations in our test sample.

Table 9 examines the market reaction to the upgrades from unfavorable initiations. Similar to Table 6, it shows that abnormal returns around the upgrade dates are significantly larger for the analysts who initiate coverage with unfavorable recommendations. The economic significance is also consistent with Table 6. Upgrades from unfavorable initiations earn

Table 8: Distribution of initiations in I/B/E/S sample for robustness check.

Recommendation	Frequency	Percentage	Cumulative
Strong buy	41,479	26.09	26.09
Buy	53,050	33.37	59.47
Hold	56,717	35.68	95.15
Sell	5,610	3.53	98.68
Strong sell	2,099	1.32	100
Total	158,955	100	

Notes: This table shows the frequency, percentage, and cumulative percentage of *strong buy*, *buy*, *hold*, *sell*, and *strong sell* initiations in the I/B/E/S sample.
Source: I/B/E/S. As of May 21, 2019.

Table 9:　Robustness check for the univariate analysis of credibility hypothesis.

XRET	Upgrades after unfavorable initiations	Upgrades after unfavorable non-initiations	Difference
Panel A: Comparison of XRET to the upgrades after unfavorable non-initiating recommendations			
Mean	0.034	0.026	0.008***
Median	0.022	0.015	0.007***
N	14,527	57,837	

XRET	Upgrade after unfavorable initiations	Favorable initiations	Difference
Panel B: Comparison of XRET to the favorable initiations			
Mean	0.034	0.013	0.021***
Median	0.022	0.009	0.013***
N	14,527	71,329	

Notes: This table checks the robustness of our univariate analysis of credibility hypothesis in a larger sample. Compared to our main sample, this larger sample is not restricted to S&P 1500 firms and has no requirement for analyst report data. Panel A compares the market reaction to *buy* or *strong buy* recommendations after unfavorable initiations and to *buy* or *strong buy* recommendations after unfavorable non-initiating recommendations. Panel B compares the market reaction to *buy* or *strong buy* recommendations after unfavorable initiations and to *buy* or *strong buy* initiating recommendations. *XRET* is the buy-and-hold abnormal return over the three trading days centered on analyst recommendations. Abnormal returns are measured over matched size, book-to-market, and momentum portfolios. A *t*-test is used to test the statistical significance of the difference in mean values. We use Wilcoxon signed-rank tests to examine the statistical significance of the difference in median values. Individual variable definitions are outlined in the Appendix.
Source: I/B/E/S, Compustat, CRSP and Thomson Reuters. As of May 21, 2019.

1–2% points higher abnormal returns than upgrades from unfavorable non-initiations and favorable initiations.

Table 10 presents the results from estimating Equation (2). The results demonstrate that analyst upgrades from unfavorable initiations are positively related to abnormal returns around the upgrade announcement date. All else being equal, investors seem to rely more on analysts who upgrade after initiating unfavorable coverage than on analysts who upgrade after an unfavorable non-initiation, or who start their coverage favorably.

Taken together, the results in this section support our main analysis, providing additional evidence that analysts tend to gain more investor

Table 10:   Robustness check for the regression analysis of credibility hypothesis.

	Dependent variable = $XRET$			
	Coefficient	t-statistics	Coefficient	t-statistics
Panel A: Favorable upgrades from unfavorable initiations and non-initiations				
Intercept	0.024***	(7.36)	0.055***	(13.08)
Unfavorable_Initiation	0.008***	(9.06)	0.006***	(7.68)
Size			−0.007***	(−30.18)
BM			0.005***	(4.18)
Ireccdn			−0.001	(−1.22)
Log_Ncover			0.001**	(2.38)
Log_Broker_Size			0.005***	(18.27)
Innovative			−0.001	(−1.56)
Industry FE	Yes		Yes	
Year FE	Yes		Yes	
N	72,364		72,364	
R-squared	2%		5%	
Panel B: .Favorable upgrades from unfavorable initiations and favorable initiations				
Intercept	0.016***	(7.73)	0.042***	(14.99)
Unfavorable_Initiation	0.021***	(24.66)	0.021***	(24.84)
Size			−0.004***	(−24.38)
BM			−0.001	(−0.21)
Ireccdn			−0.004***	(−6.02)
Log_Ncover			−0.001	(−0.67)
Log_Broker_Size			0.004***	(17.66)
Innovative			−0.003***	(−5.99)
Industry FE	Yes		Yes	

Table 10:   *(Continued)*

| | Dependent variable = *XRET* | | | |
	Coefficient	*t*-statistics	Coefficient	*t*-statistics
Year FE	Yes		Yes	
N	85,856		85,856	
R-squared	2%		4%	

Notes: This table checks the robustness of our regression analysis of credibility hypothesis in a larger sample. Compared to our main sample, this larger sample is not restricted to S&P 1500 firms and has no requirement for analyst report data. The dependent variable (*XRET*) is the buy-and-hold abnormal return over the three trading days centered on analyst recommendations. In Panel A, the sample includes *buy* or *strong buy* recommendations that are either upgrades from unfavorable initiations or upgrades from unfavorable non-initiating recommendations. In Panel B, the sample includes *buy* or *strong buy* recommendations that are either upgrades from unfavorable initiations or favorable initiating recommendations. *Unfavorable_Initiation* is equal to 1 if the *buy* or *strong buy* recommendations are upgraded from unfavorable initiations, and 0 otherwise. Heteroscedasticity-robust *t*-statistics adjusted for clustering within firms are in parentheses. ***, **, and * denote significance at the 1%, 5%, and 10% levels, respectively. Variables are defined in the Appendix.
Source: I/B/E/S, Investex, Compustat, CRSP and Thomson Reuters. As of May 21, 2019.

credibility when they start their coverage with a recommendation below *buy*. In addition, we show that our sample of analyst recommendations used for textual analysis has a representative distribution of recommendations similar to the overall I/B/E/S population.

5. Conclusion

Analysts' unfavorable coverage initiations represent a significant portion of their initiations. However, there is little research examining the economic reasons that underlie such unfavorable initiations. In this chapter, we provide two hypotheses and find empirical evidence consistent with both. First, anecdotal evidence from analyst reports suggest that when analysts regard a firm as a potentially good investment but are concerned about some ongoing uncertainty in that company, they often initiate with a *hold* opinion to inform the market that the stock has been added to their watch list. Empirical results show that analysts are indeed more likely to initiate unfavorable coverage when they perceive the firm to be of higher uncertainty. Second, we find that market reactions to analysts' subsequent recommendation upgrades are stronger after an analyst initiates unfavorable coverage. This suggests that unfavorable coverage initiations help analysts gain credibility from investors and further explains why some analysts choose to issue an unfavorable recommendation rather than to remain quiet.

Appendix: Variable Definitions

Variable	Definition
Unfavorable	Dummy variable: equal to 1 if an analyst stock recommendation is *hold*, *sell*, or *strong sell*; and 0 if an analyst recommendation is *strong buy* or *buy*.
Unfavorable_Initiation	Dummy variable: equal to 1 if an analyst starts following a stock with a *hold*, *sell* or *strong sell* recommendation and then upgrades the recommendation to either *buy* or *strong buy*; and 0 otherwise.
Ireccdn	Equal to 1–5 when the recommendation is *strong buy*, *buy*, *hold*, *sell* and *strong sell*, respectively.
Uncertainty	The frequency of "uncertain" words from the Loughran and McDonald Sentiment Word Lists in the main content of an analyst report.
Size	The natural logarithm of the market value of equity.
BM	The book value of equity divided by the market value of equity.
Leverage	The book value of debt divided by the sum of the book value of debt and the market value of equity.
Sales_Growth	The compounded 12- to 20-quarter sales growth rate (depending on data availability).
SUE	The difference between actual EPS and analyst consensus forecast EPS divided by the stock price.
Stock_Return	Compounded 12-month stock returns less the compounded 12-month returns from the CRSP value-weighted index.
Stock_Volatility	Annualized standard deviation of stock returns during the 365 days prior to the analyst recommendation date.
Institutional_Ownership	The ratio of institutional ownership, measured as shares held by institutional investors divided by total shares outstanding.
Avgrec	The mean of recommendations (from 1 to 5, i.e., *Ireccdn*) issued for a stock by other analysts in the 365 days before an analyst starts following a stock (i.e., an initiation).

Variable	Definition
Stdrec	The standard deviation of recommendations (from 1 to 5, i.e., *Ireccdn*) issued for a stock by other analysts in the 365 days before an analyst starts following a stock (i.e., an initiation).
Nrec	The number of recommendations (from 1 to 5, i.e., *Ireccdn*) issued for a stock by other analysts in the 365 days before an analyst starts following a stock (i.e., an initiation).
Broker_Size	The number of analysts affiliated with a certain broker.
Ncover	The number of stocks an analyst covers.
Unfavorable_Pct	The percentage of stocks that get *hold*, *sell*, or *strong sell* recommendations in an analyst's portfolio.
Innovative	The difference between an analyst's recommendation and the consensus recommendation, which is the average recommendation over the prior 365 days.
XRET	Buy-and-hold abnormal return over the three trading days centered on analyst recommendations and measured over matched size, book-to-market, and momentum portfolios.

References

Barber, B., Lehavy, R., and McNichols, M. (2006). Buys, holds, and sells: The distribution of investment banks' stock ratings and the implications for the profitability of analysts' recommendations. *Journal of Accounting and Economics*, 41(1), 87–117.

Brown, L.D., Call, A.C., Clement, M.B., and Sharp, N.Y. (2015). Inside the "Black Box" of sell-side financial analysts. *Journal of Accounting Research*, 53(1), 1–47.

Chen, S. and Matsumoto, D.A. (2006). Favorable versus unfavorable recommendations: The impact on analyst access to management-provided information. *Journal of Accounting Research*, 44(4), 657–689.

Clement, M.B. (1999). Analyst forecast accuracy: Do ability, resources, and portfolio complexity matter? *Journal of Accounting and Economics*, 27(3), 285–303.

Cowen, A., Groysberg, B., and Healy, P. (2006). Which types of analyst firms are more optimistic? *Journal of Accounting and Economics*, 41(1–2), 119–146.

Crawford, S.S., Roulstone, D.T., and So. E.C. (2012). Analyst initiations of coverage and stock return synchronicity. *Accounting Review*, 87(5), 1527–1553.

Daniel, K. and Titman, S. (1997). Evidence on the characteristics of cross-sectional variation in stock returns. *Journal of Finance*, 52(1), 1–33.

Demiroglu, C. and Ryngaert, M. (2010). The first analyst coverage of neglected stocks. *Financial Management*, 39(2), 555–584.

Dugar, A. and Nathan, S. (1995). The effect of investment banking relationships on financial analysts' earnings forecasts and investment recommendations. *Contemporary Accounting Research*, 12(1), 131–160.

Ertimur, Y., Muslu, V., and Zhang, F. (2011). Why are recommendations optimistic? Evidence from analysts' coverage initiations. *Review of Accounting Studies*, 16(4), 679–718.

Fama, E.F. and French, K.R. (1993). Common risk factors in the returns on stocks and bonds. *Journal of Financial Economics*, 33, 3–56.

Francis, J. and Philbrick, D. (1993). Analysts' decisions as products of a multi-task environment. *Journal of Accounting Research*, 31(2), 216–230.

Green, T.C., Russell, J., Stanimir, M., and Musa, S. (2014). Access to management and the informativeness of analyst research. *Journal of Financial Economics*, 114(2), 239–255.

Hong, H. and Kubik, J.D. (2003). Analyzing the analysts: Career concerns and biased earnings forecasts. *Journal of Finance*, 58(1), 313–351.

Huang, A.H., Zang, A.Y., and Zheng, R. (2014). Evidence on the information content of text in analyst reports. *Accounting Review*, 89(6), 2151–2180.

Irvine, P.J. (2003). The incremental impact of analyst initiation of coverage. *Journal of Corporate Finance*, 9(4), 431–451.

Jegadeesh, N. and Kim, W. (2009). Do analysts herd? An analysis of recommendations and market reactions. *Review of Financial Studies*, 23(2), 901–937.

Lang, M.H. and Lundholm, R.J. (1996). Corporate disclosure policy and analyst behavior. *Accounting Review*, 71(4), 467–492.

Li, K.K. and Haifeng, Y. (2015). What is the value of sell-side analysts? Evidence from coverage initiations and terminations. *Journal of Accounting and Economics*, 60(2–3), 141–160.

Mayew, W.J. (2008). Evidence of management discrimination among analysts during earnings conference calls. *Journal of Accounting Research*, 46, 627–659.

McNichols, M. and O'Brien, P.C. (1997). Self-selection and analyst coverage. *Journal of Accounting Research*, 35(Supplement), 167–199.

O'Brien, P.C. and Bhushan, R. (1990). Analyst following and institutional ownership. *Journal of Accounting Research*, 28(Supplement), 55–76.

Trueman, B. (1994). Analyst forecasts and herding behavior. *The Review of Financial Studies*, 7(1), 97–124.

Part III

Individuals' Behavior

Chapter 7

Annuity or Lump Sum: Getting Retiring Smokers to Make Better Savings Distribution Decisions

Abigail Hurwitz[*], Yaniv Hanoch[†], Andrew Barnes[‡], and Orly Sade[§]

[*]*Hebrew University of Jerusalem (corresponding author),
Environmental Economics and Management, Robert H. Smith
Faculty of Agriculture, Food and Environment,
Jerusalem 91905, Israel
abigail.hurwitz@mail.huji.ac.il*

[†]*Yaniv Hanoch, Center for Business in Society,
Coventry University
yaniv.hanoch@coventry.ac.uk*

[‡]*Health Behavior and Policy Virginia Commonwealth
University, Richmond, VA 23298, USA
abarnes3@apps.vcu.edu*

[§]*Hebrew University of Jerusalem, Hebrew University
Business school Finance Department, Mount Scopus,
Jerusalem 91905, Israel
orlysade@mail.huji.ac.il*

Abstract

Despite the link between smoking and reduced lifespan, the effect of smoking on retirement savings withdrawal remains understudied. We investigate the impact of various leaflets on smokers' retirement choices: (a) smoker vs. non-smoker life expectancies, (b) smoking's health effects, (c) health impact with

161

government's advice to consider health upon retirement, or (d) combined smoker's life expectancy and health info. Analyzing data from 2,000 smokers, we find that those informed about smoking's lifespan impact, alone or with health consequences, were likelier to opt for lump sum over annuity. This suggests that informing smokers about smoking's harms can influence their retirement choices.

Keywords: Annuity, Financial decisions, Lump sum, Retirement savings, Smoking

1. Introduction

Approximately 17.5% of adult males and 13.5% of adult females in the United States report being smokers. According to the Centers for Disease Control and Prevention, smoking is linked to a host of serious illnesses, such as cancer, and accounts for close to half a million deaths every year (U.S. Department of Health and Human Services, 2014). Using data from over 200,000 individuals, Jha *et al.* (2013) reported that smoking is associated with a 10-year reduction in life expectancy.[1] Smokers' shorter life expectancy, in particular, should play a key role in financial decisions including decisions related to long-term savings. In fact, there is evidence (Challenger Retirement Income Research, 2019) that individuals in general find it difficult to assess life expectancy.[2] One particular decision that involves longevity estimations is the choice between a lump sum or an annuity upon retirement. Annuities are insurance products typically aimed at protecting against longevity risk, providing yearly or monthly pension payments. In many countries, health condition is not part of the annuity pricing mechanism. Smokers confront, thus, not only difficult decisions about their health but also challenging ones about their financial well-being.

The impact of smoking on financial retirement savings withdrawal has, to date, garnered only limited attention. Hurwitz and Sade (2020a), examining real-life insurance company data from Israel, revealed that despite smokers' reduced life expectancy, smokers and non-smokers

---

[1] Life expectancy in the U.S. is 76.1 years for males and 81.1 years for females (Dyer, 2018). Assuming a retirement age of 65, all the rest equals, a smoker with a life expectancy that is lower in 6–10 years (conditional on age) may prefer the lump sum options (in countries where smoking is not a part of the annuitization pricing mechanism).

[2] A survey conducted in Australia in 2014, reveals a gap of about 5 years between senior's assessment of life expectancy and actual life expectancy.

exhibit similar preferences, all the rest equals, both choosing an annuity over a lump sum. To shed light on this conundrum, Hurwitz and Sade (2020b) solicited smokers' and non-smokers' opinions regarding their health status and life expectancy. They found that smokers were optimistic about their own expected health and life expectancy. As smokers' financial retirement decisions might be driven by erroneous assumptions, providing them with precise data could alter their decisions.

Perception of one's life expectancy and knowledge about the health risks associated with smoking are likely to be key factors involved in financial retirement savings decisions (Hurwitz *et al.*, 2021, 2022). But it is possible that smokers lack this knowledge, and a large body of evidence suggests this is the case (e.g., Weinstein, 1988; Viscusi, 2002; Cummings *et al.*, 2004). They might not know, more importantly, that smoking can lead to a shorter lifespan. Moreover, even if they do, they might not be aware of the precise magnitude: 10 years. Smokers might be under the impression that their life expectancy, as found by Hurwitz and Sade (2020b), is equal to that of the average population (that includes non-smokers).

Challenging this possibility, however, Arpino *et al.* (2018) have shown based on data derived from the University of Michigan Health and Retirement Study (HRS) of the U.S. population — that smokers report lower a subjective survival probability, suggesting that they might be cognizant of their shorter life expectancy and, furthermore, incorporate these estimates into their decision making. The nature of Arpino *et al.*'s work, however, precluded them from revealing how many years less smokers believed they would live, as they asked participants to indicate an age group rather than a specific age to which they would live. In contrast to these results, an earlier analysis by Khwaja *et al.* (2007) — using an earlier set of the HRS data — revealed that smokers tended to be more optimistic in their predictions and non-smokers somewhat more pessimistic in their predictions about life expectancy.

Another possibility is that smokers are aware of the risks but discount the probability that it will happen to them. Support for this possibility emerges from two lines of research. First, there is evidence demonstrating that smokers exhibit higher discount rates (Baker *et al.*, 2003; Bickel *et al.*, 2008; for a review see Bickel *et al.*, 2014). That is, they show a present bias. More importantly, researchers (Arnett, 2000) have reported that smokers often exhibit optimism bias — that is, they underestimate the health risks of smoking (e.g., lung cancer). In one study, Weinstein *et al.*

(2005) asked smokers and non-smokers about the probability that they would develop lung cancer, and how smokers would fare compared to non-smokers. Their results demonstrate that smokers judged their own risk of developing lung cancer as significantly lower compared to the average smoker, as well as providing more optimistic (lower) estimates regarding their probability of developing lung cancer compared to non-smokers. In a review of the literature, Weinstein (1998) reported that while smokers acknowledged that smoking poses health risks, they tended to diminish the applicability of these risks to themselves. The above suggests a tension between smokers' desire for immediate rewards (and hence the probability of them opting for a lump sum in retirement decisions) vs. their tendency to underestimate their likelihood of experiencing smoking-related diseases (and hence the decision to choose annuities).

In addition to showing optimism bias, smokers might also exhibit higher risk-taking proclivities. Using the Balloon Analogue Risk Task, Lejuez *et al.* (2003; see also Ryan *et al.*, 2013 for additional results) found that smokers exhibited higher financial risk-taking tendencies. Further evidence that smokers might be higher risk takers comes from research on smoking and cancer screening. Rolison *et al.* (2012) examined the link between smoking and prostate cancer screening among smokers and non-smokers. As smokers are at a higher risk of developing prostate cancer, one might expect them to have higher screening rates. Their data showed that non-smokers — despite being at a lower objective risk of developing prostate cancer — were almost twice as likely to undergo screening compared to smokers. In line with these findings, it is possible that at retirement, when making the choice of how much to annuitize (rather than cash out), smokers assume that they will live as long as non-smokers do.

Other lines of investigation have found that cognitive ability, financial literacy, numeracy, and retirement knowledge could help explain differences in financial decisions, including those related to retirement. A large corpus of data collected by Lusardi and Mitchell (2007, 2011, 2014) has repeatedly shown an association between financial literacy, numeracy, retirement knowledge, and actual savings for retirement. Analyzing panel data from the HRS, the National Financial Capability Survey, and the RAND American Life Panel, Lusardi and Mitchell (2007, 2011, 2014) found that individuals with higher numeracy skills, financial literacy, and retirement knowledge made better financial retirement decisions and were better prepared financially for their retirement. Banks and Oldfield (2007), likewise, reported similar trends, showing that cognitive ability is associated with higher and improved financial retirement savings. One might wonder, then, whether differences in cognitive ability, numeracy, financial knowledge, and financial literacy between smokers and non-smokers might help explain smokers' retirement savings decisions. To the best of our knowledge, no previous studies have examined these links.

Building on Hurwitz and Sade (2020, 2020a, 2020b) earlier work, the present investigation extends their study design and findings in an important way. Here, we focus on ways to remedy or alter smokers' decisions about annuity, rather than simply observe their tendencies. As smokers tend to be unfamiliar with or do not internalize the health consequences of smoking, or the reduced life expectancy associated with smoking, one mechanism to alter their retirement savings distribution decisions is to clearly inform them about both consequences, particularly at the time when the retirement decision is being made. Capitalizing on this idea, we developed four different leaflets (see Appendix 1) that contain information about (a) the life expectancies of smokers vs. non-smokers, (b) the health consequences of smoking, (c) the health consequences plus a message from the government about the importance of considering health needs in retirement decisions, or (d) a combination of life expectancy and health consequences information; we also included a control condition (i.e., no additional data provided in the leaflet). After reading one of the five leaflets, participants were asked to imagine that they had managed to save $250,000 and were now faced with a decision about their retirement savings: to take a lump sum or to receive a monthly payment for the rest of their lives.

Several predictions guided our research. As annuities are priced according to the average life expectancy in the population and smokers' expected lifetime is predicted to be lower, we assumed that all four leaflets would increase the rate of smokers opting for a lump sum compared to the control condition. Second, we hypothesized that the combination of health consequences plus life expectancy would lead to more smokers choosing the lump sum compared to smokers who were given information on life expectancy or health consequences alone. We also hypothesized that the leaflet with only life expectancy information would be more effective than the leaflet with only health consequences information, as it provides succinct information without additional health information that they could discount.

2. Method

To investigate the effect of smokers' perceptions of their life expectancy and the health consequences of smoking on their retirement savings distribution decisions, we conducted an online experiment using Amazon's Mechanical Turk (MTurk) with 2,020 U.S.[3] smokers in March 2018. Our initial sample consisted of 2,449 individuals, but over 500 were removed from the final analysis as they were either not a smoker or did not complete the study. Our only eligibility criteria were that participants were current smokers, lived in the United States, and had a human intelligence task (HIT) approval rate equal to or greater than 95%. There is now a large body of research indicating that the data collected through MTurk are reliable and comparable to those obtained through surveys using other common convenience sample approaches (Gibson *et al.*, 2011; Casler *et al.*, 2013). Participants were paid $0.50 for completing the study.

2.1. *Experimental Conditions*

Following Hurwitz and Sade (2020a), the main task participants were asked to perform was to divide the total sum of money that was saved for retirement between a monthly annuity and a lump sum (an amount of money paid immediately upon retirement).[4] Participants were assigned to one of five conditions. Participants in the first group were informed about the life expectancies of smokers and non-smokers (Condition 1: life expectancy gap). Participants in the second group were informed about some of the illnesses associated with smoking (Condition 2: health

---

[3] Using Mturk ID, we ensured no participant completed the study more than once.

[4] The annuity was calculated using a conversion factor of 200 (a conversion factor is the value that determines the annuity a retiree is able to purchase from a certain lump sum; it is specified in terms of either years or months). This parameter was chosen, to be consistent with Hurwitz *et al.* (2020). Two-hundred months is an equivalent of 16.67 years of conditional life expectancy, while according to 2017 life tables published by the U.S. social security, conditional life expectancy upon retirement (age 67) is about 17.

consequences). In the third group, we combined health consequences with a message from the government stressing the importance of planning for future medical and health needs (Condition 3: health and governmental message), while in the fourth group, participants were informed about both the life expectancies of smokers vs. non-smokers and illnesses associated with smoking (Condition 4: life expectancy and health consequences). Finally, we had a control group of participants who were not given any additional information (Condition 5: control).

2.2. *Materials*

2.2.1. *Smoking status*

Participants' current smoking status was determined by asking if they currently used tobacco every day, some days, or not at all and if they had smoked 100 or more cigarettes in their lifetime (Centers for Disease Control and Prevention, 2017; see also Bondy *et al.*, 2009 for a review). Smokers were defined as those who had smoked at least 100 lifetime cigarettes and also currently smoked some days or every day.

2.2.2. *Numeracy*

Participants completed a four-item numeracy measure taken from a larger scale developed by Lipkus *et al.* (2001). In the present version, participants answered four questions pertaining to basic probability calculations (e.g., "Imagine that we roll a fair, six-sided die 1,000 times. Out of 1,000 rolls, how many times do you think the die would come up even [2, 4, or 6]?").

2.2.3. *Risk-taking*

Risk-taking was assessed using the gambling domain of the Domain-Specific Risk-Taking Scale (Weber *et al.*, 2002). The risk-taking score was the average of responses on a 7-point Likert-type scale (anchored at 1, extremely unlikely, and 7, extremely likely) to 15 questions about how likely respondents were to engage in various risky financial and health-related activities (e.g., a day's income in a high-stakes poker game, riding a bicycle without a helmet).

2.2.4. *Discount rates*

Discount rates were evaluated using four questions about preferences for winning and losing various amounts of money immediately vs. a year later (i.e., win \$20 vs. \$30, lose \$20 vs. \$30, win \$1,000 vs. \$1,500, lose \$1,000 vs. \$1,500; Khwaja *et al.*, 2007). Individuals who reported they would rather win less money now and lose more money later were considered to have higher discount rates and thus had higher scores on this 0–4 scale.

2.3. *Financial Planning and Literacy*

Participants completed six items using a 7-point Likert-type scale (anchored at 1, *strongly disagree*, and 7, *strongly agree*) to rate their own financial retirement knowledge (e.g., "I am knowledgeable about how private investment plans work" (Hershey and Mowen, 2000). Participants also rated their own retirement savings tendencies using five items on an identical 7-point Likert-type scale, with items such as "Relative to my peers, I have saved a great deal for retirement" (Neukam and Hershey, 2002). As a measure of financial services participation, we asked if participants currently had a bank account.

Finally, five items assessed financial literacy. In the first item, participants used a 7-point Likert-type scale to self-assess financial knowledge. In four additional items, participants answered financial knowledge questions (e.g., "buying a single company's stock usually provides a safer return than a stock mutual fund", with response options of "true", "false", "do not know", and "refuse to answer"). All items were summed into a scale, with correct answers on the four knowledge questions corresponding to higher scores on the scale.

2.3.1. *Nicotine dependence*

Three indicator variables were included to control for nicotine dependence. First, we controlled for whether a participant smoked cigarettes daily, with those who smoked less than daily as the reference group. Second, we included two items from the Fagerström Test for Nicotine Dependence (Heatherton *et al.*, 1991): whether the hardest cigarette to give up would be the first cigarette in the morning or any other cigarette, and the time from waking to the first cigarette.

2.3.2. *Demographics*

Demographic characteristics assessed for smokers included their age, gender, and whether they spoke English as their main language at home, as well as their total monthly household income, having a bank account, and household size.

2.3.3. *Statistical analyses*

Our adjusted analyses regress a smoker's decision to choose a lump-sum payment instead of an annuity on condition assignment and participant characteristics. In subsequent analyses, we estimated the same model for a subgroup of more educated participants (those with a bachelor's or graduate degree), as past studies suggested a correlation between smoking and education (Jamal *et al.*, 2016); furthermore, our conjecture was that more educated individuals might be more aware of the consequences of smoking. We also studied a subgroup who reported being in excellent health, as their subjective health reporting might have been influenced by optimism (Weinstein *et al.*, 2005) and therefore they might have been affected more by the information on the health outcomes of smoking.

3. Results

3.1. *Participant Characteristics*

The mean age of the respondents was 36.7 years (*Mdn* = 34 years, *SD* = 11.39) and 48% were male. With regard to the marital status of the respondents, 45% were married, 11% divorced, 2.2% separated, 1.9% widowed, and the rest were never married. While a few participants (16%) had a high school diploma or less, 33.6% had some college education and 35.4% held a bachelor's degree. The mean total monthly household income was $9,571 (*Mdn* = $3,500, *SD* = 22,144). Of the respondents, 10.5% believed that their health was excellent, 31.6% reported that their health was very good, 42% believed that their health was good, and the rest said that their health was fair or poor. On average our participants smoked 10.6 cigarettes each day, and 66% of the participants smoked their first cigarette less than 60 min after waking up.

3.2. *Unadjusted Associations between Information Conditions and Retirement Decisions*

Figure 1(a) presents our main result, namely, that the percentage of daily smokers who made the lump-sum choice was higher among those who were provided information about smoking consequences compared to those who were not. We calculated the Z statistic for a two-sample

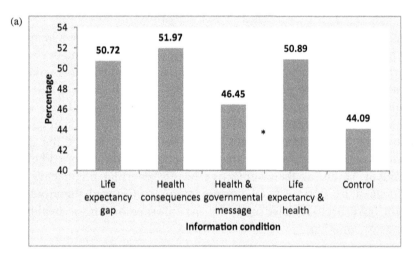

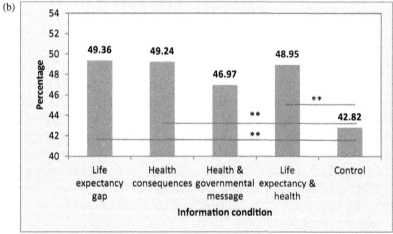

Figure 1: Unadjusted differences in choice of lump-sum payment across information conditions for (a) daily smokers and (b) all smokers.

proportion test comparing the control group to each of the treatment groups (i.e., Conditions 1–4; $Z_1 = 1.56$; $Z_2 = 1.86$; $Z_3 = 0.56$; $Z_4 = 1.61$). A significant effect of three leaflets (Figure 1(b)) was found for all (daily and occasional) smokers ($Z_1 = 1.85$; $Z_2 = 1.82$; $Z_3 = 1.18$; $Z_4 = 1.72$). The unadjusted results suggest that our informational nudge that merely mentioned that smokers can expect shorter lives and the health consequences associated with smoking had a weak effect on participants' hypothetical financial decision on how to allocate money aimed for retirement. We next analyzed the association between these informational nudges and smokers' retirement decisions, after adjusting for participants' numeracy, risk-taking, discount rates, financial planning and literacy, nicotine dependence, and demographic characteristics, before examining these effects across specific subgroups of more educated and healthier participants.

3.3. *Adjusted Associations between Information Conditions and Retirement Decisions*

As shown in Table 1, the information condition effects on smokers choosing the lump-sum payment were consistent after controlling for numeracy, risk-taking, discount rates, financial planning and literacy, nicotine dependence, and demographic characteristics. As expected, compared to smokers receiving no additional information, the tendency to choose the lump-sum was higher after adjustment when we included information regarding smokers' life expectancy gap — either by itself ($\beta = 0.347$, $SE = 0.150$, $p < 0.05$) or together with information regarding the health consequences of smoking ($\beta = 0.314$, $SE = 0.152$, $p < 0.05$; see Table 1).

Regarding participant characteristics and choosing a lump–sum payment in our model that included all smokers in our sample, significantly fewer separated individuals chose the lump-sum option ($\beta = -0.598$, $SE = 0.345$, $p < 0.1$). Further, numeracy ($\beta = 0.0914$, $SE = 0.0493$, $p < 0.1$), risk-taking ($\beta = 0.171$, $SE = 0.050$, $p < 0.001$), and discount rate indices ($\beta = 0.199$, $SE = 0.038$, $p < 0.001$) each had significant positive associations with choosing the lump sum. Conversely, knowledge of financial planning was negatively related to the decision to cash out the retirement funds ($\beta = -0.0513$, $SE = 0.0276$, $p < 0.1$).

Turning to the subgroup analyses, no significant associations were found between information conditions and financial retirement decisions

Table 1:   Adjusted associations of information about smoking consequences and choosing a lump-sum retirement payment over an annuity.

Variable	All smokers $\beta(SE)$	Bachelor's or graduate degree $\beta(SE)$	In excellent health $\beta(SE)$
Condition			
Life expectancy gap	0.347**	0.360	0.149
	(0.150)	(0.230)	(0.548)
Health consequences	0.256*	−0.0916	0.329
	(0.149)	(0.223)	(0.538)
Health consequences and governmental messaging	0.160 (0.149)	0.207 (0.221)	0.992* (0.565)
Life expectancy gap and health consequences	0.314** (0.152)	0.0157 (0.226)	0.564 (0.530)
Demographic			
Age	0.0200	0.0816*	0.0317
	(0.0284)	(0.0484)	(0.102)
Age^2	−0.000299	−0.00106*	−0.000164
	(0.000330)	(0.000565)	(0.00117)
Male gender	0.167	0.120	0.485
	(0.104)	(0.158)	(0.367)
English is the main language spoken at home	0.0417 (0.547)	−0.141 (0.621)	— —
Married	−0.0466	−0.130	0.0872
	(0.124)	(0.189)	(0.400)
Widowed	−0.0221	−0.282	0.00418
	(0.373)	(0.637)	(1.963)
Divorced	−0.0864	−0.00743	−0.190
	(0.187)	(0.312)	(0.777)
Separated	−0.598*	−0.374	—
	(0.345)	(0.564)	—
Tobacco use			

Table 1: (*Continued*)

Variable	All smokers β(SE)	Bachelor's or graduate degree β(SE)	In excellent health β(SE)
Smoke daily	0.0861	0.0602	−0.657*
	(0.109)	(0.158)	(0.392)
Time to first cigarette	−8.32e−05	−8.97e−05	0.315*
	(0.000792)	(0.00110)	(0.172)
Hardest cigarette to give up is the first in the morning	0.152 (0.0997)	0.0780 (0.149)	0.126 (0.395)
Socioeconomic status			
Monthly household income	9.24e−07	−5.95e−07	3.00e−05**
	(2.21e−06)	(3.37e−06)	(1.19e−05)
Household size	0.00965	−0.00772	−0.156
	(0.0369)	(0.0578)	(0.124)
Has a bank account	0.386	0.546	−0.0850
	(0.336)	(0.897)	(1.939)
Economic traits and knowledge			
Numeracy	0.0914*	0.111	0.167
	(0.0493)	(0.0779)	(0.183)
Risk taking	0.171***	0.115	0.207
	(0.0507)	(0.0775)	(0.139)
Retirement knowledge	−0.0513*	−0.0225	−0.0960
	(0.0276)	(0.0430)	(0.0975)
Financial literacy	0.00551	0.0439	−0.369*
	(0.0520)	(0.0814)	(0.201)
Discount rate	0.199***	0.253***	0.00983
	(0.0383)	(0.0557)	(0.137)
Constant	−2.220**	−3.217**	−1.679
	(0.894)	(1.487)	(3.113)
Observations	1,882	836	188

Notes: Standard errors are in parentheses. Experimental conditions are compared to the control condition. Marital status is compared to never married. ***$p < 0.01$, **$p < 0.05$, *$p < 0.10$.

among the highly educated subsample ($p > 0.1$). In addition, among the subgroup of smokers in self-reported excellent health, information regarding smokers' life expectancy or smoking-related illnesses did not affect the propensity to cash out the retirement funds. Rather, smokers in excellent health were significantly more likely to withdraw a lump sum than to choose an annuity when they read the leaflet that included the health consequences together with the governmental recommendation ($\beta = 0.992$, $SE = 0.565$, $p < 0.1$).

Similar to the full sample, among highly educated participants, higher discount rates were associated with choosing the lump-sum payment ($\beta = 0.253$, $SE = 0.0557$, $p < 0.01$). In the sample of those in excellent health, higher financial literacy scores were associated with a lower probability of choosing the lump-sum payment over the annuity ($\beta = -0.369$, $SE = 0.201$, $p < 0.10$).

4. Discussion

The individual- and population-level health and economic costs of smoking are well documented (U.S. Department of Health and Human Services, 2014; Xu *et al.*, 2015), but whether having this information affects smokers' financial decisions, and in particular retirement withdrawals, has been largely unknown. The present research addressed this gap by examining whether smokers choose an annuity or a lump-sum payment after they are presented with different information about the consequences of smoking: life expectancy, health consequences, a combination of the two, or governmental advice including a nudge to increase the salience of retirement decisions. Our data indicate that providing information about the life expectancy gap between smokers and non-smokers as well as information about the life expectancy gap plus the health consequences of smoking significantly increased smokers' likelihood of taking a lump sum instead of an annuity compared to providing no additional information. However, simply providing information about the potential health consequences of smoking or providing a leaflet that contained both the health consequences and a message from the government highlighting the need to financially plan for one's retirement was no more effective than providing no additional information. This result indicates that the specific content of the additional information on how smoking affects life expectancy matters.

Our research extends earlier findings in two important ways. First, while Hurwitz and Sade's (2020a) work focused on exposing an unexpected relationship between smoking and disbursement choices, the present study demonstrated how a simple manipulation that consisted of specific information about smoking-associated harms could alter this preference. The results from the current study demonstrate the utility of discussing life expectancy when helping smokers make retirement distribution choices, a financial decision that is complex and relies on life expectancy estimation. Second, our investigation provides support for earlier work (Weinstein, 1988; Viscusi, 2002; Cummings *et al.*, 2004) indicating that smokers lack information about their shorter life expectancy and the health consequences of smoking.

Our main results remain consistent even after controlling for discount rates, risk-taking, numeracy, retirement knowledge, financial literacy, and other demographic characteristics. Overall, the data highlight a number of interesting trends. For example, men were significantly more likely to choose the lump sum compared to women. This may have been because women live, on average, 5 years longer than men. It is possible that women were cognizant of their greater life expectancy and incorporated it into their decision-making. Furthermore, women tend to be more conservative or less risky in the financial domain — for example, investing less often in the stock market (Charness and Gneezy, 2012; Almenberg and Dreber, 2015).

Likewise, our data revealed that numeracy was associated with a greater likelihood of choosing a lump sum. These results align with a growing body of work (Lusardi and Mitchell, 2007, 2011, 2014) showing that higher numeracy is associated with better financial decisions, such as saving for retirement, credit card payments, and participating in the stock market, as well as better overall financial outcomes. Higher retirement knowledge was associated with lower likelihood of choosing a lump sum over an annuity. This may reflect that the typical financial advice given to the general population steers retirees toward receiving annuities, even though this advice may not apply to those with shorter life expectancies (assuming that the pricing mechanism does not take health condition or smoking status into account). Our findings were also consistent with previous work showing that higher discount rates and higher risk-taking were each associated with greater likelihood of choosing a lump sum over an annuity (Ohmura *et al.*, 2005; Bütler and Teppa, 2007). Thus, our data highlight the importance of gender, numeracy, retirement knowledge, time discounting, and risk-taking in smokers' retirement withdrawal decisions. Finally, our results point to the importance of education in financial decision-making, as more educated smokers were less affected by our informational nudges (see also Barnes *et al.*, 2017 for supporting evidence). These results could be consistent with our conjecture that more educated individuals are more cognizant of the consequences of smoking.

Our investigation has several limitations to consider. First, the use of online surveys precluded us from verifying that participants were, in fact, smokers, our main eligibility criterion. Second, participants in this study were asked to engage in a hypothetical decision, and young participants might not have given much thought to their retirement savings or withdrawal decisions. However, using hypothetical scenarios to investigate decision-making in general (Rolison *et al.*, 2017) and whether to accept annuities in particular (Cappelletti *et al.*, 2013) is common in the extant literature. Still, future research should attempt to recruit participants whose decision about their retirement withdrawal method is imminent. We also did not control for smokers' perceived life expectancy or baseline knowledge of the consequences of smoking for life expectancy, which may have played a role in how much our informational leaflets affected participants' decisions. Finally, participants were presented with limited information and did not have the ability to ask questions. Future research should explore whether face-to-face interactions with financial counselors or institutions might prove even more effective than our informational leaflets and result in an even greater likelihood of choosing a lump-sum withdrawal option.

Smoking poses serious consequences for individuals' physical and financial health. In an economic environment in which health conditions are not part of the annuity pricing mechanism (as in most countries), if two retirees are exactly the same in any feature other than smoking, then due to the shorter life expectancy, the smoker may be better served choosing a lump-sum withdrawal over an annuity. However, smokers may lack or do not understand the relevant information needed to make this critical financial decision. In this study, we demonstrate that providing information about the life expectancy gap between smokers and non-smokers (alone or in combination with information on the health consequences of smoking) increases the understanding of the consequences of smoking on financial decisions that are closely linked to life expectancy. Future research should examine new ways of protecting individuals with impaired health from longevity risk. Deferred lifetime income annuities (commencing lifetime income starting in advanced old age), suggested by Horneff *et al.* (2018), may be a good way to do so and should be better investigated considering the needs of this population.

Appendix 1: Leaflets

Version 1: Life Expectancy Gap

Nowadays, when people retire they have to make important financial decisions. One of the most important financial decisions they make is whether to take a lump sum or withdraw a monthly amount from their retirement savings. Many factors influence people's decision to take one option or another. Whether a person is a smoker or not is one such factor. This is because, on average, smokers live about 6–10 years less than non-smokers do. For example, a non-smoker can expect to live to about 77 years old in the U.S. In comparison, a smoker can expect to live to about 67 years old.

We would like you to imagine that you have just retired from your workplace. Please take a moment to imagine your retirement day. Now that you are retired, you need to make an important financial decision. Please imagine that you have managed to save $250,000 in your retirement savings account. You are now faced with two options. Please take a moment to think which of the two options you prefer, and indicate the option you would choose:

(1) Withdraw the entire $250,000 all at once.
(2) Withdraw a monthly sum of $1,250 (equal to $15,000 yearly) for the rest of your life.

Version 2: Health Consequences

Nowadays, when people retire they have to make important financial decisions. One of the most important financial decisions they make is whether to take a lump sum or withdraw a monthly amount from their retirement savings. Many factors influence people's decision to take one option or another. Whether a person is a smoker or not is one such factor. This is because, on average, smokers are much more likely to develop cancer (e.g., lung cancer), respiratory disease (e.g., asthma), cardiovascular disease (e.g., heart attack), and many other diseases that are associated with premature deaths.

We would like you to imagine that you have just retired from your work place. Please take a moment to imagine your retirement day. Now that you are retired, you need to make an important financial decision. Please imagine that you have managed to save $250,000 in your retirement savings account. You are now faced with two options. Please take a moment to think which of the two options you prefer, and indicate the option you would choose:

(1) Withdraw the entire $250,000 all at once.
(2) Withdraw a monthly sum of $1,250 (equal to $15,000 yearly) for the rest of your life.

Version 3: Health Consequences and Governmental Message

Nowadays, when people retire they have to make important financial decisions. One of the most important financial decisions they make is whether to take a lump sum or withdraw a monthly amount from their retirement savings. Many factors influence people's decision to take one option or another. Whether a person is a smoker or not is one such factor. This is because, on average, smokers are much more likely to develop cancer (e.g., lung cancer), respiratory disease (e.g., asthma), cardiovascular disease (e.g., heart attack), and many other diseases that are associated with premature deaths.

Furthermore, the U.S. Government is working to ensure individuals make the right financial decisions for their future. Financial experts and policymakers agree that individuals need to plan for the different financial expenses they will face during their retirement. So, it is important that everyone plans for their future to ensure that they can financially support themselves after they retire.

We would like you to imagine that you have just retired from your work place. Please take a couple of minutes to imagine your retirement day and yourself in your retirement. Try to picture how you might live in your retirement. Think about how important aspects of your life will be in retirement. In particular, we would like to imagine you medical and health needs in years to come.

Now that you are retired, you need to make an important financial decision. Please imagine that you have managed to save $250,000 in your retirement savings account. You are now faced with two options. Please take a moment to think which of the two options you prefer, and indicate the option you would choose:

(1) Withdraw the entire $250,000 all at once.
(2) Withdraw a monthly sum of $1,250 (equal to $15,000 yearly) for the rest of your life.

Version 4: Life Expectancy Gap and Health Consequences

Nowadays, when people retire they have to make important financial decisions. One of the most important financial decisions they make is whether to take a lump sum or withdraw a monthly amount from their retirement savings. Many factors influence people's decision to take one option or another. Whether a person is a smoker or not is one such factor. This is because, on average, smokers live about 6–10 years less than non-smokers do. For example, a non–smoker can expect to live to about 77 years old in the U.S. In comparison, a smoker can expect to live to about 67 years old. The life expectancy gap is related to the fact that, on average, smokers are much more likely to develop cancer (e.g., lung cancer), respiratory disease (e.g., asthma), cardiovascular disease (e.g., heart attack), and many other diseases that are associated with premature deaths.

We would like you to imagine that you have just retired from your workplace. Please take a moment to imagine your retirement day. Now that you are retired, you need to make an important financial decision. Please imagine that you have managed to save $250,000 in your retirement savings account. You are now faced with two options. Please take a moment to think which of the two options you prefer, and indicate the option you would choose:

(1) Withdraw the entire $250,000 all at once.
(2) Withdraw a monthly sum of $1,250 (equal to $15,000 yearly) for the rest of your life.

Version 5: Control

Nowadays, when people retire they have to make important financial decisions. One of the most important financial decisions they make is whether to take a lump sum or withdraw a monthly amount from their retirement savings. Many factors influence people's decision to take one option or another.

We would like you to imagine that you have just retired from your workplace. Please take a moment to imagine your retirement day. Now that you are retired, you need to make an important financial decision. Please imagine that you have managed to save $250,000 in your retirement savings account. You are now faced with two options. Please take a moment to think which of the two options you prefer, and indicate the option you would choose:

(1) Withdraw the entire $250,000 all at once.
(2) Withdraw a monthly sum of $1,250 (equal to $15,000 yearly) for the rest of your life.

References

Almenberg, J. and Dreber, A. (2015). Gender, financial literacy and stock market participation. *Economics Letters*, 137, 140–142.

Arnett, J.J. (2000). Optimistic bias in adolescent and adult smokers and nonsmokers. *Addictive Behaviors*, 25, 625–632.

Arpino, B., Bordone, V., and Scherbov, S. (2018). Smoking, education and the ability to predict own survival probabilities. *Advances in Life Course Research*, 37, 23–30.

Baker, F., Johnson, M.W., and Bickel, W.K. (2003). Delay discounting in current and never–before cigarette smokers: Similarities and differences across commodity, sign, and magnitude. *Journal of Abnormal Psychology*, 112, 382–392.

Banks, J. and Oldfield, Z. (2007). Understanding pensions: Cognitive functions, numerical ability and retirement saving. *Fiscal Studies*, 28, 143–170.

Barnes, A., Hanoch, Y., Rice, T., and Long, S.K. (2017). Moving beyond blind men and elephants: Providing total estimated annual costs improves health insurance decision-making. *Medical Care Research and Review*, 74, 625–635.

Bickel, W.K., Koffarnus, M.N., Moody, L., and Wilson, G.A. (2014). The behavioural-and-neuro-economic process of temporal discounting: A candidate behavioural marker of addiction. *Neuropharmacology*, 76, 518–527.

Bickel, W.K., Yi, B., Kowal, B.P., and Gatchalian, K.M. (2008). Cigarette smokers discount past and future rewards symmetrically and more than controls: Is discounting a measure of impulsivity? *Drug and Alcohol Dependence*, 96, 256–262.

Bondy, S.J., Victor, J.C., and Diemert, L.M. (2009). Origin and use of the 100 cigarette criterion in tobacco surveys. *Tobacco Control*, 8, 317–323.

Bütler, M. and Teppa, F. (2007). The choice between an annuity and a lump sum: Results from Swiss pension funds. *Journal of Public Economics*, 91, 1944–1966.

Cappelletti, G., Guazzarotti, G., and Tommasino, T. (2013). What determines annuity demand at retirement? *Geneva Papers on Risk and Insurance — Issues and Practice*, 38, 777–802.

Casler, K., Bickel, L., and Hackett, E. (2013). Separate but equal? A comparison of participants and data gathered via Amazon's MTurk, social media, and face-to-face behavioral testing. *Computers in Human Behaviour*, 29, 2156–2160.

Centers for Disease Control and Prevention (2017). Glossary. National Health Interview Survey. Retrieved from https://www.cdc.gov/nchs/nhis/tobacco/tobacco_glossary.htm

Challenger Retirement Income Research (2019). Understanding life expectancies — A big financial literacy gap for retirees. Retrieved from https://www.challenger.com.au/-/media/Challenger/Documents/Thought-leadership/Understanding-life-expectancies-paper-B.pdf

Charness, G. and Gneezy, U. (2012). Strong evidence for gender differences in risk-taking. *Journal of Economic Behavior and Organization*, 83, 50–58.

Cummings, K.M., Hyland, A., Giovino, G.A., Hastrup, B., Bauer, J.E., and Bansal, M.A. (2004). Are smokers adequately informed about the health risks of smoking and medicinal nicotine? *Nicotine Tobacco Research*, 6(Suppl. 3), S333–S340.

Dyer, O. (2018). US life expectancy falls for third year in a row. *BMJ*, 363, k5118.

Gibson, E., Piantadosi, S., and Fedorenko, K. (2011). Using mechanical Turk to obtain and analyze English acceptability judgments. *Language and Linguistics Compass*, 5, 509–524.

Heatherton, T.F., Kozlowski, L.T., Frecker, R.C., and Fagerström, K.-O. (1991). The Fagerstrom test for nicotine dependence: A revision of the Fagerström tolerance questionnaire. *British Journal of Addiction*, 86, 1119–1127.

Hershey, D.A. and Mowen, J.C. (2000). Psychological determinants of financial preparedness for retirement. *The Gerontologist*, 40, 687–697.

Horneff, V., Maurer, R., and Mitchell, O.S. (2018). Putting the pension back in 401(k) retirement plans: Optimal versus default longevity income annuities. Working Paper No. 607. Frankfurt, Germany: Center for Financial Studies.

Hurwitz, A., Mitchell, O.S., and Sade, O. (2021, May). Longevity perceptions and saving decisions during the COVID-19 outbreak: An experimental investigation. *AEA Papers and Proceedings*, 111, 297–301.

Hurwitz, A., Mitchell, O.S., and Sade, O. (2022). Testing methods to enhance longevity awareness. *Journal of Economic Behavior & Organization*, 204, 466–475.

Hurwitz, A. and Sade, O. (2021). Smokers' life expectancy and annuitization decisions. In Venezia, I. (Ed.), *Behavioral Finance: A Novel Approach*, World Scientific Publishers, London, pp. 349–364.

Hurwitz, A. and Sade, O. (2020a). An investigation of time preferences, life expectancy, and annuity versus lump sum choices: Can smoking harm long-term saving decisions? *Journal of Economic Behavior & Organization*, 180, 812–825.

Hurwitz, A., Sade, O., and Winter, E. (2020). Unintended consequences of minimum annuity laws: An experimental study. *Journal of Economic Behavior & Organization*, 169, 208–222.

Jamal, A. King, B.A., Neff, L.J., Whitmill, J., Babb, S.D., and Graffunder, C.M. (2016). Current cigarette smoking among adults — United States, 2005–2015. *Morbidity and Mortality Weekly Report*, 65, 1205–1211.

Jha, P., Ramasundarehettige, C., Landsman, V., Rostron, B., Thun, M., Anderson, R.N., McAfee, T., and Peto, R. (2013). 21st-century hazards of smoking and benefits of cessation in the United States. *New England Journal of Medicine*, 368, 341–350.

Kennedy, R., Clifford, S., Burleigh, T., Waggoner, P., and Jewell, R. (2018). The shape of and solutions to the MTurk quality crisis. Retrieved from https://papers.ssrn.com/sol3/papers.cfm?abstract_id=3272468.

Khwaja, A., Silverman, D., and Sloan, F. (2007). Time preference, time discounting, and smoking decisions. *Journal of Health Economics*, 26, 927–949.

Khwaja, A., Sloan, F., and Chung, S. (2007). The relationship between individual expectations and behaviors: Mortality expectations and smoking decisions. *Journal of Risk and Uncertainty*, 35, 179–201.

Lejuez, C.W., Aklin, W.M., Jones, H.A., Richards, J.B., Strong, D.R., Kahler, C.W., and Read, J.P. (2003). The Balloon Analogue Risk Task (BART) differentiates smokers and nonsmokers. *Experimental and Clinical Psychopharmacology*, 11, 26–33.

Lipkus, I.M., Samsa, G., and Rimer, B.K. (2001). General performance on a numeracy scale among highly educated samples. *Medical Decision Making*, 21, 37–44.

Lusardi, A. and Mitchell, O.S. (2007). Baby boomer retirement security: The roles of planning, financial literacy, and housing wealth. *Journal of Monetary Economics*, 54, 205–224.

Lusardi, A. and Mitchell, O.S. (2011). Financial literacy and planning: Implications for retirement wellbeing (Report No. w17078). Cambridge, MA: National Bureau of Economic Research.

Lusardi, A. and Mitchell, O.S. (2014). The economic importance of financial literacy: Theory and evidence. *Journal of Economic Literature*, 52, 5–44.

Neukam, K.A. and Hershey, D.A. (2002). Fear- and goal-based planning motives: A psychological model of financial planning for retirement. Paper presented at the Annual Meeting of the Gerontological Society of America, Boston, MA.

Ohmura, Y., Takahashi, T., and Kitamura, N. (2005). Discounting delayed and probabilistic monetary gains and losses by smokers of cigarettes. *Psychopharmacology*, 182, 508–515.

Rolison, J.J., Hanoch, Y., and Miron-Shatz, T. (2012). Smokers: At risk for prostate cancer but unlikely to screen. *Addictive Behaviors*, 37, 736–738.

Rolison, J. Hanoch., Y., and Wood, S. (2017). Saving for the future: Dynamic effects of time horizon. *Journal of Behavioral and Experimental Economics*, 70, 47–54.

Ryan, K.K., Mackillop, J., and Carpenter, M.J. (2013). The relationship between impulsivity, risk-taking propensity and nicotine dependence among older adolescent smokers. *Addictive Behaviors*, 38, 1431–1434.

U.S. Department of Health and Human Services (2014). The health consequences of smoking: 50 years of progress. A report of the Surgeon General. Atlanta, GA: U.S. Department of Health and Human Services, Centers for Disease Control and Prevention, National Center for Chronic Disease Prevention and Health Promotion, Office on Smoking and Health. Retrieved from https://www.surgeongeneral.gov/library/reports/50-years-of-progress/full-report.pdf

Viscusi, W.K. (2002). *Smoke-Filled Rooms: A Postmortem on the Tobacco Deal*. Chicago, IL: University of Chicago Press.

Weber, E.U., Blais, A., and Betz, N.E. (2002). A domain-specific risk-attitude scale: Measuring risk perceptions and risk behaviors. *Journal of Behavioral Decision Making*, 15, 263–290.

Weinstein, N.D. (1988). Accuracy of smokers' risk perception. *Annals of Behavioural Medicine*, 20, 135–140.

Weinstein, N.D., Marcus, S.E., and Moser, R.P. (2005). Smokers' unrealistic optimism about their risk. *Tobacco Control*, 14, 55–59.

Xu, X., Bishop, E.E., Kennedy, S.M., Simpson, S.A., and Pechacek, T.F. (2015). Annual healthcare spending attributable to cigarette smoking: An update. *American Journal of Preventive Medicine*, 48, 326–333.

https://doi.org/10.1142/9789811290633_0008

Chapter 8

The Effect of Income Inequality on Individuals' Loan Decision

Shirit Katav Herz[*] and Binyamin Berdugo[†]

*The School of Management and Economics,
The Academic College of Tel Aviv-Yaffo, Yaffo, Israel*
*shirit@mta.ac.il
†Benny.berdugo@gmail.com

Abstract

This study explores the impact of relative scarcity on borrowing decisions through experiments involving a Brick Breaker computer game. Participants receiving messages about others' superior achievements exhibited a greater inclination toward larger loans. Gender differences were observed with females showing a heightened tendency to borrow when informed about peers' accomplishments. These findings underscore the significance of upward social comparisons in loan choices. Notably, high-income inequality may deplete household savings, increasing the risk of debt crises. Effective credit market regulation assumes greater importance in addressing income inequality's implications.

Keywords: Scarcity theory, Conspicuous consumption, Inequality, Overborrowing, Experiment

1. Introduction

Scarcity theory explores a wide range of behaviors of individuals who suffer from scarcity. Mullainathan and Shafir (2013) define scarcity as "having less than you feel you need" (p. 4). Scarcity theory is defined as "the condition of having insufficient resources to cope with demands" (Zhao and Tomm, 2018) or "resource scarcity" (Hamilton *et al.*, 2019), where scarcity exists in different contexts and different areas of life. The fundamental idea of this theory is that since the poor live under severe financial conditions and face tight budgets and income volatility, they are required to struggle with concurrent and upcoming expenditures, which affects their psychology and decision-making (De Bruijn and Antonides, 2022). Such behavior includes reductions in medical care (Lusardi *et al.*, 2010), short reliance on welfare programs (Bertrand *et al.*, 2006), and spending very little on education while spending relatively large amounts on tobacco and alcohol (Banerjee and Duflo, 2007). Scarcity theory also predicts that poor households save too little and overborrow, at high interest rates[1] (Banerjee and Duflo, 2007; Skiba and Tobacman, 2008; Shurtleff, 2009; Shah *et al.*, 2012).

Several explanations have been offered for these behaviors, such as rational adaptations, norms and values, low human capital and lack of education, lack of work experience, and lack of financial literacy (De Bruijn and Antonides, 2022). Mullainathan and Shafir (2013) proposed that poverty itself induces a "scarcity mindset" in which thought patterns and choices are reshaped. They suggested that "when scarcity captures the mind, we become more attentive and efficient" (p. 13).

In recent years, a body of literature on scarcity theory has emerged that attempts to explain why poverty leads to overborrowing. Shah *et al.* (2012) conducted two laboratory experiments to examine the hypothesis that poverty leads to overborrowing through attentional focus on some problems while neglecting others.[2] Attentional focus was defined as allocating attention to the most pressing financial problems and needs, whereas neglect consisted of ignoring future needs; from this perspective,

---

[1] For example, see Skiba and Tobacman (2008), who describe how the poor rely on payday loans even when the annualized costs of these loans exceed 7,000%.

[2] In the first experiment, participants played a follow-up of the Angry Blueberries game. Participants were not only randomly assigned to small or large budgets of shots but also to some borrowing options (no borrowing, or borrowing shots with or without paying interest). In the second experiment, they examined the same mechanism using a follow-up of the Family Feud game. In this version, some of both the time-rich and time-poor participants could borrow time from future rounds while others could not.

borrowing, even at high-interest rates, appears to be a suitable solution to meet pressing needs. Indeed, their results showed that the poor borrowed a higher proportion of their budget than the rich, and gradually increased borrowing when their budget shrank. Furthermore, participants performed best when they did not have the opportunity to borrow, not as well when they could borrow without interest, and worst when they could borrow with interest. Thus, borrowing under scarcity was counterproductive, especially when it was expensive. Meanwhile, the rich performed similarly under these various conditions. The authors also found that scarcity itself leads people to overborrow and enter into cycles of debt, whereas this behavior disappears under abundance. These results were replicated in Shah *et al.* (2019).

This chapter explores a different form of scarcity that impacts borrowing decisions — *relative* scarcity — and can be associated with income inequality, where research on the effect of income inequality on household debt has found a high correlation between the two (Christen and Morgan, 2005; Coibion *et al.*, 2008; Iacoviello, 2008; Van Treeck, 2014). Christen and Morgan (2005) proposed that rising income inequality forces households with smaller income gains to use debt to maintain their consumption at the level of households with larger income gains; this results from consumers' need to maintain or improve their social position through conspicuous consumption. Veblen (1899) introduced the idea that individuals' consumption patterns may vary depending on their relative position in their group's income distribution. He argued that all individuals crave status, which is obtained by displays of wealth. Therefore, the social benefit from consumption depends on the income level of other consumers. Veblen contended that the demand for goods and services by consumers arises from both a desire to establish social networks and an aspiration to imitate higher social classes and economic groups (Patsiaouras and Fitchett, 2012).

Here, we explore how *relative* scarcity (as opposed to absolute scarcity) affects borrowing decisions. We conducted experiments to examine whether and how individuals' exposure to messages with information about *relative* scarcity (or relative low income) affects their borrowing decisions. In these experiments, individuals played Brick Breaker computer games in which their income (payments) depended on their ability to knock down bricks with game balls. During these games, they were offered to borrow game balls as a means to increase their scores and payments. We examined how the individuals' borrowing choice was affected by: (i) messages of other participants' higher success, (ii) the size of the gap between other participants' success and the individual's success, and (iii) the framing of the messages about that gap. Participants were 137 undergraduate students from the Academic College of Tel Aviv-Yaffo, 58 women and 79 men.

Consistent with scarcity theory (Shah *et al.*, 2012, 2019), we found that lower income (payments) increases the propensity to borrow. We also found a positive impact of a message about other participants' higher success on the individual's propensity to borrow, emphasizing the importance of the relative scarcity effect on borrowing decisions. The relative scarcity effect differed across genders; specifically, women exhibited a greater propensity to borrow than men when receiving information about the achievements of others. We also found differences in significance between the effects of message framing on individuals' borrowing choices. However, we did not find a significant effect of gap size on borrowing choices.

This chapter sheds light on the relative aspect of scarcity by strengthening our understanding of how perceived scarcity relative to others affects human behavior. It also contributes to the literature relating income inequality to credit consumption. It is important for policymakers, financial regulators, banks, and other credit providers, to be aware of the impact of inequality (relative scarcity) on credit risk and financial crises. High inequality in income distribution may result in a decrease in household savings, thereby potentially leading to a debt crisis, such as the subprime mortgage crisis that occurred in 2008 (see Van Treeck, 2014).

The rest of the chapter is organized as follows. In Section 2, we describe the experiments, and in Section 3, we present and analyze the results. Concluding remarks are provided in Section 4.

2. The Experiments

The experiments were conducted in the computer laboratories of the School of Management and Economics of the Academic College of Tel Aviv-Yaffo. Participants played a number of computer games similar to Atari's video game Breakout. The game begins with an endowment of balls. Using a ball, the player must knock down as many bricks as possible from a number of rows of bricks by using a springboard to hit the ball

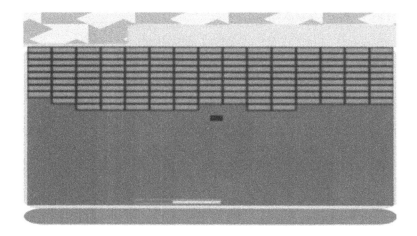

Figure 1:   The game screenshot.

against the bricks and eliminate them. If the rebounding ball misses the player's springboard, it is lost (see Figure 1). The greater the number of bricks they knock down, the higher the players' achievement is and the higher their payment.

To continue play, a threshold number of bricks must be knocked down. Subjects (players) were offered the opportunity to borrow balls in order to increase the chance of surpassing this threshold. The number of borrowed balls plus a certain interest were subtracted from the subsequent endowment of game balls. The subjects were promised payment according to their rewards in the game (i.e., the number of bricks that were knocked down), with a minimum amount of 30 new Israeli shekels (NIS)). Subjects were paid 10 agorot (0.01 NIS) for each knocked-out brick in all games in which they participated.[3] During the experiment, each subject played three rounds of games, each round consisting of three games. When each game (in each round) was over, the subjects received information about their scores (achievements) in that game. Overall, the experiment included 418 rounds of games.

---

[3] The call to participate in the experiment was: "You can earn money in the game depending on the results you achieve. A minimum payment of 30 NIS is guaranteed for those who finish the entire experiment."

2.1. *The Experimental Structure*

In every game, participants initially received an equal allocation of 10 balls unless they chose to alter it by borrowing or repaying prior loans. To progress from the second game to the third game, they had to knock down at least 30 bricks. At the end of the first game in each round, participants were given the opportunity to borrow balls from the third game's endowment, with the aim of increasing their second game's endowment and thereby improving their chances of advancing to the third game. For each ball borrowed, participants had to return two balls from the third game's endowment, essentially incurring a 100% interest rate. As already noted, at the end of each game, all participants were provided with information about their own achievements. However, in the treatment groups, participants *also received a message stating that all other participants earned, on average, more than they did, along with details on the extent of this achievement gap.* Conversely, participants in the control group only received notifications of their own achievements, without receiving reports about their peers' earnings or the earning gaps between them.

Before starting the experiment, an initial group of 40 individuals participated in a technical trial round consisting of 3 games (Round 0). During this trial, no points were accumulated, and no messages were provided. The purpose of this trial was to familiarize the participants with the technical aspects of the game. However, we found this time-consuming round to be unnecessary, because the participants reported that they quickly learned to operate the game without it. Consequently, we chose to exclude this round for all subsequent participants. It is crucial to emphasize that retaining or removing this sample had no bearing on the direction of the variables' effects on borrowing. It only affected the sample size and significance level. Furthermore, a Chow–Fisher stability test confirmed the robustness of our results.[4] At the end of each round, we implemented a brief timeout to explain the upcoming round and ensure that all participants resume simultaneously.

Figure 2 illustrates the experiment's structure: 3 rounds (rounds 1, 2, 3), each consisting of 3 games and sets of messages after each game.

---

[4]The restricted model consists of all observations (with and without Round 0), whereas the two unrestricted models consist of those with and without Round 0. The Chow–Fisher results are: F-statistic = 0.6415906 and p-value = 0.8225351.

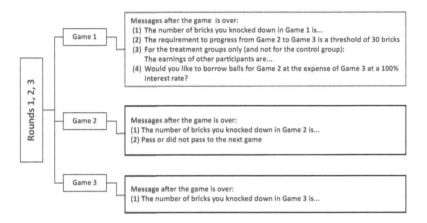

Figure 2:   The experiment's structure.

2.2. *Experimental Groups*

The experiment comprised three treatment groups, denoted groups 2, 13, and 19, and one control group designated Group 17. The three treatment groups varied with respect to the content of the messages that they received regarding their achievement gaps in comparison to other participants. As previously mentioned, the control group did not receive notifications regarding the earnings of other participants. In addition, we examined the impact of message framing on borrowing decisions. Messages were presented in two ways: as small gap or large gap and as distributional gap framing or average gap framing. Table 1 lists the messages received by each group.

3. Results

We explored the impact of messages regarding achievement gaps on borrowing decisions. Through regression analysis, we assessed borrowing size as the dependent variable while considering messages about the achievement gap, subject success, and gender as control variables. Our analysis revealed significant insights into how these factors influence borrowing behavior.

Each participant played three rounds, with three games in each round.[5] Since Game 3 solely reflected the consequences of the decision

---

[5] Except for the 40 participants who also played the trial Round 0.

Table 1. Messages received by each group.

Round number	Control group (17)	Group number 2	Group number 13	Group number 19
Round 1	There was no message about the achievements of other participants.	There was no message about the achievements of other participants.	There was no message about the achievements of other participants.	There was no message about the achievements of other participants.
Round 2	There was no message about the achievements of other participants.	The total amount earned by other participants so far is about 4% more than that earned by you. ★ ■	The total amount earned by other participants so far is about 4% more than that earned by you. ★ ■	The total amount earned by other participants so far is about 8% more than that earned by you. ★★ ■
Round 3	There was no message about the achievements of other participants.	The total amount earned by other participants so far is about 9% more than that earned by you. ★★ ■	50% of the participants have so far earned an amount similar to yours and the other 50% have earned about 8% more than you. ★ ◖	50% of the participants have so far earned 4% more on average than your total earned amount and 50% of the participants have so far earned about 14% more than you. ★★ ◖

Notes: ★ Small gap; ★★ Large gap; ◖ Distribution gap framing; ■ Average gap framing. (1) No messages were sent to any of the groups during the first round; (2) During the second and third rounds, subjects in the treatment groups (2, 13, 19) received messages highlighting a positive gap between themselves and their peers. However, there were variations in gap size and message framing; (3) In the second round, treatment groups 2 and 13 received identical messages, while treatment Group 19 received a message indicating a larger gap; (4) In treatment Group 2, the gap between peers and the subject increased from the second round to the third round. In treatment groups 13 and 19, the messages concerning the gaps were framed in terms of distribution rather than an average, as was the case in the second round.

made in Game 2 and did not involve any active decision, we excluded Game 3 in every round from our analysis. Since Game 1 and Game 2 were one unit in the decision-making system, we considered each pair of games (Game 1 and Game 2) within each round as a single observation, resulting in a total of 424 observations.

The control group for our analysis was Group 17 in all three rounds, and Round 1 of all other groups (2, 13, 19) because their loan offers did not include messages about the other subjects' achievements. Therefore, we assigned a message value of 0 to these observations. The treatment groups for our analysis comprised all other rounds (rounds 2 and 3 of groups 2, 13, and 19), as their loan offers included messages about other subjects' achievements (Table 1). Consequently, we assigned a message value of 1 to all of these observations.

As previously mentioned, the primary focus of this study was to examine the impact of relative scarcity on borrowing decisions. To investigate this, we conducted a regression analysis — Model 1 (see Table 2) — where the dependent variable is the number of balls borrowed by participants. We considered the messages they received, controlled by their achievements in the previous game (interpreted as absolute scarcity), and their gender as independent variables. In this model, we did not differentiate between message versions.[6] In subsequent models, we examined the differences between message versions, taking into account small vs. large achievement gaps, and framing of the gap as an average vs. a distribution.

In detail, loan size was regressed against the following variables:

(1) The dummy variable "Message" indicated whether the subject received or did not receive a message about the achievement gap in Game 1 (value 1 and 0, respectively).
(2) The dummy variable "Gender" received a value of 1 for male participants, and 0 for female participants.
(3) The participant's success in Game 1, marked as "RRR," was measured as the difference between the participant's achievement in

---

[6]Note that all treatment groups received messages conveying a positive achievement gap (indicating relative scarcity).

Game 1 and the threshold required to continue from Game 2 to Game 3. This represented the effect of absolute scarcity.

(4) In addition, we introduced a regression variable that indicates the interaction between the two dummy variables: gender and message ("GenderMessage").

Model 1 is described in Equation (1):

$$\text{Borrow}_i = \alpha + \beta_1 \text{RRR}_i + \beta_2 \text{Gender}_i + \beta_3 \text{Message}_i \\ + \beta_4 \text{Gender}_i : \text{Message}_i + \varepsilon_i \qquad (1)$$

where the variable "borrow" indicates the number of balls borrowed by the subjects. Of the 424 observations in our estimation, 6 were omitted due to missing gender data. The average number of borrowed balls in the experiment was 1.445.

As expected, participants' performance in Game 1, denoted "RRR" which represents absolute scarcity, exerted a negative influence on the number of borrowed balls. While the effect size was relatively modest, its significance was remarkably high ($p = 1.13\text{e-}09$). This outcome suggests that the greater a participant's success (which implies greater income) in the preceding game, the higher their self-confidence in playing Game 2 with reduced, or even no borrowing. This finding aligns with the principles of scarcity theory (Shah *et al.*, 2012, 2019), which imply that absolute scarcity tends to lead to overborrowing.

However, the most important finding from this model analysis was the significant impact of the message sent to participants regarding their inferior performance relative to other participants ($p = 0.01278$). On average, those who received this message borrowed 0.5 more balls than those who did not, regardless of gender. This supports our hypothesis that relative scarcity significantly influences borrowing decisions. When examining the impact of gender on borrowing decisions, we obtained mixed results that were contingent on whether participants received a message regarding the achievement gap. When participants did not receive such messages, males exhibited a greater inclination to take loans, borrowing, on average, 0.451432 more balls than their female counterparts. This finding suggests that males may display lower risk aversion compared to females, which aligns with previous research findings (Byrnes *et al.*, 1999; Eckel and Grossman, 2002; Croson and Gneezy, 2009).

Table 2:   The effects of messages and gender on borrowing decisions.

Variable	Model 1 Messages	Model 2 Small/large messages	Model 3 Avg/Dst messages	Model 4 Model 1 (or Model 3) without Dst message variable
Intercept	0.962502***	0.959334***	0.961991***	0.954661***
RRR	-0.026971***	-0.027215***	-0.027011***	-0.026762***
Gender	0.451432*	0.453010*	0.451687*	0.482561**
Message	0.500281*	—	—	—
GenderMessage	-0.816728**	—	—	—
Message_Small	—	0.552422*	—	—
Message_Large	—	0.423108	—	—
Message_Small:Gender	—	-0.840389**	—	—
Message_Large:Gender	—	-0.778972*	—	—
Message_AVG	—	—	0.599314**	0.609589**
Message_DST	—	—	-0.102066	—
Message_AVG:Gender	—	—	-1.004602***	-1.036926***
Message_DST:Gender	—	—	0.344664	—
N	424	424	424	424
R^2	0.1046	0.1051	0.1167	0.1156

Note: Significance codes are those defined by the "R" software: 0 "***"; 0.001 "***"; 0.01 "**"; 0.05 "*"; 0.1 "·" 1. Avg, average; Dst, distributional.

However, the dynamics shifted when the achievement gap message was delivered. For females, this message seemed to encourage higher borrowing, while it had a moderating effect on males' borrowing behavior. Specifically, among participants who received the message, males borrowed, on average, 0.365 fewer balls than females who received the message. Furthermore, females who received the message borrowed, on average, 0.5 more balls than females who did not receive it. Additionally, Males who received the message borrowed, on average, 0.316447 fewer balls than their male counterparts who did not receive the message.[7]

There are several potential explanations for the observed differences between males and females. Females may exhibit heightened sensitivity to contextual cues within the experimental environment (Croson and Gneezy, 2009). They could also lean toward being more inequality-averse (Croson and Gneezy, 2009) or more susceptible to jealousy (Sagarin et al., 2003; Ruffle and Shtudiner, 2015) compared to males. Alternatively, males may be responsive to contextual cues as well. When not receiving messages, they might approach the game on a personal level. Conversely, when receiving messages, they might shift to a competitive mindset, characterized by increased self-confidence, driven by the motivation to succeed in the game without depending on costly loans.

We further examined whether the way the messages (regarding achievement gaps) were phrased affected borrowing size. We tested two different message versions: (i) different gap sizes (large/small) and (ii) different framing of the gap size (distributional gap framing vs. average gap framing).

In Model 2 (see Table 2) we examined the effect of the size of the achievement gap reported in the messages on the borrowing size. Some messages reported a relatively large gap (see Table 1, Group 2 Round 3, and Group 19 rounds 2 and 3), and some messages reported a relatively small one (Table 1, Group 2 Round 2, Group 13 rounds 2 and 3). Model 2 is described in Equation (2) as:

---

[7]Males borrowed, on average, 0.45 more balls than females. Furthermore, individuals who received a message tended to borrow, on average, 0.5 more balls compared to those who did not receive a message. Consequently, when males received a message, their borrowing behavior was influenced by three factors: (i) their gender, (ii) the receipt of a message, and (iii) the interaction between these two characteristics. In this scenario, the interaction term diminished the cumulative effect arising from both being male and receiving a message.

$$\text{Borrow}_i = \alpha + \beta_1 \text{RRR}_i + \beta_2 \text{Gender}_i + \beta_3 \text{Mesaage Small}_i$$
$$+ \beta_4 \text{Mesaage Large}_i + \beta_5 \text{Gender}:\text{Mesaage Small}_i$$
$$+ \beta_6 \text{Gender}:\text{Mesaage Large}_i + \varepsilon_i \tag{2}$$

Running the regression with separation into message types (small gap/large gap) did not add an explanation to the main regression — Model 1. *F*-test implied that the gap size has an insignificant effect on borrowing and therefore there is no advantage to distinguishing between small/large gaps.[8]

Aside from the large and small gaps which were found to be insignificant in Model 2, we also included messages reporting the gap as an average (Group 2 rounds 2 and 3, Group 13 Round 2, Group 19 Round 2) or as a distribution (Group 13 Round 3, Group 19 Round 3). In Model 3, we analyzed the effect of framing the reported achievement gaps as averages or distributions. Model 3 is described in Equation (3) as:

$$\text{Borrow}_i = \alpha + \beta_1 \text{RRR}_i + \beta_2 \text{Gender}_i + \beta_3 \text{Message}\_\text{AVG}_i$$
$$+ \beta_4 \text{Message}\_\text{DST}_i + \beta_5 \text{Gender}:\text{Message}\_\text{AVG}_i$$
$$+ \beta_6 \text{Gender}:\text{Message}\_\text{DST}_i + \varepsilon_i \tag{3}$$

Average framing was found to significantly influence borrowing behavior. Distribution framing had the opposite effect, but the effect was not significant. This raises the possibility that participants found the distributional framing of the achievement gap difficult to understand. We therefore decided to run another regression — Model 4, in which we omitted the variable for messages with distributional framing, and we treated those observations who received average framing messages as the only observations with messages. Model 4 is described in Equation (4) as:

$$\text{Borrow}_i = \alpha + \beta_1 \text{RRR}_i + \beta_2 \text{Gender}_i + \beta_3 \text{Message}\_\text{AVG}_i$$
$$+ \beta_4 \text{Message}\_\text{AVG}:\text{Gender}_i + \varepsilon_i \tag{4}$$

The results of this regression intensified the effects and reinforced the significance of the estimators in the main regression — Model 1

---

[8] See ANOVA test in Appendix A.

(see Table 2).[9] Furthermore, the separation into message types (small gap/large gap) that was found insignificant in Model 2, remained insignificant even when the variable of the messages with distributional framing was omitted.[10]

4. Conclusions and Summary

In this study, we investigated whether, and to what extent, exposure to the gap between participants' achievements, reflecting relative scarcity, influences participants' borrowing decisions. Our experiment was designed to assess the impact of receiving a message reporting an achievement gap between a participant and all other participants, on that participant's borrowing decisions. Our experiments yielded the following key findings:

- The disparity between participants' achievements in the first game and the threshold required in the second game (referred to as "RRR," reflecting absolute scarcity) has a negative effect on loan size. Although the effect size was relatively small (-0.026971), its significance was very pronounced ($p = 1.13e{-}09$). This suggests that as participants become more confident in their ability to gain without borrowing, they tend to opt for smaller loans or no loans at all.
- Males tend to borrow more than females when they do not receive a message. This difference may be attributed to higher risk-seeking behavior among males vs. females.
- The message sent to participants regarding their achievements in comparison to other participants has a significant effect, resulting in an average increase of 0.5 balls borrowed compared to participants who did not receive the message. Simply being aware of the existence of inequality and recognizing that their achievements lag behind those of their peers encourages higher borrowing. This implies that the mere knowledge of one's lower achievements relative to peers motivates increased borrowing.
- The size of the gap between participants' achievements and those of their peers, had no significant effect on credit consumption.

---

[9] We also analyzed another regression — Model 5 — with all four types of messages (small/large achievement gap, average/distribution framing). Again, we found that the effect of messages with distributional framing of the gap was insignificant. See Appendix B.

[10] See Model 6 and ANOVA test in Appendix C.

- The effect of messages with achievement gaps framed as distributions contrasted with that of messages with gaps framed as averages. Nevertheless, the influence of the former messages was statistically insignificant. Omitting this distributional framing message variable reinforced the effects and significance levels of gender and messages presenting average gaps.
- Notably, it was observed that the awareness of lower achievements relative to peers has a more pronounced impact on females than males. This difference may be attributed to factors such as inequality aversion, heightened sensitivity to contextual cues within the experimental environment, or potentially heightened jealousy.

In a future study, one might conduct a comparative analysis of the effect of the achievement gap on borrowing taking into account peer gender vs. participant gender. The effect of conformity might be explored as well, by informing participants about the loan amounts taken by their peers, rather than just the achievement gap as in this study. This approach would allow for an examination of conformity based on the action itself, rather than its consequences (such as bricks or money), on credit consumption.

Acknowledgment

We thank Sharon Hadad and Oren Shaphir for their helpful comments, discussions, and statistical advice.

Funding

This chapter was funded by the Academic College of Tel Aviv-Yaffo's internal research fund.

Appendix A

ANOVA Test: Achievement Gap Size Has an Insignificant Effect on Borrowing

Note that the difference between the coefficients Message_Small:Gender (−0.840389) and Message_Large:Gender (−0.778972) is small, while their standard deviations, 0.310859 and 0.359100, respectively, are relatively high. This suggests that the disparity in the effects of small and large messages is insignificant. This observation is further confirmed by the subsequent ANOVA test.

We tested the difference between Models 1 and 2:

	Res. Df	RSS	Df	Sum of Sq	F	Pr(>F)
Model 1	413	717.98				
Model 2	411	717.56	2	0.42074	0.1205	0.8865

The p-value of the F test is 0.8865, indicating a probability of 88% for the hypothesis that the split into two separate regressions does not contribute added information.

Appendix B

Model 5: Analyzing the Effect of the Four Types of Messages (Small/Large, Average/Distribution) on Borrowing

In this model, we have three dummy variables: Gender, Message Type (Small/Large), and Message Framing (Average/Distribution). This model combines Models 2 and 3.

Model 5 is described in Equation (5) as:

$$\begin{aligned}
\text{Borrow}_i = {} & \alpha + \beta_1 \text{RRR}_i + \beta_2 \text{Message\_AVG\_Large}_i \\
& + \beta_3 \text{Gender}_i + \beta_4 \text{Message\_AVG\_Small}_i \\
& + \beta_5 \text{Message\_DST\_Large}_i \\
& + \beta_6 \text{Message\_DST\_Small}_i \\
& + \beta_7 \text{Gender}:\text{Message\_AVG\_Large}_i \\
& + \beta_8 \text{Gender}:\text{Message\_AVG\_Small}_i \\
& + \beta_9 \text{Gender}:\text{Message\_DST\_Large}_i \\
& + \beta_{10} \text{Gender}:\text{Message\_DST\_Small}_i \\
& + \varepsilon_i
\end{aligned} \tag{5}$$

The results are as follows:

Variable	Model 5	Std. Error	t value	Pr(>|t|)
Intercept	0.959947	0.144684	6.635	1.04e−10***
RRR	−0.027168	0.004503	−6.034	3.61e−09***
Message_AVG_Large	0.483719	0.277980	1.740	0.08259.
Gender	0.452705	0.175573	2.578	0.01028*
Message_AVG_Small	0.687858	0.251389	2.736	0.00649**
Message_DST_Large	−0.457339	0.950905	−0.481	0.63081
Message_DST_Small	−0.020320	0.460911	−0.044	0.96486
Gender:Message_AVG_Large	0.995028	0.372462	−2.671	0.00785**
Gender:Message_AVG_Small	−1.019608	0.330356	−3.086	0.00216**
Gender:Message_DST_Large	1.035631	1.094725	0.946	0.34470
Gender:Message_DST_Small	0.014537	0.663296	0.022	0.98253

Notes: Significance codes are those defined by the "R" software: 0 '***'; 0.001 '**'; 0.01 '*'; 0.05 '.'; 0.1 ' ' 1. Residual standard error: 1.317 on 407 DF. Multiple R-squared: 0.1202, Adjusted R-squared: 0.09861. F-statistic: 5.562 on 10 and 407 DF, *p*-value: 8.688e−08.

Again, as in Model 3, the coefficients of the distributional framing of the message are insignificant.

Appendix C

We re-examined the impact of message size (small and large) on borrowing in the subsequent regression — Model 6, excluding the variable of messages with distributional framing. We treated those observations who received average framing messages as the only observations with messages.

Model 6 is described in Equation (6) as:

$$
\begin{aligned}
\text{Borrow}_i = {} & \alpha + \beta_1 \text{RRR}_i + \beta_2 \text{Message\_AVG\_Large}_i + \beta_3 \text{Gender}_i \\
& + \beta_4 \text{Message\_AVG\_Small}_i \\
& + \beta_5 \text{Gender} : \text{Message\_AVG\_Large}_i \\
& + \beta_8 \text{Gender} : \text{Message\_AVG\_Small}_i \\
& + \varepsilon_i
\end{aligned}
\tag{6}
$$

The results are as follows:

Variable	Model 6	Std. Error	t value	Pr(>|t|)
Intercept	0.94840	0.13486	7.032	8.53e–12***
RRR	–0.02730	0.00436	–6.263	9.53e–10***
Message_AVG_Large	0.49352	0.27398	1.801	0.07239.
Gender	0.48590	0.16622	2.923	0.00366**
Message_AVG_Small	0.69791	0.24693	2.826	0.00494**
Gender:Message_AVG_Large	–1.02821	0.36720	–2.800	0.00535**
Gender:Message_AVG_Small	–1.05147	0.32494	–3.236	0.00131**

Notes: Significance codes are those defined by the "R" software: 0 '***'; 0.001 '**'; 0.01 '*' 0.05 '.' 0.1 ' ' 1. Residual standard error: 1.312 on 411 DF. Multiple R-squared: 0.1173, adjusted R-squared: 0.1044. F-statistic: 9.104 on 6 and 411 DF, p-value: 2.317e-09.

We compared Model 6 to Model 4 using an ANOVA test:

	Res. Df	RSS	Df	Sum of Sq	F	Pr(>F)
Model 4	413	709.11				
Model 6	411	707.75	2	1.3575	0.3942	0.6745

Again (as in Model 2), F-test implied that the gap size has an insignificant effect on borrowing decisions and therefore there is no advantage in distinguishing between small and large achievement gaps.

References

Banerjee, A.V. and Duflo, E. (2007). The economic lives of the poor. *Journal of Economic Perspectives*, 21(1), 141–167.

Bertrand, M., Mullainathan, S., and Shafir, E. (2006). Behavioral economics and marketing in aid of decision making among the poor. *Journal of Public Policy & Marketing*, 25(1), 8–23.

Byrnes, J.P., Miller, D.C., and Schafer, W.D. (1999). Gender differences in risk taking: A meta-analysis. *Psychological Bulletin*, 125(3), 367–383.

Christen, M. and Morgan R.M. (2005). Keeping up with the Joneses: Analyzing the effect of income inequality on consumer borrowing. *Quantitative Marketing and Economics*, 3, 145–173.

Coibion, O., Gorodnichenko, Y., Kudliyak, M., and Mondragon, J. (2008). Does greater inequality lead to more household borrowing? New evidence from household data. NBER Working Paper No. 19850.

Croson, R. and Gneezy, U. (2009). Gender differences in preferences. *Journal of Economic Literature*, 47(2), 448–474.

De Bruijn, E.J. and Antonides, G. (2022). Poverty and economic decision making: A review of scarcity theory. *Theory and Decision*, 92(1), 5–37.

Eckel, C.C. and Grossman, P.J. (2002). Sex differences and statistical stereotyping in attitudes toward financial risk. *Evolution and Human Behavior*, 23(4), 281–295.

Hamilton, R.W., Thompson, D., Bone, S., Chaplin, L.N., Griskevicius, V., and Goldsmith, K. (2019). The effects of scarcity on consumer decision journeys. *Journal of the Academy of Marketing Science*, 47(3), 532–550.

Iacoviello, M. (2008). Household debt and income inequality, 1963–2003. *Journal of Money Credit and Banking*, 40(5), 929–965.

Lusardi, A., Schneider, D.J., and Tufano, P. (2010). The economic crisis and medical care usage. Working Paper No. w15843. National Bureau of Economic Research.

Mullainathan, S. and Shafir, E. (2013). *Scarcity: Why Having Too Little Means So Much*. Macmillan.

Patsiaouras, G. and Fitchett, J.A. (2012). The evolution of conspicuous consumption. *Journal of Historical Research in Marketing*, 4(1), 154–176.

Ruffle, B.J. and Shtudiner, Z. (2015). Are good-looking people more employable? *Management Science*, 61(8), 1760–1776.

Sagarin, B.J., Becker, D.V., Guadagno, R.E., Nicastle, L.D., and Millevoi, A. (2003). Sex differences (and similarities) in jealousy: The moderating influence of infidelity experience and sexual orientation of the infidelity. *Evolution and Human Behavior*, 24(1), 17–23.

Shah, A.K., Mullainathan, S., and Shafir, E. (2012). Some consequences of having too little. *Science*, 338(6107), 682–685.

Shah, A.K., Mullainathan, S., and Shafir, E. (2019). An exercise in self-replication: Replicating Shah, Mullainathan, and Shafir (2012). *Journal of Economic Psychology*, 75, 102127.

Shurtleff, S. (2009). Improving savings incentives for the poor. National Center for Policy Analysis. https://www.policyarchive.org/download/20342.

Skiba, P.M. and Tobacman, J. (2008). Payday loans, uncertainty, and discounting: Explaining patterns of borrowing, repayment, and default. Vanderbilt University Law School Working Paper, 08–33.

Van Treeck, T. (2014). Did inequality cause the U.S. financial crisis? *Journal of Economic Surveys*, 28, 421–448.

Veblen, T. (1899). *The Theory of the Leisure Class*. Penguin.

Zhao, J. and Tomm, B.M. (2018). Psychological responses to scarcity. In *Oxford Research Encyclopedia of Psychology* (pp. 1–21). Oxford University Press.

© 2025 World Scientific Publishing Company
https://doi.org/10.1142/9789811290633_0009

Chapter 9

Individual Differences and the Repayment of High- and Low-Consequences Debt: Replication and Extension[*]

Yoav Ganzach[†] and Asya Pazy[‡]

†*School of Management and Economics,
The Academic College of Tel Aviv Yaffo,
Rabenu Yeruham St.,
P.O.B 8401, Yaffo 6818211, Israel
yoavga2@mta.ac.il*

‡*Coller School of Management, Tel Aviv University,
Tel Aviv 69978, Israel
asyap@tau.ac.il*

Abstract

We replicate the results of a previous study about the effect of intelligence and financial resources on the repayment of High- and Low-Consequence Debts (HCD and LCD, respectively), and extend the scope of the individual differences that are examined to include personality characteristics, and particularly the big-five personality dimensions. Our results from the first study are replicated showing that intelligence is more strongly (negatively) related to HCD repayment difficulty than to LCD repayment difficulty, whereas financial resources tend to be more strongly (negatively) related to LCD repayment difficulty than to HCD repayment difficulty. We also find that personality has a stronger effect on HCD than LCD repayment difficulties. These results are explained by the positive

---

*Financial support was provided by the Alrov Institute of Real Estate Research

relationship between involvement and quality of financial decision-making in general, and debt-taking decisions in particular. The relationships between the big five and HCD and LCD payment difficulties are also explained by the relationship between involvement and decision quality. Of special interest in this set of findings were the more positive [negative] effect of conscientiousness [neuroticism] on the repayment of HCD [LCD]. These results are consistent with the idea that the self-discipline and deliberation associated with conscientiousness on the one hand, and impulsivity and emotionality associated with neuroticism on the other hand, affect people's debt-taking decision making.

Keywords: Loan repayment, High and low involvement financial decisions, Intelligence, Personality, Big five, Conscientiousness, Neuroticism, Self-discipline, Impulsivity

1. Introduction

In a previous study, Ganzach and Amar (2017) found that intelligence has a positive effect on the quality of financial decision, that this effect is reflected in debt repayment difficulty, but that it occurs for High Consequences Debt (HCD), such as mortgage debt, but not for Low Consequences Debt (LCD), such as credit card debt. We explain this difference as resulting from the effect of involvement on the level of deliberation in making high- vs. low-consequences decisions, and by the idea that the higher the deliberation, the more significant the effect of intelligence.

If involvement is indeed the mediator of the effect of intelligence on the difference in repayment of HCD and LCD, then we should expect that non-cognitive individual differences, and particularly personality, will affect the repayment of HCD and LCD. Thus, the main purpose of the current work is to examine the effect, operationalized in terms of the big five personality dimensions, on debt repayment, and in particular to compare the repayment of mortgage debt to the repayment of credit card debts.

In addition, we aim to replicate and extend the results of our previous study in a number of directions. First, in Study 1, the evaluations of LCD and HCD repayment difficulties were made at different points in time (2004 and 2008). In the current study, the evaluations of these two types of repayment difficulties were elicited at the same point in time. And second, in the current study, LCD repayment difficulty — postponing some of the payment on credit card bills to the next month — involves even less consequential outcomes than the LCD repayment difficulty in Study 1 (it involves only some extra finance charges, but no threat to one's credit rating or danger of dispossession of assets).

2. Method

2.1. *Data*

The data were taken from the 1997 cohort of the National Longitudinal Survey of Youth (NLSY97), conducted by the Center of Human Resource Research with a probability sample of 8,804 Americans (with over-sampling of African Americans, Hispanics, and economically disadvantaged whites) born between 1980 and 1984. The participants were interviewed annually since 1997 and bi-annually since 2011. Data about debt repayment difficulty and financial resources were taken from a special module of the study that was administered in the first interview after the respondent's 30th birthday. Thus, all respondents in our sample are about 30 years old, although there is a three-year range with regard to the year in which they were interviewed.

In addition to measures of debt-repayment difficulty we obtained from the 1997 survey participants' scores in an intelligence test (the Armed Forces Qualifying Test (AFQT)) as well as background and demo-graphic information, from the 2008 survey we obtained measures of the big-five personality dimensions.

2.2. *Measures*

HCD repayment difficulty was measured based on the question: "Thinking of all the various loans or mortgage payments made during the last year, were all payments made the way they were scheduled, or were payments on any of the loans sometimes made later or missed?" Answers were coded as 0 if subjects indicated that all payments were made on schedule and as 1 if they indicated that payments were sometimes made late or missed. After omitting the 18% of the participants who indicated that no payments were due, the number of valid responses was 5,018. Of these, about 2,000 had educational loans, about 2,000 had car loans, about 1,500 had mortgages, about 300 owed money to non-active credit cards, and about 1,800 owed money to other establishments such as banks, stores, and doctors' offices.

LCD repayment difficulty was operationalized in terms of paying credit card bills, based on the question: "Thinking of your most recent credit card statements, did you or will you pay off all of your balances in full?" Answers were coded as 0 if subjects indicated that they paid their debt in full and 1 if they did not. After omitting subjects who did not report that they, their spouses, or their partners had a credit card, the number of valid responses was 2,743 valid responses.

Intelligence. As in Study 1, the measure of intelligence was derived from respondents' test scores on the AFQT that was given to participants in the first survey of the study. The test was administered as a Computer Adaptive Test, and its results were normed by age by the NLS staff to obtain an age-independent score. As in Study 1, we use a standard IQ scale with a mean of 100 and standard deviation of 15.

The big five personality dimensions were measured in 2008 using the Ten-Item Personality Inventory (TIPI), two items for each of the big five dimensions (conscientiousness, openness to experience, extraversion, agreeableness, and neuroticism). The TIPI consists of 10 pairs of personality traits that the respondents are asked to rate regarding the extent to how well they describe themselves on a scale from 1 (Disagree strongly) to 7 (Agree strongly).

Financial resources. *Net worth* was calculated by the NLS staff based on participants' reports about the various assets and debts of the participants. *Income* was obtained from participants' reports about their family income. *Parents' income* was obtained from the reports of the parents of the participants in the first (1997) interview about their 1996 income.

Demographic information. Included sex (coded as 1 for males and 2 for females), ethnicity (Black, Hispanic, and White, the latter served as a reference group), and parents' income (taken from the 1997 survey).

2.3. *Analyses*

As in Study 1, we used logistic regressions with listwise deletion. We also used partial correlation to assess the strength of the association between debt repayment difficulty and our independent variables. However, because in the current study partial correlations could be derived from the same group of participants measured at the same time, we conducted significance tests to compare relationships involving LCD repayment difficulty to relationships involving HCD repayment difficulty.

2.3.1. *Results and discussion*

Table 1 presents a correlation matrix among the study variables (correlations involving HCD and LCD repayment difficulties are point-biserial correlations). The data indicate that 48.9% of the participants had LCD repayment difficulty whereas only 24% encountered HCD repayment difficulty. Like Study 1, the basic thrust of our findings is already apparent in this table: Intelligence is more strongly (negatively) related to HCD repayment difficulty than to LCD repayment difficulty, whereas financial resources tend to be more strongly (negatively) related to LCD repayment difficulty than to HCD repayment difficulty. The data in the table also suggest that big-five dimensions tend to be more strongly related to HCD than LCD repayment difficulty.

Table 2 presents the results of regression analyses predicting LCD and HCD repayment difficulties. It is clear from this table that, even after adding other individual differences variables, intelligence had a significant negative effect on HCD repayment difficulty but did not have a significant effect on LCD repayment difficulty. This was the case both for the exogenous variables model and the full model that includes the financial assets.

The results in this table also indicate that conscientiousness and neuroticism had, respectively, significant negative and positive effects on HCD repayment difficulties, but did not have significant effects on LCD repayment difficulty. Thus, it appears that individual differences in general, and not only intelligence, are important in predicting of HCD but not LCD repayment difficulty. Note also that the direction of the effects of conscientiousness and neuroticism in the HCD model makes theoretical sense. Debt repayment difficulty is positively related to conscientiousness since conscientious people are careful, self-disciplined, organized, and deliberate (Roberts *et al.*, 2009). On the other hand, debt repayment difficulty is negatively related to neuroticism since neurotic people are irrational, impulsive, emotionally unstable, and lack self-control (Andrews *et al.*, 1990).

Table 1: Descriptive statistics and intercorrelation of Study 2 variables.

	Mean	Std err	1	2	3	4	5	6	7	8	9	10	11	12	13
1. HCD difficulty	0.240	0.427	1.00	0.16	-0.11	-0.02	-0.05	0.00	-0.11	0.13	0.12	-0.01	0.09	-0.09	-0.16
2. HCD difficulty	0.489	0.500	0.16	1.00	-0.04	0.00	-0.01	-0.02	-0.03	0.09	0.00	0.01	0.12	-0.10	-0.17
3. Intelligence	97.59	15.01	-0.11	-0.04	1.00	0.06	0.10	0.02	-0.04	-0.16	-0.33	-0.15	0.03	0.36	0.16
4. Openness	4.981	1.133	-0.02	0.00	0.06	1.00	0.05	0.12	0.12	-0.26	-0.01	-0.04	0.21	0.03	0.00
5. Conscientiousness	4.654	1.363	-0.05	-0.01	0.10	0.05	1.00	0.16	0.10	-0.13	-0.10	0.00	0.10	0.10	0.06
6. Extraversion	5.738	1.261	0.00	-0.02	0.02	0.12	0.16	1.00	0.12	-0.17	0.03	0.04	-0.01	0.03	-0.01
7. Agreeableness	5.688	1.131	-0.11	-0.03	-0.04	0.12	0.10	0.12	1.00	-0.26	0.07	-0.01	0.06	-0.01	0.05
8. Neuroticism	3.043	1.340	0.13	0.09	-0.16	-0.26	-0.13	-0.17	-0.26	1.00	-0.01	0.01	0.12	-0.06	-0.08
9. Black	0.260	0.439	0.12	0.00	-0.33	-0.01	-0.10	0.03	0.07	-0.01	1.00	-0.31	0.01	-0.23	-0.12
10. Hispanic	0.212	0.408	-0.01	0.01	-0.15	-0.04	0.00	0.04	-0.01	0.01	-0.31	1.00	0.00	-0.18	-0.03
11. Sex	1.488	0.500	0.09	0.12	0.03	0.21	0.10	-0.01	0.06	0.12	0.01	0.00	1.00	-0.01	-0.02
12. Parents' income	46.36	42.14	-0.09	-0.10	0.36	0.03	0.10	0.03	-0.01	-0.06	-0.23	-0.18	-0.01	1.00	0.18
13. Net worth	45.62	125.26	-0.16	-0.17	0.16	0.00	0.06	-0.01	0.05	-0.08	-0.12	-0.03	-0.02	0.18	1.00
14. Net income	65.14	57.31	-0.14	-0.07	0.31	0.00	0.14	0.03	0.05	-0.07	-0.22	-0.01	-0.01	0.29	0.31

Table 2: HCD and LCD repayment difficulty models — Study 2.

	LCD				HCD			
	b	Std. err.	b	Std. err.	b	Std. err.	b	Std. err.
Intercept	0.448	0.682	-0.008	0.756	-0.005	0.567	-0.138	0.632
Intelligence	-0.004	0.004	-0.001	0.005	-0.011**	0.004	-0.008*	0.004
Openness	-0.052	0.045	-0.043	0.050	0.085	0.039	0.092*	0.043
Conscientiousness	-0.060	0.050	0.003	0.056	-0.209***	0.041	-0.208***	0.046
Extraversion	0.005	0.038	0.046	0.043	-0.046	0.034	-0.004	0.038
Agreeableness	-0.006	0.050	-0.017	0.055	-0.047	0.043	-0.064	0.048
Neuroticism	0.079	0.045	0.044	0.050	0.149***	0.037	0.137***	0.042
Black	-0.100	0.165	-0.025	0.190	0.466***	0.117	0.378*	0.134
Hispanic	-0.184	0.140	-0.086	0.155	-0.126	0.130	-0.122	0.143
Sex	0.459***	0.109	0.440***	0.120	0.400***	0.097	0.414***	0.107
Parents income	-0.005***	0.001	-0.004**	0.001	-0.003*	0.001	-0.001	0.001
Net worth			-0.004***	0.001			-0.003***	0.001
Net income			-0.0002***	0.0011			-0.003***	0.001
N	1,649		1,382		2,927		2,423	

Note: * $p < 0.05$, ** $p < 0.01$, *** $p < 0.001$.

Financial resources had significant effects on both HCD and LCD repayment difficulties. For LCD repayment difficulty the effects of parents' income, net income, and net worth were significantly negative (see Table 2); for HCD repayment difficulty the effects of net worth and net income were significantly negative (see Table 2). However, like Study 1, a pattern of a stronger negative effect of financial resources on HCD repayment difficulty emerges. Controlling for the rest of the variables in our full model, the partial correlations between LCD [HCD] repayment difficulty, net worth, net income, and family income were, respectively, −0.161 [−0.085], −0.096 [−0.054] and −0.112 [−0.032]. Because there was a large group of participants (n = 1339) who reported both LCD and HCD repayment difficulty, we could conduct significance tests to examine the difference between these two sets of correlation. Like the trend we found in Study 1, these tests indicated that with regard to net worth and family income these correlations were significantly more negative for LCD than for HCD repayment difficulty (p < 0.05). For net income the difference was not significant.

3. General Discussion

Consistent with previous studies in the literature, the current results suggest that intelligence has a positive effect on the quality of financial decisions and that this effect is reflected in debt repayment difficulty. However, the results also suggest that this effect of intelligence occurs for high- but not for low-consequences debts. We explain this difference as resulting from the effect of involvement on the level of deliberation in making high- vs. low-consequences decisions, and by the idea that the higher the deliberation, the more significant the effect of intelligence.

In addition to this differential effect of intelligence on debt repayment difficulty, we found two additional differences between HCD and LCD. First, we found that personality predicts HCD, but not LCD, repayment difficulty, suggesting that individual differences in general, and not only intelligence, are more strongly associated with HCD than LCD financial decisions. Second, we found that the effect of financial resources is stronger for LCD than for HCD.

These effects, like the effects of intelligence on debt repayment, are also explained by the difference in involvement with the decisions. First, the effect of individual differences on debt repayment difficulty is best understood by analyzing repayment decisions at the time the debt is due. Since the higher the involvement with the decision, the stronger the relationship between individual characteristics and decision outcome (Cooper and Withey, 2009; Beaty *et al.*, 2001), HCD repayment difficulty is more strongly related to individual differences than LCD repayment difficulty. Take for example the effect of conscientiousness on debt decision at the time the debt was taken. When taking an HCD, people high on conscientiousness are relatively more careful in assuming debt, while people low on conscientiousness are relatively more careless. As a result in repaying HCD, but not in repaying LCD, the low conscientiousness people are more likely to face debt difficulties.

Second, the effect of financial resources is best understood by analyzing repayment decisions at the time the debt is due. At this time financial resources will have a strong effect on LCD repayment: LCD will be paid when financial resources are available (why not repay a debt when money is available) but not when finances are limited (why repay an unimportant debt when resources are limited). On the other hand, at the time of repayment, financial resources will have a relatively weak effect on HCD repayment difficulty — because the repaying of such debt is important people will try to repay it no matter what are the available financial resources. Note that this explanation also suggests that as LCD repayment depends primarily on financial resources, it will have a weak dependence on individual differences.

Third, quite often the difference between HCD and LCD is perceptual rather than real. In particular, debts that appear to have low consequences may be of substantial importance to consumers. In particular, credit card debt may appear as non-significant debt, leading to low consumer involvement and insufficient deliberation, resulting in debt burden that is incongruent with consumers' preferences and with their ability to service the debt (Prelec and Loewenstein, 1998). This is further exacerbated by credit card suppliers who complicate the debt terms, making deliberation more effortful, thus rendering consumers even more susceptible to the consequences of low involvement. Raising consumers' involvement and regulatory actions to simplify the terms of seemingly low consequences debt could help alleviate these problems.

Finally, the analyses in the chapter were based solely on American samples. As international differences in intelligence (e.g., Lynn and Vanhanen, 2002), debt markets (e.g., Bacchetta, and Gerlach, 997), and social attitudes toward debt (e.g., Lea *et al.*, 1995) may be large, it is an open question whether the effects observed in the current U.S. data generalize to other countries.

References

Andrews, G., Stewart, G., Morris-Yates, A., Holt, P., and Henderson, S. (1990). Evidence for a general neurotic syndrome. *The British Journal of Psychiatry*, 157(1), 6–12.

Bacchetta, P. and Gerlach, S. (1997). Consumption and credit constraints: International evidence. *Journal of Monetary Economics*, 40(2), 207–238.

Beaty Jr, J.C., Cleveland, J.N., and Murphy, K.R. (2001). The relation between personality and contextual performance in "strong" versus "weak" situations. *Human Performance*, 14(2), 125–148.

Cooper, W.H. and Withey, M.J. (2009). The strong situation hypothesis. *Personality and Social Psychology Review*, 13(1), 62–72.

Ganzach, Y. and Amar, M. (2017). Intelligence and the repayment of high- and low-consequences debt. *Personality and Individual Differences*, 110, 102–108.

Lea, S.E., Webley, P., and Walker, C.M. (1995). Psychological factors in consumer debt: Money management, economic socialization, and credit use. *Journal of Economic Psychology*, 16(4), 681–701.

Lynn, R. and Vanhanen, T. (2002). *IQ and the Wealth of Nations*. Greenwood Publishing Group.

Prelec, D. and Loewenstein, G. (1998). The red and the black: Mental accounting of savings and debt. *Marketing Science*, 17(1), 4–28.

Roberts, B.W., Jackson, J.J., Fayard, J.V., Edmonds, G., and Meints, J. (2009). *Conscientiousness*. In Mark R. Leary and Rick H. Hoyle (Eds.), *Handbook of Individual Differences in Social Behavior*. New York/London: The Guildford Press, pp. 257–273.

https://doi.org/10.1142/9789811290633_0010

Chapter 10

It's Not about the Money…: Behavioral Aspects of Tipping

Hana Medler-Liraz

School of Management and Economics,
Academic College of Tel-Aviv-Yaffo,
Tel-Aviv-Yaffo, Israel
hanamedl@mta.ac.il

Abstract

Tipping behavior continues to intrigue economists, psychologists, and hospitality management researchers primarily because tipping is a voluntary payment that does not buy something real in return. Yet, it is still a major source of income for millions of workers. This chapter offers a glimpse into the main reasons why people tip. Since consumers' psychological and social motivations can better account for tipping behavior than economic considerations, the following sections present key studies on the behavioral factors that affect tips. Future directions are discussed.

Keywords: Tipping behavior, Motives, Behavioral factors

1. Introduction

Consumers often leave voluntary sums of money (tips) for their service provider (e.g., waiters, bartenders, delivery drivers). Although each customer typically only leaves a small amount of money, the total amount tipped in the U.S. food industry alone was estimated at roughly $47 billion annually (Azar, 2011). The Treasury Inspector for Tax Administration

(2018) estimated a total of $44 billion in individual tip income in 2006 in the United States (including unreported tips, and not only in the food industry; Azar, 2020). Tipping is a major source of income for millions of workers and thus accounts for economists', psychologists', and hospitality management researchers' interest (for a review, see Lynn, 2006).

Tipping behavior dates back to the 16th century, where brass urns with the inscription "**T**o **I**nsure **P**romptitude" were placed in coffeehouses and local pubs. Clients tipped in advance to get good service (Brenner, 2001).

Contemporary research on tipping focuses on several issues: motivations for tipping (Azar, 2008; Saunders and Lynn, 2010), the disparity between tip size and service evaluation (Chapman and Winquist, 1998; Bodvarsson and Gibson, 1999; Lynn, 2000a, 2001, 2003; Lynn and McCall, 2000; Lynn and Gregor, 2001; Green *et al.*, 2003; Lynn and Sturman, 2003), personality differences and its effects on tipping attitudes (Lynn, 2000b, 2008, 2009), as well as consumer demographics and their impact on tipping behavior (Lynn and Thomas-Haysbert, 2003; McCall and Lynn, 2009).

This chapter examines why people tip and what factors influence consumers' tipping behavior (Azar, 2008; Saunders and Lynn, 2010) based on the current psychological, social, and to a lesser extent economics literature.

2. Motivations to Tip

Think about the last time you ate in a restaurant. You finished the meal, got the bill, paid, and left a tip. Why did you tip? Actually, the meal had ended. Is it because you had a great time? Is it because you are considering returning and want to be remembered as a generous customer? Is it because of the fear of what people will think if you don't leave a tip? These questions continue to intrigue researchers, mostly because tipping behavior challenges the economic assumption that people strive to maximize their utility subject to a budget constraint. Hence, people should only pay when they receive something in return. This is not the case, however, when people tip: the service has already been provided by the time the tip is given, so the tip is a voluntary payment that does not buy something real (such as improved service) in return (Azar, 2010).

Skinner's operant conditioning or instrumental conditioning paradigms are one way of accounting for tipping (Skinner, 1953). In Skinnerian terms, people tip because this behavior is reinforced (rewarded), or to avoid punishment. Clearly tipping is a social norm. People in cultures that consider tipping to be customary adhere to this societal rule, which enables individuals to feel they are a part of society. Azar (2010) compared American to Israeli motivations to tip and found that conforming to the social norm was the most frequent reason for tipping in both groups.

Alternatively, people who know that service workers typically earn low wages may feel empathy, compassion, and consider that by giving a tip they can reinforce their own self-image as good-hearted people who contribute to another person's welfare (Azar, 2004; Becker *et al.*, 2012). Correlatively, giving a generous tip enables people to view themselves as generous and be perceived as generous by their social circles. Tipping generously enhances tippers' self-esteem and may prompt them to tip even more than the norm. Tipping generously often impresses others (e.g., waiters and customers at the table).

Researchers have also posited that people show gratitude and appreciation toward those who help them out of a sense of reciprocity and fairness. Equity Theory, for example, suggests that individuals tip an amount equal to the service they believe they received (Becker *et al.*, 2012). For example, a customer who had a wonderful time at a restaurant and felt that the waiter served well and made a real effort, the tip is a way to show gratitude.

However, people also tip out of fear of punishment; i.e., they fear the negative consequences of not tipping. People who avoid tipping may find themselves embarrassed by others' looks or whispers. They also may feel guilty because they did not repay the waiter for his services. In some cases, the waiter may respond negatively (e.g., yell, shout) at customers who do not leave a tip. While embarrassment, guilt, and shame are felt at the end of the service encounter, the fear of avoiding tipping may also be related to apprehension of poor future service. According to Becker *et al.* (2012), consumers' tips are motivated by the desire to control future service. The thought of coming back to the same restaurant may motivate customers to give a tip so that they feel comfortable on their next visit.

Interestingly, findings suggest that tipping for positive reasons is more frequent than tipping for negative ones. Azar (2010) reported that social norms, showing gratitude, and supplementing waiters' income are the three most important reasons for tipping in both the U.S. and Israel. That is, people tip more because of the positive outcomes they experience if they tip than because of the negative consequences of not tipping. These findings also help explain why economic models fail to account satisfactorily for tipping behavior. Improving future service may maximize self-interested consumer utility, but surprisingly, did not emerge as a significant reason for tipping. Moreover, this economic motivation does not apply to customers who do not intend to return to the same service provider, despite the fact that they tip. According to Azar (2010), psychological motivations such as the desire to conform to the social norm or to show gratitude need to be invoked to explain tipping (see also Azar, 2007a, 2007b). A study by Lynn (2018) supports Azar's assumption by showing that for a wide array of professions (e.g., restaurant workers, installation personnel, appliance delivery providers), where future-service motives are plausible, tipping is rare. Azar (2020) concluded that "the vast majority of tipping is not motivated by economic considerations of a selfish and emotionless consumer, but rather by psychological and social motivations" (p. 219).

3. Behavioral Factors Affecting Tips

Studies on the psychological-social aspects of tipping only date back to the late 1990s. Earlier work focused primarily on the elusive relationship between service quality and tip size, which was confirmed in some studies but not in others. Various explanations have been put forward including methodological reasoning relating to the distribution of service ratings, its ordinal scale, and the interpersonal comparability of ratings (Bodvarsson and Gibson, 1999; Lynn, 2000a, 2003), the size of the bill (Chapman and Winquist, 1998), consumer sensitivity to the costs of tipping (Lynn and McCall, 1998 in Lynn and Sturman, 2003), differences between flat and percentage tippers (Lynn and Sturman, 2003), and the familiarity of customers with service providers (Lynn and McCall, 2000).

Lynn and McCall (2000) were the first to hypothesize that because consumers' moods affect evaluations of food as well as service, mood could also affect the service–tipping relationship. Their results showed that although food ratings were positively correlated with service ratings, the service–tipping relationship remained significant after statistically controlling for food evaluations. Medler-Liraz (2012) drew on the notion of selective attention (Berlyne, 1951) and suggested that both service quality and food quality could act as strong stimuli. Specifically in restaurants where the food was defined as "superb," consumers were more likely to shift their attention toward food-related stimuli rather than service quality, resulting in only normatively acceptable tip sizes. In cases where the food was rated "reasonable," consumers' attention focused on the service, which influenced tip size. In these cases, tip size depended on the customers' evaluation of service quality.

Studies on the interactions between the server and consumer have found that an interpersonal connection with the server is a critical determinant of tip percentage. In an experimental study, Crusco and Wetzel (1984) found a positive effect of interpersonal touch on tip percentage: tip percentages were significantly higher in the interpersonal touch condition than in either the control or the no-touch conditions. Similar results were found in Stephen and Zweigenhaft (1986), who also reported that the effect of interpersonal touch was stronger when the server touched a female consumer than a male consumer. Other studies on the effect of employees' light tactile contact have found that employees can increase tips in a restaurant or in a bar (Hornik, 1992; Guéguen and Jacob, 2005; Guéguen and Jacob, 2014) or increase the sale of products (Guéguen *et al.*, 2007) simply by touching a client. Seiter (2007) found that food servers received significantly higher tips when they complimented their customers' choice of menu items than when they did not. Similar studies on hairstyling salons indicated that stylists received significantly smaller tips when they did not compliment customers, compared to when they did (Seiter and Dutson, 2007). Seiter and Weger (2010) indicated that food servers received significantly higher tips when complimenting their parties than when not complimenting them, although as the size of the party increased, the effectiveness of compliments decreased.

Besides the physical connection between the server and the consumer, there is evidence that interpersonal behavior can be effective without direct contact. A display of gratitude by writing "Thank You" or drawing a happy face on the bill also increased tips (Rind and Bordia, 1995, 1996). However, a replication of this study using a scenario-based approach found that adding a personalized message significantly lowered tip percentages. This negative effect was magnified when service quality failed to meet customer expectations (Kinard and Kinard, 2013). Strohmetz *et al.* (2002) examined the impact of a different interpersonal connection, where a server gave out candies with the bill. The results indicated that consumers who were given candy with their bills tipped more on average than those who did not. There was also a positive linear relationship between the number of candies and tip size. Seiter *et al.* (2011) examined the impact of gratuity guidelines on tip percentages. When diners finished their meals, they were given checks that either did or did not include cal- culated examples informing them what various percentages of their bill would amount to in tips. The results indicated that parties who received the gratuity examples left significantly higher tips than those who did not.

In the last ten years, research on tips has expanded to include emo- tional factors. Medler-Liraz (2014) found that hospitality employees char- acterized by negative affectivity (i.e., individuals who experience more negative than positive emotions and have a tendency to dwell on the nega- tive side; Watson and Clark, 1984; George, 1992) who engaged in surface or deep acting (i.e., faked or suppressed emotional regulation strategy) received a higher tip percentage than negative affectivity employees who engaged to a lesser extent in emotional labor strategies. Medler-Liraz (2014) suggested that the positive relationship between negative affectiv- ity and tip size was related to these employees' ability to pay attention to details, which may enable negative affectivity hospitality employees to be more aware of their customers' needs and thus serve them better than positive affectivity hospitality employees. However, awareness and sensi- tivity are not enough. For example, negative affectivity hospitality employees may be aware that a customer has spilled wine on the table- cloth but may react negatively by being upset and displaying negative emotions toward the customer. Engaging in surface/deep acting enables service providers with negative affectivity to be cognizant of and sensitive to customers' needs without displaying these emotions. Customers thus only perceive the outward emotional labor strategies, and will receive quick quality service, which makes for an enjoyable experience, and in turn may encourage them to leave a generous tip.

Medler-Liraz (2020) explored the association between customer inci- vility and tipping. This study also examined the role of agreeableness as a personal resource in coping with instances of incivility. The findings indi- cated that agreeable waiters and waitresses who served customers catego- rized as exhibiting low/medium incivility reported a higher tip percentage than disagreeable hospitality employees. Unexpectedly, the findings also suggested that when hospitality employees served customers who manifested high incivility, the tip percentages for high agreeableness were lower than for low agreeableness. Thus being a sympathetic, kind, courteous, and tolerant waiter/waitress does not "do the trick." By contrast, disagreeable (in the sense of less outgoing) hospitality employees who are more practical, look for solutions, are less emotional, and less apologetic, seem to handle these aggressive situations in a better way, which was manifested in higher tips.

In a qualitative study on flirting in bar interactions involving 40 interviews with bartenders and customers, Seger-Guttmann and Medler-Liraz (2018) found that most of the bartenders flirted for instrumental reasons and that they used flirting to get customers to either spend more money or leave larger tips. However, only customers who enjoyed flirting and feeling courted left large tips. The findings suggest that flirting can also create a sense of misunderstanding on the part of the customer, who may feel insulted, confused or embarrassed when the employee flirts. Most of these customers reported flirting to be mostly negative. In more recent follow-up Medler-Liraz and Seger-Guttmann (2021) found that flirting displays resulted in higher tips in the presence of deep acting, but not surface acting. Customers who considered the service employees' flirting displays as authentic and genuine courtesy left higher tips, whereas customers who had doubts about the service employees' intentions saw these displays as overstepping the bounds of commercial friendship, which led to negative feelings, lower tips for the employee and fewer benefits overall for the restaurant. Since flirting is laden with sex-role stereotypes, Seger-Guttmann and Medler-Liraz (2022) examined the combined effect of flirting type (faked vs. authentic) and the flirter's gender on tip size. Male servers engaging in fake flirting tended to generate adverse customer responses, resulting in a lower tip size than female servers in the fake condition. By contrast, for authentic flirting, no significant difference was found in tip size between customers interacting with male servers and those interacting with female servers. Table 1 summarizes these studies.

4. Conclusion and Future Directions

This chapter presented the state of the art on tipping in empirical literature. It classified tip motivations according to Skinner's operant conditioning paradigm where tipping is either rewarded or punished. The reward category includes conforming to social norms, contributing to

Table 1:   Behavioral factors affecting tips.

Surface-level behaviors	Emotional behaviors
• Interpersonal touch (Crusco and Wetzel, 1984; Stephen and Zweigenhaft, 1986) • Light tactile contact (Hornik, 1992; Guéguen and Jacob, 2005; Guéguen et al., 2007; Guéguen and Jacob, 2014) • Compliments (Seiter and Dutson, 2007; Seiter and Weger, 2010) • Writing "Thank You" or drawing a happy face on the bill (Rind and Bordia, 1995, 1996) • Placing candies on the salver with the bill (Stohmetz et al., 2002) • Incorporating gratuity guidelines on tip percentages on the printed bill (Seiter et al., 2011)	• Negative affectivity (Medler-Liraz, 2014) • Emotional regulation strategies (i.e., engaging in surface or deep acting; Medler-Liraz, 2014; Medler-Liraz and Seger-Guttmann, 2021) • Flirting (Seger-Guttmann and Medler-Liraz, 2018; Medler-Liraz and Seger-Guttmann, 2021; Seger-Guttmann and Medler-Liraz, 2022)

another person's welfare, strengthening one's own self-image as a good-hearted person, and impressing others by being generous and showing gratitude, and appreciation of employees out of a sense reciprocity and fairness. The negative reasons that nevertheless prompt people to tip include the fear of embarrassment, a sense of guilt, shame, and concerns over poor future service.

The literature in the last 10 years indicates that psychological-social motivations can better account for tipping behavior than economic motivations. One compelling explanation can be derived from the Vilnai-Yavetz and Rafaelis (2003) framework. In their framework, analyses of interactions can be divided into the skeleton of an interaction and the tissue of an interaction. The skeleton is the basic core of interactions that comprises routine business behaviors. These behaviors are taken for granted and are likely to be explicitly noted only if an interaction somehow goes astray. For example, placing one's order with a waiter or receiving the bill are the key components or the skeleton of restaurant interactions between waiters and customers. The tissue comprises overtly social behaviors that do not replace the skeletal behaviors but instead follow or accompany them. Tissue components can include expressions of positive emotion, eye contact, and smiling. In this theoretical framework, formal role demands can be viewed as the skeleton, while extra role behaviors are the tissue of the relationship between employees and the organization (Rafaeli and Zilberman, 2004 in Vilnai-Yavetz and Rafaelis, 2005).

Thus, employees' light tactile contact (Crusco and Wetzel, 1984; Stephen and Zweigenhaft, 1986; Hornik, 1992; Guéguen and Jacob, 2005; Guéguen *et al.*, 2007; Guéguen and Jacob, 2014), complimenting the customer (Seiter, 2007; Seiter and Dutson, 2007; Seiter and Weger, 2010), gratitude displays (Rind and Bordia, 1995, 1996; Stohmetz *et al.*, 2002; Seiter *et al.*, 2011), are all parts of the tissue, and have been found to increase tip size.

While the behaviors described above are mainly technical/physical and intended to create surface-level relationships, recent studies reviewed above also examined behaviors that embrace an emotional layer such as negative affectivity (Medler-Liraz, 2014), emotional regulation strategies (i.e., engaging in surface or deep acting; Medler-Liraz, 2014; Medler-Liraz and Seger-Guttmann, 2021), and flirting (Seger-Guttmann and Medler-Liraz, 2018; Medler-Liraz and Seger-Guttmann, 2021; Seger-Guttmann and Medler-Liraz, 2022), that also enhanced tip size. Future studies should explore the differences between "surface-level service" and "emotional service" on tip size. Since studies have found that the authenticity of the behavior is also important beyond the behavior itself, future studies should examine the effects of authentic behaviors on tip size. Note that Groth *et al.* (2009) found that surface acting (i.e., faking emotions) is effective as long as customers do not identify it as such. Medler-Liraz (2014) showed that since service encounters in restaurants may be characterized as a cluster of relatively short, technical interactions (e.g., waiters bring the menu, suggest beverages and describe the restaurant specials, take orders, bring food, and finally the bill), hospitality employees can engage in both surface and deep acting without "paying a price" for faking emotions. However, the nature of the interaction depends on the restaurant type (e.g., luxury vs. non-luxury restaurant), so that the authenticity deserves to be further investigated.

    The behavioral factors reviewed above that affect tips can all be sub-
sumed under the concept of rapport. Rapport in the service sector refers
to "a customer's perception of having an enjoyable interaction with the
service provider employee, characterized by a personal connection
between the two interactants" (Gremler and Gwinner, 2000, p. 92). For
example, hospitality workers foster rapport with their clients by showing
special attention, finding a shared ground for exchanges, being courteous,
relating to them, and providing information tailored to these clients
(Gremler and Gwinner, 2008). Compliments, displays of gratitude, and
flirting may also contribute to the personal connection and enjoyable
interaction with the service employee, and hence enhance rapport.
Positive rapport is known to augment loyalty, generate positive word of
mouth (Gremler and Gwinner, 2000), contribute to enhancing service
recovery (DeWitt and Brady, 2003), prompt positive future behavioral
intentions (Gremler *et al.*, 2001), and positively affects revisit intentions
(Hwang *et al.*, 2013). In a recent study in restaurants, Medler-Liraz (2020)
found a positive significant relationship between rapport and tip size.
Future studies should further explore whether these "tissued behaviors"
when translated into positive rapport can enhance tip size.
    Despite the importance of physical service relationships to tips, the
online service revolution cannot be ignored. New technologies, in particular digital service platforms, have disrupted the low-tech norms of tipping
(Warren and Hanson, 2023). Until recently, tipping involved a customer
using analog technologies, such as cash or a credit card. However, payment platforms for tipped services are no longer limited to cash, credit,
and the occasional tip jar (Rifkin *et al.*, 2021). In fact, in the age of credit
card payment, tips in cash are rapidly becoming a thing of the past. On
some digital service platforms, customers can choose to tip before or after
receiving the service. Research exploring tip sequencing effects has indicated that customers tip more after service (Warre *et al.*, 2020), but service
workers provide better service when they are tipped before service
(Lavoie *et al.*, 2020). Some platforms allow customers to renege on preservice tips after the service is completed, a practice that frustrates
employees (O'Brien and Yurieff, 2020). Future research should explore
how digital tipping affects tipping practices. Specifically, these works
could examine the factors that affect tip size when gestures such as light
tactile contact, compliments, and flirting are no longer relevant, how the

service provider can create rapport in this new reality, and how tip size is affected by the fact that customers are also rated on their tip size and not only the employees.

Finally, service robots are increasingly being integrated into hospitality service encounters both in the front (e.g., hosting, serving) and at the back (e.g., cooking, washing dishes) of the restaurant (Kim *et al.*, 2021). These robots tend to be considered a disruptive innovation in the restaurant context (Choi *et al.*, 2020), and may change traditional conventions of tipping behavior. Is tipping a dying custom? Only time will tell.

References

Azar, O.H. (2004). What sustains social norms and how they evolve? The case of tipping. *Journal of Economic Behavior and Organization*, 54(1), 49–64.

Azar, O.H. (2007a). Do people tip strategically, to improve future service? Theory and evidence. *Canadian Journal of Economics*, 40(2), 515–527.

Azar, O.H. (2007b). The social norm of tipping: A review. *Journal of Applied Social Psychology*, 37(2), 380–402.

Azar, O.H. (2008). Do people tip because of psychological or strategic motivations? An empirical analysis of restaurants tipping. *Applied Economics*, May, 1–6.

Azar, O.H. (2010). Tipping motivations and behavior in the U.S. and Israel. *Journal of Applied Social Psychology*, 40, 421–457.

Azar, O.H. (2011). Business strategy and the social norm of tipping. *Journal of Economic Psychology*, 32, 515–525.

Azar, O.H. (2020). The economics of tipping. *Journal of Economic Perspectives*, 34(2), 215–236.

Becker, C., Bradley, G.T., and Zantow, K. (2012). The underlying dimensions of tipping behavior: An exploration, confirmation, and predictive model. *International Journal of Hospitality Management*, 31(1), 247–256.

Berlyne, D.E. (1951). Attention, perception and behavior theory. *Psychological Review*, 58, 137–146.

Bodvarsson, O.B. and Gibson, W.A. (1999). An economic approach to tips and service quality: Results of a survey. *Social Science Journal*, 36, 137–147.

Brenner, M.L. (2001). *Tipping for Success: Secrets for How to Get in and Get Great Service*. Sherman Oaks: Brenmark House.

Chapman, G.B. and Winquist, J.R. (1998). The magnitude effect: Temporal discount effects and restaurant tips. *Psychonomic Bulletin and Review*, 5, 119–123.

Choi, Y., Choi, M., Oh, M., and Kim, S. (2020). Service robots in hotels: Understanding the service quality perceptions of human–robot interaction. *Journal of Hospitality Marketing Management*, 29, 613–635.

Crusco, A.H. and Wetzel, C.G. (1984). The Midas Touch: The effects of interpersonal touch on restaurant tipping. *Personality and Social Psychology Bulletin*, 10(4), 512–517.

DeWitt, T. and Brady, M.K. (2003). Rethinking service recovery strategies: The effect of rapport on consumer responses to service failure. *Journal of Service Research*, 6(2), 193–207.

George, J.M. (1992). The role of personality in organizational life: Issues and evidence. *Journal of Management*, 18, 185–213.

Green, L., Myerson, J., and Schneider, R. (2003). Is there a magnitude effect in tipping? *Psychonomic Bulletin and Review*, 10, 381–386.

Gremler, D.D. and Gwinner, K.P. (2000). C–E rapport in service relationships. *Journal of Service Research*, 3(1), 82–104.

Gremler, D.D. and Gwinner, K.P. (2008). Rapport-building behaviors used by retail employees. *Journal of Retailing*, 84(3), 308–324.

Gremler, D.D., Gwinner, K.P., and Brown, S.W. (2001). Generating positive word-of-mouth communication through C–E relationships. *International Journal of Service Industry Management*, 12(1), 44–59.

Groth, M., Hennig-Thurau, T., and Walsh, G. (2009). Customer reactions to emotional labor: The roles of employee acting strategies and customer detection accuracy. *Academy of Management Journal*, 52, 958–974.

Guéguen, N. and Jacob, C. (2005). The effect of touch on tipping: An evaluation in a French's bar. *International Journal of Hospitality Management*, 24, 295–299.

Guéguen, N. and Jacob, C. (2014). Clothing color and tipping: Gentlemen patrons give more tips to waitresses with red clothes. *Journal of Hospitality and Tourism Research*, 38(2), 275–280.

Guéguen, N., Jacob, C., and Boulbry, G. (2007). The effect of touch on compliance with a restaurant's employee suggestion. *International Journal of Hospitality Management*, 26, 1019–1023.

Hornik, J. (1992). Tactile stimulation and consumer response. *Journal of Consumer Research*, 19, 449–458.

Hwang, J.H., Kim, S.S., and Hyun, S.S. (2013). The role of server–patron mutual disclosure in the formation of rapport with and revisit intentions of patrons at full-service restaurants: The moderating roles of marital status and educational level. *International Journal of Hospitality Management*, 33, 64–75.

Kim, S., Kim, J., Badu-Baiden, F., Giroux, M., and Choi, Y. (2021). Preference for robot service or human service in hotels? Impacts of the COVID-19 pandemic. *International Journal of Hospitality Management*, 93, 102795.

Kinard, B.R. and Kinard, J.L. (2013). The effect of receipt personalization on tipping behavior. *Journal of Consumer Behaviour*, 12(4), 280–284.

Lavoie, R., Main, K., Hoegg, J., and Guo, W. (2020). Employee reactions to preservice tips and compliments. *Journal of Service Research*, 1094670520960231.

Lynn, M. (2000a). The relationship between tipping and service quality: A comment on Bodvarsson and Gibsons' article. *The Social Science Journal*, 37, 131–135.

Lynn, M. (2000b). National character and tipping customs: The needs for achievement, affiliation and power as predictors of the prevalence of tipping. *International Journal of Hospitality Management*, 19, 205–210.

Lynn, M. (2001). Restaurant tipping and service quality: A tenuous relationship. *Cornell Hotel and Restaurant Administration Quarterly*, 42, 14–20.

Lynn, M. (2003). Restaurant tips and service quality: A weak relationship or just weak measurement. *International Journal of Hospitality Management*, 22, 321–325.

Lynn, M. (2006). Tipping in restaurants and around the globe: An interdisciplinary review. In Altman, M. (Ed.), *Handbook of Contemporary Behavioral Economics: Foundations and Developments*. M.E. Sharpe (Chapter 31), pp. 626–643.

Lynn, M. (2008). Personality effects on tipping attitudes, self-reported behaviors and customs: A multi-level inquiry. *Personality and Individual Differences*, 44, 989–999.

Lynn, M. (2009). Individual differences in self-attributed motives for tipping: Antecedents, consequences, and implications. *International Journal of Hospitality Management*, 28, 432–438.

Lynn, M. (2018). How motivations for tipping vary with occupational differences in descriptive tipping norms. *Journal of Behavioral and Experimental Economics*, 77, 1–10.

Lynn, M. and Gregor, R. (2001). Tipping and service: The case of hotel bellmen. *International Journal of Hospitality Management*, 20, 299–303.

Lynn, M. and McCall, M. (2000). Gratitude and gratuity: A meta-analysis of research on the service-tipping relationship. *The Journal of Socio-Economics*, 29, 203–214.

Lynn, M. and Sturman, M.C. (2003). It's simpler than it seems: An alternative explanation for the magnitude effect in tipping. *International Journal of Hospitality Management*, 22, 103–110.

Lynn, M. and Thomas-Haysbert, C. (2003). Ethnic differences in tipping: Evidence, explanations and implications. *Journal of Applied Social Psychology*, 33, 1747–1772.

McCall, M. and Lynn, A. (2009). Restaurant servers' perceptions of customer tipping intentions. *International Journal of Hospitality Management*, 28, 594–596.

Medler-Liraz, H. (2012). Service quality and tipping: The moderating role of the quality of food. *International Journal of Hospitality Management*, 31, 1327–1329.

Medler-Liraz, H. (2014). Negative affectivity and tipping: The moderating role of emotional labor strategies and leader-member exchange. *International Journal of Hospitality Management*, 36, 63–72.

Medler-Liraz, H. (2020). Customer incivility, rapport and tipping: The moderating role of agreeableness. *Journal of Services Marketing*, 34(7), 955–966.

Medler-Liraz, H. and Seger-Guttmann, T. (2021). The joint effect of flirting and emotional labor on customer service-related outcomes. *Journal of Retailing and Consumer Services*, 60(2), 102497.

O'Brien, S.A. and Yurieff, K. (2020). People are luring Instacart shoppers with big tips — And then changing them to zero. *CNN Business* (April 9).

Rifkin, J.R., Du, K.M., and Berger, J. (2021). Penny for your preferences: Leveraging self-expression to encourage small prosocial gifts. *Journal of Marketing*, 85(3), 204–219.

Rind, R. and Bordia, P. (1995). Effect of server's "Thank you" and personalization on restaurant tipping. *Journal of Applied Social Psychology*, 25, 745–751.

Rind, R. and Bordia, P. (1996). Effect on restaurant tipping of male and female servers drawing a happy, smiling face on the backs of customers' checks. *Journal of Applied Social Psychology*, 26, 218–225.

Saunders, S.G. and Lynn, M. (2010). Why tip? An empirical test of motivations for tipping car guards. *Journal of Economic Psychology*, 31, 106–113.

Seger-Guttmann, T. and Medler-Liraz, H. (2018). Hospitality service employees' flirting displays: Emotional labor or commercial friendship? *International Journal of Hospitality Management*, 73, 102–107.

Seger-Guttmann, T. and Medler-Liraz, H. (2022). Flirting in service encounters: Does the server's sex matter? *Journal of Services Marketing*, 37(5), 549–562.

Seiter, J.S. (2007). Ingratiation and gratuity: The effect of complimenting customers on tipping behavior in restaurants. *Journal of Applied Social Psychology*, 37(3), 478–485.

Seiter, J.S., Brownlee, G.M., and Sanders, M. (2011). Persuasion by way of example: Does including gratuity guidelines on customers' checks affect restaurant tipping behavior? *Journal of Applied Social Psychology*, 41(1), 150–159.

Seiter, J.S. and Dutson, E. (2007). The effect of compliments on tipping behavior in hairstyling salons. *Journal of Applied Social Psychology*, 37(9), 1999–2007.

Seiter, J.S. and Weger H. Jr. (2010). The effect of generalized compliments, sex of server, and size of dining party on tipping behavior in restaurants. *Journal of Applied Social Psychology*, 40(1), 1–12.

Skinner, B.F. (1953). *Science and Human Behavior*. Macmillan.

Stephen, R. and Zweigenhaft, R.L. (1986). The effect on tipping of a waitress touching male and female customers. *The Journal of Social Psychology*, 126(1), 141–142.

Strohmetz, D.B., Rind, B., Fisher, R., and Lynn, M. (2002). Sweetening the till: The use of candy to increase restaurant tipping. *Journal of Applied Social Psychology*, 32(2), 300–309.

Vilnai-Yavetz, I. and Rafaeli, A. (2003). Organizational interactions: A basic skeleton with spiritual tissue. In R. A. Giacalone & C. L. Jurkiewicz (Eds.), *Handbook of Workplace Spirituality and Organizational Performance*. Armonk, NY: M.E. Sharpe Publications, pp. 76–92.

Vilnai-Yavetz, I. and Rafaeli, A. (2005). Emotion in spirituality of organizational interactions. In Kumar, C. & K. Sreenath (Ed.). *Spirituality in the Workplace*. Hyderabad, India: ICFAI Books, pp. 92–113.

Treasury Inspector for Tax Administration (2018). *Billions in Tip-Related Tax Noncompliance are Not Fully Addressed and Tip Agreements are Generally Not Enforced*. Washington, DC: Department of the Treasury.

Warren, N.B. and Hanson, S. (2023). Tipping, disrupted: The multi-stakeholder digital tipped service journey. *Journal of Service Research*, 26(3), 389–404.

Watson, D. and Clark, L. (1984). Negative affectivity: The disposition to experience aversive emotional states. *Psychological Bulletin*, 96, 465–490.

Warren, N.B., Hanson, S., and Yuan, H. (2020). Feeling manipulated: How tip request sequence impacts customers and service providers. *Journal of Service Research*, 24(1), 66–83.

Part IV

Innovative Technology
Driven Markets

Chapter 11

Non-Fruitful Token? Market Reactions to NFT-Related Disclosures

Smadar Siev

*Ono Academic College, Department of Business
Administration, HaNamal 32 Street,
Haifa 3303142, Israel
smadar.si@ono.ac.il*

Abstract

This study analyzes market reactions to firms' "NFT" or "Non-Fungible Token" disclosures filed with the SEC. The analysis distinguishes "Clear" disclosures, indicating actual NFT engagement, from "Vague" ones, referring to vague future intentions. Both types exhibit similar non-significant CAAR behavior upon announcement, followed by a significant decline. Positive cash flow firms experience initial positive CAAR, reversing by day 4. Segmenting by traits shows varied CAAR patterns, but overall, the study suggests skepticism toward NFTs. Firms in or entering this space face consistent negative CAAR over 30 days post-publication, indicating market mistrust.

Keywords: NFT, Non-fungible token, SEC disclosures, Stock returns, Abnormal return, Cumulative average abnormal return, Market model, Market-adjusted model

1. Introduction

1.1. *The Evolution of NFTs*

Non-fungible tokens, most commonly referred to as NFTs, came to prominence in 2017 with the launch of Crypto Kitties, a blockchain[1]-based game in which players can collect and breed virtual cats. Each CryptoKitty was represented by a unique NFT, which could be bought, sold, and traded on the Ethereum blockchain. Since then, NFTs have expanded beyond the world of gaming and into other industries such as art, music, and sports. NFTs enable creators, owners, potential purchasers, and others to verify the ownership and authenticity of their digital assets (including digital images, video and audio files, characters and objects in computer games, and more), making it possible to sell them as unique, identifiable assets. Ownership is recorded using smart contracts on a blockchain. This has opened new revenue streams for creators and created a new market for collectors who are interested in owning unique digital assets.

In early 2021, NFTs gained popularity with several high-profile sales, including a digital artwork by Beeple that sold for $69.3 million at Christie's. The increased attention on NFTs has led to more companies and individuals exploring their potential uses, sparking a debate about the benefit of digital ownership and the future of the art and collectibles markets. As of 2023, there are approximately fifty NFT marketplaces, such as OpenSea, one of the most popular among them. According to Laycock (2022), in the United States, 6.6 million people (3% of the population) own an NFT. India leads in NFT adoption rates, with 7% of the population owning these assets. At the other end of the spectrum, only 1% of Germans own an NFT.

1.2. *Market Size and Anticipated Growth*

According to the DappRadar industry report (2022), the NFT market in 2022 generated a value of approximately $24.7 billion in organic trading volume across various blockchain platforms and marketplaces. Trades

---

[1] Blockchain technology, which is both decentralized and immutable, has the potential to revolutionize industries by providing secure and transparent transactions and data management.

suspected of being wash trades[2] or manipulated transactions are excluded from these figures, which represents a slight decline compared to 2021. In that year, trading volume in NFTs surged to an estimated $25.1 billion as tokenized collectibles gained wider recognition and became more than a niche interest.

It seems that the NFT market followed a similar trajectory to the cryptocurrency market, which witnessed significant losses throughout 2022 with the collapse in May of that year of the Terra network's LUNA and UST, as well as the collapse of the crypto exchange FTX in November. According to the DappRadar industry report (2022), there were about 101 million NFT trades during 2022, compared to about 58.6 million NFT trades in 2021. While the number of NFT trades increased over this period, the average value of the trades fell.

Forecasts regarding the growth of the NFT market differ between research groups producing different reports, but most predict double-digit annual growth in the coming years. For example, BCC Research (2022) estimates an annual growth rate of 27.3% until 2027, with the value of the NFT market reaching over $100 billion in 2027; Grand View Research (2022) forecasts that the value of the global NFT market will reach $211.72 billion by 2030, growing at a compound annual growth rate (CAGR) of 34.2% from 2023 to 2030; and EMERGEN Research (2022) forecasts a CAGR of 34.2% through 2030.

1.3. *(Lack of) Regulation*

NFT trading operates within a regulatory grey zone, lacking clear guidelines, and oversight. Unlike in traditional financial markets, where wash trading is explicitly prohibited, the crypto market currently lacks any such regulatory restrictions. This absence of regulation allows individuals to artificially inflate the value of specific NFT collections by engaging in activities such as opening multiple crypto wallets and conducting transactions between them. Hildobby (2022) characterizes the situation as follows:

> The NFT space is quickly evolving and maturing. In 2022 it became ever more competitive, and it has become obvious that capturing trade

---

[2] Wash trading involves an individual or group trading with themselves to create a false impression of market activity.

volume market share is a top priority for platforms. Well-intentioned schemes to incentivize usage quickly emerged as a way to pull ahead in the race to attract this volume and become the most successful marketplace. A byproduct of this has been the rise of wash trading, which is still in a legal gray area and distorts key metrics used by analysts to measure usage and performance. Many widely quoted statistics have therefore been misleading at best, painting a picture of organic usage which hasn't perfectly matched reality.

According to Hildobby (2022), over $430 billion of NFT trading volume in 2022 resulted from wash trading. The practice peaked in January 2022, when more than 80% of trading volume was attributed to wash trading, accounting for 58% of the entire year's trading volume. These unresolved issues, such as wash trading arising from the lack of regulation, highlight the challenges and concerns surrounding NFT trading practices.

Radman (2023) suggests that the true number of wash trading transactions is likely to be even higher than this, noting that the Hildobby (2022) review does not include groups of fraudulent actors who artificially inflated the prices of certain NFT projects on Discord[3] or Reddit.[4] These findings regarding the large percentage of wash trades are particularly concerning for investors in the stock market, who may be influenced by news of large trading volumes in NFTs, deceptively inflated in wash trading, when making investment decisions.

China was the first country to take a clear position against the crypto market and its derivatives by imposing a number of regulations banning cryptocurrency transactions and mining activities. In May 2021, China's State Council prohibited financial institutions from engaging in any crypto transactions, mining, or trading. It cited concerns about the environmental impact of cryptocurrency mining, which requires vast amounts of electricity, as well as apprehensions about the use of cryptocurrencies for illegal activities such as money laundering and tax evasion. China banned all domestic crypto mining in June 2021 and outlawed cryptocurrencies in September of that year. The ban on cryptocurrency mining in China has had a significant impact on the global cryptocurrency market,

---

[3] Discord is a private chat platform for communities.
[4] Reddit is a public forum for discussion and content sharing.

as China had been one of the largest producers of Bitcoin and other cryptocurrencies. In addition, because NFTs are often bought and sold using cryptocurrencies, China's restrictions have made it difficult for Chinese citizens to engage in NFT transactions.

1.4. *Research Rationale*

The future of NFTS, which is driven by opposing factors, remains intriguing to investors. On one hand, the growth of platforms dedicated to creating and minting NFTs, as well as secondary marketplaces, hints at a promising trajectory. As discussed above, forecasts project double-digit annual growth rates in the NFT industry. However, several factors could potentially impede the market's expansion. Recent discoveries concerning wash trading within the NFT market have raised concerns and highlighted the need for increased transparency. This is in addition to the introduction of new regulations in China described above which can significantly affect the market.

Considering that the NFT market is characterized by substantial uncertainty, with no prevailing consensus regarding whether it will ultimately prosper or collapse, I sought to explore the reaction of financial markets to corporate disclosures regarding their involvement in the NFT field, encompassing activities such as minting and selling NFTs, as well as involvement in NFT-related platforms and applications. I follow recent literature that explores the reaction of financial markets to corporate involvement in new and promising technologies. Cheng *et al.* (2019), Cahill *et al.* (2020), and Klöckner *et al.* (2022) analyze the contribution of the novel blockchain technology to company value, and Aharon *et al.* (2022) explore the market reaction to corporate involvement in the virtual world of the metaverse. To the best of my knowledge, this chapter is the first to examine the market reaction to NFT disclosures.

By examining the reaction of stock prices to disclosures submitted to the SEC that contain the expression "NFT" or "Non-Fungible Token," I seek to provide insights surrounding financial market reactions to NFT-related corporate disclosures and shed light on the potential risks and opportunities associated with investing in firms that are involved in the NFT field.

1.5. *Research Method and Overview*

I segmented the sample to analyze the market reaction in terms of various factors such as the characteristics of the disclosures and disclosing companies. Disclosure characteristics were analyzed in two ways. First, in line with Cheng *et al.* (2019), Cahill *et al.* (2020), Klöckner *et al.* (2022), and Aharon *et al.* (2022), I classified disclosures according to their content: "Vague" (announcements of vague future intentions to develop NFT technology in the future or general statements of involvement); or "Clear" (announcements stating existing specific involvement in NFTs). Secondly, I distinguish between companies that primarily focus on the creation and sale of NFTs, which typically are short-term or one-time activities, and firms that are involved in developing trading platforms or other infrastructure for NFTs, which represents a long-term strategic approach. Regarding corporate characteristics, I explored potentially relevant factors, such as cash flow, leading vs. lagging companies, the sector in which the company operates, and the geographical location its corporate headquarters, among other factors.

Although there are clear differences between the behavior of different subsamples, as detailed later, the overall picture indicates a negative price reaction following NFT disclosures, with the entire sample experiencing a negative cumulative average abnormal return (CAAR) of −4.93% ($t = 3.69$) in the [2, 20] time window.

My findings indicate that, for the period I considered, the market does not believe that involvement in NFTs is beneficial and "punishes" companies that are engaged, or plan to engage, in NFT-related activities by devaluing their stock prices, which leads to a negative CAAR. Will this perception of NFTs continue in the future? Only time will tell.

The remainder of the chapter is organized as follows. In Section 2, I review the relevant literature; in Section 3, I describe the sample construction and the data sources; in Section 4, I describe the methodology; in Section 5, I report the main findings; and in Section 6, I summarize the results.

2. Literature Review

Together with media reports, the disclosure of information by companies plays a crucial role in shaping investors' perceptions and influencing stock prices. In this chapter, I present what is, to my knowledge, the first effort to examine the response of stock prices to NFT-related corporate disclosures. I conducted this study using a similar methodology to related studies that explore the reaction of stock markets to companies' disclosures about their involvement in new and promising technologies. These studies include those by Cheng *et al.* (2019), Cahill *et al.* (2020), Yen and Wang (2021), and Klöckner *et al.* (2022), which explore the stock market reaction to disclosures related to blockchain and/or cryptocurrencies. I also refer to a study conducted by Aharon *et al.* (2022), who explore the market reaction to companies' involvement in the virtual world of the metaverse. Below is a chronological overview of some of this research.

Cheng *et al.* (2019) extracted 82 blockchain-related 8-K[5] disclosures and categorized them as "speculative" (vague plans) and "existing" (actual products). They found that investors react positively to "speculative" disclosures in the seven-day event window with buy-and-hold abnormal returns (BHAR) of 7.5%, with a reverse reaction in the 30 days following the disclosure. They argue that this implies an overreaction by investors to "speculative" disclosures. The reaction is stronger during periods of positive Bitcoin returns. However, there is almost no market reaction to "existing" disclosures.

Cahill *et al.* (2020) used a global sample of 713 companies between 2016 and 2018 to explore the market reaction to blockchain-related disclosures. The authors found that corporate disclosures related to blockchain positively affect companies' stock prices by 5% on the announcement day, indicating a favorable market response. Additionally, the study reveals that the market response is influenced by factors such as company size, the level of prior involvement in blockchain technology, and trends in the price of Bitcoin. These findings suggest that companies can benefit from signaling their interest in blockchain technology to investors and stakeholders.

Yen and Wang (2021) examine the impact of 10-K[6] disclosures related to blockchain technology and cryptocurrencies on stock prices. The authors find that disclosures about blockchain technology positively affect

---

[5]Form 8-K, known as a "current report" is the report that companies must file with the SEC to announce major events that shareholders should know about.
[6]The annual report on Form 10-K provides a comprehensive overview of the company's business and financial condition and includes audited financial statements.

stock prices, while disclosures concerning cryptocurrencies had no statistically significant effect on stock prices. The authors suggest that "blockchain disclosures could be more related to a firm's involvement in blockchain technology. Relatively, cryptocurrency disclosures could be more related to a firm's investment strategy (e.g., investment in cryptocurrencies) or payment solutions (e.g., accepting cryptocurrencies)" (Yen and Wang, 2021, p. 10). Their findings also indicate that the stock price is influenced by factors such as book value, industry classification, and financial performance.

Klöckner *et al.* (2022) examine the impact of 175 blockchain-related announcements by 100 firms in 15 countries on their market value between 2015 and 2019. Their findings reveal that 59% of the sample experienced positive abnormal returns on the announcement day, with a positive significant AAR of 0.3%. There was no significant abnormal return for the two days before and two days after the announcement day. They found that the announcement of blockchain applications used to trace physical objects or to share sensitive information is associated with a decrease in abnormal returns, while involvement with an external information technology service provider in a blockchain project is associated with an increase in abnormal returns.

Regarding factors affecting the interest of the public in NTFs, Pinto-Gutiérrez *et al.* (2022) examined the factors that attracted attention to NFTs between December 2017 and July 2021 and found that Bitcoin and Ethereum[7] returns significantly predicted interest in NFTs during the following week, as measured by Google search queries. They concluded that "the remarkable increase in prices of major cryptocurrencies can explain the hype around NFTs" (Pinto-Gutiérrez *et al.*, 2022, p. 1).

Luo *et al.* (2022) found a positive relationship between the number of tweets (of NFT Twitter Communities) mentioning NFTs and the price of more than half of the 19 top genuine projects which are authentic, original products created by legitimate creators, compared to insufficient causality for most of the copycat projects referring to projects that imitate already existing authentic NTF products. Most recently, the research of von Wachter *et al.* (2022) addresses fraudulent trading activity in the context of blockchain-based assets and examines wash trading behavior in the NFT market. Their study covers the period from January 2018 to

---

[7]Ethereum is the second largest digital currency by market cap apart from Bitcoin.

mid-November 2021 and focuses on data from the 52 largest NFT collections by volume. Their findings indicate that within their sample "3.93% of addresses,[8] processing a total of 2.04% of sales transactions, trigger suspicions of market abuse" (von Wachter *et al.*, 2022, p. 1).

3. Sample Construction

I compiled a sample of SEC filings (forms 6-K, 8-K, 10-K, 10-Q, and 20-F) that include the terms "NFT" or "Non-Fungible Token" using the EDGAR system available on the SEC website. I collected data spanning the period from 2013 to August 2022. Although blockchain NFTs have existed only since the first NFT — *Quantum* — was minted in 2014, I searched for disclosures starting in 2013 to remove any risk of ignoring previous disclosures. This resulted in a sample of 1916 disclosures, beginning in March 2021. To refine the sample, I manually checked and read each result and employed a screening procedure outlined in Appendix A. I excluded disclosures submitted by trusts, funds, ETFs, Over-the-counter (OTC) firms, and private companies. I also filtered out disclosures in which the NFT is used as an abbreviation of other terms such as "non-flow-through," "no further treatment," "non-firm transmission," and so on. Furthermore, I excluded disclosures in which the term "NFT" was referenced only in connection with the career experience of corporate officers in the NFT field and disclosures containing only a general mention of the term NFT. Lastly, I removed duplicate disclosures that were submitted multiple times within the same day. The remaining disclosures either indicate the company's intention or plan for involvement with NFTs or disclose active involvement with NFTs through their sale or creation, or the management of trading marketplace platforms. Following this screening process, a final sample of 331 disclosures from 109 companies remained. The stock daily prices and data from the financial reports were extracted from Yahoo Finance.

I constructed several subsamples from the original sample and also categorized the sample into groups based on the disclosure content to examine the consistency of results across different subsamples and groups.

---

[8]The term "address" typically refers to a unique party associated with a digital wallet or account on a blockchain network.

3.1. *Subsamples*

To construct the subsamples, I applied the following exclusions and classifications:

Full excluding financial reports: I excluded disclosures where the NFT was mentioned as part of an overlapping financial report. This resulted in a subsample consisting of disclosures that were not included in financial reports.

Full excluding repetitive a range of five days: If multiple disclosures were sent within a 5-day time range, I excluded the later ones to avoid repetition. This led to a subsample that excluded duplicate disclosures.

Full excluding price < \$1: For disclosures where the share price was less than \$1 within the time window of $[-10, 9]$, I created a subsample excluding such cases.

3.2. *Segmentation by Disclosure Content*

3.2.1. *Vague and clear*

In line with the works of Cahill *et al.* (2020), Cheng *et al.* (2019), and Aharon *et al.* (2022), I categorized the disclosures into "Clear" or "Vague" based on the content of the disclosure. "Clear" disclosures refer to explicit information about selling NFTs or available services, such as operating a marketplace, minting capabilities, or any other NFT-related platform. They also include investments in companies through mergers and acquisitions. "Vague" disclosures encompass ambiguous statements about potential future opportunities and statements regarding exploring options, allocating resources for research and development, or general intentions. Examples of "Clear" and "Vague" disclosures can be found in Appendix B.

3.2.2. *NFT sales vs. platform*

I distinguished between companies focusing on the one-time *creation and sale* of NFT collections and companies that are considering a long-term approach to NFTs and are therefore developing and maintaining platforms for NFT minting, trading, or management. Examples of disclosures concerning NFT creation and sales and those concerning NFT platforms are presented in Appendix C.

3.2.3. *Disclosures with and without warnings*

The regulatory landscape for blockchain technologies, NFTs, cryptocurrencies, and digital assets is uncertain. Undoubtedly, these uncertainties and new regulations or policies pose risks to the NFT market's development and value, particularly for those companies heavily reliant on cryptocurrencies, and could have a substantial adverse impact on their future. Other risks may include shifts in consumer preferences and the failure to implement innovations to maintain the competitiveness of products and services. It is possible that some investors are not aware of all these uncertainties involved with NFTs; therefore, drawing their attention to these issues may affect their investment decisions. Therefore, I distinguished between disclosures that explicitly include warnings or present uncertainties directly associated with NFTs and disclosures that lack such warnings or messages. Examples for disclosures that contain warnings are presented in Appendix D.

Panel A in Table 1 shows the types of disclosures that compose the sample. Of the total 331 disclosures, 189 are classified as Clear while 142 are Vague. A total of 218 disclosures are classified as a platform while only 110 deal with creation and sales of NFTs. During 2021, 120 disclosures were submitted, but the number of disclosures submitted between January and August 2022 reached 211. This is a 2.8-fold increase on an annual basis, which highlights the increasing interest of listed firms in the field of NFTs. Only 41 out of 331 disclosures, accounting for 12% of the total, addressed the inherent risks within the NFT field and contained explicit warnings. Panel B in Table 1 shows that most of the companies in the sample (69%) are headquartered in the United States and 18% in China. Most companies (nearly 55%) are in the communication services or technology sectors Together with the consumer cyclical and financial services sectors, these account for 99% of the sample.

Table 2 displays financial descriptive statistics of the companies included in the sample. The average assets value is of $3,800,922 thousand and a market capitalization of $5,043,157 thousand. The average

Table 1:   Sample characteristics.

Type	2021	2022	Total
Panel A: Disclosure type			
Clear disclosures	70	119	189
Vague disclosures	50	92	142
Total disclosures	**120**	**211**	**331**
Platform	88	130	218
Creations & sales of NFTs	32	78	110
Total disclosures	**120**	**208**	**328**
Disclosures without warning	112	178	290
Disclosures with warning	8	33	41
Total disclosures	**120**	**211**	**331**

Headquarters		Sector	
Panel B: Firms headquarters and sector segmentation			
USA	75	Communication services	30
China	20	Technology	29
Europe (EU)	9	Consumer cyclical	23
Cayman Islands	1	Financial services	16
Singapore	1	Industrials	7
Malaysia	1	Consumer defensive	2
Korea	1	Basic materials	1
Australia	1	Healthcare	1
Total	**109**	**Total**	**109**

Note: Panel A lists the number of *Clear* and *Vague* disclosures, *platform* and *creation & sales* disclosures, and disclosures with and without warnings. The figures for 2022 are up to August 2022, as the construction of the sample ended in August 2022. Panel B shows the number of companies by headquarters locations and sector. There are a total of 331 disclosures from 109 companies in 8 sectors. Some disclosures did not fit into either of the "platform" or "creation & sales of NFTs" categories, such as those dealing with the organization of conferences and clients who deal with NFTs; therefore, the total of these two categories does not add up to 331.

Table 2: Descriptive statistics.

Company characteristics	Mean	Median	Std. dev.
Total assets (thousands of USD)	3,800,922	134,461	19,023,417
Market capitalization (thousands of USD)	5,043,157	162,375	19,254,168
Share price at $t = -30$	24.07	7.79	48.54
Free cash flow (thousands of USD)	196,212	−4,538	1,341,241
Company sales growth	18.62%	9.51%	50.67%
Book to market	15.58	0.80	52.64
Leverage	2.03	0.88	2.93

Notes: The table presents financial descriptive statistics for the companies in the sample. Total assets and Free cash flow are for the most recent fiscal year before the announcement. Drawing on Cahill *et al.* (2020), market capitalization is calculated as the number of shares at the end of the most recent quarter prior to the announcement, multiplied by the closing share price 30 trading days prior to the announcement. Following Klöckner *et al.* (2022), I calculate firm growth as the annual percentage change in total revenues in the fiscal year prior to the announcement. The book-to-market ratio is the ratio of book value per share at the end of the most recent quarter to the stock closing price at the announcement date, and firm leverage ratio is the ratio of total debt to total equity at the of the fiscal year prior to the announcement.

(median) share price is $24.07 ($7.79) and the average (median) financial leverage is 2.03 (0.88). The standard deviation of the examined variables and a comparison of median and mean values suggest that the sample consisted of a wide variety of companies.

4. Methodology

For this study, I utilized event study methodology to investigate the effect of NFT disclosures on stock prices around the disclosure day ($t = 0$). To establish the event date ($t = 0$), I compared the filing date when the form was submitted to the SEC and the date mentioned in the disclosure itself. If the date on the form was earlier and a matching press release was published on the company's website on that same date, I considered the earlier date as the event date. This is because it signifies the initial public availability of the information. However, if there is no corresponding press release on the company's website, the filing date was considered the event date.

For each firm "i" on day "t", I estimated abnormal return AR_{it} by subtracting the expected return according to the market model from the real return, as described in Equation (1):

$$AR_{it} = R_{it} - \left(\hat{\alpha}_i + \hat{\beta}_i R_{mt}\right) \tag{1}$$

where R_{it} is the log daily return of the firm stock i on day t, R_{mt} is the log daily return of the S&P 500 index for day t, $\hat{\alpha}_i$ and $\hat{\beta}_i$ are regression estimates for the true parameters using data from 252 historical trading days ending 30 days before the event date. For each firm, I aggregated the abnormal returns for selected time windows [T1, T2] around the event to obtain the cumulative abnormal return ($CAR_{i,T}$). That is,

$$CAR_{i,T} = \sum_{t=T1}^{T2} AR_{it} \tag{2}$$

The cumulative average abnormal return ($CAAR_T$) across a subsample of n firms is calculated as follows:

$$CAAR_T = \frac{1}{n}\sum_{i=1}^{n} CAR_{i,T} \tag{3}$$

The cross-sector standard deviation t-test is expressed in Equation (4).

$$t_{CAAR} = \frac{CAAR_T}{\hat{\sigma}_{CAAR_T}/\sqrt{N}} \tag{4}$$

where $\hat{\sigma}_{CAAR_T}$ is estimated as follows:

$$\hat{\sigma}^2_{CAAR_T} = \frac{1}{N-1}\sum_{i=1}^{N}\left(CAAR_{i,T} - \frac{1}{N}\sum_{i=1}^{N}CAAR_{i,T}\right)^2 \tag{5}$$

I computed CAAR using the CAPM and the adjusted market model where $\hat{\alpha}_i$ is set to 0 and $\hat{\beta}_i$ is set to 1.

5. Empirical Results

To begin with, I observed a prominent trend concerning the public and firms' interest in NFTs. Figure 1 shows the prevalence of monthly

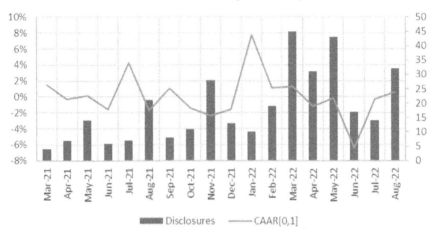

Figure 1: The prevalence of NFT disclosures.

Note: Following Aharon *et al.* (2022), the graph displays the monthly prevalence of NFT disclosures and the corresponding CAAR [0, 1].

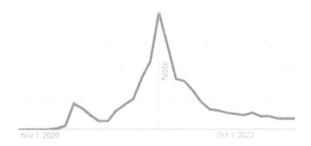

Figure 2: Google Searches of "NFT."

Note: This figure indicates worldwide interest in NFTs according to Google Trends for "What is an NFT?" Interest peaked in January 2022 with 1,447,774 searches then declined sharply to less than 140,000 by April 2023.

disclosures during the sample period along with parallel CARR in the [0, 1] time window. The number of corporate NFT-related disclosures reached a peak in March 2022 with 45 disclosures. From then onward a decline began, although this decline was not monotonic. Figure 2 shows public interest in NFT as reflected in Google searches. It seems very clear that public interest peaked in January 2022 with 1,447,774 searches.

By April 2023, eight months after my sample period ended on August 22, this number had declined to less than 140,000. These figures demonstrate the gradual loss of public interest in NFTs.

Figure 3 and Table 3 refer to the same subsamples and groups classified by the disclosure content and therefore should be read and understood as a set. Figure 3 shows CAAR for the period [−3, 30] days around the disclosure date and Table 3 presents the market response for selected time

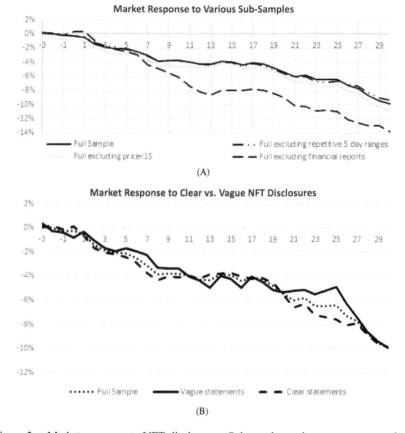

Figure 3: Market response to NFT disclosures: Subsamples and content segmentation. Panel (A) Market response to various sub-samples, panel (B) market response to clear vs. vague disclosures, panel (C) market response to NFT sales vs. platform disclosures, and panel (D) market response to NFT disclosures with and without warnings.

Note: These figures present CAAR for the [−3, 30] time window around the disclosure day, as estimated by the market model. Panel A shows CAAR for various sub-samples and Panels B to D show CAAR for groups classified by disclosure content.

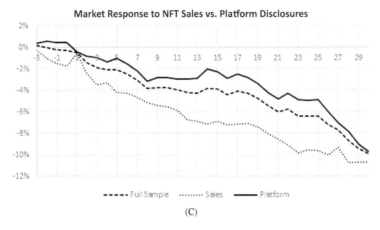

(C)

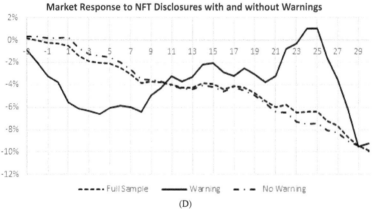

(D)

Figure 3: (*Continued*)

windows around the event. Panels A and B in Table 3 present CAAR calculated using the CAPM market model and adjusted market model,
respectively, as a benchmark. Based on the similarity of the results, I will
refer here only to Panel A.

Figure 3 Panel A shows CAAR for the full sample and three subsample
classifications, as explained in section 3.1: full sample excluding repetitive
5-day ranges, full sample excluding companies whose share price was
below \$1, and full sample excluding financial reports. As can be seen from
the graph and Table 3, Panel A, the full sample and its sub-samples exhibit
similar behavior. There is no significant change in CAAR during days
[0, 1] with CAAR $= -0.26 \%(t = -0.40)$ for the entire sample. However,
CAAR starts to decrease on day 1 and the decrease continues over the next

Table 3: Market response to NFT disclosures — market models — subsamples and content segmentation.

	Panel A: CAAR market model				Panel B: CAAR market adjusted model			
	[−3, −1]	[0, 1]	[2, 6]	[2, 20]	[−3, −1]	[0, 1]	[2, 6]	[2, 20]
Full sample	−0.24% (−0.36)	−0.26% (−0.40)	−1.96% (−2.18**)	−4.93% (−3.69***)	−0.99% (−1.48)	−0.41% (−0.63)	−2.99% (−3.32***)	−8.89% (−7.14***)
N	331	331	331	331	331	331	331	331
Full excluding repetitive 5-day range	−0.12% (−0.17)	−0.27% (−0.40)	−2.10% (−2.23**)	−5.02% (−3.76***)	−0.89% (−1.27)	−0.43% (−0.64)	−3.05% (−3.25***)	−9.03% (−7.06***)
N	309	309	309	309	309	309	309	309
Full excluding price<$1	−0.83% (−1.24)	−0.32% (−0.51)	−1.95% (−2.09**)	−4.93% (−3.64***)	−1.52% (−2.24**)	−0.42% (−0.67)	−2.89% (−3.10***)	−8.62% (−6.74***)
N	305	305	305	305	305	305	305	305
Full excluding financial reports	−0.17% (−0.14)	0.50% (0.46)	−3.27% (−2.10**)	−9.35% (−4.69***)	−0.63% (−0.52)	0.41% (0.38)	−3.70% (−2.37**)	−11.57% (−6.26***)
N	133	133	133	133	133	133	133	133
Clear plans	−0.15% (−0.18)	−0.47% (−0.57)	−2.26% (−1.82*)	−4.90% (−2.96***)	−0.88% (−1.07)	−0.61% (−0.73)	−3.59% (−2.87***)	−9.51% (−6.24***)
N	189	189	189	189	189	189	189	189
Vague plans	−0.37% (−0.33)	0.02% (0.02)	−1.57% (−1.22)	−4.97% (−2.25**)	−1.14% (−1.03)	−0.15% (−0.14)	−2.19% (−1.72*)	−8.06% (−3.89***)
N	189	189	189	189	189	189	189	189

N	142	142	142	142	142	142	142	142
Platform	0.42%	-0.85%	-1.11%	-3.80%	-0.54%	-0.98%	-2.49%	-8.19%
	(0.57)	(-1.15)	(-1.07)	(-2.28**)	(-0.71)	(-1.31)	(-2.36**)	(-5.2***)
N	218	218	218	218	218	218	218	218
Creation & Sales of NFT	-1.52%	0.98%	-3.72%	-7.51%	-1.88%	0.79%	-4.04%	-10.60%
	(-1.12)	(0.80)	(-2.13**)	(-3.33***)	(-1.38)	(0.63)	(-2.35**)	(-5.21***)
N	110	110	110	110	110	110	110	110
Disclosures without warning	0.19%	0.04%	-2.20%	-5.88%	-0.51%	-0.10%	-3.16%	-9.72%
	(0.27)	(0.05)	(-2.20**)	(-4.19***)	(-0.72)	(-0.14)	(-3.18***)	(-7.55***)
N	290	290	290	290	290	290	290	290
Disclosures with Warning	-3.25%	-2.32%	-0.31%	1.78%	-4.43%	-2.62%	-1.80%	-3.00%
	(-1.59)	(-1.29)	(-0.18)	(0.43)	(-2.09**)	(-1.47)	(-0.99)	(-0.73)
N	41	41	41	41	41	41	41	41

Note: This table presents CAAR for the entire sample, selected subsamples, and various sample segmentations based on the disclosure content. For a detailed explanation please refer to Section 3. CAAR was calculated for selected time windows around the event as estimated by both the Market Model and the Market Adjusted Model. The *t*-stats are in parentheses, and ***, **, and * denote significance at the 1%, 5%, and 10% levels, respectively, using two-tailed tests.

30 days. The CAAR for the entire sample is −1.96% (t = −2.18) and −4.93% (t = −3.69) for [2, 6] and [2, 20] time windows respectively. CAAR for the sub-sample without financial reports decreases somewhat faster and reaches −3.27% (t = −2.10) and −9.35% (t = −4.69) for [2, 6] and [2, 20] time windows respectively. This result is not ambiguous: the market "punishes" companies that are involved in NFTs. This is evident in the significant negative CAAR in the days following the disclosure.

I now turn to the groups that were classified by the disclosure content. It seems that investors do not make a distinction between Clear and Vague disclosures, with the market reacting in a similar way to both, as presented in Figure 3 Panel B, and Table 3. CAAR for Clear and Vague disclosures reach a low of −4.9% (t = −2.96) and −4.97% (t = 2.25), respectively, in the [2, 20] time window.

Figure 3 Panel C describes the evolution of CAAR for NFT sales disclosures, which are generally associated with one-off events, in contrast to platform disclosures, which indicate a longer-term engagement in NFTs. Both types of disclosures exhibit a significant CAAR decline through the 30 days after disclosure. The CAAR decline for platform disclosures is slower than for sales disclosures. It may be that investors assume that technology that was developed for a platform could later be used in tangential fields, and therefore the decrease in CAAR is more moderate. CAAR reaches a low of −3.80% (t = −2.28) for platform disclosures and −7.51% (t = −3.33) for sales disclosures during the [2, 20]-daytime window.

The market response to the 41 disclosures that contain warnings (12.4% of the sample) is volatile. It seems that the information about the warning is generally expected, as the market begins to respond at least 3 days before the disclosure, with a low of −6.64% (t = −2.08) on the 4th day after the disclosure. The market then corrects this overreaction with a constant increase in CAAR until the 25th day when CAAR is 1.01% (t = 0.17). CAAR then falls again, reaching a low of −9.23% (t = −1.91) on the 30th day after the disclosure. Disclosures without warning present a constant CAAR decline with −5.88% (t = −4.19) in the [2, 20]-daytime window, which is similar to the entire sample (see Figure 3 Panel D).

5.1. Robustness Tests

To check the robustness of the results, I recalculated CAAR according to the Fama–French three-factor model (Fama and French, 1993). The results are presented in Table 4. As can be seen from the table, the results are very similar to those obtained from the market model and the market-adjusted model. The entire sample exhibits CAAR of −5.01% ($t = −3.79$) for the [2, 20] time window. CAAR for the full sample excluding financial reports decreases faster than the entire sample, reaching a low of −9.10% ($t = −4.40$) in the [2, 20] time window. Clear and Vague disclosures both demonstrate a similar decrease in CAAR with −4.67% ($t = −2.78$) and

Table 4: Market response to NFT disclosures — Fama–French Three-Factor Model — subsamples and content segmentation.

	CAAR Fama–French three-factor model			
	[−3, −1]	[0, 1]	[2, 6]	[2, 20]
Full sample	−0.11%	−0.53%	−1.76%	−5.01%
	(−0.16)	(−0.84)	(−1.95*)	(−3.79***)
N	331	331	331	331
Full excluding repetitive 5-day range	0.02%	−0.49%	−1.91%	−5.25%
	(0.03)	(−0.75)	(−2.04**)	(−3.85***)
N	309	309	309	309
Full excluding price<$1	−0.67%	−0.61%	−1.67%	−4.8%
	(−1.04)	(−1.02)	(−1.78*)	(−3.56***)
N	305	305	305	305
Full excluding financial reports	0.18%	0.10%	−3.26%	−9.1%
	(0.15)	(0.10)	(−2.07**)	(−4.40***)
N	133	133	133	133
Clear statement	−0.01%	−0.59%	−2.10%	−4.67%
	(−0.01)	(−0.71)	(−1.67*)	(−2.78***)
N	189	189	189	189
Vague statement	−0.24%	−0.46%	−1.30%	−5.47%
	(−0.23)	(−0.47)	(−1.03)	(−2.58**)
N	142	142	142	142
Platform	0.66%	−1.10%	−0.66%	−3.41%
	(0.91)	(−1.51)	(−0.65)	(−2.08**)
N	218	218	218	218
Creation & Sales of NFT	−1.60%	0.70%	−3.93%	−8.48%
	(−1.25)	(0.58)	(−2.22**)	(−3.78***)
N	110	110	110	110

(*Continued*)

Table 4:   (*Continued*)

CAAR Fama–French three-factor model			
	[−3, −1]	[0, 1]	[2, 6]	[2, 20]
Disclosures without warning	0.38%	−0.25%	−2.02%	−5.86%
	(0.56)	(−0.37)	(−2.02**)	(−4.17***)
N	290	290	290	290
Disclosures with warning	−3.46%	−2.52%	0.13%	1.04%
	(−1.72*)	(−1.44)	(0.08)	(0.28)
N	41	41	41	41

Note: This table presents CAAR for selected time windows around the event according to the Fama–French (1993) three-factor model. The t-stats are in parentheses, and ***, **, and * denote significance at the 1%, 5%, and 10% levels, respectively, using two-tailed tests. For the remaining definitions, please refer to Table 3.

−5.47% ($t = -2.58$) respectively in the [2, 20] time window. Disclosures of NFT sales exhibit a CAAR of −8.48% ($t = -3.78$) vs. −3.41% ($t = -2.08$) for platform disclosures in the [2, 20] time window. Disclosures without warnings show similar behavior to the entire sample, with a CAAR of −5.86% ($t = -4.17$), and disclosures that contain warnings exhibit a positive yet insignificant CAAR of 1.04% ($t = 0.28$) in the [2, 20]-daytime window.

5.2. *Further Examinations*

Market's reactions to corporate disclosures are often influenced by factors other than the content of the disclosure, such as the timing of the disclosure and firms' financial characteristics. Consequently, it is worthwhile to examine some of these factors.

5.2.1. *Financials and timing*

Financial data enable investors to evaluate a company's performance and potential profitability. In this context, I chose to study the market response to NFTs-related disclosures in terms of companies' *market capitalization* and *free cash flow*. Large companies are likely to have more experienced management, possess greater available resources, and have a larger, more diverse product portfolio. These factors are likely to enhance a large company's potential for future success, as well as attract greater attention from investors. Cash flow is an essential indicator of a company's financial health. Negative free cash flow can indicate potential financial risks and constraints for a company, whereas positive free cash flow suggests financial stability and the ability to invest or distribute profits.

Thus, I classified companies according to their market capitalization 30 days prior to the NFT disclosure, with two size groups: large-cap ("Big") and small-cap ("Small"), composed of companies above and below the median size, respectively. I also classified them based on positive or negative free cash flow in the most recent quarter before the disclosure. I assumed that companies with strong financials receive a more positive response from investors, as investors perceive their ability to leverage NFTs more effectively.

The timing of the disclosure can also be a critical factor in investors' response; hence, I examined three aspects of timing that may have an impact on the market's reaction.

(1) If a company announces its NFT initiatives during a period of high market optimism or positive sentiment, the reaction may be more favorable. Conversely, if the disclosure occurs during a market downturn or negative sentiment, the reaction is likely to be more negative. The current sample includes two distinct periods: a bullish period from March to December 2021, followed by a bearish and more volatile period from December 2021 to August 2022, when my sample ends.

(2) I explore whether the market response differs between disclosures made by Early Adopters — the *"leading"* companies that unveil their NFT information at the very beginning or during the initial wave of NFT disclosures — and disclosures made subsequently by companies considered to be *"lagging."*

(3) In 2021, the Chinese government implemented regulatory measures prohibiting the use of cryptocurrencies, as described in Section 1.3. In May 2021, the country prohibited financial institutions from engaging in any crypto transactions; in June 2021 it banned all domestic crypto mining; and finally outlawed cryptocurrencies outright in September. The Chinese government's crackdown on cryptocurrency and NFTs caused a drop in prices and trading volumes for both. I chose the date May 21, when the regulatory measures began, as a cut-off point and calculated CAAR before and after the Chinese regulation starting

date. It is worth noting that some experts believe that these regulatory measures may ultimately benefit the NFT market in the long run by encouraging more stable and regulated trading practices.

Figure 4 and Table 5 refer to the same groups, segmented by market cap, cashflow, and the timing of the disclosure. Thus, they should be read and understood as a set. Figure 4 depicts CAAR for the period [−3, 30] around the disclosure day and Table 5 presents the market's response for selected time windows around the event. Panels A, B, and C in Table 5 present CAAR calculated using the CAPM market model, the adjusted market model, and the Fama–French three-factor model, respectively,

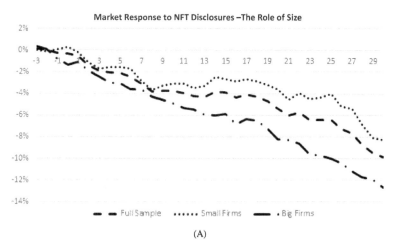

(A)

Figure 4:   Market response to NFT disclosures — Financials and timing. Panel (A) Market response to NFT disclosures — the role of size, panel (B) market response to NFT disclosures — the role of negative/positive free cash flow, panel (C) market response to NFT disclosures during bullish and bearish market sentiment, panel (D) market response to leading vs. lagging disclosures, and panel (E) market response to NFT disclosures — before and after Chinese ban of cryptocurrencies.

Note: These figures present CAAR for the [−3, 30] time window around the disclosure day, as estimated by the market model. Panel A relets to the firms' size. *Small and big* companies are below and above the median of the market capitalization at day $t = -30$. Panel B refers to firms' cash flow. *Negative and positive free cash flow* refer to the most recent quarter before the disclosure date. Panels C–F refers to the disclosure timing. *Leading* disclosures can be regarded as disclosures by "early adopters" of NFTs, while lagging disclosures are issued by "late adopters." March 14, 2022, is the determining point for the division of the two groups. The last segmentation relates to the Chinese government's ban on financial institutions from engaging in any crypto transactions starting on May 21, 2021.

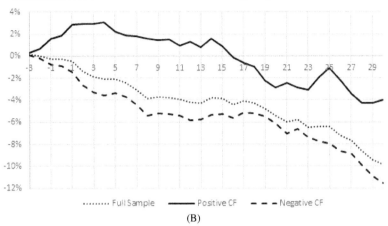

(B)

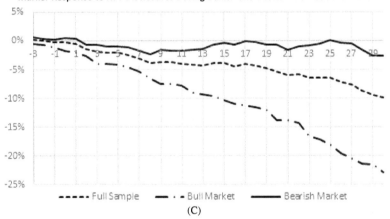

(C)

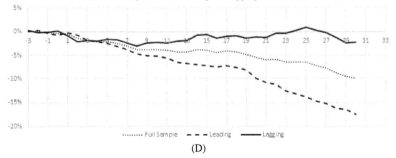

(D)

Figure 4: (*Continued*)

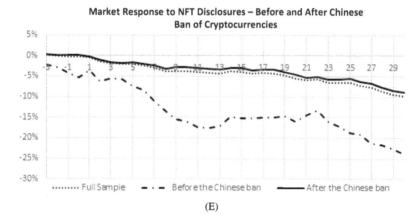

Figure 4: (*Continued*)

Table 5: Market response to NFT disclosures — Financials and timing.

	[−3, −1]	[0, 1]	[2, 6]	[2, 20]
Panel A: CAAR market model				
Small companies	0.06%	−0.22%	−1.03%	−3.47%
	(0.05)	(−0.23)	(−0.66)	(−1.72*)
N	163	163	163	163
Big companies	−0.65%	−0.32%	−2.92%	−6.56%
	(−0.97)	(−0.36)	(−3.13***)	(−3.63***)
N	162	162	162	162
Negative free cash flow	−0.78%	−0.69%	−2.23%	−4.70%
	(−0.94)	(−0.93)	(−2.04**)	(−2.98***)
N	257	257	257	257
Positive free cash flow	1.61%	1.25%	−1.03%	−5.73%
	(2.01**)	(1.03)	(−0.79)	(−2.39**)
N	74	74	74	74
Bull market period	−1.18%	−0.87%	−2.65%	−11.8%
	(−1.5)	(−0.93)	(−1.86*)	(−5.04***)
N	118	118	118	118
Bear market period	0.28%	0.09%	−1.58%	−1.12%
	(0.3)	(0.1)	(−1.37)	(−0.72)
N	231	231	231	231

Table 5: (*Continued*)

	[−3, −1]	[0, 1]	[2, 6]	[2, 20]
Lagging	−0.16%	−0.64%	−0.98%	−0.26%
	(−0.14)	(−0.69)	(−0.72)	(−0.15)
N	166	166	166	166
Leading	−0.33%	0.14%	−2.95%	−9.63%
	(−0.45)	(0.15)	(−2.50**)	(−4.89***)
N	165	165	165	165
After the Chinese ban	0.05%	−0.31%	−1.75%	−4.38%
	(0.07)	(−0.46)	(−1.85*)	(−3.16***)
N	308	308	308	308
Before the Chinese ban	−4.06%	0.44%	−4.82%	−12.33%
	(−1.98*)	(0.21)	(−1.97*)	(−2.59**)
N	23	23	23	23
Panel B: CAAR market-adjusted model				
Small companies	−0.78%	−0.48%	−2.61%	−8.84%
	(−0.66)	(−0.5)	(−1.65)	(−4.7***)
N	163	163	163	163
Big companies	−1.34%	−0.36%	−3.45%	−9.28%
	(−1.92*)	(−0.39)	(−3.74***)	(−5.54***)
N	162	162	162	162
Negative free cash flow	−1.52%	−0.84%	−3.32%	−8.94%
	(−1.84*)	(−1.11)	(−3.02***)	(−6.07***)
N	257	257	257	257
Positive free cash flow	0.83%	1.09%	−1.83%	−8.70%
	(0.93)	(0.89)	(−1.46)	(−3.98***)
N	74	74	74	74
Bull market period	−1.03%	−0.63%	−2.44%	−10.82%
	(−1.32)	(−0.67)	(−1.73**)	(−5.2***)
N	118	118	118	118
Bear market period	−0.97%	−0.29%	−3.3%	−7.81%
	(−1.02)	(−0.33)	(−2.84)	(−5.05)
N	231	231	231	231

(*Continued*)

Table 5:   (*Continued*)

Lagging	−1.45%	−1.15%	−3.03%	−8.28%
	(−1.28)	(−1.23)	(−2.21**)	(−4.69***)
N	166	166	166	166
Leading	−0.53%	0.34%	−2.96%	−9.50%
	(−0.74)	(0.38)	(−2.54**)	(−5.42***)
N	165	165	165	165
After the Chinese ban	−0.77%	−0.52%	−2.92%	−8.94%
	(−1.10)	(−0.77)	(−3.07***)	(−6.91***)
N	308	308	308	308
Before the Chinese ban	−3.92%	1.05%	−3.96%	−8.22%
	(−1.96*)	(0.50)	(−1.67)	(−1.82*)
N	23	23	23	23

Panel C: CAAR Fama–French three-factor model

Small companies	0.3%	−0.53%	−0.75%	−3.67%
	(0.26)	(−0.56)	(−0.48)	(−1.84*)
N	163	163	163	163
Big companies	−0.6%	−0.58%	−2.85%	−6.67%
	(−0.98)	(−0.67)	(−3.04***)	(−3.75***)
N	162	162	162	162
Negative free cash flow	−0.62%	−1.01%	−1.94%	−4.79%
	(−0.77)	(−1.38)	(−1.77*)	(−3.07***)
N	257	257	257	257
Positive free cash flow	1.67%	1.15%	−1.10%	−5.76%
	(2.17**)	(0.96)	(−0.84)	(−2.46**)
N	74	74	74	74
Bull market period	−0.45%	−0.6%	−1.64%	−8.58%
	(−0.57)	(−0.68)	(−1.2)	(−3.87***)
N	118	118	118	118
Bear market period	0.09%	−0.49%	−1.82%	−3.03%
	(0.1)	(−0.58)	(−1.55)	(−1.55)
N	231	231	231	231
	[−3, −1]	[0, 1]	[2, 6]	[2, 20]

Table 5: (*Continued*)

Lagging	−0.37%	−1.11%	−1.20%	−2.50%
	(−0.35)	(−1.23)	(−0.88)	(−1.44)
N	166	166	166	166
Leading	0.17%	0.06%	−2.32%	−7.54%
	(0.23)	(0.06)	(−1.96**)	(−3.82***)
N	165	165	165	165
After the Chinese ban	0.15%	−0.58%	−1.60%	−4.54%
	(0.23)	(−0.88)	(−1.68*)	(−3.32***)
N	308	308	308	308
Before the Chinese ban	−3.47%	0.17%	−3.87%	−11.26%
	(−1.58)	(0.09)	(−1.63)	(−2.30**)
N	23	23	23	23

Note: This table presents CAAR estimations for various time windows and sample segmentations. Panels A, B, and C present CAAR that was calculated by the market model, the market-adjusted model, and the Fama–French three-factor model, respectively. *Small and big* companies are below and above the median of the market capitalization at day $t = -30$. *Negative and positive free cash flow* refer to the most recent quarter before the disclosure date. *Leading* disclosures can be regarded as disclosures by "early adopters" of NFTs, while lagging disclosures are issued by "late adopters." March 14, 2022, is the determining point for the division of the two groups. The last segmentation relates to the Chinese government's ban on financial institutions from engaging in any crypto transactions starting on May 21, 2021. The *t*-stats are in parentheses. ***, **, and * denote significance at the 1%, 5%, and 10% levels, respectively, using two-tailed tests.

as a benchmark. Due to the similarity of the results, I will refer here only to Panel A of Table 5 results.

Figure 4, Panel A, indicates a decline in CAAR from day 1 onwards for both groups: small-cap and big-cap companies. Contrary to my assumption that big-cap companies would perform better, they underperform the small companies with a CAAR of −6.56% ($t = -3.63$) vs. −3.47% ($t = -1.72$) in the [2, 20] time window (Table 5, Panel A).

Free cash flow appears to be a more prominent factor in its effect on the market's reaction to disclosures, as can be seen in Figure 4, Panel B. Companies with positive free cash flow experienced an increase in CAAR over the six days from day −3, with a CAAR of 1.61% ($t = 2.01$) in the [−3, −1] time window. From day 3 onwards, CAAR started to decline,

262   *S. Siev*

turning negative on the 16th day. CAAR for [0, 1] time window is 1.25% ($t = 1.03$) for the positive free cash flow group, compared with −0.69% ($t = -0.93$) for the negative free cash flow group (Table 5, Panel A). The picture reversed completely in the [2, 20] time window, with CAAR of −5.73% ($t = -2.39$) for the positive free cash flow group and −4.70% ($t = -2.98$) for the negative free cash flow group. It is interesting to note that most of the disclosures, 257 out of 331 (78%), were submitted by companies with negative cash flow. To summarize, the positive reaction to disclosures from companies with positive cash flow is short-lived, slowing down the rate of CAAR decline but not preventing it. In the end, investors express their lack of confidence in NFT-related activity, resulting in a negative CAAR. This lends further support to the conclusion that NFT-related activity is received poorly by investors.

I turn now to the segmentation according to the timing of disclosures. As described earlier, the current sample spans the period from March 2021 to August 2022, which is a relatively short period of 18 months. The market was bullish for the first ten months but turned bearish in the last eight months. These periods largely overlap with the classification into leading (the first 12 months) and lagging (the last 6). Therefore, I analyzed both classifications simultaneously. Since the abnormal return is measured vs. a market index, investors' negative reaction to NFT disclosures is more pronounced during a bull market period. This is clear from the fast decline in CAAR during the bullish period relative to the response observed during the bear market period when benchmark indices are already declining. See Figure 4, Panel C.

The same trend can be seen in Figure 4, Panel D. The CAAR of leading companies, as mentioned above, is measured largely in the period of the bull market. It deteriorates faster than that of lagging companies (mainly during the bear market period) whose CAAR does not significantly differ from zero. Table 5 Panel A shows that lagging companies exhibit CAARs of −0.98% ($t = -0.72$) and −0.26% ($t = -0.15$) in the time windows [2, 6] and [2, 20] vs. leading companies whose CAAR is −2.95% ($t = -2.50$) and −9.63% ($t = -4.89$), for the respective periods.

The last distinction regarding timing refers to the period before and after the Chinese ban on cryptocurrency transactions and mining activities which, like leading and lagging, partly overlap the periods of bullish and bearish market sentiment. As shown in Figure 4, Panel E, prior to the ban, the CAAR exhibited a faster decline after NFT-related disclosures, reaching a low of −25.22% ($t = -3.31$) within the [−3, 30] time window around the date of the disclosure. After the ban, the market's response was less severe, with a decline of −8.78% ($t = -4.44$) during the same period.

The market reaction is somewhat surprising, as one might have expected a more pronounced negative response following the ban due to increased uncertainty in NFT markets. However, it is important to interpret these results with caution, given that only 23 companies (7%) were included in the sample that submitted disclosures before the ban. Moreover, as mentioned earlier, these periods largely overlapped with bullish and bearish periods in capital markets.

5.2.2. *Headquarters and sectors*

More factors worth examining are the location of a company's *headquarters* and the *sector* to which the company belongs. Headquarters location can influence investor sentiment, as it may provide insights into the regulatory environment, market accessibility, and the company's strategic positioning. Different sectors may vary due to their unique risks and regulations.

Figure 5, Panel A provides a clear visualization of the average market reaction to NFT disclosures across various sectors within the sample. Notably, the technology sector, which comprises 29% of the companies in the sample, demonstrates the fastest and largest deterioration of CAAR within the [−3, 30] time window, reaching a low of −13.00% ($t = -3.70$). On the other hand, the financial services sector, which comprises 7.5% of the sample, exhibits a positive yet insignificant CAAR until day 26. Over the [2, 20]-daytime window, the communication services industry presents the largest negative CAAR of −6.84% ($t = -2.74$), followed by the consumer cyclical industry with a CAAR of −4.91% ($t = -1.69$) and the technology industry with CAAR of −4.40% ($t = -1.63$). These findings are summarized in Table 6 Panel A.

The role of location is presented in Figure 5, Panel B. Among the 109 companies, 75 companies (69%) are headquartered in the United States, whereas 25 companies (23%) are based in China, representing a three-fold difference. Chinese companies display the highest underperformance relative to the market with a CAAR of −9.21% ($t = -2.70$) for the [2, 20]

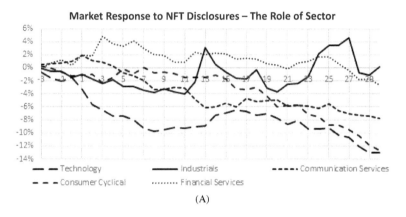

(A)

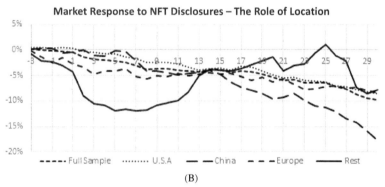

(B)

Figure 5: Panel (A) Market response to NFT disclosures — the role of sector and panel (B) market response to NFT disclosures — the role of location.

Table 6: Market response to NFT disclosures — Industry and headquarters locations.

	[−3, −1]	[0, 1]	[2, 6]	[2, 20]
Panel A: CAAR market model				
Communication services	0.81%	1.13%	−3.18%	−6.84%
	(0.79)	(1.03)	(−2.47**)	(−2.74***)
N	97	97	97	97
Technology	−2.00%	−1.37%	−4.59%	−4.40%
	(−1.20)	(−1.03)	(−2.32**)	(−1.63)
N	95	95	95	95

Table 6: (*Continued*)

	[−3, −1]	[0, 1]	[2, 6]	[2, 20]
Consumer cyclical	−0.7%	−0.38%	0.22%	−4.91%
	(−0.62)	(−0.26)	(0.11)	(−1.69*)
N	79	79	79	79
Financial services	1.21%	0.70%	2.26%	−1.45%
	(0.61)	(0.41)	(0.95)	(−0.41)
N	25	25	25	25
Industrials	−0.50%	−0.55%	−1.87%	−2.66%
	(−0.26)	(−0.24)	(−0.63)	(−0.71)
N	18	18	18	18
USA	0.22%	0.10%	−1.79%	−5.25%
	(0.30)	(0.12)	(−1.80*)	(−3.23***)
N	223	223	223	223
China	0.22%	−0.69%	0.18%	−9.21%
	(0.22)	(−0.39)	(0.07)	(−2.70***)
N	50	50	50	50
Europe	−2.43%	−0.32%	−0.93%	−3.63%
	(−2.34**)	(−0.34)	(−0.67)	(−1.65)
N	26	26	26	26
Rest	−2.33%	−2.02%	−7.35%	2.91%
	(−0.53)	(−1.01)	(−1.54)	(0.54)
N	32	32	32	32

Panel B: CAAR market-adjusted model

	[−3, −1]	[0, 1]	[2, 6]	[2, 20]
Communication services	−0.13%	0.57%	−4.32%	−12.04%
	(−0.12)	(0.52)	(−3.42***)	(−5.16***)
N	97	97	97	97
Technology	−3.07%	−1.65%	−6.11%	−9.93%
	(−1.82*)	(−1.23)	(−3.10***)	(−3.74***)
N	95	95	95	95
Consumer cyclical	−0.88%	0.05%	−0.17%	−6.10%
	(−0.79)	(0.03)	(−0.08)	(−2.46**)
N	79	79	79	79

(*Continued*)

Table 6:   (Continued)

	[−3, −1]	[0, 1]	[2, 6]	[2, 20]
Financial services	0.52%	0.69%	2.31%	−1.81%
	(0.26)	(0.40)	(0.98)	(−0.67)
N	25	25	25	25
Industrials	−1.17%	−0.98%	−4.91%	−9.63%
	(−0.57)	(−0.43)	(−1.55)	(−2.58**)
N	18	18	18	18
USA	−0.57%	−0.06%	−2.60%	−9.25%
	(−0.79)	(−0.07)	(−2.63***)	(−6.17***)
N	223	223	223	223
China	−0.21%	−0.48%	−1.09%	−11.80%
	(−0.21)	(−0.28)	(−0.45)	(−3.87***)
N	50	50	50	50
Europe	−2.94%	−0.78%	−1.93%	−6.91%
	(−2.96***)	(−0.86)	(−1.34)	(−3.11***)
N	26	26	26	26
Rest	−3.59%	−2.42%	−9.59%	−3.40%
	(−0.82)	(−1.23)	(−2.03*)	(−0.63)
N	32	32	32	32

Panel C: CAAR Fama–French three-factor model

	[−3, −1]	[0, 1]	[2, 6]	[2, 20]
Communication services	0.95%	0.68%	−3.10%	−6.58%
	(0.98)	(0.63)	(−2.37**)	(−2.65***)
N	97	97	97	97
Technology	−1.49%	−1.86%	−3.89%	−4.86%
	(−0.93)	(−1.42)	(−1.97*)	(−1.79*)
N	95	95	95	95
Consumer cyclical	−1.03%	−0.10%	0.30%	−5.24%
	(−0.92)	(−0.07)	(0.15)	(−1.87*)
N	79	79	79	79
Financial services	1.18%	0.38%	2.39%	−0.51%
	(0.61)	(0.23)	(1.05)	(−0.16)
N	25	25	25	25

Table 6: (*Continued*)

	[−3, −1]	[0, 1]	[2, 6]	[2, 20]
Industrials	−0.47%	−0.40%	−2.17%	−3.90%
	(−0.25)	(−0.17)	(−0.73)	(−0.99)
N	18	18	18	18
USA	0.28%	−0.14%	−1.75%	−5.62%
	(0.42)	(−0.17)	(−1.78*)	(−3.56***)
N	223	223	223	223
China	0.44%	−0.82%	1.31%	−7.37%
	(0.43)	(−0.49)	(0.59)	(−2.26**)
N	50	50	50	50
Europe	−2.66%	−0.57%	−1.07%	−4.10%
	(−2.54**)	(−0.63)	(−0.82)	(−1.9*)
N	26	26	26	26
Rest	−1.53%	−2.79%	−7.11%	2.18%
	(−0.36)	(−1.32)	(−1.43)	(0.38)
N	32	32	32	32

Note: This table presents CAAR based on companies' segmentation due to their sector and headquarters location. Panel A presents CAAR estimations calculated by the market model, Panel B by the market-adjusted model, and Panel C by the Fama–French three-factor model. The CAAR is calculated for selected time windows around the event, *t*-stats are in parentheses, and ***, **, and * denote significance at the 1%, 5%, and 10% levels, respectively, using two-tailed tests.

period, vs. −5.25% (−3.23) in the U.S. and −3.63% ($t = -1.65$) in Europe. This suggests that Chinese companies are the most affected by the Chinese regulation, and thus exhibit weaker market performance compared to their counterparts.

6. Summary and Conclusions

NFTs are a relatively new and evolving concept, and market participants may have varying perceptions and sentiments regarding their value and potential. Examining the market's response to NFT disclosures can shed light on how investors interpret and evaluate the strategic importance of NFTs for different types of companies. It can also provide insights into market sentiment toward NFT-related developments and their perceived impact on a company's prospects. This study is the first known effort to examine the market's reaction to NFT-related disclosures between March 2021 and August 2022 using an event study methodology and employing three benchmarks for calculating the abnormal return: the market model, the market-adjusted model, and the Fama–French three-factor model. The overall picture that emerges from the various analyses is unambiguous. There is a constant CAAR decline from day 1 onward with a significant negative CAAR of -4.93% ($t = -3.69$) during the [2, 20] time window for the entire sample.

The message conveyed by these results is clear: the market does not believe that corporate involvement in NFTs is beneficial, thus leading to a negative CAAR in the days following disclosures. Interestingly, despite the decisive reaction in the weeks after the disclosure, the CAAR on the day of the event itself and the subsequent day is not statistically significant.

The delayed response from the market could indicate a lower level of market efficiency which can be attributed to the newness and relatively niche nature of the NFT market. Many investors may not yet possess a comprehensive understanding of NFTs and their implications. However, as investors are given more time to react, they may begin considering other relevant uncertainties associated with NFTs. These uncertainties include the loosely regulated nature of the NFT market and potential legal issues related to intellectual property, contract law, and taxation. Taking these uncertainties into account, it is plausible that the subsequent days could witness a significant negative CAAR as investors weigh these factors and reassess their position.

Factors such as the specific content of the NFT-related disclosures, the characteristics of the sample companies, and broader market conditions have been investigated and appear to play a role in the market's reaction to NFT-related disclosures.

As the NFT market continues to evolve and investors gain a deeper understanding of its complexities, future studies could extend the period investigated and engage in an in-depth investigation of the factors that may drive the abnormal returns experienced around NFT disclosures. Will the NFT market prove to be a lucrative opportunity for investors, or will it be perceived as a cynical and environmentally detrimental scam? Only time will tell.

Appendix A. Sample Screening Procedure

	Observations
Total extractions from the SEC website	**1,916**
Less	
Trusts/Funds/EFT's	735
Not relevant	392
OTC (67 companies)	369
Multiple identical disclosures sent on the same day	83
Price data is missing	6
Final sample	**331**

Note: This table outlines the process used to create the sample, starting with 1916 disclosures obtained from the SEC website and culminating in the 331 disclosures considered after the filtering process.

Appendix B. Clear and Vague Disclosures

Examples for *"Clear"* Disclosures

AeroCentury Corp. (ACY) December 10, 2021

..."AeroCentury" or the "Company" (NYSE American: ACY), today announced that it launched its GameFi business in the metaverse ecosystem through its wholly-owned subsidiary, Mega Metaverse Corp... MEGA plans to release its first NFT game "Mano" in first quarter of 2022. Mano is a competitive idle role-playing game (RPG) deploying the concept of GameFi in the innovative combination of NFTs (non-fungible token) and DeFi (decentralized finance) based on blockchain technology, with a "Play-to-earn" model that the players can earn while they play in MEGA's metaverse universe "alSpace". The Company believes it is the first NYSE AMEX listed company with GameFi business operations..."

CompoSecure, Inc. (CMPO) May 9, 2022

"...Key Highlights — Q1 2022 Adjusted EBITDA1 of $33M, 14% higher than Q1 '21 due to increased customer acquisitions by our clients and a focus on operational excellence and process improvement Strong momentum from Fintechs and traditional banks in the payment card business along with initial Arculus B2B momentum from multiple cryptocurrency platforms selecting Arculus as their digital authentication partner Significant enhancements for Arculus wallet enabling NFT viewing, sending, and receiving, connection to DeFi..."

Examples for "*Vague*" Disclosures

AGM GROUP HOLDINGS, INC. (AGMH) June 30, 2021

"...In blockchain and fintech application areas, we launched a financial training network web service back to June 2019. It targets the beginner and intermediate users and help them to improve their basic trading skills and be more familiar with knowledge of modern trading software and financial markets. Fintech product team remain actively research and seek opportunities to introduce blockchain-based NFT and Defi technologies into existing products, aiming to provide more values to clients and bring more knowledge of blockchain and crypto assets to clients..."

GameStop Corp. (GME) December 8, 2021

"... We are pursuing, and expect to continue to pursue, business and strategic initiatives, some of which may expose us to new or enhanced risks. For example, we are exploring opportunities in blockchain, NFT, and Web 3.0 technology..."

Appendix C. Sales of NFTs vs. a Long-Term Approach (Platform or Marketplace) Disclosures

Examples for *NFT sale* (248,824)

Allied Esports Entertainment, Inc. (AESE) August 15, 2022

"...The Company's NFT revenue was generated from the sale of non-fungible tokens (NFTs). The Company's NFTs exist on the Ethereum

Blockchain under the Company's EPICBEAST brand, a digital art collection of 1,958 unique beasts inspired by past and present e-sport games. The Company uses the NFT exchange, OpenSea, to facilitate its sales of NFTs. The Company, through OpenSea, has custody and control of the NFT prior to the delivery to the customer and records revenue at a point in time when the NFT is delivered to the customer and the customer pays. The Company has no obligations for returns, refunds or warranty after the NFT sale..."

AMC ENTERTAINMENT HOLDINGS, INC. (AMC) March 1, 2022

".... During the fourth quarter of 2021, we partnered with Sony Pictures to become the first theatrical exhibition company to offer AMC Stubs members a limited number of exclusive Spider-Man: No Way Home non-fungible tokens ("NFTs") based on a ticket purchase and redemption of a Spider-Man ticket on the opening night of the film. Some 86,000 exclusive and limited edition NFTs offer guests a tradeable collectible commemorating the most successful film of 2021. This NFT is tradeable and in the future will offer discounts or other benefits to the then-current holders to generate future attendance. We will continue to implement innovative NFT offers to further engage and build loyalty with our guests."

Examples of NFT Platform

Medigus Ltd. (MDGS) October 13, 2021

"Medigus Enters NFT Space with a First Investment in Blockchain Company Safee Medigus to invest $400,000 in Safee, an NFT-based ownership social network aiming to bring its unique technology to mass market creators and audiences..."

Mogo Inc. (MOGO) March 23, 2022

".... On January 11, 2022, Mogo announced a strategic investment in NFT Trader. Mogo's initial investment is through a convertible note which, if converted, will represent a 25% interest in NFT Trader. Mogo also has an option to acquire an additional interest in NFT Trader through a secondary purchase from the founders of NFT Trader of 25% within six months of the initial investment. ...."

Appendix D. Warning Disclosures

> **Dunxin Financial Holdings Ltd (DXF)** May 2, 2022
>
> "... For example, NFTs raise various intellectual property law considerations, including adequacy and scope of assignment, licensing, transfer, copyright, and other right of use issues. The creator of an NFT will often have all rights to the content of the NFT and can determine what rights to assign to a buyer, such as the right to display, modify, or copy the content. To the extent we are directly or indirectly involved in a dispute between creators and buyers on our NFT platform, it could materially and adversely affect the success of our NFT platform and harm our business and reputation. NFTs, and our NFT platform, may also be an attractive target for cybersecurity attacks. For example, a perpetrator could seek to obtain the private key associated with a digital wallet holding an NFT to access and sell the NFT without valid authorization, and the owner of the NFT may have limited recourse due to the nature of blockchain transactions and of cybercrimes generally. NFT marketplaces, including our NFT platform, may also be vulnerable to attacks where an unauthorized party acquires the necessary credentials to access user accounts. The safeguards we may implement in the future to protect against cybersecurity threats may be insufficient. If our NFT platform were to experience any cyberattacks, it could negatively impact our reputation and market acceptance of our platform. We, or our service providers, may deposit, transfer, and custody customer's NFT in multiple jurisdictions..."

References

Aharon, D. Y., Demir, E., and Siev, S. (2022). Real returns from unreal world? Market reaction to Metaverse disclosures. *Research in International Business and Finance*, 63, 101778.

BCC Research (2022, November). Non-fungible tokens (NFT). Global market (report no. IFT248A). Retrieved from https://www.bccresearch.com/market-research/information-technology/nft-market.html.

Cahill, D., Baur, D.G., Liu, Z.F., and Yang, J.W. (2020). I am a blockchain too: How does the market respond to companies' interest in blockchain? *Journal of Banking & Finance*, 113, 105740.

Cheng, S.F., De Franco, G., Jiang, H., and Lin, P. (2019). Riding the blockchain mania: Public firms' speculative 8-K disclosures. *Management Science*, 65(12), 5901–5913.

DappRadar (2022). DappRadar 2022 industry report. Retrieved from https://dappradar.com/blog/dapp-industry-report-2022-dapp-industry-proves-resilient-in-crypto-winter.

EMERGEN Research (2022, December). Non-fungible token market, by category (collectibles, utility, art, metaverse, game), by application (real estate, medical, academic, gaming), and by region forecast to 2030. Retrieved from https://www.emergenresearch.com/industry-report/non-fungible-token-market.

Fama, E.F. and French, K.R. (1993). Common risk factors in the returns on stocks and bonds. *Journal of Financial Economics*, 33(1), 3–56.

Grand View Research (2022, April). Non-fungible token market size worth $211.72 Billion By 2030. Retrieved from https://www.grandviewresearch.com/press-release/global-non-fungible-token-market.

Hildobby (2022, December). Analysis NFT wash trading on ethereum. Retrieved from https://community.dune.com/blog/nft-wash-trading-on-ethereum.

Klöckner, M., Schmidt, C.G., and Wagner, S.M. (2022). When blockchain creates shareholder value: Empirical evidence from international company announcements. *Production and Operations Management*, 31(1), 46–64.

Laycock, R. (2022, October), NFT statistics. Finder's NFT adoption report: 2.8% of American internet users own NFTs. Retrieved from https://www.finder.com/nft-statistics.

Luo, J., Jia, Y., and Liu, X. (2022). Understanding NFT price moves through social media keywords analysis. arXiv preprint arXiv:2209.07706.

Pinto-Gutiérrez, C., Gaitán, S., Jaramillo, D., and Velasquez, S. (2022). The NFT hype: What draws attention to non-fungible tokens? *Mathematics*, 10(3), 335.

Radman, M. (2023). The market that was not: This is how the world of digital art revolved around the NFT. *Globes*, 22 (in Hebrew).

Von Wachter, V., Jensen, J.R., Regner, F., and Ross, O. (2022). NFT wash trading: Quantifying suspicious behaviour in NFT markets. arXiv preprint arXiv:2202.03866.

Yen, J.C. and Wang, T. (2021). Stock price relevance of voluntary disclosures about blockchain technology and cryptocurrencies. *International Journal of Accounting Information Systems*, 40, 100499.

https://doi.org/10.1142/9789811290633_0012

Chapter 12

The Alternative Meat Industry: Fad or Disruption?

Shlomith D. Zuta

The Academic College of Tel Aviv-Yaffo, Tel-Aviv, Israel
shlomitz@mta.ac.il

Abstract

Consumption of plant-based meat has been booming over the past few years, accompanied by surging interest on the part of investors, traditional meat producers, and the media. But is the alternative meat industry a true disruptive force in the meat industry, or is it just a fad? The case sets out to explore this question. Following an introduction of the issue at hand, it provides an overview of the reasons for the increase in popularity of meat substitutes. Next, industry structure and competition are explored. An examination of the different types of investors is warranted since behavioral considerations might govern some of their decisions. The case concludes with a discussion of the challenges facing the industry and potential policy issues.

Keywords: Alternative meat, Disruptive innovation, Market transition, Investments

1. Introduction

I do think that all rich countries should move to 100% synthetic beef.

— Bill Gates, February 14, 2021 (Temple, 2021).

The third-most impactful industry is the animal agriculture industry.
And we have to find a better way to source protein for people.

— Prince Khaled bin Alwaleed of Saudi Arabia,
February 11, 2020 (Turak, 2020).

The alternative meat industry has been all the rage over the past few years. But is this industry a true disruptive force in the meat industry, or is alternative meat just a blip in the history of meat? Should CEOs of large traditional meat companies be worried, devising strategies to fight back, or can they dismiss the threat? This is the question at hand.

The popularity of meat substitutes is part of a growing trend toward plant-based diets (Kerle, 2021). Over the past few years, consumption of plant-based proteins has been booming and the onset of the COVID-19 pandemic gave plant-based products a boost, with young people leading the way. Boston Consulting Group estimates that by 2035 at least 11% of the global protein market will be alternative (Morach *et al.*, 2021). A sign that animal-free diets are in vogue is the menu at one of New York City's most prestigious restaurants. Eleven Park Madison, a Michelin 3-star restaurant, is offering, as of June 2021, a plant-based tasting menu at $335 per person, and reservations are hard to come by.[1]

Consumer demand for plant-based meat, in particular, is surging. According to The Good Food Institute, global sales of plant-based meat grew 24% in 2020 to $4.2 billion, up from $3.4 billion in 2019. In the U.S., sales grew 45%, from $962 million in 2019 to $1.4 billion in 2020. Looking into the future, projections regarding market size and growth as well as market share are optimistic, to different degrees. Union Bank of Switzerland (UBS) projects a market size of $85 billion in 2030 with an impressive compound annual growth rate (CAGR) of 28%, noting that this estimate might be conservative (Khan, 2019). A. T. Kearney holds a particularly bullish view. The company projects that by 2040, alternative meat will constitute 60% of the global meat market (Gerhardt, 2020; Warschun *et al.*, 2020).

In spite of its rapid growth, the alternative meat market accounts currently for only about 1% of the total meat market. However, demographics are in favor of this sector. A U.S. survey found that young people are

---

[1] https://www.elevenmadisonpark.com.

the largest consumers of alternative meat and the most inclined to increase their consumption, with 54% of U.S. consumers aged 24–39 self-identifying as meat reducers vs. 47% of U.S. consumers of all ages (Sprouts Farmers Market, 2021). A U.K. survey reveals similar trends — an increase in the number of people adopting a meat-free diet, with young people most likely to follow this lifestyle (Johnson, 2021). Exposure to plant-based meat is high: a Gallup poll found that 41% of Americans have tried plant-based meat, with an even higher exposure among upper-income, young adults, and suburbanites (McCarthy and Decoster, 2020a). This reflects the transition of alternative meat from a niche product to the mainstream.

The increase in demand for alternative meat has brought about a proliferation of outlets selling it, both retail and food service. Plant-based meat products can now be purchased in grocery stores and supermarkets such as Kroger, Whole Foods, and Costco as well as in restaurants — primarily fast-food restaurants such as McDonald's, Pizza Hut, and Burger King. The variety of alternative meat products is increasing at a fast pace as well. Existing products include burgers, meatballs, sausages, and chicken, and new products are rolled out frequently, though the holy grail of sizzling steak is yet to come.

Investment has skyrocketed as well, running the gamut from corporate behemoths to the public at large. Early backers, who recognized the industry's market potential over a decade ago, include high-tech moguls and financiers such as Bill Gates of Microsoft and Sergey Brin of Google. Nowadays, venture capital funds and others investing in private alternative meat companies abound. Some investors, especially angel investors, might have been guided, at least in part, by behavioral and non-financial considerations such as climate change, food insecurity, health, sentiment, and animal welfare.

Contributing to industry visibility and attracting media interest was the successful Initial Public Offering of Beyond Meat, a dedicated plant-based meat company and a market leader in the space, in May 2019, at a valuation of $1.5 billion. This IPO was the entry point of the public to the space of alternative meat. So why is the alternative meat market expanding at such a high rate and spurring so much interest on the part of consumers, investors, and the media? Will the novelty of alternative meat wear off or will the growth in consumption continue to the point where it poses a real threat to the traditional meat industry?

2. The Meat Industry

Meat is a staple food in Western diets and is fast becoming more and more popular in developing countries.[2] Since the early 1970s, per capita meat consumption has almost tripled, with the increase stemming in large part from the growing middle class in Southeast Asia (particularly China and India) (FAO, 2017; OECD-FAO, 2017). Looking ahead, a 2021 OECD-FAO report projects further growth in global consumption of meat proteins in the coming decade, driven largely by income and population growth (OECD-FAO, 2021).[3,4]

At the same time, the 2021 OECD-FAO report anticipates some dietary shifts in consumption over the coming decade. In particular, per capita consumption of animal-based proteins in high-income countries is expected to level off. Moreover, the report projects a shift away from animal-based products and toward plant-based ones among young consumers in high-income countries. Consequently, vegetarian, vegan or "flexitarian" lifestyles are expected to be on the rise among these consumers.

As noted earlier, consumption of alternative meat has already been on the rise. In what follows, the reasons for this trend, and how COVID-19 has impacted it, will be described and substantiated.

The reasons for the increase in demand for alternative meat over the past few years are three-fold. First, an increasing understanding of the detrimental effects of meat production on the environment. Second, an enhanced awareness of the impact of meat consumption on human health. Third, a growing concern for animal welfare. The onset of the COVID-19 pandemic further fueled the demand, providing a body of evidence regarding the environmental hazards inflicted by the animal industry. These hazards range from greenhouse gas emissions to loss of biodiversity, with the latter likely to have been a major factor in the emergence of COVID-19.

---

[2] The term "meat" refers to all types of meat, including beef, pork, poultry, lamb, etc., but does not refer to fish. The term "livestock" refers to all types of meat as defined above with the exception of poultry. The impacts discussed in this chapter are most pronounced for livestock.

[3] United Nations, Department of Economic and Social Affairs, Population Division (2015). Population 2030: Demographic challenges and opportunities for sustainable development planning (ST/ESA/SER.A/389).

[4] The United Nations projects a population of 8.6 billion in 2030, compared to 7.9 in 2021.

What is this body of evidence? Let us examine it briefly, starting with the environmental impacts of the meat industry.

According to a report by the Food and Agriculture Organization (FAO) of the United Nations, the contribution of animal agriculture to global warming, air pollution, land and water depletion, and biodiversity loss is enormous (Steinfeld *et al.*, 2006; Gerber *et al.*, 2013; For European data see Leip *et al.*, 2015). The report, appropriately titled "Livestock's Long Shadow," singles out the animal industry as "one of the top two or three most significant contributors to the most serious environmental problems, at every scale from local to global" (Wynes and Nicholas, 2017).

Starting with greenhouse gas emissions, the essence of livestock's impact on climate change was succinctly captured by *The Economist*: "Treating cattle like coal would make a big dent in greenhouse-gas emissions" (*The Economist*, 2021). Livestock supply chains account for 14.5% of global greenhouse gas emissions originating from human activity (Masson-Delmotte *et al.*, 2018; Crippa *et al.*, 2021; McClure, 2021; On the accelerating increase in emissions, see World Meteorological Organization, 2021).[5-8] This compares with 14% of global anthropogenic emissions from the transportation sector as a whole (United States Environmental Protection Agency, 2023; For the impact of the global food system see Clark *et al.*, 2020).

What's more, the role of livestock in methane emissions is especially significant. Livestock contributes about 37% of methane emissions originating from human activity (Steinfeld *et al.*, 2006; For Europe, see Leip, 2015).[9] This is crucial since methane is a potent greenhouse gas that has at least 80 times more warming power than carbon dioxide over a 20-year period (UNECE, 2021; UNEP, 2021). In the words of Senator

---

[5] Cattle are responsible for about two-thirds of that total, largely due to their methane emissions. About 44% of livestock emissions are in the form of methane.

[6] Key Facts and Figures", FAO website, http://www.fao.org/news/story/en/item/197623/icode/.

[7] More generally, a third of global greenhouse gas emissions come from the food system.

[8] Moreover, the amount of greenhouse gas emissions originating in animal agriculture is increasing. To illustrate, greenhouse gases released by New Zealand's cows on New Zealand dairy farms just hit an all-time high.

[9] Livestock contributes about 9% of total carbon dioxide emissions, 37% methane, and 65% nitrous oxide.

Chuck Schumer, "Methane is like carbon dioxide on steroids" (Tabushi, 2021). Although methane has received less attention than carbon dioxide so far, recent reports have been shining the spotlight on its impact on climate change. According to the 2021 Intergovernmental Panel on Climate Change (IPCC) report, at least a third (a half by some estimates) of global warming originates in methane (Masson-Delmotte, 2021). The UN Emissions Gap Report 2021 concludes that since methane is relatively short-lived, slashing methane emissions would significantly contribute to reducing global warming in the near term (United Nations Environment Programme, 2021).[10] John Kerry, the US climate envoy, called cutting methane the "single fastest strategy that we have to keep a safer, 1.5-degree centigrade future within reach," referring to the target of the 2015 Paris Agreement to limit global warming to 1.5 degrees centigrade compared to pre-industrial levels (Friedman, 2021). Indeed, at COP26, the 2021 United Nations climate change conference, more than 100 countries pledged to reduce methane emissions by 30% by 2030.

In light of the leading role of livestock in methane emissions, and in turn the impact of methane emissions on global warming, an obvious way to achieve this goal would be to reduce animal-based proteins in our diet. Indeed, the UN Emissions Gap Report 2021 points out the potential for large cuts in methane emissions from the agriculture sector and notes that "substantial mitigation of livestock-related methane could be achieved through widespread changes in human dietary choices" (Ocko *et al.*, 2021).

The environmental hazards of meat production do not stop at greenhouse gas emissions. Animal agriculture is also responsible for excessive land and water use, leading to food insecurity and loss of biodiversity. The livestock industry accounts for about 70% of all agricultural land and about 30% of global freshwater consumption (Steinfeld *et al.*, 2006; Gerbens-Leenes, 2013). In addition, the animal industry is a leading source of water pollution and degradation. As a result, livestock actually detract more from the total food supply than they provide, hence being a key driver of food insecurity (Steinfeld *et al.*, 2006). According to the 2018 Intergovernmental Panel on Climate Change (IPCC) report, a global food transition to less meat, let alone a complete switch to plant-based

---

[10] The half-life of Methane is 9.1 years vs. 120 for carbon dioxide.

protein, could have a dramatic effect on land use and consequently play a role in delivering food security (Masson-Delmotte, 2018).

Beyond its impact on climate change, the animal industry plays a major role in biodiversity loss by being a key driver of deforestation and destruction of habitat (Díaz *et al.*, 2019).[11] Diversity loss is accelerating and its scale is enormous: the Global Living Planet Index of the World Wildlife Fund (WWF) shows an average of a 68% decrease in population sizes of mammals, birds, amphibians, reptiles, and fish between 1970 and 2016.[12] The fact that 70% of previously forested land in the Amazon is now occupied by pastures attests to the contribution of animal agriculture to habitat destruction (FAO, 2017).[13]

The damage to biodiversity brings about zoonotic diseases, that is, diseases transmitted by certain animals, such as bats, to humans. This happens because the damage to the natural habitat of these animals forces them to migrate. The US Centers for Disease Control and Prevention (CDC) estimates that 75% of new or emerging infectious diseases in people are zoonotic (United Nations Environment Programme and International Livestock Research Institute, 2020).[14,15] According to multiple sources, among them a UN report titled "Preventing the next pandemic," COVID-19 is one of these diseases (United Nations Environment Programme and International Livestock Research Institute, 2020). In the words of David Quammen, the well-known science and nature writer, at the onset of the COVID-19 pandemic: "We invade tropical forests and other wild landscapes, which harbor so many species of animals and

---

[11] According to the 2019 report by Intergovernmental Science-Policy Platform on Biodiversity and Ecosystem Services, current negative trends in biodiversity and ecosystems will undermine progress toward 80% of UN Sustainable Development Goals.

[12] WWF (2020) Living Planet Report 2020 — Bending the curve of biodiversity loss. Almond, R.E.A., Grooten M. and Petersen, T. (Eds). WWF, Gland, Switzerland.

[13] According to the report "Beef, banks and the Brazilian Amazon" by Global Witness In just one Amazon state over three years, beef giants JBS, Marfrig, and Minerva bought cattle from a combined 379 ranches containing 20,000 football fields' worth of illegal deforestation."

[14] For information on zoonotic diseases, see Centers for Disease Control and Prevention (CDC). https://www.cdc.gov/onehealth/basics/zoonotic-diseases.html.

[15] World Organization for Animal Health (OIE). https://www.oie.int/en/one-world-one-health/.

plants — and within those creatures, so many unknown viruses. We cut the trees; we kill the animals or cage them and send them to markets. We disrupt ecosystems, and we shake viruses loose from their natural hosts. When that happens, they need a new host. Often, we are it" (Carrington, 2020; Quammen , 2020).

Zoonotic diseases are not the only health hazard caused by the meat industry. Excessive consumption of meat, especially red and processed meat, has been shown in numerous studies to increase the probability of certain diseases such as cancer, cardiovascular disease, and type-2 diabetes (FAO, 2017; On cancer see, e.g., Bouvard *et al.*, 2015; Crimarco, 2020; On diabetes see, e.g., Feskens, 2013; Wolk, 2017). Furthermore, meat often contains high quantities of antibiotics, contributing to antibiotic resistance (Wallinga and Kar, 2020).

Last but not least is the growing awareness of the suffering of animals and the ensuing desire to end this cruelty and pursue cruelty-free alternatives.[16] This has been a prevalent motivation in the community of early backers of the alternative meat industry. Sergey Brin of Google said, "When you see how these cows are treated, it's certainly something I'm not comfortable with" (One Green Planet, 2013). Jeremy Coller of Coller Capital, the private equity investor and philanthropist who established the FAIRR (Farm Animal Investment Risk and Return) initiative, said "People are human animals" (Rose-Smith, 2016; Klein, 2021; Han, 2022).[17,18]

Plant-based meat significantly improves, and in some cases eliminates, the environmental and health hazards associated with animal-based meat discussed above. The environmental benefits of a plant-based diet vs an animal-based diet, such as reduced emissions and reduced use of land and water, have been widely recognized (Poore and Nemecek, 2018;

---

[16]Number of animals slaughtered. https://faunalytics.org/global-animal-slaughter-statistics-and-charts-2020-update/.

[17]Ezra Klein of the New York Times wrote: "If we could produce the meat we want without the suffering we now inflict, it would be one of the great achievements of our age."

[18]Surprising evidence for the growing awareness of animal suffering in the business world, though not directly related to alternative meat, is the recent activism of the billionaire investor and corporate raider Carl Icahn. Icahn, famous for putting pressure on firms in order to achieve financial goals, launched a proxy fight against McDonald's in connection to its treatment of pigs.

The Good Food Institute, 2019; IPCC, 2019; Clark, 2020; Xu *et al.*, 2021). Just to illustrate, the amount of carbon dioxide (CO_2) emitted by beef per calorie is 31 times larger than the amount emitted by tofu (*The Economist*, 2021). In addition, studies comparing a regular beef burger to the plant-based burgers produced by the market leaders Beyond Meat and Impossible Foods yielded impressive results, showing that these plant-based burgers significantly reduce land and water use relative to regular burgers (For Beyond Meat, Heller and Keoleian, 2018; For Impossible Foods, see Dettling *et al.*, 2016; For some differences between the burgers of Beyond Meat and Impossible Foods see *The Economist*, 2021). Furthermore, elimination of animal agriculture alone, without any changes in other sources of anthropogenic activity, would freeze increases in global warming for 30 years (Eisen and Brown, 2022).

As for health benefits, many studies document that a plant-based diet is associated with a lower risk of various diseases such as diabetes, high blood pressure, and heart disease compared to a meat-based diet (Battaglia *et al.*, 2015; Melina *et al.*, 2016; Satija and Hu, 2018; Tello, 2018). Indeed, the Intergovernmental Panel on Climate Change (IPCC) reports of 2019 and 2022 highlight the positive impacts of plant-based foods on both the environment and human health (IPCC, 2019; The Good Food Institute, 2022).[19]

Finally, alternative meat spares the lives of millions of animals. The non-profit World Animal Protection (WAP) documented that in 2021, alternative meat spared nearly one million lives in the US alone (Bazzi, 2022).

Considering the above discussion, the increasing popularity of alternative meat with consumers, scientists, investors, and the media should not come as a surprise.

3. Industry Structure and Competition

Which population is the target market of alternative meat companies? If you thought it was the vegetarian and vegan population, think again.

---

[19] The EAT-Lancet diet was developed with both human health and the environment in mind. For a discussion see Vaidyanathan, G. What humanity should eat to stay healthy and save the planet," *Nature* magazine, March 17, 2022, in *Scientific American*.

In fact, the target market is the enormous segment of flexitarians, meat eaters who reduce their consumption of animal-based meat and replace it with its alternative counterpart. The segment most likely to adopt a plant-based diet is young consumers. A One Poll survey found that 54% of respondents ages 24–39 identified themselves as flexitarians vs. 47% of all Americans who describe themselves as such (Sprouts Farmers Market, 2021). Around 63% of the U.S. consumers aged 24–39 believe that a plant-based diet fulfills their nutritional needs (Sprouts Farmers Market, 2021). Comparing meat consumption in 2019 and 2018, a Gallup poll found that 23% of Americans have cut back on eating meat, with the trend more pronounced in women, non-whites, and urban consumers (McCarthy and Decoster, 2020b). Another Gallup poll documented a high household exposure to plant-based meat with 41% of Americans having tried plant-based meat, and a higher exposure among upper-income, young adults, and suburbanites (McCarthy and Decoster, 2020a).

Hence, one could argue that the alternative meat industry poses a significant challenge to the animal-based meat industry. Indeed, the CNBC Disruptor 50 list contains alternative meat companies.[20] It should not come as a surprise, then, that traditional meat companies began moving into the plant-based meat space, much like the entrance of legacy car manufacturers such as General Motors to the electric vehicles market following the disruption introduced by the electric car manufacturer Tesla. In effect, these companies, among them Brazilian JBS, the world's largest meat company, Tyson Foods, Cargill, Smithfield, and Hormel, are attempting to hedge against a decrease in their meat business by grabbing a share of the growing alternative meat market. David MacLennan, CEO of Cargill, said plainly on June 4, 2021: "Our analysis is that in ... three to four years plant-based will be perhaps 10% of the market. We're a large beef producer and that is a big part of our portfolio. So there's some cannibalization that will occur" (*Reuters*, 2021).

How do traditional meat companies establish their presence in this increasingly crowded field? Methods include developing their own brands, buying shares in alternative meat companies, and forming collaborations. Cargill, for example, launched its own plant-based meat

---

[20] CNBC Disruptor 50, https://www.cnbc.com/2021/05/25/these-are-the-2021-cnbc-disruptor-50-companies.html. Note that the list consists only of private companies.

brand PlantEver for consumers in China and invested in alternative meat companies such as Memphis Meats (now Upside Foods). It went a step further and got involved in the emerging field of alternative seafood, as did Tyson Foods and JBS (Wright *et al.*, 2021).[21] This massive entry of conventional meat companies into the field of meat substitutes may be interpreted as a positive signal that alternative meat is making its way from being a niche product to the mainstream.

Not surprisingly, traditional meat companies such as Tyson Foods and Smithfield clearly state their intention to continue to sell conventional meat products and emphasize that they see alternative meat products as a business opportunity (Yaffe-Bellany, 2019[22]; Sorvino, 2020). This stands in stark contrast to the mission statements of the dedicated alternative meat companies such as the market leaders Beyond Meat and Impossible Foods which emphasize their commitment to the environment and health.

Indeed, in an interview conducted in October 2020 Patrick Brown, the CEO of Impossible Foods and former Stanford University biochemistry professor, said of his main competitor: "Beyond Meat is not our competition, the incumbent animal industry is" (Yahoo finance, 2020). He also stated that his mission was to eradicate the animal industry by 2035 (Greenfield, 2021; Reiley, 2021).[23] Ethan Brown, CEO of Beyond Meat and former clean energy executive (no relation to Patrick Brown), said, referring to the big meat producers: "I don't want to collaborate with them. I want to be them" (Yaffe-Bellany, 2019).

4. The Different Types of Alternative Meat at a Glance

The term "alternative meat" actually refers to several different products, most commonly plant-based meat and cultivated meat (also known as

---

[21] Cargill announced that it is committed to transforming its agricultural supply chains to be free of deforestation by 2030. However, the Guardian sharply criticized the company for its practices.

[22] The article also raises the concern that meat companies would "swallow" the stand-alone plant-based meat companies, in much the same way that big oil companies bought clean energy start-ups and closed them down.

[23] Among other things, Mr. Brown said in this interview "put it on your calendar, because Impossible Foods is going to do it."

lab-grown meat or cultured meat) (Firth, 2020).[24] The goal of these products is identical: create an alternative to animal-based meat that tastes and
looks like the real thing with the aim of replacing it, for the sake of mitigating the environmental, health and animal welfare hazards associated
with real meat. However, the similarity between the different products
ends there. Differences between these products abound, among them
ingredients, processes, costs, and regulations.

Plant-based meat is made of ingredients such as peas, chickpeas,
beans, and soy. Products made from these ingredients have been around
for centuries (Smith, 2014; Hunt, 2020). The difference between these
products and the current day plant-based meat products is that the new
products are meant to mimic real meat in terms of taste, texture, and looks
and to be marketed to meat eaters, whereas their predecessors were meant
mostly for vegans and vegetarians. The transformation to a new generation of substitute meat products was enabled by the development of new
formulations and novel ways of using ingredients. The new meat-like
products first came to the market in 2013.

Cultivated meat is based on a completely different concept. It
involves taking a small number of cells from living animals and growing
them in a bioreactor in a lab. Thus, it is real meat, without the slaughter
of animals. Cultivated meat is currently produced and sold on a very
small scale for a variety of reasons, not the least of which is regulation.
While, for the most part, plant-based meat products require little regulation, cultivated meat is subject to heavy regulation.[25] The only country
that has granted approval to sell lab-grown meat so far is Singapore, with
the approval granted in November 2020 specifically to a chicken product

---

[24] Another process used in the production of alternative meat is fermentation, a process
similar to the one used in the production of bread and beer. It is sometimes used in the
production of plant-based meat, for example in the case of Impossible Foods, to create a
hybrid product, but it can also be used by itself. The term "hybrid product" may also refer
to a blend of plant-based meat and cultivated meat. Another type of hybrid meat is real
meat blended with plants such as the one brought to the market by Tyson Foods in 2019.

[25] The exception for plant-based meat products is the regulation required for ingredients
defined as "novel food." Impossible Foods needed regulatory approval to use an ingredient
known as "heme" that causes the burger to bleed like a real meat burger, and is considered
"novel food."

by the U.S. company Eat Just. Regulatory approval is in process in the U.S., Europe, Canada, Israel, and more.

5. Investments throughout the Years

Alternative meat has been attracting investments from the get-go. Financiers and tech moguls, existing meat companies, celebrities, the public — they all want to grab a piece of this fast-growing market. In 2020, investment in alternative proteins reached a record high of $3.1 billion, three times more than the amount raised in the previous year and 4.5 times more than in 2018, according to the Good Food Institute. Of this amount, roughly half went to alternative meat companies.[26] In 2021, a new record high of $5 billion was set, exceeding previous year's record high by 60%.[27]

Early backers of the industry were motivated in large part by ideology. The list of early investors includes high-tech moguls and financiers such as Bill Gates of Microsoft, Sergey Brin of Google, Peter Thiel of PayPal, Richard Branson of Virgin, and the billionaire entrepreneur Mark Cuban, as well as entrepreneurs and philanthropists such as Jeremy Coller. Gates, a long-time proponent of sustainability as a whole, set a concrete goal for meat consumption: "I do think that all rich countries should move to 100% synthetic beef" (Temple, 2021).

Many of these investors have bought shares in more than one company in the alternative meat space. Bill Gates invested in both Beyond Meat and Impossible Foods as well as in a handful of smaller companies. Recently, he invested, together with Jeff Bezos of Amazon, in Nature's Fynd, a company using fungus as the key ingredient in its products (Woods, 2021). Peter Thiel invested in a few alternative meat companies as well, among them Wild Earth, a company developing alternative meat for pets.

Another notable investor in the field is the former vice president of the US and long-time environmental activist Al Gore, whose work on climate change earned him the Nobel Prize in 2007. Gore has been a

---

[26]Notable beneficiaries include Impossible Foods which got about one-fourth of the total investments.

[27]Of the $11.1 billion invested in alternative proteins since 2010, 73% was raised since the onset of the pandemic in 2020, according to the Good Food Institute.

strong proponent of plant-based diets, a lifestyle he has adopted personally, for the sake of the environment. Recently he invested in the emerging
company Natura's Fynd along with Gates and Bezos.

Conventional meat companies have been investing in alternative meat
companies as well. Tyson Foods invested in Beyond Meat as early as 2016
and sold its stake in the company in 2019, soon after announcing it would
launch its own meat substitute and a week prior to Beyond Meat's IPO
(El-Bawab, 2019). It also invested in Memphis Meats (along with Richard
Branson). Other conventional meat companies investing in alternative
meat companies include Cargill and JBS.

Very few alternative meat companies are traded on public markets.
The most notable is Beyond Meat which filed a high-profile initial public
offering (IPO) in 2019 valuing the company at $1.5 billion.[28] Beyond
Meat is practically the only way for the public at large to gain exposure to
this sector. Its big rival, Impossible Foods, is not publicly traded as of yet,
but it has raised capital in a few successful rounds. In 2020 alone, it raised
$700 million from investors such as Bill Gates and the Qatar Investment
Authority. As of October 2021, it is reportedly (though not confirmed by
the firm) in talks to raise about $500 million at a valuation of $7 billion.
Its founder and CEO, Pat Brown, acknowledged that going public at some
point in the future is inevitable (Sorvino, 2021).

What better indication is there for the trendiness of a sector
than investment by celebrities? Many celebrities have been fond of alter-
native meat companies, among them Leonardo DiCaprio, Jay-Z, Serena
Williams, and Ashton Kutcher. DiCaprio, a long-time environmental
activist, invested in Beyond Meat as early as 2017 (Garfield, 2017).
Since then he has backed other companies such as the Dutch Mosa Meat.
Impossible Foods is especially popular among celebrity investors: Jay Z,
Serena Williams, Trevor Noah, and Katy Perry all participated in its
March 2020 financing round.

6. Challenges Facing the Alternative Meat Industry and Policy Issues

Perhaps the biggest challenge facing the alternative meat industry is to
deliver the sensory experience of meat in terms of taste, texture, and looks

---

[28] The other public alternative meat companies are relatively small.

to the flexitarian consumer. Though significant progress has been made since the days of the veggie burger, there is still a way to go. Views on the similarity of existing plant-based products to the "real thing" diverge greatly. The experts at Food & Wine tried four different plant-based burgers and found two out of the four, the ones by Beyond Meat and Impossible Foods, good meat replacements in terms of taste (Hallinan, 2019). Not everyone shares their view, however.

Then there is the issue of perception: How are the products perceived by consumers and what will it take to convince consumers to try the products? A One Poll survey conducted in the US found that 47% of people polled were hesitant to taste plant-based meat because they did not think it would taste like real meat, and a similar percentage hesitated to try it because of its texture (Sprouts Farmers Market, 2021).

The other big obstacle is price. Currently, alternative meat products cost more than their real meat counterparts, mostly due to higher costs of production and ingredients. As production is scaled up costs are expected to go down, and the goal is to bring plant-based meat to price parity with animal-based meat. Beyond Meat, the publicly traded market leader, announced that it would make at least one of its products cost-competitive with its meat counterpart by 2024. Dennis Woodside, President of Impossible Foods, said on the issue of pricing: "We will be able to price at the same level or lower than the cow. Our entire production process starts with plants — we turn it into meat without using the cow as the middleman … Our ingredients require a small fraction of water, small fraction of the land and energy than it takes to raise a cow" (Cohen, 2021).

Scaling up production is also necessary to meet rising demand. As the popularity of plant-based products has soared, fast food behemoths such as McDonald's and Burger King have introduced these products into their menus. If the current physical production capacity of plant-based product suppliers cannot meet the increased demand, supply shortages would happen and hinder the growth momentum of the industry (Breakthrough Institute, 2020). Beyond Meat experienced such shortages in 2017 and 2018 as demand for its products surged, while Impossible Foods had its own share of shortages in 2019 (Lucas, 2019; Taylor, 2019).

Related to price is the contentious issue of government subsidies granted to the animal agriculture industry. A 2021 UN report found that nearly 90% of global subsidies given to farmers each year, a majority of which are granted to animal agriculture, are harmful, asserting that they cause damage to human health, fuel the climate crisis, destroy nature, and drive inequality (Carrington, 2021; FAO, UNDP, and UNEP, 2021). Consequently, the report calls for phasing out of this distortive and harmful support and for repurposing subsidies for good uses, such as supporting healthy food. The 2022 Intergovernmental Panel on Climate Change (IPCC) report makes a similar recommendation (The Good Food Institute, 2022). The idea of subsidies being distortive is not new, and in the context of the environment it is best demonstrated in the statement of the United Nations Development Programme (UNDP) pertaining to fossil fuels — "Moving away from subsidies is a critical step to show the true cost of using fossil fuels, to both society and the environment".[29] This argument is perfectly applicable to meat subsidies.

Furthermore, some commentators have suggested levying taxes on meat, similar to those levied on cigarettes and sugary drinks because of their negative impact on health (Ivanova, 2018; Samuel; 2019; For a study on the optimal tax levels on red and processed meat based on the marginal health costs associated with their consumption see Springmann *et al.*, 2018). Because of this impact, taxes on cigarettes and sugary drinks are sometimes referred to as "sin taxes" (Parker and Abboud, 2019; Allen, 2015).

Taxes on meat should not be viewed as fines but rather as a mechanism to internalize the environmental and health externalities associated with meat, that is, to incorporate the true costs of negative health and environmental consequences into meat's price. The European Union is considering applying the Polluters Pay Principle to agriculture, with the backing of the Agricultural Commissionaire (Foote, 2021).[30]

In some countries, such as Germany, Sweden, and Denmark, these suggestions have come up in parliamentary and regulatory discussions (Charlton, 2019; FAIRR, 2020; BBC News, 2019).[31] There have also been calls for public investment in alternative protein, specifically in alternative meat (Smith, 2021; Klein, 2021). Tax incentives for alternative meat producers, such as those included in the social safe net and climate bill

---

[29] See UNDP web page: https://feature.undp.org/breaking-up-with-fossil-fuels/.

[30] The Polluter Pays Principle: Inconsistent application across EU environmental policies and actions. Special Report, European Court of Auditors, December 2021.

[31] The issue was especially hotly debated in Germany. See, e.g., Deutsche Welle (DE) (2019) and BBC News (2019).

recently approved by the U.S. House of Representatives for producers of clean energy, are another potential avenue of public support. As in the case of most subsidies and taxes, political issues are involved (Shapiro, 2016; see Vaidyanathan (2022) regarding the meat industry pressure in response to the attempt of the United States Department of Agriculture (USDA) to revise its dietary guidelines so that they take into account the environment).

Will these obstacles be overcome? The answer depends on who you ask. Richard Branson of Virgin Group said: "I believe that in 30 years or so we will no longer need to kill any animals and that all meat will either be clean or plant-based, taste the same and also be much healthier for everyone" (Singh, 2017).

References

Allen, L. (2015). Rejection of sugar tax is based on faulty logic about the poor. *The Conversation*, University of Oxford. https://www.ox.ac.uk/research/rejection-sugar-tax-based-faulty-logic-about-poor-0

Battaglia, R.E., Baumer, B., Conrad, B., Darioli, R., Schmid, A., and Keller, U. (2015). Health risks associated with meat consumption: A review of epidemiological studies. *International Journal for Vitamin and Nutrition Research*, 85(1–2), 70–78.

Bazzi, M. (2022). Plant-based offerings in the food industry are sparing the lives of nearly a million animals per year. World Animal Protection, January 6. https://www.worldanimalprotection.us/blogs/plant-based-offerings-food-industry-are-sparing-lives-nearly-million-animals-year

BBC News (2019). Climate change: German MPs want higher meat tax. August 8.

Bouvard, V., Loomis, D., Guyton, K.Z., Grosse, Y., Ghissassi, F.E., Benbrahim-Tallaa, L., Guha, N., Mattock, H., and Straif, K. (2015). International Agency for Research on Cancer Monograph Working Group. Carcinogenicity of consumption of red and processed meat. *Lancet Oncology*, 16(16), 1599–1600.

Breakthrough Institute (2020). For more on this issue see "Can Alternative Proteins Scale?"

Carrington, D. (2020). Deadly diseases from wildlife thrive when nature is destroyed, study finds. *The Guardian*, August 5.

Carrington, D. (2021). Nearly all global farm subsidies harm people and planet — UN. *The Guardian*, September 14.

Charlton, E. (2019). This is why Denmark, Sweden and Germany are considering a meat tax. *World Economic Forum*, August 28.

Clark, M.A., Domingo, N.G.G., Colgan, K., Thakrar, S.K., Tilman, D., Lynch, J., Azevedo, I.L., and Hill, J.D. (2020). Global food system emissions could preclude achieving the 1.5° and 2°C climate change targets. *Science*, 370(6517), 705–708.

Cohen, M. (2021). Impossible foods, beyond meat battle to achieve price parity with real meat. *CNBC*, August 25.

Crimarco, A., Springfield, S., Petlura, C., Streaty, T., Cunanan, K., Lee, J., Fielding-Singh, P., Carter, M.M., Topf, M.A., Wastyk, H.C., Sonnenburg, E.D., Sonnenburg, J.L., and Gardner, C.D. (2020). A randomized crossover trial on the effect of plant-based compared with animal-based meat on tri-methylamine-N-oxide and cardiovascular disease risk factors in generally healthy adults: Study With Appetizing Plantfood-Meat Eating Alternative Trial (SWAP-MEAT). *American Journal of Clinical Nutrition*, 112(5), 1188–1199.

Crippa, M., Solazzo, E., Guizzardi, D., Monforti-Ferrario, F., Tubiello, F.N., and Leip, A. (2021). Food systems are responsible for a third of global anthropogenic GHG emissions. *Nature Food*, 2, 198–209.

Deutsche Welle (DE) (2019). Germany: "meat tax" is on the table to protect the climate. August 7.

Díaz, S., Settele, J., Brondízio E.S., Ngo, H.T., Guèze, M., Agard, J., … and Zayas, C.N. (Eds.) (2019). Summary for policymakers of the global assessment report on biodiversity and ecosystem services of the intergovernmental science-policy platform on biodiversity and ecosystem services. IPBES Secretariat, Bonn, Germany.

Eisen, M.B. and Brown, P.O. (2022). Rapid global phaseout of animal agriculture has the potential to stabilize greenhouse gas levels for 30 years and offset 68 percent of CO_2 emissions this century. *PLOS Climate*, 1(2), e0000010. https://doi.org/10.1371/journal.pclm.0000010

El-Bawab, N. (2019). Tyson Foods sold its stake in alternative protein company Beyond Meat. *CNBC*, April 24.

FAIRR (2020). The livestock levy: progress report. A Coller initiative, June 2020.

FAO (2017). The future of food and agriculture — Trends and challenges. Rome: FAO.

FAO, UNDP and UNEP (2021). *A Multi-Billion-Dollar Opportunity — Repurposing Agricultural Support to Transform Food Systems*. Rome: FAO.

Feskens, E.J.M., Sluik, D., and van Woudenbergh, G.J. (2013). Meat consumption, diabetes, and its complications. *Current Diabetes Reports*, 13, 298–306.

Firth, N. (2020). Your first lab-grown burger is coming soon — and it'll be "blended." *MIT Technology Review*, December 18.

Foote, N. (2021). Agri Commissioner backs call for polluter pays principle in farming. *Euractive*, July 7. https://www.euractiv.com/section/agriculture-food/news/agri-commissioner-backs-call-for-polluter-pays-principle-in-farming/

Friedman, L. (2021). More than 30 countries join US pledge to slash methane emissions. *New York Times*, October 11.

Garfield, L. (2017). Leonardo DiCaprio just invested in the Bill Gates-backed veggie burger that "bleeds" like beef — here's how it tastes. *Business Insider*, October 17.

Gerber, P.J., Steinfeld, H., Henderson, B., Mottet, A., Opio, C., Dijkman, J., Falcucci, A., and Tempio, G. (2013). Tackling climate change through livestock — A global assessment of emissions and mitigation opportunities. Rome: Food and Agriculture Organization of the United Nations (FAO).

Gerbens-Leenes, P.W., Mekonnen, M.M., and Hoekstra, A.Y. (2013). The water footprint of poultry, pork and beef: A comparative study in different countries and production systems. *Water Resources and Industry*, 1–2, 25–36.

Gerhardt, C., Suhlmann, G., Ziemßen, F., Donnan, D., Warschun, M. and Kühnle, H.J. (2020). How will cultured meat and meat alternatives disrupt the agricultural and food industry? *Industrial Biotechnology*, 16(5), 262–270.

Greenfield, P. (2021). Let's get rid of friggin' cows' says creator of plant-based "bleeding burger". *The Guardian*, January 8.

Hallinan, B. (2019). Plant-based burger taste test: We tried four vegan 'meat' brands ahead of grilling season. *Food & Wine*, May 13.

Han, Y. (2022). McDonald's goes on the defense against activist investor Carl Icahn in escalating battle over pork production. *Business Insider*, 2022.

Heller, M.C. and Keoleian, G.A. (2018). Beyond meat's beyond burger life cycle assessment: A detailed comparison between a plant-based and an animal-based protein source. *CSS Report*, University of Michigan, pp. 1–38.

Hunt, E. (2020). From tofu lamb chops to vegan steak bakes: the 1,000-year history of fake meat. *The Guardian*, January 12.

Ivanova, I. (2018). Is it time to put a tax on meat? *CBS News*, November 20.

Johnson, G.R. (2020). UK diet trends 2021. *The Finder*, February 12.

Kerle, A. (2021). Plant-based proteins: Building a sustainable future. *The Economist Intelligence Unit*, April 13.

Khan, Y. (2019). UBS predicts plant-based meat sales could grow by more than 25% a year to $85 billion by 2030. *Business Insider*, July 19.

Klein, E. (2021). Let's launch a moonshot for meatless meat. *New York Times*, April 24.

Leip, A., Billen, G., Garnier, J., Grizzetti, B., Lassaletta, L., Reis, S., Simpson, D., Sutton, M.A., de Vries, W., Weiss, F., and Westhoek, H. (2015). Impacts of European livestock production: Nitrogen, sulphur, phosphorus and greenhouse gas emissions, land-use, water eutrophication and biodiversity. *Environmental Research Letters*, 10, 11.

Masson-Delmotte, V., Zhai, P., Pörtner, H.-O., Roberts, D., Skea, J., Shukla, P.R., Pirani, A., Moufouma-Okia, W., Péan, C., Pidcock, R., Connors, S., Matthews, J.B.R., Chen, Y., Zhou, X., Gomis, M.I., Lonnoy, E., Maycock, T., Tignor, M., and Waterfield, T. (Eds.) (2018). *Global Warming of 1.5°C. An IPCC Special Report on the Impacts of Global Warming of 1.5°C above Pre-Industrial Levels and Related Global Greenhouse Gas Emission Pathways, in the Context of Strengthening the Global Response to the Threat of Climate Change, Sustainable Development, and Efforts to Eradicate Poverty.* Cambridge University Press, Cambridge, UK and New York, NY, USA.

Masson-Delmotte, V., Zhai, P., Pirani, A., Connors, S.L., Péan, C., Berger, S., Caud, N., Chen, Y., Goldfarb, L., Gomis, M.I., Huang, M., Leitzell, K., Lonnoy, E., Matthews, J.B.R., Maycock, T. K., Waterfield, T., Yelekçi, O., Yu R., and Zhou B. (Eds.) (2021). Summary for policymakers. In: *Climate Change 2021: The Physical Science Basis*. Contribution of Working Group I to the Sixth Assessment Report of the Intergovernmental Panel on Climate Change. IPCC: Cambridge University Press.

McCarthy, J. and Decoster, S. (2020a). Four in 10 Americans have eaten plant-based meats. *Gallup*, January 28. https://news.gallup.com/poll/282989/four-americans-eaten-plant-based-meats.aspx.

McCarthy, J. and Decoster, S. (2020b). Nearly one in four in US have cut back on eating meat. *Gallup*, January 27.

McClure, T. (2021). Emissions from cows on New Zealand dairy farms reach record levels. *The Guardian*, August 5.

Melina, V., Craig, W., and Levin, S. (2016). Position of the academy of nutrition and dietetics: Vegetarian diets. *Journal of the Academy of Nutrition and Dietetics*, 116(12), 1970–1980.

Morach, B., Witte, B., Walker, D., von Koeller, E., Grosse-Holz, F., Rogg, J., Brigl, M., Dehnert, N., Obloj, P., Koktenturk, S., and Schulze, U. (2021). Food for thought: The protein transformation. Boston Consulting Group, March 24.

Ocko, I.B., Sun, T., Shindell, D., Oppenheimer, M., Hristov, A.N., Pacala, S.W., Mauzerall, D.L., Xu, Y., and Hamburg, S.P. (2021). Acting rapidly to deploy readily available methane mitigation measures by sector can immediately slow global warming. *Environmental Research Letters*, 16, 054042.

OECD-FAO (2017). *OECD-FAO Agricultural Outlook 2017–2026*. OECD Publishing. Paris, France.

OECD-FAO (2021). OECD-FAO Agricultural Outlook 2021–2030, OECD Publishing. https://doi.org/10.1787/19428846-en. In particular, Chapter 6 "Meat", in OECD/FAO (2021), OECD-FAO Agricultural Outlook 2021–2030, OECD Publishing. Paris, France.

One Green Planet (2013). Google's Sergey Brin funded test-tube burger for animal welfare reasons. August 5.

Parker, G. and Abboud, L. (2019). Boris Johnson vows review of "sin taxes". *Financial Times*, July 3.

Poore, J. and Nemecek T. (2018). Reducing food's environmental impacts through producers and consumers. *Science*, 360(6392), 987–992.

Quammen, D. (2012). *Spillover: Animal Infections and the Next Human Pandemic*. Norton & Co. New York, NY, USA.

Quammen, D. (2020). We made the coronavirus epidemic. *New York Times*, January 28.

Reiley, L. (2021). Why the CEO of Impossible Foods thinks he can eliminate all animal-based meat in 15 years. *The Washington Post*, July 16.

Reuters (2021). Plant-based protein to cannibalize meat demand, Cargill CEO says. *Reuters*, June 4.

Rose-Smith, I. (2016). Private equity veteran Jeremy Coller champions farm animal welfare. *Institutional Investor*, January 14.

Samuel, S. (2019). We put a "sin tax" on cigarettes and alcohol. Why not meat? *Vox*, August 11.

Satija, A. and Hu, F.B. (2018). Plant-based diets and cardiovascular health. *Trends in Cardiovascular Medicine*, 28(7), 437–441.

Shapiro, P. (2016). The elephant-sized subsidy in the race. *National Review*, February 17.

Shukla, P.R., Skea, J., Calvo Buendia, E., Masson-Delmotte, V., Pörtner, H.-O., Roberts, D.C., Zhai, P., Slade, R., …. and Malley, J. (Eds.) (2019). *Climate Change and Land: An IPCC Special Report on Climate Change, Desertification, Land Degradation, Sustainable Land Management, Food Security, and Greenhouse Gas Fluxes in Terrestrial Ecosystems*. IPCC. Cambridge University Press, Cambridge, UK and New York, NY, USA.

Singh, S.D. (2017). "No longer kill animals": Bill Gates, Richard Branson back "clean meat" start-up. *The Sydney Morning Herald*, August 24.

Smith, A. (2014). The history of the veggie burger. *Smithsonian Magazine*, March 19.

Smith, A., Shah, S., and Blaustein-Rejto, D. (2021). The case for public investment in alternative proteins. Breakthrough Institute, March 30.

Sorvino, C. (2020). The world's largest meat seller embraces plant-based proteins as pandemic demand surges. *Forbes*, June 18.

Sorvino, C. (2021). Impossible foods' CEO says going public is "inevitable." So why have most of 2021's food listings spoiled? *Forbes*, November 4.

Springmann, M., Mason-D'Croz, D., Robinson, S., Wiebe, K., Godfray, H.C.J., Rayner, M., and Scarborough, P. (2018). Health-motivated taxes on red and processed meat: A modelling study on optimal tax levels and associated health impacts. *PLoS One*, 13(11), e0204139.

Sprouts Farmers Market (2021). Survey by Sprouts looks into new year eating habits, reveals young Americans are likely to shift away from meat. January 18.

Steinfeld, H., Gerber, P., Wassenaar, T., Castel, V., Rosales, M., and de Haan, C. (2006). *Livestock's Long Shadow: Environmental Issues and Options*. Food and Agriculture Organization of the United Nations. Rome, Italy.

Tabushi, H. (2021). Halting the vast release of methane is critical for climate, U.N. says. *New York Times*, April 24.

Taylor, K. (2019). A looming problem has plagued Beyond Meat for years. Here's how the CEO says it plans to deal with demand as its rival Impossible Foods faces shortages. *Business Insider*, May 3.

Tello, M. (2018). Eat more plants, fewer animals. *Harvard Health Blog*, November 29.

Temple, J. (2021). Bill Gates: Rich nations should shift entirely to synthetic beef. *MIT Technology Review*, February 14.

The Economist (2021a). Treating cattle like coal would make a big dent in greenhouse-gas emissions. October 2.

The Economist (2021b). Cows are no longer essential for meat and milk. September 28.

The Good Food Institute (2019). *Plant-Based Meat for a Growing World*. Washington, DC, USA.

The Good Food Institute (2022). IPCC report highlights critical role of sustainable proteins in adapting to climate change. February 28.

Turak, N. (2020). The son of Saudi Arabia's Warren Buffett sees a big future for Beyond Meat and plant-based foods. *CNBC*, 2020.

UN Economic Committee for Europe (UNECE). Sustainable Developments Goals. Supporting climate action on the road to COP26. https://unece.org/unece-and-sdgs/supporting-climate-action-road-cop-26

UN Environmental Programme (2021). Methane emissions are driving climate change. Here's how to reduce them. August 20. https://www.unep.org/news-and-stories/story/methane-emissions-are-driving-climate-change-heres-how-reduce-them#:~:text=Rather%20than%20allowing%20the%20continuous,water%2C%20making%20it%20more%20economical

United States Environmental Protection Agency (2023). Global emissions by economic sector. https://www.epa.gov/ghgemissions/global-greenhouse-gas-emissions-data

United Nations Environment Programme (2021). *Emissions Gap Report 2021: The Heat Is On — A World of Climate Promises Not Yet Delivered*. Nairobi, Kenya.

United Nations Environment Programme and International Livestock Research Institute (2020). *Preventing the Next Pandemic: Zoonotic Diseases and How to Break the Chain of Transmission*. UNEPILRI. Nairobi, Kenya.

Vaidyanathan, G. (2022). What humanity should eat to stay healthy and save the planet. *Nature* magazine, March 17. Scientific American.

Vidal, J. (2020). "Tip of the iceberg": Is our destruction of nature responsible for Covid-19? *Guardian*, March 18.

Wallinga, D. and Kar, A. (2020). New data: Animal vs. human antibiotic use remains lopsided. Natural Resources Defense Council expert blog, June 15. https://www.nrdc.org/experts/david-wallinga-md/most-human-antibiotics-still-going-us-meat-production

Warschun, M., Donnan, D., and Ziemßen, F. (2020). When consumers go vegan, how much meat will be left on the table for agribusiness? A.T. Kearney website, https://www.de.kearney.com/consumer-retail/article/?/a/when-consumers-go-vegan-how-much-meat-will-be-left-on-the-table-for-agribusiness-.

Wolk A. (2017). Potential health hazards of eating red meat. *Journal of Internal Medicine*, 281(2), 106–122.

Woods, B. (2021). Bezos, Gates back fake meat and dairy made from fungus as next big alt-protein. *CNBC*, July 3.

World Meteorological Organization (WMO) (2021). Greenhouse gas bulletin, No. 17, October 25.

Wright, G., Olenick, L., and Westervelt, A. (2021). The dirty dozen: meet America's top climate villains. *The Guardian*, October 27.

Wynes, S. and Nicholas, K.A. (2017). The climate mitigation gap: education and government recommendations miss the most effective individual actions. *Environmental Research Letters*, 12, 7.

Xu, X., Sharma, P., Shu, S. *et al.* (2021). Global greenhouse gas emissions from animal-based foods are twice those of plant-based foods. *Nature Food*, 2, 724–732.

Yaffe-Bellany, D. (2019). The new makers of plant-based meat? Big meat companies. *New York Times*, October 14.

Yahoo finance (2020). Impossible Foods CEO: "Beyond Meat is not our competition", the incumbent animal industry is. October 21.

Chapter 13

Understanding and Mitigating Biases in AI Systems: Insights and Recommendations

Ruti Gafni*, Boris Kantsepolsky† and Sofia Sherman‡

*The Academic College of Tel Aviv – Yaffo,
Yaffo 6818211, Israel
rutigafn@mta.ac.il
†boriskn@mta.ac.il
‡sofiash@mta.ac.il

Abstract

Artificial Intelligence has become an inseparable part of civilization and rapidly changes every field of human activities. In addition to the positive impact of AI on humankind, it also may have negative consequences or unintentionally harm businesses, individuals, or parts of society. Through this chapter, we explain how the embedded human nature biases may become inherited in AI systems. Then, we raise the attention of AI practitioners to the dangers of ignoring human and machine biases and provide actionable recommendations on how to mitigate this phenomenon and thus contribute to increasing trust and adoption of AI systems.

Keywords: Artificial intelligence, AI biases, ML biases, AI biases mitigation, AI lifecycle, AI human cognitive biases, AI algorithmic biases, AI systems, Applications biases

1. Introduction

Artificial Intelligence (AI) challenges every aspect and field of human activities. While there are multiple pieces of evidence about the positive change AI creates in areas such as education, medicine, finance, and business, it also has the potential for negative impacts. It even harms individuals and society (Van Wynsberghe, 2021). The growing stream of research deals with ethical and practical concerns about the fairness and applicability of AI systems. These concerns are rooted in understanding and acknowledging that human psychological and cognitive biases may affect the entire lifecycle of AI systems, from the idea generation throughout the development and up to the government of their application (Schwartz *et al.*, 2022). Moreover, the results of human-generated biases might be strengthened with a machine or algorithmic biases, leading to repeatable errors in the systems' outcomes (Park *et al.*, 2021).

The goal of this chapter is two-fold. First, we aim to create awareness and raise the attention of AI practitioners to the dangers of ignoring the biases embedded in human nature. Second, we discuss how these biases may affect the fairness and applicability of AI systems and provide actionable recommendations to mitigate them. This chapter is organized as follows. We begin with an introduction to cognitive biases and mental models to explain how humans make decisions based on heuristics. Then, we present the main stages of the AI systems lifecycle. In the chapter's central section, we describe nine representative types of human and algorithmic biases and discuss how these biases may affect AI systems and the users' decisions. In the last section, we summarize the insights derived from the AI systems biases analysis, conclude about the multifaceted challenges faced by AI systems stakeholders, and provide actionable recommendations on addressing these challenges, increasing trust, and facilitating AI-based systems adoption.

1.1. *Introduction to Cognitive Biases and Mental Models*

1.1.1. *Cognitive biases*

Cognitive biases represent the tendency of the human mind to perceive and interpret information subjectively, leading to errors, distortions, or illogical reasoning (Ellis, 2018; Neal *et al.*, 2022). Cognitive biases can arise from a range of factors, such as the brain's limited processing capacity, the need for quick decision-making in complex situations, social influences, emotional factors, and mental models that simplify information processing (Neal *et al.*, 2022). These biases often operate on an unconscious level, influencing our thoughts and actions without awareness, and can lead to deviation from rationality or objectivity in judgment and decision-making. After decades of psychology and behavioral economics research, about 200 cognitive biases were identified and studied (Manoogian *et al.*, 2018; Neal *et al.*, 2022). Some examples discussed in this chapter are confirmation, availability, and anchoring biases. Since cognitive biases can lead to errors in judgment, flawed decision-making, and distorted perceptions of reality, recognizing and mitigating these biases is vital in fields such as medicine, finance, law, and artificial intelligence (Schwartz *et al.*, 2022).

1.1.2. *Mental models*

Mental models are cognitive frameworks or representations individuals use to understand and make sense of the world around them. Mental models are composed of beliefs, assumptions, knowledge, and expectations about how things work or how particular phenomena are related (Jones *et al.*, 2011; Rouse and Morris, 1986). People heavily rely on mental models to perceive, interpret, and predict events and guide their decision-making processes (Johnson-Laird *et al.*, 2017). When there is a need for quick decision-making, individuals relate the newly arrived information to an existing model and then classify the uncertain events into categories of the known events. The shortcut of connecting new information to an existing one, also known as heuristic, may negatively affect optimal decision-making (Singh *et al.*, 2022).

Mental models are not static but can undergo maintenance and building processes. Individuals tend to maintain or reinforce their current beliefs and decision-making rules, actively seeking information that aligns with their existing mental models. When faced with novel and disconfirming information, individuals may restructure or build new mental models (Bauer *et al.*, 2023). Mental model adjustments are subject to *confirmation bias* so that misconceptions can persist and accumulate, possibly leading to suboptimal or biased decisions. Understanding the role of mental models in cognition and decision-making is crucial, particularly in human interaction with AI systems. Explanations provided by AI systems can potentially reshape users' mental models and influence their information-processing and problem-solving approaches (Bauer *et al.*, 2023; Müller, 2021).

1.2. *The Main Stages of the AI Systems Lifecycle*

The literature provides several classifications of AI products' lifecycles. For example, one of the recent concepts is the three-phase approach of design, development, and deployment (Chen *et al.*, 2023). Each phase is divided into several stages representing a series of activities related to (a) data collection, selection, and annotation; (b) the model's design, development, testing, and evaluation; (c) the AI system's deployment, operationalization, monitoring, and integration of feedback loops. Another perspective on the AI products' lifecycles is a four-stage approach, including predesign, design and development, testing and validation, and deployment (Schwartz *et al.*, 2022). The predesign stage consists of planning, problem specification, background research, and identification of data. The next stage includes requirements, design, and development of the model. It is worth mentioning that this stage is the most critical for identifying, documenting, and mitigating data-related biases. Throughout the entire AI lifecycle, the testing and evaluation stage is continuous. Data scientists should be aware of the consequences of new data introduction for a specific context and act proactively to identify any potential new sources of bias. Finally, the deployment stage relates to the human interaction with the AI systems. Because of the iterative nature of the AI systems lifecycle, the development teams must ensure continuous feedback and the solution's applicability monitoring to eliminate unintended use and outcomes. This stage should also serve as a basis for setting specific governing policies and guidelines. A similar four-stage approach stands for data creation, problem formulation, data analysis, validation, and testing (Srinivasan and Chander, 2021). Finally, the five-stage concept includes idea generation, training, re-tuning, implementation, and governance (Van Wynsberghe, 2021). Adding governance as a separate stage was acknowledged in the later literature as a vital phase for overcoming so-called systemic biases — a set of policies and procedures to monitor how organizations implement and control decision-making processes related to uncovering and overcoming human cognitive biases and group heuristics and throughout the AI lifecycle (Schwartz *et al.*, 2022).

Despite the seeming differences in the formulations, they have an evident commonality. Data engineers must be aware of the unconscious effect of various human biases on data collection, selection, and annotation. The representative types of human biases discussed in this chapter are confirmation, availability, automation, and anchoring biases. Data scientists should be cautious about not introducing datasets or algorithmic biases during the model design, development, training, and evaluation stages. We discussed sampling, model selection, and design, including overfitting and underfitting biases as typical representatives of this type of bias. Finally, to cover the stage of the AI systems deployment, we addressed the biases of appropriate use and presentation, as well as ethical and social considerations. In the following section, we describe each of the representative biases, discuss the specific impact of these biases on AI products, and offer recommendations for mitigation practices.

2. Biases in AI: Challenges and Opportunities

2.1. *Confirmation Bias*

Confirmation bias is a cognitive bias that occurs when individuals seek or interpret information to confirm their pre-existing beliefs or hypotheses (Bauer *et al.*, 2023; Chen *et al.*, 2023). Because of the unconscious nature of the phenomenon, this bias can happen when the newly arrived information is different or contradicts the existing perceptions, associations, or stereotypes (Schwartz *et al.*, 2022). As a result, confirmation bias affects how humans process information and make decisions, thus affecting rational judgment and behavior (Park *et al.*, 2021). Since the human cognitive system is naturally susceptible to various cognitive biases, researchers are prone to confirmation bias, regardless of their intentions or conscientiousness (Nguyen and Benjamin-Chung, 2023). In the particular case of data scientists, whose objective and rational decision-making are crucial at every stage of developing and training AI algorithms, confirmation bias poses a particularly significant challenge.

2.1.1. *Confirmation bias in AI*

Although AI is desired to be free from the qualitative nature of individual human judgments, several studies have reported how confirmation bias can impact the outcomes of AI decision-making processes. Researchers can unconsciously exhibit confirmation bias by imposing personal preferences during training data sample selection (Park *et al.*, 2021; Srinivasan and Chander, 2021), analysis, or interpretation of results (Schwartz *et al.*, 2022). In addition, the decision to adopt algorithmic advice when it matches the researchers' subjective expectations, although the data is not optimal, may also be biased (Park *et al.*, 2021; Schwartz *et al.*, 2022). For example, educators may consider AI-based tools as the ultimate truth for grading students' work and skip manual validation of the system's outcome (Nazaretsky *et al.*, 2021). Another example is reliance on AI systems for property price prediction only based on the building parameters (Bauer *et al.*, 2023). These and additional cases documented in the literature stress the importance of mitigating biases and ensuring fairness in AI systems.

Since confirmation bias can lead data scientists and analysts to selectively choose or interpret data that aligns with their initial assumptions, it may lead to biased algorithms and decision-making (Chen *et al.*, 2023; Collins *et al.*, 2022). Moreover, modern AI methods can transfer knowledge from AI systems to human users by offering answers alongside predictions. In the case of faulty conclusions or recommendations, AI users may gain wrong insights about the relationship between variables (Müller, 2021). Designing effective regulations surrounding AI is one of the ways to tackle the challenge. Meanwhile, the researchers should apply practical means to address confirmation bias to ensure objectivity and fairness in AI development, analysis, explainability, and transparency (Bauer *et al.*, 2023).

2.1.2. *Mitigating confirmation bias in AI*

Gaps in transparency and fidelity of data used in training and developing AI algorithms create a lack of trust in the model's outcome (Mylrea and Robinson, 2023). To overcome this lack of trust, one must ensure that the data used to train and validate AI models is free of cognitive bias and representative of a diverse population (Mylrea and Robinson, 2023;

Nihei, 2022). Although the present literature does not yet contain standardized guidance to mitigate confirmation bias, it helps understand the nature of the phenomenon and provides some practical recommendations. For example, acknowledging confirmatory information search and evaluation phenomena as the core of the confirmation bias, dedicated tests such as the selective exposure paradigm or confirmatory information evaluation can serve to establish baseline measures of confirmation bias presence (Bedek *et al.*, 2018). However, even trained and aware of cognitive biases, data scientists may refuse to acknowledge that certain biases could affect their decisions (Kretz, 2018). This phenomenon is known in the literature as blind spot bias (Ellis, 2018) or an illusion of control (Singh *et al.*, 2022). It leads to overestimating the researcher's confidence in analysis while discarding the signals that disconfirm their decision. To find an optional debiasing strategy and enable new perspectives to the existing challenges, ongoing research focuses on the discovery and empirical validation of debiasing techniques. One example is structured analytical techniques (de Melo, 2021; Pili, 2023). Broadly discussed representatives of these techniques are argument mapping (Ellis, 2018; Zografistou *et al.*, 2022) and analysis of competing hypotheses (Robinson, 2022; Whitesmith, 2022). Because of the apparent difficulty in influencing cognitive behavior, some studies discuss how combining visualization techniques, statistical information, and evidence-based reasoning might help mitigate certain cognitive biases, particularly those affecting decision-making objectivity (Ellis, 2018).

2.2. *Availability Bias*

Availability bias is a cognitive bias in which individuals tend to give more weight to information that is easily accessible or available in their minds (Rastogi *et al.*, 2022; Sunstein, 2022; Varona and Suárez, 2022). As a result, people allot measlier importance to more abstract information (Singh *et al.*, 2022). Factors such as familiarity, salience, and recency influence availability bias. Because humans rely on the information that comes to mind quickly rather than considering a broader range of relevant factors, availability bias can lead to distorted decision-making (Austin *et al.*, 2023; Li, 2020).

The literature provides multiple descriptions of how availability bias can affect decision-making in various human activities. For example, in the context of financial trading, traders may be inclined to give more importance to readily available information, as acquiring new information can be costly and time-consuming in financial markets (Sharma *et al.*, 2022). Additional examples are in the field of education (Austin *et al.*, 2023), gender and military operations (Brown *et al.*, 2020), and ecological studies about the abundance of narwhals (Heide-Jørgensen and Lage, 2022).

Numerous medical studies discussed the challenge of availability bias. Experienced physicians often utilize this bias to simplify their decision-making process by focusing on information that comes to mind easily, which can improve efficiency. However, it can also lead to diagnostic errors and influence therapeutic decisions, as doctors may prescribe familiar treatments, be influenced by recently encountered data, or assess the probability of an event based on the ease with which relevant instances can be recalled (Elston, 2020; Monteiro *et al.*, 2020; Pot *et al.*, 2021).

2.2.1. *Availability bias in AI*

Availability bias in AI can lead to overemphasizing specific patterns or data points that are more easily accessible, potentially overlooking important but less accessible information. For example, if the training data is biased in recommendation systems, the system may perpetuate that bias in its suggestions (Mueller *et al.*, 2022). Availability bias can also lead to the inclusion of notable cases in the Machine Learning (ML) database, causing exceptional cases to be over-represented in the ML database, hence leading to missing usual cases. This may happen because people tend to search only where it is easiest to look (Schwartz *et al.*, 2022). For example, if AI systems are trained only on data received from the most active users (Schwartz *et al.*, 2022), then some relevant variables and corresponding features are not included in the model (Mehrabi *et al.*, 2021; Srinivasan and Chander, 2021). Another example is weighing available evidence more than newly arrived one (Park *et al.*, 2021). Convenience data sampling techniques used in statistics could be seen as exemplifying the availability bias in AI (Park *et al.*, 2021).

Despite the advancements and accuracy of current AI systems, they are more likely to augment rather than replace human decision-making in specific fields. One example is medicine, which remains an art that requires personalized patient care (Hoard *et al.*, 2021; Kyere *et al.*, 2022). Nevertheless, it became a consensus that AI has the potential to revolutionize fields like medicine by enhancing diagnostic and treatment decisions (Mamede *et al.*, 2021; Pisciotta *et al.*, 2023). Understanding the nature of availability bias and employing the appropriate strategies can help mitigate its impact and promote more rational decision-making processes.

2.2.2. *Mitigating availability bias in AI*

Algorithms can mitigate availability and other cognitive biases, offering more reliable and unbiased decision-making processes. However, human-engineered algorithms and the biases introduced during their creation have constrained the development and implementation of AI systems. While Machine-Learning (ML) based AI is seen as a solution to mitigate human biases, it can also introduce its own biases. The "garbage in, garbage out" problem highlights that ML algorithms are only as good as the data they are trained with, meaning biases present in training data can be reinforced and exacerbated by AI applications. Therefore, availability bias constitutes a significant concern in implementing ML technologies (Pot *et al.*, 2021).

To overcome the availability bias and focus on relevant information, unsupervised ML clustering techniques can be utilized. These techniques help group information with similar features, allowing labeling and categorizing it based on its significance. Additionally, hierarchical clustering can assist in prioritizing and analyzing abstract information effectively. One can make more informed decisions by clustering and creating a hierarchical information structure, reducing the influence of availability bias (Sharma *et al.*, 2022).

2.3. *Automation Bias*

Automation bias occurs when users rely on and favor recommendations from automated systems as a heuristic replacement for their own information-seeking and processing and disregarding information from non-automated sources. (Nourani *et al.*, 2021; Passi and Vorvoreanu, 2022; Schwartz *et al.*, 2022). Humans over-rely on automated systems or have

their skills attenuated by such over-reliance (Schwartz *et al.*, 2022), causing users to accept incorrect AI recommendations (Passi and Vorvoreanu,
2022). Thus, this bias is also called overreliance bias.

Automation sometimes leads humans to a loss of situational awareness bias. This occurs when users are unaware of their situation when the
control of a system is given back to them when humans and systems
cooperate, and then they are unprepared to assume their duties (Schwartz
et al., 2022). Users have difficulties determining appropriate levels of
trust in the system because they lack awareness of what the system can do,
how it works, and how good the output is (Passi and Vorvoreanu, 2022).

2.3.1. *Automation bias in AI*

AI systems used to assist in decision-making by users in different domains
are black boxes not understood by the users. This lack of transparency and
the users' trust in the systems leads to overreliance on the outputs of these
systems. Generally accepting AI advice would also include accepting
incorrect or inaccurate AI advice (Schemmer *et al.*, 2023).

Automation bias refers to determining the value of a decision based
solely on the outcome, disregarding the generation process because of the
lack of transparency (Park *et al.*, 2021). When individuals make decisions
based on the outcomes of the events and not the process, which describes
the rationale for such an outcome, they are said to suffer from outcome
bias, which is a kind of automation bias (Singh *et al.*, 2022). The overreliance is affected by the users' characteristics, such as demographic, social,
cultural, and professional characteristics, and on their literacy on AI, how
much they understand the system, their expertise in the relevant domain,
and familiarity with the task (Passi and Vorvoreanu, 2022).

2.3.2. *Mitigating automation bias in AI*

AI models are expected to provide accurate predictions, and in order to
offer decision-makers meaningful support, the black boxes need to
become more transparent, giving the user a notion of how a particular
decision has been derived to empower users to develop an appropriate
reliance on the AI systems (Yin *et al.*, 2019). Explaining the rationale
behind an AI decision should enable the user to learn when to trust the

recommendations of the AI and when to question it (Schemmer *et al.*, 2022). These kinds of explanations need to consider the characteristics of the user, the familiarity with the task, and the user's expertise. Hence, the explanations must be adapted to each user (Passi and Vorvoreanu, 2022). Researchers who identified the automation bias introduced eXplainable AI (XAI) models, which try to explain to the users the process of the system's decision-making (Nourani *et al.*, 2021). According to the researchers, the explanations should help users build a better mental model of the system and, thus, understand the reason and rationale of the system's outputs, allowing them to make more based and solid decisions. Rastogi *et al.* (2022) found that informing users about the AI system confidence mitigates the automation bias and makes the users' decisions better. The explanations can be based on different information, such as feature importance-based, example-based, rule-based methods, and others (Schemmer *et al.*, 2022). The explanations provided to the users can be shown in various formats, using visualization and other means (Nourani *et al.*, 2021). A better understanding of how the AI's decision was derived should subsequently enable the user to appropriately rely on the AI's suggestions (Nourani *et al.*, 2021; Rastogi *et al.*, 2022; Schemmer *et al.*, 2022). Explanations contradicting the system's prediction could cause the user to become skeptical, considering the AI prediction less in the final decision-making process. However, the complexity of AI systems is growing, and explaining the processes to human users in a beneficial manner is getting harder (Nourani *et al.*, 2021); therefore, more instructions and explanations are needed.

Schemmer *et al.* (2022) conducted a meta-analysis to find the effect of the explanations on the users according to published research. They found a statistically positive impact of XAI on users' performance. However, they found no effect of explanations on users' performance compared to using sole AI. As a consequence of prior research, a new concept was defined — the appropriate reliance — human decision-makers should not simply rely on AI advice but should be empowered to differentiate when to rely on AI advice and when to rely on their own (Schemmer *et al.*, 2023). Rastogi *et al.* (2022) claim that reducing the trust users have in the AI system leverages their judgment in making the decision, thus reducing the automation bias, as well as the anchoring bias. They found that when the AI is incorrect, the information it provides the human distracts them from the correct decision, thus reducing their performance. They performed some experiments in which they informed the users about the algorithm's confidence in its decision. Giving the users information about the AI system confidence as an explanation alleviates some of the automation and anchoring bias, making the decisions of the human-system team better than AI alone or only humans' decisions.

2.4. *Anchoring Bias*

Anchoring is a cognitive bias, which refers to the tendency of individuals to rely on the first (Park *et al.*, 2021), last, or recent (Singh *et al.*, 2022) shown piece of information they receive when making decisions and ignore the requirement of a rigorous process to make decisions. This initial information, known as the anchor, often influences subsequent thoughts and assessments, even if the anchor is arbitrary or unrelated to the decision at hand (Chinander and Schweitzer, 2003). Another kind of anchoring bias is the "peak end," a type of memory-related cognitive bias in which people judge an experience based largely on how they felt at its peak, the most intense point, and at its end, rather than based on the total sum or average of every moment of the experience (Srinivasan and Chander, 2021).

For a decision to be made, both the setup of the task and the information shown within the task can be an anchor for the decision-maker (Echterhoff *et al.*, 2022). The anchoring bias is universal and exists in various contexts relating to decision-making and message processing, independently of individual personality and intelligence differences (Adame, 2016). Tversky and Kahneman (1974) proposed that individuals rely on an initial value and then make adjustments to arrive at an acceptable decision and that biased estimates occur from perpetually insufficient adjustment. It is often referred to as anchoring-and-adjustment, or anchoring-and-adjusting: after an anchor is set, people adjust insufficiently from that anchor point to arrive at a final answer (Schwartz *et al.*, 2022).

Decision Support Systems were aware of this limitation on decision-making, either with both novice and expert decision-makers; consequently, systems try to mitigate the anchoring bias (George *et al.*, 2000) by working on the data with specific algorithms or by training the users, trying to make users aware of their own bias, and explaining how to work with these kinds of systems. However, unfortunately, the remedy for the bias was not found. Studies demonstrate that making individuals aware of the potential for anchoring has no mitigation effect (Adame, 2016).

2.4.1. *Anchoring bias in AI*

It is assumed that AI systems can avoid anchoring biases by taking decision-making away from humans and giving it to algorithms. However, it was found that AI has not eliminated the anchoring bias, but it reflects the problem and sometimes enhances it (Romanov *et al.*, 2023). AI-assisted decision-making tasks are prone to anchoring bias, where the human decision-maker is irrationally anchored to the AI-generated decision (Rastogi *et al.*, 2022). This phenomenon can be caused by two reasons: training data bias and user interaction bias.

The training data bias: This refers to when using human-generated data sets to train the algorithm. The training datasets are commonly prepared by humans, exhibiting conscious or subconscious human biases. Following this, the AI system may learn and reinforce those biases. The algorithm inherits the biases caused by the order of the data. When making decisions or providing recommendations, the AI system could be anchored to the biased information it was trained on, potentially leading to unfair or inaccurate outcomes (Rastogi *et al.*, 2022).

User interaction bias: When interacting with AI systems, users may be influenced by the initial information or suggestions provided by the system, according to their trust in the system (Rastogi *et al.*, 2022). AI recommendations may act as anchors and significantly influence users' decision-making processes to align with the system recommendations (Passi and Vorvoreanu, 2022). This can lead to users accepting or relying heavily on the initial outputs without critically evaluating or considering alternative options, potentially reinforcing biases present in the AI system.

2.4.2. *Mitigating anchoring bias in AI*

To mitigate anchoring bias in AI, it is crucial to arrange the data sets and/ or the algorithms and/or the outputs:

Data sets order: Ensuring the training data is diverse, representative, and free from biases to the best extent possible will help to mitigate anchoring biases caused by data. Researchers (Echterhoff *et al.*, 2022; Romanov *et al.*, 2023) propose methods to remove the order of the information in the process of ML by using various algorithms for order change, which impacts human decisions in AI systems, avoiding the system being influenced by the previously made decisions. Thus eliminating this cognitive bias and improving automated decision-making.

Algorithms: Algorithms can also mitigate bias retrospectively for already-made decisions by capturing the anchoring state of a reviewer with a probabilistic model and adapting decisions with a logical strategy (Echterhoff *et al.*, 2022). Regularly evaluating and auditing AI systems for biases in decision-making processes to update algorithms will help mitigate biases caused by the system. Teaching users to critically assess AI-generated outputs and consider alternative perspectives or information can help mitigate users' interaction biases.

Output: Factor models and principal component analysis tools of unsupervised ML may assist users in putting emphasis not only on recent events but also on prior events. The required dimensionality reduction can be applied with the help of ML techniques to assist the users in considering only relevant aspects of information. A thorough analysis of all or most of the past strategies by the user will help the user reduce the influence of recent events on decision-making (Singh *et al.*, 2022).

2.5. *Sampling Bias*

Sampling bias is one of the most common types of dataset biases. It occurs when a dataset is created by selecting or ignoring particular types of instances and does not represent the entire population or phenomenon of study (Srinivasan and Chander, 2021; Vokinger *et al.*, 2021). Sampling bias may also arise due to non-random sampling of subgroups or the addition of synthetic or redundant samples to a dataset. Sampling bias is similar to representation bias and negative set biases, depends on the data collection process, and may cause faulty trends that do not apply to the entire population or phenomenon of study (Mehrabi *et al.*, 2021; Schwartz *et al.*, 2022). This type of bias can also be caused by human erroneous measurement, sample selection, or inappropriate labeling during the validation and testing procedures (Mehrabi *et al.*, 2021; Srinivasan and Chander, 2021).

2.5.1. *Sampling bias in AI*

Sampling bias in AI occurs when the data used to train or analyze AI systems does not represent the entire population or phenomenon under study (Ntoutsi *et al.*, 2020; Vokinger *et al.*, 2021). It can arise from self-selection bias, survivorship bias, or dataset bias (Hellström *et al.*, 2020). For example, online surveys may attract individuals with specific interests, creating bias in the collected data and leading to performance differences and systematic errors for under-represented groups. The skewed or not reflecting diversity of the target population data can lead to biased models and inaccurate predictions. The sampling bias in ML models has been demonstrated in various studies across different domains and can have significant implications.

One specific type of sampling bias is under-sampling, which occurs when certain groups are under-represented in the sample. For example, racial and ethnic minorities may be under-sampled, resulting in a model that heavily relies on data and variable interrelationships associated with the over-represented group (Buolamwini and Gebru, 2018; Fletcher *et al.*, 2021; Vokinger *et al.*, 2021). Another example is spatial data analysis, where geological subsurface characterization is based on sparse and non-representative sampling. In such cases, bias in the training data can result in biased predictions by ML models (Liu *et al.*, 2021). In the context of metrology, sampling bias can result in algorithmic bias, where biases in the data propagate into AI-based systems, leading to discriminatory outcomes or skewed decisions (Tancev and Pascale, 2020). In turn, uncertainty bias results from predictive algorithms favoring groups that are better represented in the training data (Schwartz *et al.*, 2022), leading to biased predictions and limited generalizability for under-represented groups (Hellström *et al.*, 2020).

2.5.2. *Mitigating sampling bias in AI*

Recognizing the problem and striving for improved representation in training data are crucial steps toward mitigating sampling bias and

R. Gafni et al.

promoting fairness in ML algorithms. Addressing sampling bias requires collecting representative and balanced datasets to minimize bias and ensure fair and accurate predictions (Sklar, 2022; Vokinger *et al.*, 2021). However, these approaches alone may not guarantee successful mitigation of bias in practice (Buolamwini and Gebru, 2018; Mehrabi *et al.*, 2021). Addressing sampling bias is also crucial for the reliable performance of ML models. For supervised ML, rather than applying ad-hoc bias correction methods after model creation, methods such as Bayesian inference can correct for bias during the learning process itself (Sklar, 2022). In medicine, to ensure suitability in specific settings, it is essential to compile diverse and large datasets that represent all patient groups, monitor error rates for different cohorts, and disclose the performance levels of ML systems (Landers and Behrend, 2022). While transparently reporting the performance levels of ML models can help identify and mitigate bias, monitoring error rates for different populations and reporting checklists can aid in assessing the risk of bias in ML-based systems (Vokinger *et al.*, 2021). For the context of spatial data sets, such as geological subsurface characterization, methods such as spatially weighted trees might be helpful to mitigate the bias in predictions and improve the accuracy evaluation. It is generally recommended to incorporate model checking and bias mitigation for all ML prediction models with sparse, spatial data sets (Liu *et al.*, 2021).

Regardless of the field of application, it is essential to avoid implicit bias resulting from unforeseen correlations between variables in models (Hellström *et al.*, 2020). Model inspection techniques and explainable AI methods can help uncover and address sampling bias in AI systems. Besides, certification and assessment procedures by independent organizations can ensure the fairness and accuracy of AI products (Tancev and Pascale, 2020). To conclude, because sampling bias can have significant implications for the reliability and fairness of ML models, researchers must carefully focus on data selection, monitoring, and transparent reporting to ensure representative and accurate predictions for all population segments. The discussion of bias in AI and ML intersects applied and social sciences, highlighting the need for transparency, explainability, and responsibility in developing AI systems to avoid discrimination and ensure accuracy (Tancev and Pascale, 2020).

2.6. *Model selection and design bias*

During the model selection and design phase, developers must decide how features should be engineered and selected for the data, what algorithms should be applied to train the machines, and what evaluation metrics or evaluation data should be developed (Chen *et al.*, 2023). Bias in the model selection and design phase can result in incorrect judgments and negative results for individuals, organizations, and society levels (Kordzadeh and Ghasemaghaei, 2021; Martin, 2019). This includes algorithmic bias, which gained significant traction in both mainstream media and public discourse surrounding technology. For example, following Martin (2019), the media increasingly features headlines highlighting algorithms' potential consequences on healthcare and employment decisions. Danks and London (2017) argued that there is a growing worry regarding the presence of biases in various algorithmic systems, such as Google searches, Facebook feeds, FaceApp, and similar applications.

2.6.1. *Algorithmic bias in AI*

Algorithmic bias in AI is defined as a bias added by the algorithm itself and not by the input data (Baeza-Yates, 2018; Srinivasan and Chander, 2021). The most common algorithmic biases discussed in academic literature refer to design-related bias, confounding bias, and overfitting/underfitting biases.

Design-related bias may arise due to algorithmic limits or other constraints within the system, such as computational power (Srinivasan and Chander, 2021). The ML algorithms are known as "black box" algorithms, where the input and output of the algorithm are observable. However, the internal process remains undisclosed. Consequently, there is a lack of transparency concerning the methodologies and underlying logic utilized in AI systems (d'Alessandro *et al.*, 2017; Favaretto *et al.*, 2019).

Confounding bias is one of the most notable biases, also called the "bias-variance trade-off" (Belkin *et al.*, 2019). The bias-variance trade-off suggests that a model should be rich enough to express underlying structure in data and simple enough to avoid fitting spurious patterns (Belkin *et al.*, 2019). There are statistical approaches that aim to minimize random errors given the sample in which modeling is performed while also maximizing predictive accuracy within the sample to provide clear and unambiguous interpretations of individual coefficients (Landers and Behrend, 2022). When such a model is applied to new data acquired from the original population, the lack of bias within the sample is related to increased variance in out-of-sample predicted accuracy, which can result in less stable out-of-sample predictive performance, a problem called overfitting (Landers and Behrend, 2022).

Overfitting and Underfitting Biases are constant and pervasive threats in ML (Bashir *et al.*, 2020). A statistical ML model overfits when it learns the systematic and noisy components in the training data to the point that it has a negative effect on the model's performance on new data. This indicates that the statistical ML model adapts effectively to both the noise and the signal contained in the training data, which introduces bias and impairs the model's ability to generalize (Massa *et al.*, 2022). On the other hand, underfitting occurs when models are trained in a very simplistic manner, resulting in low variance but high bias estimates (Ghojogh and Crowley, 2019). Although training data sets are frequently discussed when discussing overfitting or underfitting biases in ML systems, there are situations when the bias may be produced or at least aggravated by the algorithm itself (Cunningham and Delany, 2021). AI practitioners try to avoid the risks of overfitting and underfitting; however, there is no formalized set of criteria for whether a particular algorithm will overfit or underfit a given dataset (Bashir *et al.*, 2020). Moreover, the theory of overfitting and underfitting remains underdeveloped, depending primarily on folk wisdom and heuristic approaches (Amini *et al.*, 2019; Bashir *et al.*, 2020).

2.6.2. *Mitigating algorithmic bias in AI*

The absence of transparent information on how algorithms and processes work makes it challenging to evaluate the fairness of the algorithms or discover discriminatory patterns in the system (Favaretto *et al.*, 2019). Developing interpretable algorithms, which provide explanations regarding the logical processes underlying a specific classification, will increase algorithmic transparency and enable individuals to anticipate how their behavior and choices will be interpreted by the algorithm (Favaretto *et al.*, 2019; Kroll *et al.*, 2017). Algorithmic bias mitigation also comes from regulatory bodies that implement measures for addressing the challenges associated with algorithmic bias. For example, the General Data Protection Regulation (GDPR) of the European Union and the Future of AI Act of 2017 in the United States enforce limitations on the processing of data and the utilization of AI in corporate operations in order to foster algorithmic responsibility and mitigate algorithmic bias (Danks and London, 2017).

In the context of overfitting and underfitting biases associated with confounding bias, several considerations must be taken into account when selecting mitigation strategies:

Regularization: Regularization techniques aim to reduce overfitting by adding a penalty term to the model's objective function. In this context, a penalty term is defined as adding a cost term to the error function, emphasizing either simplification or complexity of the cost function to reduce the overfit or underfit phenomenon (Ghojogh and Crowley, 2019).

Early Stopping: Early stopping technique refers to defining the stopping criteria that need to be established for testing and validation sets in addition to the quantity of training data that must be learned. Training-wise, one should train neural networks past the underfitting point and before the overfitting starts. Early stopping is a simple yet effective technique to prevent overfitting (Jabbar and Khan, 2015).

Dropout: The dropout technique randomly "drops out" (deactivates) a fraction of neurons in a neural network during each training iteration. By dropping out neurons, the network becomes less reliant on specific neurons and instead learns to rely on combinations of neurons. This encourages the network to learn more robust and generalized representations (Srivastava *et al.*, 2014).

Cross-Validation: Cross-validation is a technique used to estimate the model's performance on unseen data. It involves partitioning the data into multiple subsets, training the model on a subset, and evaluating its performance on the remaining subset. By averaging the performance across different subsets, cross-validation provides a more reliable estimate of the model's generalization ability (Ghojogh and Crowley, 2019).

Ensemble Methods: Ensemble methods combine multiple models to improve generalization performance. Techniques like bagging (bootstrap aggregating) and boosting create an ensemble of models trained on different subsets of the data or with different weightings, thereby reducing overfitting and improving overall performance (Ghojogh and Crowley, 2019).

2.7. *Appropriate Use Bias*

Appropriate use bias belongs to human biases where a system is used outside the initially intended application's domain. The literature provides additional definitions of the phenomenon, such as deployment bias (Suresh and Guttag, 2019), drift, or emergent bias (Schwartz *et al.*, 2022). This bias typically arises when data representatives are questionable, and the context or system's user population may differ from the original target population (Mehrabi *et al.*, 2021). For example, a medical system designed and tested to diagnose a specific type of cancer is later used to diagnose a different type of cancer (Fletcher *et al.*, 2021). As a result, this bias may cause inaccurate or even faulty system outputs (Schwartz *et al.*, 2022).

2.7.1. *Appropriate use bias in AI*

In AI, the appropriate use bias can occur during the development and deployment of ML systems. Since ML systems should target particular scopes and be developed using specific data, using them beyond this scope can lead to biased or incorrect results (Fletcher *et al.*, 2021; Yan and Zeleznikow, 2022). For example, if, due to sampling bias, certain parts of the population are not represented in the dataset, then applying the model for these parts of the population is not appropriate concerning how the model was developed (Schwartz *et al.*, 2022). The same principle applies to using inappropriate or disproportionate benchmarks during model testing and evaluation (Mehrabi *et al.*, 2021).

During model development, appropriate bias may also become an inherited or error propagation bias if a certain application is improperly used to generate inputs for another ML algorithm (Schwartz *et al.*, 2022).

For example, in dynamic environments, such as financial markets, AI systems trained on historical data may not perform well when market dynamics change (Singh *et al.*, 2022). Another possibility may occur when specific scenarios were not considered during the initial model's training. The further improper use of the model makes it unprepared and unreliable for these cases (Cummings, 2023; Yan and Zeleznikow, 2022).

2.7.2. *Mitigating appropriate use bias in AI*

Although the present literature does not contain specified guidance to mitigate the appropriate use bias, it helps in deriving some practical recommendations. Concerning data security and quality, researchers should precisely assess and document the appropriateness of the selected training datasets (Roselli *et al.*, 2019). They must ensure no manipulation or inappropriate use of datasets for building AI models (Kahlawi, 2022; Suciu *et al.*, 2018). Surrogate data should be substantiated and accompanied by quantitative evidence to ensure that this data is appropriate for its intended use in the model. Any limitations in the data should be documented and considered for the prediction results (Kiritz and Sarfati, 2018). Training data should be validated for trustworthiness, including accuracy, relevancy, credibility, reliability, and consistency (Kahlawi, 2022). In turn, incomplete or ambiguous samples must be eliminated.

Regarding the model's intended use, it should be trained with a range of datasets covering various scenarios it might encounter in the real world. The system's intended use cases and limitations during its design and development should be documented to ensure the model's interpretability or explainability (Vokinger *et al.*, 2021). The appropriateness for each use case should be accompanied by quantitative external evidence that supports it, along with any known limitations of the validation methodology (Kiritz and Sarfati, 2018). Following the system's deployment, it is recommended to continuously monitor and evaluate the system's performance in different contexts and adjust as necessary (Koh *et al.*, 2022). These and additional safeguards related to the model's methodology may contribute to a model's transferability assessment (Varadharajan *et al.*, 2022).

2.8. *Presentation Bias*

Users' decision-making can be affected based on how the information is presented, either on the Web, via a user interface, or due to rating or ranking of the output. These kinds of biases are called presentation biases (Schwartz *et al.*, 2022), framing biases, when the framing of words alters the decision-making process (Singh *et al.*, 2022), and interaction biases (Schwartz *et al.*, 2022). The presentation bias is derived from the fact that the user can receive feedback only on items that have been presented to the user (Srinivasan and Chander, 2021).

Ranking biases are also closely related to presentation bias. Ranking is a form of bias that occurs when more popular items are more exposed and less popular items are under-represented (Schwartz *et al.*, 2022). This is often called popularity bias (Klimashevskaia *et al.*, 2023) or position bias (J. Chen *et al.*, 2023), both occurring specifically in recommender systems. The idea that top-ranked results are the most relevant and important will result in the attraction of more clicks than others results (Schwartz *et al.*, 2022). However, popularity metrics are subject to manipulation — for example, by fake reviews or social bots (Mehrabi *et al.*, 2021). Therefore, this bias also affects search engines and crowd-sourcing applications (Mehrabi *et al.*, 2021).

User interaction bias is a type of bias derived from presentation and ranking biases and is affected by anchoring and automation biases. It is triggered from the user interface and through the user itself by imposing his/her self-selected biased behavior and interaction (Mehrabi *et al.*, 2021). The user interaction is based on the interface and the presentation, which can confuse human operators, who misunderstand which mode the system is using, taking actions that are correct for a different mode but incorrect for their current situation (Schwartz *et al.*, 2022).

2.8.1. *Presentation bias in AI*

The presentation of outputs, including the ranking mechanism, can affect AI systems because of the feedback loop and the ML from previous actions. According to Chen *et al.* (2023), three components in AI systems are affected during the feedback loop related to presentation biases: (1) Collection of data from users, including user-item interactions; (2) Learning from the collected biased data, which affects the model; and (3) Returning the recommendation results to users.

2.8.2. *Mitigating presentation bias in AI*

Presentation biases, including ranking and popularity biases, can be mitigated by including moderating algorithms in the AI system or by introducing randomness into the recommendations and learning better models.

Proper text or visual recognition by users can help them resolve the consequences of framing bias (Singh *et al.*, 2022). Users should not make decisions based on how the information is presented to help them mitigate the impact of the framing bias. Presentation bias can also be addressed at the output stage by adjusting how certain outputs are labeled and presented (Fletcher *et al.*, 2021).

2.9. *Ethical and Social Biases*

In today's rapid technological development, ethics is critical in understanding how technologies affect individuals, businesses, groups, society, and the environment (John-Mathews *et al.*, 2022; Sætra and Danaher, 2022). Ethical issues in computer-based technologies are gaining much attention in academic studies and industry. Ethics is defined as the discipline dealing with "right" vs. "wrong" and entities' moral obligations and duties (Siau and Wang, 2020). Therefore, ethical bias represents the risk of harm if misused or deployed without careful consideration.

2.9.1. *Ethical bias in AI*

Following Sætra and Danaher (2022), digital ethics was positioned at the height of inflated expectations in the 2021 version of Gartner's *hype cycle* for AI (Gartner, 2021, as cited in Sætra and Danaher, 2022). Concerns about the ethical implications of AI are growing as more sectors employ automation processes. For example, self-driving vehicles, which promise to promote personal mobility and save lives by minimizing driver errors, present the dilemma of who should be prioritized in an emergency situation: pedestrians or passengers (Bonnefon *et al.*, 2016). Banking Chatbots can be manipulated or exploited in such a way that the hackers may try to impersonate a banking officer, get the details of a customer, and commit fraud (Nasim *et al.*, 2022). Algorithm biases, discrimination, and, consequently, unfairness have been identified in various AI applications (John-Mathews *et al.*, 2022; Mehrabi *et al.*, 2021).

Nasim *et al.* (2022) analyzed the AI Incident Database. They identified eight categories of common ethical biases: inappropriate use, racial discrimination, physical safety, unfair algorithm, gender discrimination, privacy, unethical (illegal use), and mental health. While trying to find a strategy for dealing with ethical bias in AI, academic works explore different categorizations of these biases (Favaretto *et al.*, 2019; Jobin *et al.*, 2019; Mehrabi *et al.*, 2021; Siau and Wang, 2020). Jobin *et al.* (2019) examined 84 ethical AI documents. They discovered that, while no single principle was present in all of them, the themes of transparency, justice and fairness, non-maleficence, responsibility, and privacy appeared in more than half.

Transparency refers to AI's inner processing and algorithm (Jobin *et al.*, 2019; Nasim *et al.*, 2022). This processing is hard to explain, leading to significant information asymmetries among AI experts and users, hindering human trust in the technology and AI agents (Siau and Wanhg, 2020). Furthermore, AI may evolve without human monitoring and guidance (Siau and Wanhg, 2020). One of the famous examples is Facebook, which discovered that its AI had constructed its own unique language, which humans could not understand and therefore had to shut down an AI engine (Bradley, 2017).

Justice and fairness relate to non-discrimination, non-biased, and impartiality (Jobin *et al.*, 2019; Nasim *et al.*, 2022). For example, racial bias is a bias in AI systems that unfairly favors or discriminates against individuals of certain racial or ethnic groups (Favaretto *et al.*, 2019).

The non-maleficence principle refers to an obligation not to cause harm to others (Jobin *et al.*, 2019; Nasim *et al.*, 2022). Responsibility and accountability refer to setting moral norms in order to avoid damage in the first place (Jobin *et al.*, 2019; Sand *et al.*, 2022). The privacy and security principle refers to data misuse. While huge amounts of data are generated in AI models, it is essential to protect this data from misuse (Siau and Wang, 2020). Ethical AI sees privacy as a value to uphold and a right to be protected (Jobin *et al.*, 2019). A health record, for example, always contains sensitive information that, if not securely protected, a rogue institution could access and hurt the patients personally and financially. As a result, data must be appropriately maintained to avoid misuse and malicious usage (Timmermans *et al.*, 2010, as cited in Siau and Wang, 2020).

2.9.2. *Mitigating ethical bias in AI*

People are generally aware of the norms and ideas behind ethics but are unaware of the consequences if they are not followed or how to apply them in AI. Various multinational organizations have established frameworks, rules, and suggestions to reduce risks in AI to create a sustainable ecosystem for technological progress. For example, The European Union has established various expert groups to promote the safe and reliable development of AI, including the European Commission-appointed Ad-hoc Committee on AI (CAHAI) and the Organization for Economic Cooperation and Development (OECD) group of AI experts (de Manuel *et al.*, 2023). These organizations seek to ensure that technology is in accordance with human rights, dignity, and specific ethical ideals such as transparency, security, and privacy, among others (de Manuel *et al.*, 2023). However, questions were raised regarding the actual impact of those guidelines on human decision-making in AI and ML (Hagendorff, 2020). Empirical experiments show that reading ethics guidelines has no significant influence on the decision-making of software developers (Hagendorff, 2020). In cases where ethics is integrated into institutions, it mainly serves as a marketing strategy (Hagendorff, 2020).

Several more focused strategies to prevent ethical bias are discussed in the literature. For example, to ensure data security, each activity taken with the data should be thorough and documented. Both the data itself and the transaction record may pose privacy problems. As a result, it is critical to examine what should be documented, who should be in charge of the recording action, and who has access to the data and records (Siau and Wang, 2020). To prevent discrimination and inequality in data analytics, technology solutions, legal solutions, and human-centered solutions are proposed (Favaretto *et al.*, 2019). Technology solutions include three stages of processing solutions, which refer to training data sanitization or distortion to remove possible biases in order to prevent the new model from learning discriminatory behaviors (pre-processing), algorithms development to avoid discriminatory predictions, overfitting or hidden model bias (in-processing), and auditing of the extracted data mining models, for discriminative patterns and eventually their sanitization (post-processing). Legal solutions suggest legislation on data protection and discrimination. Human-centered solutions suggest keeping humans in the loop of data mining (Favaretto *et al.*, 2019).

Researchers have pursued an innovative path by developing tools that can determine the amount of fairness in an AI system (Mehrabi *et al.*, 2021). For example: (a) Aequitas is a toolset that allows users to evaluate models against various biases and fairness measures for different demographic subsets (Saleiro *et al.*, 2018); (b) AI Fairness 360 (AIF360) aims to facilitate the transition of fairness research algorithms for use in an industrial setting and to provide a common framework for fairness researchers to share and evaluate algorithms (Bellamy *et al.*, 2019); and (c) Fairkit is a python toolkit aiming to evaluate ML models based on various fairness metrics (Johnson *et al.*, 2023).

3. Summary, Conclusions, and Recommendations

This chapter had two primary goals. The first was to create awareness and raise the attention of AI practitioners to the dangers of human biases. To address this goal, we explained the nature of cognitive biases, mental models, and how humans make decisions based on heuristics. Understanding how these biases may affect thoughts and decisions is crucial to mitigate possible unintended errors in judgment and flawed decision-making across the entire community of AI systems developers and users.

The second goal was to discuss the effects of biases on the fairness and applicability of AI systems and provide actionable recommendations to mitigate them. To meet this goal, we first described the main stages of the AI systems lifecycle, emphasized the risks associated with the human, data set, and algorithmic biases according to each phase of the AI systems lifecycle, and listed the representative types of these biases. Then, for each of the representative biases, we provided a detailed description, explained the dangers of having these biases in AI systems, and provided practical recommendations for mitigating each type of bias.

One can derive several conclusions and recommendations from this paper. First, due to the human nature of decision-making processes and embedded in their biases, the earlier educators will raise attention to these processes among future AI practitioners, the sooner they will become aware of it. Second, awareness alone without practice does not provide immunity, and even trained people may still fall into biased decisions. Hence, there is a need for a set of practical guidelines and procedures for each one of the AI systems' lifecycle phases. One of the ways to achieve these guidelines is through the unified sets of compulsory requirements documented as standards or other types of regulatory decisions. Finally, no regulation or standards can be fulfilled without a detailed mechanism of auditing or certifications. Hence, similar to the concept of security-by-design and the corresponding frameworks for verifying the cybersecurity aspects of software products, we propose leveraging the fairness-by-design approach for AI systems. The ultimate goal of leveraging this concept is to provide AI systems users the trust that the AI product they purchased or used has passed the necessary validation or certification approvals and probably will not supply harmful outcomes.

References

Adame, B.J. (2016). Training in the mitigation of anchoring bias: A test of the consider-the-opposite strategy. *Learning and Motivation*, 53, 36–48.

Amini, A., Soleimany, A.P., Schwarting, W., Bhatia, S.N., and Rus, D. (2019, January). Uncovering and mitigating algorithmic bias through learned latent structure. In *Proceedings of the 2019 AAAI/ACM Conference on AI, Ethics, and Society*, Honolulu, HI, USA, January 27–28, pp. 289–295.

Austin, T., Rawal, B.S., Diehl, A., and Cosme, J. (2023). AI for equity: Unpacking potential human bias in decision making in higher education. *AI, Computer Science and Robotics Technology*, 2(May), 1–17.

Baeza-Yates, R. (2018). Bias on the web. *Communications of the ACM*, 61(6), 54–61.

Bashir, D., Montañez, G.D., Sehra, S., Segura, P.S. and Lauw, J. (2020). An information-theoretic perspective on overfitting and underfitting. In *AI 2020: Advances in Artificial Intelligence: 33rd Australasian Joint Conference*, AI 2020, Canberra, ACT, Australia, November 29–30, 2020, Proceedings 33. Springer International Publishing, pp. 347–358.

Bauer, K., von Zahn, M., and Hinz, O. (2023). Expl(AI)ned: The impact of explainable artificial intelligence on users' information processing. *Information Systems Research*, 34(4), 1–21.

Bedek, M.A., Nussbaumer, A., Huszar, L. and Albert, D. (2018). Methods for discovering cognitive biases in a visual analytics environment. In Ellis, G. (Ed.), *Cognitive Biases in Visualizations*, pp. 61–73. Cham, Switzerland: Springer.

Belkin, M., Hsu, D., Ma, S., and Mandal, S. (2019). Reconciling modern machine-learning practice and the classical bias-variance trade-off. *Proceedings of the National Academy of Sciences*, 116(32), 15849–15854.

Bellamy, R.K., Dey, K., Hind, M., Hoffman, S.C., Houde, S., Kannan, K., ... and Zhang, Y. (2019). AI fairness 360: An extensible toolkit for detecting and mitigating algorithmic bias. *IBM Journal of Research and Development*, 63(4/5), 4–1.

Bonnefon, J.F., Shariff, A., and Rahwan, I. (2016). The social dilemma of autonomous vehicles. *Science*, 352(6293), 1573–1576.

Bradley, T. (2017). Facebook AI creates its own language in creepy preview of our potential future. *Forbes*. Retrieved from https://www.forbes.com/sites/tonybradley/2017/07/31/facebook-ai-creates-its-own-language-in-creepy-preview-of-our-potential-future/

Brown, B., Carlucci, R., and Stewart, S. (2020). The consequences of bias. *Phalanx*, 53(4), 26–33.

Buolamwini, J. and Gebru, T. (2018, January). Gender shades: Intersectional accuracy disparities in commercial gender classification. In *Conference on Fairness, Accountability and Transparency*, pp. 77–91. PMLR. New York University, NYC, USA.

Chen, Y., Clayton, E.W., Novak, L.L., Anders, S., and Malin, B. (2023). Human-centered design to address biases in artificial intelligence. *Journal of Medical Internet Research*, 25, e43251.

Chen, J., Dong, H., Wang, X., Feng, F., Wang, M., and He, X. (2023). Bias and debias in recommender system: A survey and future directions. *ACM Transactions on Information Systems*, 41(3), 1–39.

Chinander, K.R. and Schweitzer, M.E. (2003). The input bias: The misuse of input information in judgments of outcomes. *Organizational Behavior and Human Decision Processes*, 91(2), 243–253.

Collins, J.W., Marcus, H.J., Ghazi, A., Sridhar, A., Hashimoto, D., Hager, G., Arezzo, A., Jannin, P., Maier-Hein, L., Marz, K., Valdastri, P., Mori, K., Elson, D., Giannarou, S., Slack, M., Hares, L., Beaulieu, Y., Levy, J., Laplante, G., ... and Stoyanov, D. (2022). Ethical implications of AI in robotic surgical training: A Delphi consensus statement. In *European Urology Focus*, 8(2), 613–622.

Cummings, M.L. (2023). Revising human-systems engineering principles for embedded AI applications. *Frontiers in Neuroergonomics*, 4, 1102165.

Cunningham, P. and Delany, S. J. (2021). Underestimation bias and underfitting in machine learning. In *Trustworthy AI-Integrating Learning, Optimization and Reasoning*: First International Workshop, TAILOR 2020, Virtual Event, September 4–5, 2020, Revised Selected Papers 1 (20–31). Springer International Publishing.

d'Alessandro, B., O'Neil, C., and LaGatta, T. (2017). Conscientious classification: A data scientist's guide to discrimination-aware classification. *Big Data*, 5(2), 120–134.

Danks, D. and London, A. J. (2017, August). Algorithmic bias in autonomous systems. *IJCAI*, 17(2017), 4691–4697.

de Manuel, A., Delgado, J., Parra Jounou, I., Ausín, T., Casacuberta, D., Cruz, M., ... and Puyol, A. (2023). Ethical assessments and mitigation strategies for biases in AI-systems used during the COVID-19 pandemic. *Big Data & Society*, 10(1), 20539517231179199.

de Melo, H.B. (2021). Does analysis of competing hypotheses (ACH) really mitigate cognitive biases? Practical implications for intelligence analysts and criminal investigators. *International Journal of Criminal Justice*, 3(2), 68–82.

Echterhoff, J.M., Yarmand, M., and McAuley, J. (2022, April). AI-moderated decision-making: Capturing and balancing anchoring bias in sequential decision tasks. In *Proceedings of the 2022 CHI Conference on Human Factors in Computing Systems*, New Orleans, LA, USA, April 30–May 5, pp. 1–9.

Ellis, G. (2018). So, what are cognitive biases? In Ellis, G. (Ed.), *Cognitive Biases in Visualizations*, Cham, Switzerland: Springer, pp. 1–10.

Elston, D.M. (2020). Availability bias and artificial intelligence. *Journal of the American Academy of Dermatology*, 1–2. https://doi.org/10.1016/j.jaad.2019.07.051

Favaretto, M., De Clercq, E., and Elger, B.S. (2019). Big data and discrimination: perils, promises and solutions. A systematic review. *Journal of Big Data*, 6(1), 1–27.

Fletcher, R.R., Nakeshimana, A., and Olubeko, O. (2021). Addressing fairness, bias, and appropriate use of artificial intelligence and machine learning in global health. *Frontiers in Artificial Intelligence*, 3(April), 1–17.

Gavrilov, A.D., Jordache, A., Vasdani, M., and Deng, J. (2018). Preventing model overfitting and underfitting in convolutional neural networks. *International Journal of Software Science and Computational Intelligence (IJSSCI)*, 10(4), 19–28.

George, J.F., Duffy, K., and Ahuja, M. (2000). Countering the anchoring and adjustment bias with decision support systems. *Decision Support Systems*, 29(2), 195–206.

Ghojogh, B. and Crowley, M. (2019). The theory behind overfitting, cross validation, regularization, bagging, and boosting. *Machine Learning*, 23.

Hagendorff, T. (2020). The ethics of AI ethics: An evaluation of guidelines. *Minds and Machines*, 30(1), 99–120.

Heide-Jørgensen, M.P. and Lage, J. (2022). On the availability bias in narwhal abundance estimates. *NAMMCO Scientific Publications*, 12. https://doi.org/10.7557/3.6518

Hellström, T., Dignum, V., and Bensch, S. (2020). Bias in machine learning — What is it good for? In *CEUR Workshop Proceedings*, Vol. 2659, pp. 3–10.

Hoard, J.C., Medus, C., and Schleiss, M.R. (2021). A 3-year-old with fever and abdominal pain: Availability bias in the time of COVID-19. *Clinical Pediatrics*, 60(1), 83–86.

Jabbar, H. and Khan, R.Z. (2015). Methods to avoid over-fitting and under-fitting in supervised machine learning (comparative study). *Computer Science, Communication and Instrumentation Devices*, 70(10.3850), 978–981.

Jobin, A., Ienca, M., and Vayena, E. (2019). The global landscape of AI ethics guidelines. *Nature Machine Intelligence*, 1(9), 389–399.

John-Mathews, J.M., Cardon, D., and Balagué, C. (2022). From reality to world. A critical perspective on AI fairness. *Journal of Business Ethics*, 178(4), 945–959.

Johnson, B., Bartola, J., Angell, R., Witty, S., Giguere, S., and Brun, Y. (2023). Fairkit, fairkit, on the wall, who's the fairest of them all? Supporting fairness-related decision-making. *EURO Journal on Decision Processes*, 11, 100031.

Johnson-Laird, P.N., Goodwin, G.P., and Khemlani, S.S. (2017). Mental models and reasoning. In Ball, L. J. and Thompson, V. A. (Eds.), *International Handbook of Thinking and Reasoning*. Routledge, NY, USA. pp. 346–365.

Jones, N.A., Ross, H., Lynam, T., Perez, P., and Leitch, A. (2011). Mental models: An interdisciplinary synthesis of theory and methods. *Ecology and Society*, 16(1), 46–59.

Kahlawi, A. (2022). Amalgamation of business intelligence with corporate strategic management. In P.M. Jeyanthi, T. Choudhury, D. Hack-Polay, T.P. Singh & S. Abujar (Eds.), *Decision Intelligence Analytics and the Implementation of Strategic Business Management*. Springer International Publishing, pp. 109–123.

Kiritz, N. and Sarfati, P. (2018). Supervisory guidance on model risk management (SR 11-7) versus enterprise-wide model risk management for deposit-taking institutions (E-23): A detailed comparative analysis. Available at SSRN 3332484.

Klimashevskaia, A., Elahi, M., and Trattner, C. (2023, June). Addressing popularity bias in recommender systems: An exploration of self-supervised learning models. In *Adjunct Proceedings of the 31st ACM Conference on User Modeling, Adaptation and Personalization*, Limassol, Cyprus, June 26–29, pp. 7–11.

Koh, D.M., Papanikolaou, N., Bick, U., Illing, R., Kahn Jr, C.E., Kalpathi-Cramer, J., ... and Prior, F. (2022). Artificial intelligence and machine learning in cancer imaging. *Communications Medicine*, 2(1), 133.

Kordzadeh, N. and Ghasemaghaei, M. (2021). Algorithmic bias: Review, synthesis, and future research directions. *European Journal of Information Systems*, 31(3), 388–409.

Kretz, D.R. (2018). Experimentally evaluating bias-reducing visual analytics techniques in intelligence analysis. In Ellis, G. (Ed.), *Cognitive Biases in Visualizations*. Springer, Cham, Switzerland. pp. 111–135.

Kroll, J.A., Huey, J., Barocas, S., Felten, E.W., Reidenberg, J.R., Robinson, D.G., and Yu, H. (2017). Accountable algorithms. *University of Pennsylvania Law Review*, 165(3), 633.

Kyere, K., Aremu, T.O., and Ajibola, O.A. (2022). Availability bias and the COVID-19 pandemic: A case study of *Legionella pneumonia*. *Cureus*. https://doi.org/10.7759/cureus.25846.

Landers, R.N. and Behrend, T.S. (2022). Auditing the AI auditors: A framework for evaluating fairness and bias in high stakes AI predictive models. *American Psychologist*, 78(1), 36–49.

Liu, W., Ikonnikova, S., Scott Hamlin, H., Sivila, L., and Pyrcz, M.J. (2021). Demonstration and mitigation of spatial sampling bias for machine-learning predictions. *SPE Reservoir Evaluation & Engineering*, 24(01), 262–274.

Mamede, S., Goeijenbier, M., Schuit, S.C.E., de Carvalho Filho, M.A., Staal, J., Zwaan, L., and Schmidt, H.G. (2021). Specific disease knowledge as predictor of susceptibility to availability bias in diagnostic reasoning: A randomized controlled experiment. *Journal of General Internal Medicine*, 36(3), 640–646.

Manoogian, J. III, Benson, B., and Tilmann, R. (2018). The cognitive bias codex – 180+ biases, designed by John Manoogian III. https://commons.wikimedia.org/wiki/File:Cognitive_bias_codex_en.svg

Martin, K. (2019). Designing ethical algorithms. *MIS Quarterly Executive*, 18(2), 129–142.

Massa, E., Jonker, M., Roes, K., and Coolen, A. (2022). Correction of overfitting bias in regression models. arXiv preprint arXiv:2204.05827.

Mehrabi, N., Morstatter, F., Saxena, N., Lerman, K., and Galstyan, A. (2021). A survey on bias and fairness in machine learning. *ACM Computing Surveys*, 54(6), 1–35. https://doi.org/10.1145/3457607

Mueller, B., Kinoshita, T., Peebles, A., Graber, M.A., and Lee, S. (2022). Artificial intelligence and machine learning in emergency medicine: A narrative review. *Acute Medicine & Surgery*, 9(1), 1–10.

Müller, Vincent C. (2021). Ethics of artificial intelligence and robotics. In Edward N. Zalta (Ed.), *The Stanford Encyclopedia of Philosophy*, Summer 2021 Edition. https://plato.stanford.edu/archives/sum2021/entries/ethics-ai. https://doi.org/10.1093/oso/9780190905033.001.0001

Mylrea, M. and Robinson, N. (2023). AI trust framework and maturity model: A zero trust approach to zero trust for AI driven autonomous human machine teams & systems (A-HMT-S). *Cybersecurity and Innovation Technology Journal*, 1(1), 1–15.

Nasim, S.F., Ali, M.R., and Kulsoom, U. (2022). Artificial intelligence incidents & ethics a narrative review. *International Journal of Technology, Innovation and Management (IJTIM)*, 2(2), 52–64.

Nazaretsky, T., Cukurova, M., Ariely, M., and Alexandron, G. (2021). Confirmation bias and trust: Human factors that influence teachers' attitudes towards AI-based educational technology. In *CEUR Workshop Proceedings*, 3042. Bozen-Bolzano, Italy, September 20, https://www.fastcompany.com/90266263/brooklyn-students-walk-out-of-school-over-zuckerberg-backed

Neal, T.M.S., Lienert, P., Denne, E., and Singh, J.P. (2022). A general model of cognitive bias in human judgment and systematic review specific to forensic mental health. *American Psychological Association*, 46(2), 99–120.

Nguyen, A. and Benjamin-Chung, J. (2023). Rigour and reproducibility in perinatal and paediatric epidemiologic research using big data. *Paediatric and Perinatal Epidemiology*, March, 322–325. https://doi.org/10.1111/ppe.12971

Nihei, M. (2022). Epistemic injustice as a philosophical conception for considering fairness and diversity in human-centered AI principles. *Interdisciplinary Information Sciences*, 28(1), 35–43.

Nourani, M., Roy, C., Block, J.E., Honeycutt, D.R., Rahman, T., Ragan, E., and Gogate, V. (2021, April). Anchoring bias affects mental model formation and user reliance in explainable AI systems. In *26th International Conference on Intelligent User Interfaces*, New York, NY, USA. pp. 340–350.

Ntoutsi, E., Fafalios, P., Gadiraju, U., Iosifidis, V., Nejdl, W., Vidal, M.E., Ruggieri, S., Turini, F., Papadopoulos, S., Krasanakis, E., Kompatsiaris, I., Kinder-Kurlanda, K., Wagner, C., Karimi, F., Fernandez, M., Alani, H., Berendt, B., Kruegel, T., Heinze, C., … and Staab, S. (2020). Bias in data-driven artificial intelligence systems — An introductory survey. Wiley Interdisciplinary Reviews: *Data Mining and Knowledge Discovery*, 10(3), e1356. https://doi.org/10.1002/widm.1356

Park, B., Rao, D.L., and Gudivada, V. N. (2021). Dangers of bias in data-intensive information systems. In *Next Generation Information Processing System: Proceedings of ICCET 2020*, Volume 2. Springer, Singapore, pp. 259–271.

Passi, S. and Vorvoreanu, M. (2022). Overreliance on AI literature review. Microsoft Research.

Pili, G. (2023). Deciphering intelligence analysis: The synthetic nature of the core intelligence function. *Intelligence and National Security*, 38(1), 128–142.

Pisciotta, W., Arina, P., Hofmaenner, D., and Singer, M. (2023). Difficult diagnosis in the ICU: Making the right call but beware uncertainty and bias. *Anaesthesia*, 78(4), 501–509.

Pot, M., Kieusseyan, N., and Prainsack, B. (2021). Not all biases are bad: Equitable and inequitable biases in machine learning and radiology. *Insights into Imaging*, 12(1), 1–10.

Rastogi, C., Zhang, Y., Wei, D., Varshney, K.R., Dhurandhar, A., and Tomsett, R. (2022). Deciding fast and slow: The role of cognitive biases in AI-assisted decision-making. *Proceedings of the ACM on Human-Computer Interaction*, 6(CSCW1), 83.

Robinson, J. (2022). Distributed hypothesis generation and evaluation. In Castagna, F., Sarkadi, J.M., and Xydis, A. (Eds.), *Online Handbook of Argumentation for AI*, pp. 38–42, https://arxiv.org/pdf/2212.07996.pdf#page=41.

Romanov, D., Molokanov, V., Kazantsev, N., and Jha, A.K. (2023). Removing order effects from human-classified datasets: A machine learning method to improve decision making systems. *Decision Support Systems*, 165, 113891.

Roselli, D., Matthews, J., and Talagala, N. (2019). Managing bias in AI. In *The Web Conference 2019 — Companion of the World Wide Web Conference, WWW 2019*, San Francisco, CA, USA. pp. 539–544.

Rouse, W.B. and Morris, N.M. (1986). On looking into the black box: Prospects and limits in the search for mental models. *Psychological Bulletin*, 100(3), 349.

Sætra, H.S. and Danaher, J. (2022). To each technology its own ethics: The problem of ethical proliferation. *Philosophy & Technology*, 35(4), 93.

Saleiro, P., Kuester, B., Hinkson, L., London, J., Stevens, A., Anisfeld, A., ... and Ghani, R. (2018). Aequitas: A bias and fairness audit toolkit. arXiv preprint arXiv:1811.05577.

Sand, M., Durán, J.M., and Jongsma, K.R. (2022). Responsibility beyond design: Physicians' requirements for ethical medical AI. *Bioethics*, 36(2), 162–169.

Schemmer, M., Hemmer, P., Nitsche, M., Kühl, N., and Vössing, M. (2022, July). A meta-analysis of the utility of explainable artificial intelligence in human-AI decision-making. In *Proceedings of the 2022 AAAI/ACM Conference on AI, Ethics, and Society*, Oxford, UK, August 1–3, pp. 617–626.

Schemmer, M., Kuehl, N., Benz, C., Bartos, A., and Satzger, G. (2023, March). Appropriate reliance on AI advice: Conceptualization and the effect of explanations. In *Proceedings of the 28th International Conference on Intelligent User Interfaces*, Sydney, NSW, Australia, pp. 410–422.

Schwartz, R., Vassilev, A., Greene, K., Perine, L., Burt, A., and Hall, P. (2022). Towards a standard for identifying and managing bias in artificial intelligence. *NIST Special Publication*, 1270(10.6028).

Sharma, A.K., Sharma, D.M., Purohit, N., Rout, S.K., and Sharma, S.A. (2022). Analytics techniques: Descriptive analytics, predictive analytics, and prescriptive analytics. In Jeyanthi, P.M., Choudhury, T., Hack-Polay, D., Singh, T.P., and Abujar, S. (Eds.), *Decision Intelligence Analytics and the Implementation of Strategic Business Management*, Cham, Switzerland: Springer, pp. 1–14. https://doi.org/10.1007/978-3-030-82763-2_1.

Siau, K. and Wang, W. (2020). Artificial intelligence (AI) ethics: Ethics of AI and ethical AI. *Journal of Database Management (JDM)*, 31(2), 74–87.

Singh, H., Singh, A., and Nagpal, E. (2022). Demystifying behavioral biases of traders using machine learning. In Jeyanthi, P.M., Choudhury, T., Hack-Polay, D., Singh, T.P., and Abujar, S. (Eds.), *Decision Intelligence Analytics and the Implementation of Strategic Business Management*, Springer International Publishing, Springer, Cham, Switzerland, pp. 179–188.

Sklar, M. (2022). Sampling bias correction for supervised machine learning: A Bayesian inference approach with practical applications. arXiv preprint arXiv:2203.06239.

Srinivasan, R. and Chander, A. (2021). Biases in AI systems. *Communications of the ACM*, 64(8), 44–49.

Srivastava, N., Hinton, G., Krizhevsky, A., Sutskever, I., and Salakhutdinov, R. (2014). Dropout: A simple way to prevent neural networks from overfitting. *The Journal of Machine Learning Research*, 15(1), 1929–1958.

Suciu, O., Marginean, R., Kaya, Y., Daume III, H., and Dumitras, T. (2018). When does machine learning {FAIL}? Generalized transferability for evasion and poisoning attacks. In 27th *USENIX Security Symposium*, USENIX Security 18, Baltimore, MD, USA, August 15–17, pp. 1299–1316.

Sunstein, C.R. (2022). Governing by Algorithm? No noise and (potentially) less bias. *Duke Law Journal*, 71(6), 1175–1205.

Suresh, H. and Guttag, J.V. (2019). A framework for understanding unintended consequences of machine learning. arXiv preprint arXiv:1901. 10002, 2(8).

Tancev, G. and Pascale, C. (2020). The relocation problem of field calibrated low-cost sensor systems in air quality monitoring: A sampling bias. *Sensors*, 20(21), 1–14.

Tversky, A. and Kahneman, D. (1974). Judgment under uncertainty: Heuristics and biases: Biases in judgments reveal some heuristics of thinking under uncertainty. *Science*, 185(4157), 1124–1131.

Van Wynsberghe, A. (2021). Sustainable AI: AI for sustainability and the sustainability of AI. *AI Ethics 1*, 213–218.

Varadharajan, C., Appling, A.P., Arora, B., Christianson, D.S., Hendrix, V.C., Kumar, V., ... and Zwart, J. (2022). Can machine learning accelerate process understanding and decision-relevant predictions of river water quality? *Hydrological Processes*, 36(4), e14565.

Varona, D. and Suárez, J.L. (2022). Discrimination, bias, fairness, and trustworthy AI. *Applied Sciences*, 12(12), 1–13.

Vokinger, K.N., Feuerriegel, S., and Kesselheim, A.S. (2021). Mitigating bias in machine learning for medicine. *Communications Medicine*, 1(1), 3–5.

Whitesmith, M. (2022). Justified true belief theory for intelligence analysis. *Intelligence and National Security*, 37(6), 835–849.

Yan, H. and Zeleznikow, J. (2022). The appropriate use of artificial intelligence in law: Investigating the liability of artificial intelligence in legal decision-making. *ANU Journal of Law and Technology*, 3(2), 8–37.

Yin, M., Wortman Vaughan, J., and Wallach, H. (2019). Understanding the effect of accuracy on trust in machine learning models. In *Proceedings of the 2019 CHI Conference on Human Factors in Computing Systems*, Glasgow Scotland, UK, pp. 1–12. ACM.

Zografistou, D., Visser, J., Lawrence, J., and Reed, C. (2022, September). ACH-Nav: Argument navigation using techniques for intelligence analysis. In *9th International Conference on Computational Models of Argument, COMMA 2022*, Wales, United Kingdom, September 14–16, pp. 377–378. IOS Press BV.

Index